What Made Pistachio Nuts?

Film and Culture

John Belton, General Editor

What Made Pistachio Nuts? Early Sound Comedy and the Vaudeville Aesthetic

Henry Jenkins

Columbia University Press

New York

Columbia University Press
New York   Oxford
Copyright © 1992 Columbia University Press
All rights reserved

Library of Congress Cataloging-in-Publication Data

Jenkins, Henry.
    What made pistachio nuts? early sound comedy and the vaudeville
    aesthetic / Henry Jenkins.
        p.   cm.—(Film and culture)
    Includes bibliographical references and index.
    ISBN 0-231-07854-4
        1. Comedy films—History and criticism.   I. Title.   II. Series.
PN1995.9.C55J46   1992
791.43'617—dc20   92-22094
                                                                          CIP

Casebound editions of Columbia Uinversity Press books
are Smyth-sewn and printed on permanent and durable
acid-free paper.

Printed in the United States of America

c 10 9 8 7 6 5 4 3 2 1

Contents

Contents

Acknowledgments

No text of this length and scope is the product of a single mind or a single hand. This book bears the imprint of hundreds of individuals who have, for better or for worse, touched me and shaped my development. Space and memory does not allow me to thank them all here but I want to take this opportunity to express my gratitude to some special people.

To all of those who have taught me film: Marilyn Schmidt (Henderson High School), Jack Creech, William R. Thomas, Richard Firda, Robert Palmer, Milton Snowenbaas, and Jackie Byers (Georgia State University); Dudley Andrew, Charles Barr, Ed Buscombe, Herbert Eagle, Richard Dyer MacCann, and John Raeburn (University of Iowa); Tino Balio, Ben Brewster, Donald Crafton, Lea Jacobs, and Vance Kepley (University of Wisconsin); and, especially, to four outstanding teachers whose impact on my thinking and development will be felt for years to come—Rick Altman, Edward Branigan, David Bordwell, and John Fiske.

To those friends and associates with whom I have debated and discussed issues relating to film, television, and popular culture: Edward McNally, Walter Reaves, Mark Flanigan, Signe Hovde, and Will Brantley (Georgia State University); Carol Flinn, Jeff Carpenter, Kathy Schwictenberg, Cassandra Amesley, and James Collins (University of Iowa); Matthew Bernstein, Mary Carbine, Julie D'Acci, K. C. D'Allasandro, Jeanne Hall, Charles Kyle, Nickianne Moody, Deb Navins, Dave Pratt, Paul Seales, Murray Smith, and Mike Wassanaar (University of Wisconsin); David Thorburn, Ed Turk, Peter Donaldson, and Martin Marks (MIT); Jane Shattuc, Ellen Draper, Susan Emanuel, Thomas Doherty, Ben Singer, and Michael Selig (Cambridge area); and John Belton, Richard deCordova, Charles Musser, Roberta Pearson, Constance Penley, Dana Polan, Tom Gunning, Janet Staiger, and Charles Wolfe (Society for Cinema Studies). I especially want to thank Kristine Karnick, Peter Kramer, and Lynn Spigel, three friends whose support and encouragement have meant more to me than they realize and who have read and commented intelligently upon much of this text.

To those institutions who actively assisted my research: Wisconsin Center for Film and Theater Research, University of Wisconsin Library, Emory University Library, Georgia State University Library, University of California, Los Angeles Library, University of Southern California Library, Academy of Motion Picture Arts and Sciences, Institute for the American Musical, Walt Disney Studio Archives, University of California, Santa Barbara Library, Harvard University Library, MIT Humanities Library, the Boston Public Library, and especially Ted Turner, without whose commitment to film this book could not have been written, and to David and Kathi Beretan, two old and dear friends, who fed and housed me for six weeks while I did research in Los Angeles.

To my father, who probably regards this book to be yet another rewrite of my seventh grade term paper, and to my mother, from whom I inherited my love of laughter and the movies.

To my brother, who certainly still thinks I am a jerk but whom I love anyway.

To my in-laws, who have understood why I have taken their daughter and grandson halfway across the country to live in a subpoverty level for nine years.

To Cynthia Jenkins, who has put up with my bragging and my complaining in equal doses, who has slaved and starved to make this possible, who will always be my "bestest friend."

To my son, who may someday understand why his father's work takes precedence over his computer games and *Dr. Who* tapes.

And, last, though certainly not least, to my grandfather, for whom my father, my son, and I are named. Your lifetime commitment to the pursuit of excellence in all things, large and small, inspired me to pursue my dreams wherever they took me. I dedicate this book to you, Papa, as a small repayment for an investment you once made in my future.

Sections of chapters 3 and 7 have previously appeared as" 'Fifi Was My Mother's Name!' *Diplomaniacs,* Anarchistic Comedy, and the Vaudeville Aesthetic," *Velvet Light Trap* 26:3–27 (Fall 1990); translated as "La Commedia Anarcha e *Diplomaniacs*" in Vito Zagarrio, ed., *"B Dreams": I B Movies RKO e Monogram anni '30 e '40* (Siena: Mostra Internazionale del Nuovo Cinema, 1990), pp. 67–77. Sections of chapter 6 previously appeared as " 'Shall We Make It for New York or for Distribution?' Eddie Cantor, *Whoopee,* and Regional Resistance to the Talkies" *Cinema Journal* 29(2):32–52 (Spring 1990). Sections of chapter 9 previously appeared as " 'Don't Become Too Intimate with That Terrible Woman!' Wild Women, Disorderly Conduct, and Gendered Laughter in Early Sound Comedy," *Camera Obscura* (Fall 1991).

What Made Pistachio Nuts?

1

The Strange Case of the Backflipping Senators

Some years ago, in one of those chance encounters that must be familiar to all film scholars and movie buffs, I was captivated by an obscure Fox musical on the late late show. *Stand Up and Cheer* (Fox, 1934) centers upon the efforts of a theatrical impresario, Lawrence Cromwell (clearly modeled after Florenz Ziegfeld), hired to head a New Deal agency, the Department of Amusements. His task is to raise public morale. Cromwell faces opposition from wealthy corporate interests and conservative congressmen who feel that government-sponsored "dog and pony shows" may not be a frugal response to the Depression. The film's narrative offers an elaborate apologia for Hollywood's own role as a central national institution during a national crisis, arguing for the social importance of entertainment and the need to "stand up and cheer" in the face of adversity.

Cromwell's assignment also motivates the film's presentation of short musical and comic performance sequences. The Shirley Temple—James Dunn number, "Baby, Take a Bow," for example, is presented as an audition to determine whether their variety act violates child labor laws (fig. 1.1). Stepin Fetchit performs a sand dance in Cromwell's office, having used his name, George Bernard Shaw, to gain admission. For the most part, dramatic actors, like Warner Baxter (Cromwell), adopt restrained acting styles and function as spectators for the performances rather than participants in their staging; these actors push the narrative forward, providing exposition and taking actions that have plot consequences. Comic and musical performers, on the other hand, play limited roles in the plot development and interact with the dramatic characters only insofar as necessary to fit their numbers into the frame story. Not until the film's climactic number do Baxter and the other dramatic actors enter into the entertainment; Cromwell leads a parade of workers, farmers, military men, children, Pullman porters, and others, all celebrating the nation's triumph over the Depression: "We're out of the red and into the black!"

Stand Up and Cheer is full of surprising moments: a talking penguin who thinks he's Jimmy Durante (fig. 1.2), chorus girls tap-dancing across the New York skyline, a spiritual sung by Aunt Jemima, and a zany scene involving Stepin Fetchit and a yodeling hillbilly (fig. 1.3). What astounded me on first and subsequent viewings, however, was a sequence that deliberately violated the film's carefully established separation between narrative and spectacle, naturalistic acting and virtuoso performance. The agency's somber-minded opponents dispatch two senators, Danforth and Short (Mitchell and Durant), to lecture Cromwell on his fiscal irresponsibility (fig. 1.4). Following a brief discussion, Cromwell leaves the room to call for his assistant, leaving the two politicians alone. Although the two senators have been played with verisimilitude throughout the earlier scenes, their performance style shifts dramatically upon Cromwell's exit. The two begin pacing and talking faster. Suddenly, Senator Danforth turns and begins to slap his colleague rhythmically in the face, a gesture Senator Short acknowledges constitutes a "sound argument." Their conversation rapidly dissolves into vaudeville crossfire: Danforth kicks his friend in the head, throws him across the room (fig. 1.5), knocks him off his feet and lifts him off the ground; Short swings at him, but his taller associate holds him at arm's length (fig. 1.6). Political back scratching is literally transformed into backflips (figs. 1.7, 1.8), and the tumbling men spout forth a bizarre blend of campaign rhetoric ("But sixteen-inch guns do not mean naval supremacy!"; "True, inflation is the best policy!") and comic patter ("What made pistachio nuts?") The two men are rocking back and forth on top of each other (fig. 1.9) when Dimwitty (Nigel Bruce), Cromwell's trusty assistant, returns and offers them a booking on the five-a-day circuit. The indignant dignitaries rise to their feet, regain their composure, and walk down the hall continuing to discuss the political ramifications of their meeting with Cromwell (fig. 1.10).

Their exit abruptly ends a major subplot, not through its resolution but through its explosion into remarkable performance spectacle. The sketch was not simply a digression from the central narrative; rather, it challenged the further development of the causal event chain, leaving central plot points unresolved in favor of our immediate pleasure in comic spectacle. The more I learned about classical film style, the more my thoughts returned to this troubling moment. I found myself actively seeking an answer to Senator Short's perplexing question, "What made pistachio nuts?" What factors could account for the disruptive function of such performances within the classical Hollywood cinema? How can we create a model of classical narrative that acknowledges the system's stability and coherence yet, at the same time, explains the local appearance of aberrant elements like these backflipping senators? Was the episode an idiosyncratic flourish of stylistic excess? Could it have been an isolated aberration within a poorly crafted film? Or might it relate to other film practices and belong to some other stylistic system? What did all of this tomfoolery mean to its original audience? Were they as surprised as I had been or had these features been so normalized within this generic tradition that they had become conventional and uninteresting?

AGEE, MAST, AND THE CLASSICAL TRADITION

A dominant tradition in the criticism of early sound comedy has viewed films like *Stand Up and Cheer* as flawed works that fail to preserve what was interesting and vital in the silent cinema or to achieve the full potential of the classical sound cinema. James Agee's 1949 *Life* essay, "Comedy's Greatest Era," set the terms for this debate: "We will discuss here what has gone wrong with screen comedy and what, if anything, can be done about it. But, mainly we will try to suggest what it was like in its glory in the years from 1912 to 1930." [1] Agee's elegy to the visual "poetry" of silent comedy elevates Chaplin, Langdon, Lloyd, and Keaton at the expense of sound comedy: "The only thing wrong with screen comedy today is that it takes place on a screen that talks." [2] Agee felt that sound comedy denied silent clowns the use of their artistry as physical performers, while exposing talking comedians to "a continual exhibition of their inadequacy as screen comedians." [3] Of all the sound comedians, Agee acknowledged only W. C. Fields as having made any substantial contribution to screen comedy; all of the others he dismissed as "semi-skilled laborers." [4]

Later critics, including Donald McCaffrey, Walter Kerr, and Gerald Mast, retained Agee's nostalgia for the silent era and his prejudices against early sound comedy. McCaffrey writes, "The special art of pantomime faded and nearly died when motion picture producers turned to the talents of the fast-talking 'stand-up' comics of vaudeville."[5] For Gerald Mast, the coming of sound becomes the defining moment in the history of screen comedy. Mast discusses silent comedy in terms of its great performers, rehearsing Agee's pantheon with nods toward several more neglected figures like Larry Semon and Raymond Griffith, and suggesting how each built upon the legacy of Mack Sennett, the "father" of slapstick comedy. Mast characterizes sound comedy, however, in terms of broader traditions and particularly in terms of the contributions of directors and screenwriters, shifting attention from slapstick or comedian comedy to romantic comedy. Sound, Mast argues, replaces the comedy of personality and performance with the comedy of structure and language. Like Agee, Mast found few great "comic minds" in early sound comedy: "American sound comedians have been more successful at creating comic character than at combining that character with a unique comic structure and a unique approach to creating comedy *through* cinema."[6] Mast grants space to only the Marx Brothers and W. C. Fields, displaying serious reservations about both and dismissing them as minor artists.

Basing their judgments on explicit appeals to classical criteria of thematic significance, character consistency, narrative unity, causal logic, and psychological realism, these critics do not find the same things to admire in the films of Wheeler and Woolsey or even the Marx Brothers that they found in the "silent classics" of Chaplin and Keaton. Andrew Sarris, for example, praises the performance skills of the Marx Brothers, "their distinctly anarchistic personalities," yet regards their films as having less merit than the "silent classics" because of their poorly constructed stories and inconsistent characterizations.[7] McCaffrey suggests that what made the silent clowns better was that "they were concerned, first of all, with the comedy character and the development of a well-motivated dramatic story that sprang from the roots of the leading comic character."[8] McCaffrey protested that sound comedians were too interested in the production of verbal gags to be concerned with the development of their narratives and that their comedy consequently lacked substance.

To treat works like *Stand Up and Cheer* or *Duck Soup* (Paramount, 1933) as failed classical narratives misses the point. While it is true that many of these films lack narrative coherence and ignore character consistency, the comedies are most pleasurable when they most openly transgress classical norms. Writing of silent slapstick, Donald Crafton has asked, "Is there not something perverse about arguing that what is 'wrong' with a film form is that which defines it to begin with?"[9] The same question could be asked in regard to sound comedy, which seems to have been perpetually judged by standards running contrary to its own aesthetic interests. Early sound comedies do not always work as logical or unified wholes, but they are filled with moments of immense fascination and satisfaction. Traditional approaches to classical works teach us to think globally, to see all segments as part of a larger narrative system, and to view their individual appeals as subordinate to the logic of the whole. *Stand Up and Cheer* can be partially understood within these terms: as a satire of the New Deal, as a justification of mass entertainment, as the story of Cromwell's struggle against outside opposition and against his own self-doubts. Some performance sequences are integrated into that narrative, providing indirect insight into the protagonist's ideals and goals or showing him in action as a producer of public amusements. However, the real vitality of the film lies in the heterogeneity of its material, the virtuosity of its performances, its wild and wonderful violations of the rules of classical storytelling. *Stand Up and Cheer* is most alive when a singer rips through Cromwell's suddenly giant-sized newspaper (fig. 1.11) or when the talking penguin runs amok in his fish tank or when the senators somersault across his carpet. The film's disintegration as a classical narrative facilitates its success as a popular amusement. To appreciate such a film, we need to think about comedy atomistically, as a loosely linked succession of comic "bits." That the parts are more satisfying than the whole may only be a criticism if we do not like the parts.

Recent critics, such as Donald Crafton, Peter Kramer, and others, acknowledge the uneasy position of comedian comedy within the classical cinema; slapstick comedy retained aspects of the earlier "cinema of attractions" long after other film genres were fully absorbed into the classical paradigm. Crafton notes the disruptive or disintegrative potential of gags, locating a basic antagonism between elements of spectacle ("the pie") and elements of narrative ("the chase").[10] Kramer is concerned with early screen comedy's foregrounding of performance and its consequent disinterest in narrative causality; the introduction of comic stars into feature-length films focused greater attention on narrative integration and character consistency, drawing the silent clowns more completely into classical Hollywood cinema.[11] Early sound comedy represented another repositioning of the comic performer within the classical cinema, an attempt to absorb an aesthetic tradition (that of

5

vaudeville and revue performance) that did not fit comfortably within its storytelling conventions. Classically oriented critics like Mast and McCaffrey see this history in terms of a rise and fall in the merits of film comedy, evaluating performers and films according to how closely they adhere to standard Hollywood practices. More recent writers, however, offer a useful corrective to this teleological model of genre history; slapstick comedies reflect alternative film practices responsive to different aesthetic impulses, striving to fulfill different functions within the larger cultural economy. An effort to reconstruct the historical norms applicable to early sound comedy might allow us a clearer picture of how it functioned in relation to the classical cinema; such an approach would also provide more appropriate criteria for evaluating these films.

ANTONIN ARTAUD AND THE ANARCHISTIC COMEDY TRADITION

Other critics have embraced the Marx Brothers' comedies precisely because of their transgressions of classical conventions and their violations of normal filmmaking practice. Richard Rowland, writing in 1947, proclaimed, "There can scarcely be too much plot for the Marx Brothers; scriptwriters may build up skyscrapers of plot; the Brothers will destroy them as easily as Harpo atomizes this building." [12] Such critics represent the Marx Brothers as rebelling against the constraints of the studio system, viewing their comedy as antagonistic to narrative and as successful only insofar as it is able to break free of plot and character. Hence, these critics value the Marx Brothers' Paramount films, such as *Animal Crackers* (1930), *Duck Soup, Horse Feathers* (1932), and *Monkey Business* (1931), over their MGM vehicles, such as *A Day at the Races* (1937), *A Night at the Opera* (1935), or *The Big Store* (1941); Irving Thalberg's classicism put too many constraints on the Marx Brothers' performances, as the comedians were asked to operate within "well-made plots" and to adopt more stable characterizations.

These critics' celebration of the antinarrative tendencies of the Marx Brothers' comedies reflects their particular readings of the clowns' "unique personalities." John Grierson wrote that the Marx Brothers were "wild men, who, if they did not find a jungle ready at hand, would certainly invent one." [13] Clifton Fadiman describes their gestures as "rapid, explosive, and extravagantly unnecessary," [14] while Francis Birrell calls them "mad and aimless . . . utterly disconnected" from the realm of everyday conduct and rational thought. [15] Colin L. Westerbeck speaks

Harpo Marx. Wisconsin Center for Film and Theater Research.

of their "recklessness," [16] Meyer Levin of their "boyishness," [17] and William Troy of their "hysteria." [18] Most persistently, however, the Marx Brothers are linked to images of anarchy and social disruption. Antonin Artaud characterized *Monkey Business* (Paramount, 1931) as a "hymn to anarchy and whole-hearted revolt," [19] and at least since Artaud, anarchy has functioned as the central metaphor in the discussion of the Marx Brothers films. For Raymond Durgnat, the Marx Brothers constitute a "three-pronged attack on society"; they "tear language, and all the conventions and assumptions which language incorporates"; they unleash "a verbal barrage whose real aim is to devastate social custom"; they "challenge the habits and the rules." [20] Gerald Weales writes of the "destructive force" and "malevolent energy" of the Marx Brothers, an energy that cannot be contained within the text. [21] Robert Warshow attributes to the Marx Brothers "an uncompromising nihilism that is particularly characteristic of the submerged and the dispossessed." Warshow continues: "The Marx Brothers are lumpen, they spit on culture, and . . . they express a blind and destructive disgust with society that the responsible man is compelled to suppress in himself." [22]

The metaphor of anarchy allows critics to draw direct connections between the Marx Brothers films' formal and thematic structures—if only by way of common analogy. Andrew Bergman can, thus, see both their style and their content as "a wild response to an unprecedented shattering of confidence" in American institutions and values. [23] Even a classicist like Gerald Mast evokes this metaphor in explaining their appeal:

> The breezy, chaotic, revolutionary activities of the comic anarchists give society's respectable calcifications a much-deserved comeuppance. . . . The Marxes' Paramount writers and producer enjoyed destroying the very conventions of their craft and the aesthetics of their employers, creating films with deliberately irrelevant plot twists, incongruous sight gags, inconclusive conclusions, red herrings, faceless and forgettable supporting players. [24]

Mast's discussion blurs the boundaries between thematic anarchy and a set of aesthetic practices that can be labeled anarchistic, although they are equally open to various other meanings. In the process, he equates screen conventions with social conventions, performers with writers, characters within the text with the production of the text, and so on.

This slippage between form and content, once started, soon assumes as well the function of explaining the spectator's relationship to the text. Gerald Weales writes that the "truly subversive element" in their comedies stems from the ability of the audience to tap into "the energy they can generate in their collective endeavor to deflate, destroy, defuse, defenestrate everything around them and in their guiltless joy in the process."[25] The suspension of formal and social convention within the Marx Brothers' comedies allows us to experience these films in a more "impulsive" fashion, frees us from the demand of rational thought, and positions us outside of culture; the spectators themselves become "anarchists" in the process of enjoying the comic anarchy of the Marx Brothers. There is nothing new or theoretically sophisticated in this claim. Meyer Levin, writing in *Esquire* in 1934, discussed the direct and instinctual appeal of Harpo, who "does everything we are inhibited from doing," allowing us to vicariously experience the transgression of social order.[26] Phillipe Soupault, who praised the surrealistic quality of their films, writes that "the comedy of the Marx Brothers lifts us out of reality,"[27] a view he shared with Salvador Dali, Antonin Artaud, and more recently, Roland Barthes.[28]

Such an approach initially seems preferable to Agee's condemnation of these films, if only because it recognizes the potential pleasures derived from their transgression of classical conventions. Yet as this discussion has already suggested, the anarchic reading of the Marx Brothers has many limitations.[29] First, comic performances are read as "spontaneous" disruptions of narrative structure, as comic "improvisations" running counter to studio expectations. Rather, the studio hired the Marx Brothers to create such comic disruptions and such moments were as carefully scripted as scenes of narrative exposition. The Marx Brothers, in practice, had little or no say over their screen vehicles, though the films were designed to showcase their particular performance skills and borrowed material from their previous stage career. The anarchic approach offers a romantic myth about the films' authorship that denies the material conditions of their production and does not allow us to ask harder questions about what might motivate the studio's tolerance of such deviations from its standard narrative formulas. Second, such an approach isolates the Marx Brothers from a much broader tradition of early sound comedies. It celebrates the "uniqueness" of the Marx Brothers while shifting focus away from their contemporaries, such as Joe Cook, Wheeler and Woolsey, or Olsen and Johnson, whose comedies were essentially similar in their style and structure.

Finally, this approach looks toward the films' thematic structures (the clown's opposition to social constraint) as explaining their formal organization (the breakdown of narrative coherence and character consistency); this approach, thus, forecloses any attempt to position the films within the aesthetic history of the American cinema. The metaphor of the Marx Brothers as anarchists survives, I suspect, because it conforms so well to the way progressive-minded academics like to remember 1930s American culture—as a period of tremendous political upheaval and, at least initially, of a succession of radical alternatives to a capitalist order that seemed on the edge of collapse. Politically charged metaphors ("anarchists," "guerrilla warriors," "Marxists," "revolutionaries") permit us to claim for the Marx Brothers a progressive voice. We must not become seduced, however, by the power of our own metaphors. Inviting as it is to imagine an American comedy of radical discontent, it is not clear in what meaningful sense the Marx Brothers films may be read as a political reaction against any particular social system or as reflecting any coherent ideological position (anarchistic or otherwise). While such an approach would see the Marx Brothers as historically responsive to the Depression, its overall effect is to isolate them from the larger history of screen comedy and the performance tradition(s) from which they emerged.

STEVE SEIDMAN AND THE COMEDIAN COMEDY MODEL

More recent work by Steve Seidman and Frank Krutnik proposes one way of positioning these films within a broader generic history. Seidman locates specific formal and thematic characteristics of the "comedian comedy" as a "tradition" in the American cinema. The comedian comedy is characterized by a tension between "the maintenance of the comedian's position as an already recognizable performer with a clearly defined extrafictional personality" and the need to integrate that performer into a character who functions within a classically linear narrative.[30] Comedian comedy, Seidman argues, is characterized by its self-consciousness and artificiality, its constant disruption of a "fictional universe" in order to acknowledge the comedian's status as a performer. These films represent a "nonhermetic" tradition within the classical cinema, a tradition that also includes "animated cartoons, some musicals" and that bears some loose connection to modernist and avant-garde aesthetics. This "counter-tendency" consistently violates classical conventions: "a nonhermetic approach to narrative . . . is comprised of a more open and expansive narrative structure which acknowledges the spectator, narrative exposition that is 'spoiled' by actors who 'step out' of character, a foregrounding of its marks of production, essential artificiality, and a deconstruction of its signifying practice." [31] Seidman and Krutnik link this formal transgressiveness to a particular narrative trajectory; Comedian comedy, Seidman argues, involves a "dialectic . . . between eccentric behavior (counter-cultural drives) and social conformity (cultural values)." [32] The comedian's "disruptiveness" is constructed as a problem blocking his full assimilation into the social and narrative order; the comic plot works to resolve these personality problems and to bring about his full integration into adult society. Just as the comedian comedy plot centers around the character's movement toward great conformity to social expectations, the film integrates the comedian more fully into a coherent character and ties performance sequences more tightly to larger plot developments.

Seidman and Krutnik have contributed a great deal to our understanding of the genre's formal and thematic structures and its complex relationship to classical Hollywood narrative. These writers, however, fail to provide an historical account of this tradition. While their emphasis on the continuity between silent and sound comedy is laudable, their focus on the "continuum" of the comedian comedy traditions leads them to group together works produced from 1914 to the present with little sense of generic development. Having identified the genre's characteristic formal devices, these writers assign them fixed meanings, as if direct address to the camera or masquerade always meant the same thing regardless of shifting studio practices or the changing expectations of the films' audience(s). While they draw examples from many films, Seidman and Krutnik typically focus their interpretation on works from the late 1940s and 1950s, films representing a particular configuration of the comedian comedy that draws heavily on pseudo-Freudian notions of character psychology. Generalizations formed through close analysis of Bob Hope, Danny Kaye, or Jerry Lewis vehicles are treated as fully applicable to interpreting the works of John Bunny, Buster Keaton, or the Marx Brothers. Most models of film genre provide some notion of differentiation and change; here, however, comedian comedy, which of all Hollywood genres seems the most dependent upon novelty and immediacy, is read as essentially stable—almost static. Moreover, while Seidman acknowledges that comedian comedy builds upon other performance traditions, especially those of vaudeville, he is not interested in exploring those traditions, their relationship to the classical aesthetic, or the institutional factors shaping their adoption by Hollywood.

COMEDIAN COMEDY AS A PROGRESSIVE GENRE

Both the strengths and limitations of the comedian comedy model are symptomatic of larger movements within post-1968 film criticism and genre theory. Jean-Luc Comolli and Jean Narboni's 1969 essay, "Cinema/Ideology/Criticism" and the *Cahiers du Cinema* editorial board's application of its approach to *Young Mr. Lincoln* (Fox, 1939) placed increased attention upon the relationship between form and ideology within the Hollywood cinema.[33] Refusing to treat the commercial cinema as a monolithic structure, these writers looked for signs of ideological and formal contestation. Comolli and Narboni proposed five different categories of texts potentially present within the commercial cinema: a) films that are conservative in both their formal and ideological construction; b) films that "attack" the dominant ideology through both their form and their context; c) films lacking explicit political content but characterized by formal deviations; d) films that have progressive content but adhere to dominant formal practices; e) films that "seem at first sight to belong firmly within the ideology and to be completely under its sway, but that turn out to be so only in an ambiguous manner."[34]

While this initial essay saw categories b and c as central to the *Cahiers*'s project and included within category c several formally "progressive" works from the popular cinema (including comedian comedies such as Jerry Lewis's *The Bellboy* (Paramount, 1960), the more slippery category e has become the focus for subsequent analysis; critics have advanced many different films, filmmakers, and genres as representing forms of "countercinema." Category e allowed the *Cahiers* editors to maintain some continuity with their earlier auteurist model (which had valued directors who were "at war" with their materials).[35] Ford the auteur became Ford the textual discourse; *Young Mr. Lincoln* the masterpiece became *Young Mr. Lincoln* the contradictory text. Claire Johnson's "Women's Cinema as Countercinema" and her subsequent readings of films by Jacques Tourneur and Dorothy Arzner linked ideological analysis with a more traditionally auteurist defense of certain exceptional filmmakers. Johnson searched not for contradictory tendencies within dominant film practice but for a model of feminist film practice.[36]

Much of the scholarly writing surrounding Jerry Lewis and Frank Tashlin fits squarely within this tradition.[37] French critics, especially, embraced their films for their reflexive gags, their performance virtuosity, their playful treatment of other Hollywood films, their narrative "openness" and their fragmented and inconsistent characterizations. Paul Willemen, for example, argues that the defining characteristics of "Tashlin's Method" are his intertextual "openness" and his construction of narratives through the combination of fragmentary material:

> A Tashlin film does not profess to be a single, unique work, entirely closed in upon itself, standing as a completely self-sufficient and organic whole. Rather, his films present themselves as compromising part of a network of visual texts produced in a particular society at a particular time (i.e., in the USA in the late 1950's/early 1960's). . . . Meaning is produced strictly through the relations between separate elements, the elements themselves being largely arbitrary. [38.]

Such intertextuality and fragmentation destroys the classical illusion of a unified, self-contained, and coherent text, allowing Willemen to claim for Tashlin the status of a modernist artist. Similarly, the *Cahiers* editors characterize Jerry Lewis's films as "an extension and a critique" of American "mythologies," a process they locate within certain characteristic themes (childhood, family, jobs, money, sports, technology), aspects of his performance style (his rubberiness, his inarticulateness, his stiffness, his "virtuosity") and aspects of the films' formal structure (their cartoonish stylization, their fragmentation, their quotation, their unusual sound-image relations).[39] As Michael Selig notes, those features of the Lewis films that critics have labeled "modernist" appear within a broad range of American film comedies, including many of the early sound comedies discussed here, and seem reasonably conventional within the genre's "tradition of 'subversion.' " [40]

This concept of ideological rupture within the classical cinema also had a tremendous influence on post-1968 genre theory, especially upon debates surrounding the melodrama, film noir, and the horror film, although it has not been broadly applied to film comedy.[41] This approach provided a constructive basis for textual analysis and a useful vehicle for shifting attention onto genres neglected or disdained by more classically oriented critics. Its failure, however, is its tendency to read any break with dominant film practice as "progressive." Deviations from classical norms are assumed to question the "naturalness" of standard techniques, to "rattle the perfect illusionism" of the Hollywood film.[42] The progressive genre argument attributes "deconstructive capabilities and a subversive effectivity" to all differences from its otherwise monolithic conception of the classical text.[43] Invention is read as a challenge—both formal and ideological—to the coherence of the classical system rather than a means by which genres generate new audiences and broaden their formal vocabulary.

As early as 1978, Dana Polan warned that this approach could sink into "a new ahistorical formalism."[44] None of the dominant Hollywood genres are perfectly "illusionistic," which has become abundantly clear as more and more of them have been subsumed into the general category of "progressive genres." What genre is not potentially readable in these terms? And, if all genres are equally "progressive," then, doesn't the distinction lose all significance since it is founded on an explicit notion of difference from dominant film practice? There has always been some place within the classical paradigm for disruptions, transgressions, "baring of the device," as a form of product differentiation and a source of novelty within formula, if nothing else. As Polan notes, "The conventional work of art does not banish contradiction; rather, it works by divorcing contradiction from its social causes. We are used to having our realities deconstructed and so too it does not bother us to see the reality of the movie screen world deconstructed."[45] The displacement or reshaping of dominant norms is how aesthetic systems grow and how they remain of active interest to their reception community. Only if we reduce the classical aesthetic to a limited and fixed range of stereotypical features can we regard such traits as posing a radical break with traditional film practice.

Perhaps most troubling has been the tendency of such critics to attribute more or less fixed effects to certain formal devices, such as direct address to the camera. Aesthetic devices gain significance both from their function within individual texts and from their place within a historically specific formal system. Formal devices are constantly open to redefinition and reapplication. Techniques alien to us today might have seemed normal and unexceptional in a different context. My experience of a rupture within the performance style of *Stand Up and Cheer* was shaped to no small degree by the fact that I did not recognize Mitchell and Durant as vaudeville performers and had little familiarity with the traditions from which they emerged. A contemporary viewer of the film might have been more disoriented by the fact that these comic acrobats were assuming a realist performance style than by their unmotivated backflips. Without determining what expectations or knowledge spectators took with them to the cinema, it is impossible to determine which textual features might seem disorientating or defamiliarizing and which might be anticipated. In examining specific devices characteristic of a given genre, then, we must ask what were the limitations of acceptable transgressiveness within the studio system at any particular historical moment, what functions these devices served within the formal and thematic system of a specific film, what institutional factors facilitated invention within classical norms, and what impact these "differences" had within a specific reception context. To answer such questions requires a constant movement between critical, theoretical, and historical treatments of the films under examination. As we have seen, the "progressive genre" debate has been waged largely in critical terms, with an eye toward its usefulness within contemporary theoretical debates, but with little or no interest in film history.

HISTORICAL POETICS, CLASSICAL NORMS, AND GENRE STUDY

Reaching a similar conclusion, Alan Williams has called upon genre critics to "return to film history and to produce individual genre studies with real historical integrity," to examine the "prehistory" of film genres in other popular culture traditions, to analyze a broad range of genre texts and not simply canonized works in order to determine the norms at work within a particular historical context, and to fit genre filmmaking into its broader institutional setting.[46] Unfortunately, so far we have relatively few models for such a genre history. Notable exceptions would be Donald Crafton's work on early animation, Lea Jacobs's discussion of the influence of the Breen office upon the "fallen woman" cycle of the early 1930s, Paul Kerr's consideration of the formal and economic determinants of film noir, and Tom Doherty's exploration of the connection between the emergence of Teen Exploitation pictures in the 1950s and the changing composition of the motion picture audience.[47] Each of these discussions builds upon methodologies and insights drawn from institutional, social, and cultural history. These scholars give theoretical rigor and historical specificity to concepts such as formula, convention, formal norms, historical transformation, institutional restraints, intertextuality, and reception.

The work of David Bordwell, Janet Staiger, and Kristin Thompson on film style and mode of production within the classical Hollywood cinema offers the most complex and far-reaching model for a more historical account of the social, cultural and institutional determinants of genre conventions. Bordwell, Thompson, and Staiger treat the classical Hollywood cinema as constituting a recognizable and distinctive "group style" that retained a high degree of consistency "across decades, genres, studios, and personnel" from 1917 to 1960.[48] Thompson traces the style's historical development, linking it to the conventions and principles of theatrical realism, showing how it emerged from the experimentation of the early cinema into a coherent set of formal norms, and suggesting ways that the system absorbed new technologies and techniques. Staiger demonstrates how this group style satisfied the studios' need to standardize their output while facilitating constant novelty and product differentiation. Bordwell concentrates on the formal consistency within the group style, attempting to locate the general principles or norms behind its film practice. Collectively, the three writers present a convincing explanation for the look and logic of the classical Hollywood cinema. For our present purposes, we must pay close consideration to the nature and function of aesthetic norms within the Bordwell, Staiger, and Thompson model and the role generic formula plays within their account of the Hollywood cinema.

Drawing on the work of Jan Mukarovsky and other Slavic formalist critics, Bordwell argues that norms are not "codified and inflexible rules"; rather, they are characterized by their "comparative flexibility."[49] Norms are the commonsense assumptions artists bring to bear upon the production of artworks; norms therefore prefer certain formal choices as more acceptable or appealing than others: "Those norms constitute a determinant set of assumptions about how a movie should behave, about what stories it properly tells and how it should tell them, about the range and functions of film technique, and about the activities of the spectator."[50] Artists' acceptance of the general logic underlying a particular formal system encourages them to make certain choices from the larger vocabulary of available options. Adherence to these general norms allows for the production of works that win easy approval both from those in power over the artist and from those who will constitute the audience or consumers of the artwork. Yet disobedience of the rules is not necessarily "a negative act" since transgressions may lead to artistic innovation and create desired novelty. Consequently, no single text will perfectly correspond to the normative system; each will represent an inflection of those codes and conventions, more or less consistent with the larger group style.

Bordwell's "historical poetics" identifies general aesthetic principles shaping the production of individual artworks; it also inventories the vocabulary of possible formal choices historically available to filmmakers. From various rule books and guides and from textual analysis of a massive body of films, Bordwell identifies the dominant principles governing the classical Hollywood cinema: its focus on causality, linearity, psychological motivation, comprehensibility, universality, coherence, and transparency. Advances in technological resources (such as sound or widescreen) or the influences of alien aesthetic systems (such as German Expressionism, Soviet montage, or European modernism) may introduce new formal devices, but these devices will be harnessed toward fulfilling such basic functions as maintaining spatial and temporal coherence, focusing attention on character response to narrative events, or creating transitions between segments of an unfolding story. As a result, the classical system remained open to limited formal or thematic innovation while remaining highly stable over time.

Bordwell suggests that any formal, thematic, or narrative choice may be motivated in various ways. Compositional motivation determines what story elements must be present in order for the narrative to proceed to a satisfactory resolution. Realistic motivation determines what story elements are necessary to preserve a sense of verisimilitude. Intertextual motivation determines choices on the basis of their adherence to the conventions of particular classes or genres of artworks. Artistic motivation determines what elements are required to produce certain aesthetic effects. The classical norms, Bordwell argues, place the greatest emphasis upon compositional motivation, though frequently any given narrative element or aesthetic choice will be motivated at multiple levels. For the most part, Bordwell contends, generic or intertextual motivation is consistent with and reinforces the causal logic of compositional motivation and therefore ensures the transparency of Hollywood style.

Where there is a conflict between intertextual and compositional determination, however, Bordwell explains, "such operations do not radically disunify the films, since each genre creates its own rules, and the spectator judges any given element in the light of its appropriateness to generic conventions." [51] Unlike the *Cahiers*'s conception of category e films, which attributed a radicalizing potential to any deviation from classical narrative, Bordwell's model contains "a great range of nondisruptive differentiation." [52] Potentially jolting moments, such as the episode with the backflipping senators, do not radically challenge the dominance of classical norms; such transgressive sequences represent the exercise of options already contained within this paradigm and are followed by a return to standard narrative construction. Bordwell writes, "Conventions of the more stylized genres operate as limited plays with the classical compositional dominant." [53] Stylization, he suggests, occurs only along limited perimeters while preserving many basic principles, especially those concerning the articulation of time and space.

While helpful, Bordwell's account of "the bounds of difference" does not yet provide a full theory of the place of generic norms within the classical Hollywood cinema. Notions of generic convention seem capable, within his account, of absorbing and justifying all formal or thematic experimentation. Bordwell's analysis of film noir, for example, locates traits others read as outside dominant film practice; his model, however, allows him to conclude that these elements are not finally subversive because they "adhere to specific and nonsubversive conventions derived from crime literature and from canons of realistic and generic motivation."[54] "Crazy comedy" (i.e., what this text calls *anarchistic comedy*), Bordwell contends, cannot be regarded as outside of the mainstream of film practice, since these comedies appeal to vaudeville traditions and since there is a constant movement back and forth between elements that are intertextually motivated and elements that are compositionally and realistically motivated. Bordwell even suggests that the modernist aspirations of contemporary American films like *The Conversation* (United Artists, 1974) are defeated because the films do not "escape" from genres: "Classical film style and codified genres swallow up art-film borrowings, taming the (already limited) disruptiveness of the art cinema."[55] The conventionality of genre becomes a catch-all justification, allowing problematic popular texts to be reread within the mainstream of American film practice.

One can raise several objections to this account. First, while elements drawn from other aesthetic traditions will certainly be conventional, those conventions are not necessarily congruent or consistent with the norms of the classical cinema. Our backflipping senators might constitute a fairly standard comic acrobat act in vaudeville, yet their insertion into an ongoing narrative may be unconventional and disruptive. Even if we accept Bordwell's general claim that the classical cinema absorbed only those elements of alternative aesthetics compatible with its dominant principles, we must posit an initial period of exploration or experimentation during which transgressive practices could have pushed over those lines. As Hollywood maps "the bounds of difference," some texts or groups of texts are likely to be produced violating a sufficient number of basic expectations that they cannot be regarded as classical works. Such local exceptions need not challenge the model's larger claim that the classical system quickly absorbed those deviations and made them functional within its own terms. By emphasizing consistency over any

18

sense of experimentation or inconsistency, however, Bordwell risks reducing his otherwise complex model to a perfectly regulated system: Hollywood always knew in what direction it was moving and what would work best to achieve its goals; Hollywood never slipped outside of its own loosely defined set of artistic norms.

Second, to accommodate these aberrant texts, Bordwell stretches his definition of the classical norms to such breadth that it may lose its value for making useful distinctions between different aesthetic traditions. As Bordwell's model admits, not all Hollywood movies are equally classical. Minimally, if we conceive of the classical norms as a hierarchically organized set of aesthetic options, there will be some classical texts that consistently make the dominant choices from that set, while others consistently choose more marginal options. How far can a given film push against the margins of dominant film practice and still be said to operate within the classical paradigm? Is it possible for a film produced under the studio system to exceed the "bounds of difference" within classical norms?

Despite these reservations, the Bordwell-Staiger-Thompson model provides a framework for constructing a historical account of the development of specific generic norms. Thompson's discussion of the formation of the classical style directs us toward a review of trade journals, technical manuals, memoirs, film reviews, and publicity releases as points of entry into historical expectations about what constituted an acceptable or meritorious work. Staiger's consideration of the mode of production indicates the importance of institutional factors in determining the range of permissible transgression. Bordwell's detailed treatment of the classical norms provides a background against which that transgression may be read. His account of "the bounds of difference" also directs our attention toward ways generic norms may be traced to other cultural practices and aesthetic traditions.

GENRE HISTORY AND THE SOCIAL CONSTRUCTION OF TASTE

A historical conception of popular genres, however, must not be content to view them exclusively in terms of formal norms or institutional constraints; generic formulas are also ways of ordering the spectator's affective and cognitive experience, ways of exploiting and resolving ideological tensions. Consequently, generic evolution needs to be understood in light of larger social and cultural processes that determine what meanings and values will be assigned to certain formal and narrative conventions. Stuart Hall writes, "The important fact, then, is not a mere descriptive inventory—which may have the negative effect of freezing popular culture into some timeless descriptive mold—but the relations of power which are constantly punctuating and dividing the domain of culture into its preferred and its residual categories."[56] Commercial entertainment, he suggests, always feeds upon older popular traditions, adopting cultural forms that previously spoke on behalf of ideological resistance and transforming them into vehicles for ideological reproduction. Yet these commercial remakings of popular forms are rarely completely successful in containing or regulating the radical impulses characterizing the earlier folk traditions; commercial texts retain "elements of recognition and identification" and continue to speak to fundamental dissatisfactions within the social formation. Popular forms are neither "wholly corrupt [n]or wholly authentic" but rather deeply "contradictory" expressions of popular sentiments; popular forms are characterized by a "double movement" of ideological "containment and resistance."

Hall contends that the study of popular culture should be the study of these cultural "transformations," the study of the "active work on existing traditions and activities, their active reworking, so that they come out a different way," and of the process by which cultural distinctions get made. Hall's account urges us against making large scale claims about the conservativeness or progressiveness of particular genres, it rather demands that such claims be historically grounded. Recent work by cultural historians, such as Michael Denning, Lawrence Levine, Peter Stallybrass and Allon White, and Robert C. Allen, has focused attention on the process by which cultural distinctions get made and by which popular forms are absorbed and transformed by the domains of commercial entertainment and high art.[57]

These works suggest how the formalist orientation of the Bordwell-Thompson-Staiger account of the classical Hollywood cinema might assume an ideological dimension. Formal practices bear social connotations, win approval or disapproval within cultural institutions, speak to or for reception communities, and resist or reinforce dominant conceptions of taste and propriety. Consequently, in tracing the appropriation of formal devices from one cultural tradition by another, we must be attentive not simply to the ways the formal system restabilizes itself following a initial period of experimentation and exploration; we must also consider the process by which previous social connotations are stripped away, the prevailing ideological order is restored, and cultural respectability is reestablished.

Within such a socially informed version of "historical poetics," a recognition of ideological transgression would not hinge on whether a formal practice could be viewed as conventional or acceptable within aesthetic or generic norms. A fairly conventional element might still bear faint traces of its earlier use and an unconventional technique might still be consistent with prevailing conceptions of appropriate taste and social propriety. Hollywood norms were never perfectly aligned with dominant taste, but rather remained open to constant controversy and subject to periodic dismissal by central cultural and social institutions. The Hollywood cinema worked to preserve the affective immediacy of popular traditions while retaining enough social respectability to insure its institutional survival. Its central challenge was to attract both the "masses" and the "classes," both men and women, both young and old, both urban and rural viewers, threading its way across diverse and often contradictory conceptions of what constituted good taste and appropriate entertainment.

Some degree of transgressiveness is already presupposed by the notion of popular entertainment. Norbert Elias and Eric Dunning have offered an important analysis of the function of recreation and sport within the civilizing process, noting that it allows an expression of emotions and desires that must otherwise be repressed in order to operate within the social order: "many of these leisure activities . . . are designed so as to produce an enjoyable and controlled de-controlling of emotions. They offer pleasurable mimetic tensions often (though not always) leading up to a mounting excitement and to a climax of heightened feeling with the help of which . . . the tension may be happily resolved." [58] Elias and Dunning stress that the release from self-control sports and other entertainments provoke must itself be regulated to insure that the untapped emotions do not become overwhelming and socially destructive. If it is in the nature of popular entertainment to provoke strong emotions by transgressing social expectations, there remain limits of acceptability, thresholds of shame, that cannot be crossed without negative reaction. Those thresholds are flexible rather than fixed. Sometimes, the construction and articulation of these limits sparks passionate debate. At other times, mass culture quietly adjusts itself to changing sensibilities. Those boundaries of good taste, like the "bounds of difference" within the formal system, tell us much about the logic of social and cultural experience at a particular historical moment.

The history of a popular genre can usefully concern itself with the ways its dominant features were positioned within prevailing community taste, with ways its materials excite and regulate audience response, and with ways it transgresses or observes the boundaries of good taste and social propriety. The transgressiveness of generic material is read not only against the formal norms of the Hollywood cinema as an aesthetic institution but also against the system of prevailing taste distinctions.

EARLY SOUND COMEDY AND THE VAUDEVILLE AESTHETIC

What Made Pistachio Nuts? examines representative works drawn from a body of comedian-centered comedies produced within the Hollywood studio system during the late 1920s and early 1930s. These films constitute a particular chapter in the larger generic history of the comedian comedy tradition. Such films are characterized by a subordination of visual and aural style, narrative structure and character development to foregrounded comic performance; they are marked by a general questioning of social norms. In short, these comedies are recognizable through their difference from or opposition to dominant film practice during the early sound period and represent the extreme example of the "nonhermetic" or transgressive tendencies Seidman, Krutnik, and others have located within the comedian comedy tradition.

Consequently, I have adopted the term, *anarchistic comedy* to refer to this particular group of films. *Anarchistic comedy* is a doubly appropriate label. First, these comedies are anarchistic in that they press against traditional film practice, moving from the classical Hollywood cinema's emphasis upon linearity and causality toward a more fragmented and episodic narrative. If a dominant tendency of classical narrative is its push to unify its materials into a coherent story, the tendency of anarchistic comedy is toward heterogeneity, even at the risk of disunity and incoherence. Second, these films are anarchistic in that they often celebrate the collapse of social order and the liberation of the creativity and impulsiveness of their protagonist. These comedies are anarchistic in both form and content, though the relationship between these formal and thematic conventions is more complex than most previous accounts have acknowledged. I prefer the term *anarchistic comedy* to the alternative form, *anarchic comedy,* for two reasons: first, my chosen term preserves a sense of process in the texts, a movement from order to disorder, while *anarchic comedy* might suggest a consistent state of anarchy; second,

Vaudevillians in Hollywood: Charles Riesner, Ed Wynn, and Jimmy Durante at MGM. Wisconsin Center for Film and Theater Research.

anarchistic comedy foregrounds the active and central role of the clowns as bringers of anarchy.

In adopting the term *anarchistic comedy*, I consciously evoke the critical tradition surrounding the Marx Brothers. In doing so, however, I remain agnostic about the potential connections between the films' thematic concerns and their formal structures, and to fit the films' "anarchistic" tendencies within a broader aesthetic tradition, I have adopted a much broader definition of *anarchistic comedy* than those earlier accounts. A significant goal of this study will be to position the well-known films of the Marx Brothers against the context of lesser-known works from other studios. Anarchistic comedy, I will claim, is simply one of several different categories of comedian comedies produced in the early sound era. It is a generic tradition, not simply a formula for constructing vehicles for any particular star performer. From time to time, the names of neglected figures, such as Eddie Cantor, Wheeler and Woolsey, Olsen and Johnson, Burns and Allen, Joe E. Brown, Jimmy Durante, Charlotte Greenwood, and Winnie Lightner, will dominate this account. Indeed, I have made a conscious decision, at places, to focus attention on works like *Palmy Days* (UA, 1931), *So Long Letty* (Warner Brothers, 1929), *Hollywood Party* (MGM, 1934), *Six of a*

Kind (Paramount, 1934) and *Diplomaniacs* (RKO, 1933) rather than develop my arguments through the use of more canonical examples of anarchistic comedy such as *Duck Soup* or *It's a Gift* (Paramount, 1934).

I base this decision on two grounds. First, genre history must move beyond its reliance upon a great masterpiece (or comic minds) approach if its potential as a means of accounting for both the conventionality and the novelty of popular entertainment is to be achieved. Exceptional works like *Duck Soup* gain their significance only against the background of more mundane films like *You Said a Mouthful* (Warner Brothers, 1932) or *Hook, Line and Sinker* (RKO, 1932). Second, the genre's existing canon was based on a misapplication of classical criteria to the evaluation of works from an alternative aesthetic tradition and as such, it is not to be trusted. Only after we have reconstructed a more appropriate set of aesthetic norms can we decide which films most fully exemplify and actively extend the perimeters of this tradition and which blindly adhere to formula.

My central claim will be that anarchistic comedy emerged from the classical Hollywood cinema's attempt to assimilate the vaudeville aesthetic, an alternative set of social and artistic norms that enjoyed an uneasy relationship with dominant film practice in the early 1930s. Neither fully contained within the classical Hollywood cinema nor fully free of its norms, these films represent a succession of uneasy compromises, painstakingly negotiated during the production process, between two competing aesthetic systems, one governed by a demand for character consistency, causal logic, and narrative coherence, the other by an emphasis upon performance, affective immediacy and atomistic spectacle. Probably no two films resolved these formal problems in precisely the same way. During this transitional period, various strategies for constructing comic texts were tested; some embraced classical conventions, while others rejected those conventions in favor of a more faithful reproduction of vaudeville performance traditions, but most texts fell somewhere between these two extremes. Spatial metaphors—attempts to describe these films as "inside" or "outside" classical cinema—confuse what is essentially a process of negotiation between competing aesthetic logics. Such logics can overlap and coexist in ways that spatial categories cannot. What is clear is that these films cannot be fully explained through reference either to classical Hollywood norms or the vaudeville aesthetic but represent some overlap or interplay between the two formal systems. These films were, after all, produced within the mainstream commercial cinema and were answerable to the same institutional constraints as any other Hollywood movie. If these films are transgressive, it is because the Hollywood studios that financed, produced, and released them allowed and even encouraged those transgressions. For the most part, even these films conform to classical Hollywood norms. They are narratives. They have goal-centered protagonists. They maintain spatial and temporal coherence. They provide at least a minimal degree of causal integration. At the same time, they contain elements that transgress classical expectations about how stories should be told and how characters should be constructed.

The history of anarchistic comedy is the history of Hollywood's attempts to absorb those aspects of the vaudeville tradition most compatible with its norms, to make its devices functional within the preexisting logic of the narrative film, and to jettison those elements that proved irreconcilable with classical conventions. This book will trace the points of intersection between these two formal systems and outline the various moral, ethical, social, and cultural meanings that became attached to these different conceptions of popular amusement. It will link the formal reworking of vaudeville aesthetic within the commercial cinema with a transformation of its basic ideological assumptions and with a redefinition of its cultural status. This book will examine ways in which this new thematic and formal material pushed against and sometimes crossed over the boundaries of social acceptability and became the focus for cultural struggle. This study has the intention of providing a theoretical and historical framework within which additional studies of the comic genre might be constructed. It strives to displace auteur-dominated studies and the ahistorical comedian comedy model with an account of the comic film that is grounded in "historical poetics" and attentive to the politics of taste. All of this, in the end, may appear to be a long and circuitous route toward explaining the appearance of a pair of backflipping senators in an obscure Fox musical. Yet there is no simpler answer to the baffling question they pose for contemporary film scholarship: "What made pistachio nuts?"

2

"How Is It Possible for a Civilized Man to Live Among People Who Are Always Joking?" Class, Comedy, and Cultural Change in Turn-of-the-Century America

Originally published in *Century Magazine* in 1910, Carolyn Wells's comic short story, "First Lessons in Humor," encapsulates contemporary debates within the popular press about the proper place and function of laughter. A young married couple enjoys a life of bliss and harmony in "one of the prettiest houses on one of the prettiest streets of the pretty village of Brookdale" until they learn their elderly Aunt Molly, from whom they anticipate a sizable inheritance, is coming to stay with them. Aunt Molly personifies late nineteenth-century American "true womanhood," sharing her generation's somber disposition. Frustrated in her efforts to achieve a rapport with the older woman, the "unusually amiable young wife" remarks to her husband: "There's only one thing the matter with Aunt Molly. . . . And that is, she has no sense of humor. At first I thought she was grumpy and sour, but she isn't at all. She is only serious minded—so much so that she can't see the funny side of anything. I believe the sense of humor was entirely left out of her make-up." [1] In the name of family harmony, the young couple conspires to teach their aunt the "New Humor." They introduce common jokes into household discourse, explaining them carefully, and repeating them until they become so familiar that even Aunt Molly feels comfortable laughing at them. Soon, however, the young couple learns the true horrors of overjocularity, as their elderly pupil begins telling jokes without satiation or mercy: "We rose in the morning to be thrown into convulsions of irrepressible mirth; we retired at night exhausted from innumerable and unconquerable fits of laughter. To be in Aunt Millarkey's presence meant to be in a constant state of giggling, with frequent spasms and paroxysms of insane mirth. . . . Like Frankenstein, we had voluntarily created a monster that now threatened catastrophe."[2] Their aunt's newfound jocularity overrode all sense of propriety or inhibition, until the woman was capable of taking nothing seriously. Only when Brookdale's "grave and dignified minister" takes her as his wife and works to repair the damage to her "womanliness" can Aunt Molly achieve a proper balance between sobriety and mirthfulness.

The two faces of Aunt Molly—the one so prim and proper that no smile ever crossed its lips, the other joking and laughing uncontrollably—exaggerate, yet do not totally distort, a polarization of cultural taste and sensitivity characteristic of the first few decades of the twentieth century. Though offering playful criticisms of its potentially adverse influences in this particular short story, Wells was a key proponent of the so-called New Humor; she defended its playful nonsense through her critical essays and her anthologies of contemporary wit. However, she was not alone in recognizing both the dangers of uncompromising puritanism and the threat of unceasing jocularity. Writing in 1926, Irwin Edman described a mounting battle between "the earnest seekers after truth and salvation" whose solemnness "puts to sleep those who might otherwise have been saved" and the "frivolists" who refuse to treat anything about life with its due respect.[3] While both represented a clear and present danger to the growth and development of the national culture, almost all commentators agreed that it was the frivolists who posed the most tangible threat. The nation's fate could not be allowed to remain in the hands of those without social mission or the ability to be aroused to action. In the words of one educator, "The end of life is work and work must be grave and serious; playfulness carried to excess becomes emptiness. . . . Humor must not intervene to relieve tension when tension is helpful to the achievement of some end."[4] The image of the frivolist as a monstrous anarchist, willing to abandon all responsibility, ready to reduce the entire nation to uncontrollable laughter, enjoyed broad currency during the period.

This chapter will examine the social and cultural dimensions of this struggle over the appropriate limits and proper functions of popular humor, a struggle that had dramatic consequences for the development of twentieth-century American comedy. I will expose the major assumptions underlying the two dominant comic aesthetics of the early twentieth century and consider how the new mass culture challenged some traditional attitudes about the place of laughter in human society. Middle-class anxiety about jokes and laughter displaced legitimate fears about social change onto the aesthetic sphere; it was a submerged discourse about the cultural transformation of American life. "Canons of good taste" and notions of restrained laughter helped to maintain class boundaries and to naturalize inequalities of economic and social opportunity. The redefinition of appropriate comedy was a feared challenge to the coherence of this system as critics sought to contain its excesses. I will outline the impact of these debates upon early conceptions of film comedy.

"A THING WHOLESOME, REFRESHING, AND EDIFYING OF CHARACTER": THE TRADITION OF THOUGHTFUL LAUGHTER

George Meredith's 1877 "An Essay on Comedy" set the terms for late Victorian and progressive era discourse on the comic, drawing a sharp contrast between the "hypergelasts," whom he characterizes as "excessive laughers, . . . who are so loosely put together that a wink will shake them" and the "agelasts," the nonlaughters who "are in that respect as dead bodies, which, if you prick them, do not bleed."[5] Meredith felt that the "comic spirit" dwelt most comfortably in a middle ground between "puritanism and Bacchanalism" and was both purposeful and restrained, a reasoned laughter that is full of "healing. . . good breeding . . . [and] wisdom"[6] Despite some reservations about the state of contemporary British stage comedy, Meredith's account is generally optimistic, partially because of his faith in the perfectibility of human society, partially because of his assumption that both agelasts and hypergelasts were fringe groups and neither could dominate. For the first time, Meredith felt, humanity had reached a level of cultural development allowing the "true comic spirit" to prosper. Meredith saw signs that the laughter of the body and of the brute passions was giving way to the more refined laughter of the intellect and the heart: "A society of cultivated men and women is required, wherein ideas are current and the perceptions quick that he [the comic playwright] may be supplied with matter and an audience. The semi-barbarism of merely giddy communities, and feverish emotional periods, repel him."[7] Such "refinement" was possible only where individuals could remove themselves from the immediacy of their environment and achieve a degree of mental distance from popular thought and follies.

Although perhaps the best-known essay to emerge from this period, Meredith's argument reflects a much larger cultural discourse. As Robert Bernard Martin notes, the nature and function of laughter had been a lively source of debate in both America and across the Atlantic throughout the Victorian era. "The Victorians were much concerned with the propriety of laughter: whether it was suitable for philosophers, for Christians, even for ladies and gentlemen. . . . By extension the validity of comedy and of the risible in literature was brought into question." [8] These literary debates, though often heated, were grounded in a "gentleman's agreement" that comedy should serve a serious purpose, laughter be subordinated to didacticism and restrained through a strong-felt sense of morality, propriety, and ethics. Certain subjects were almost universally deemed inappropriate for comic treatment. The foundation uniting Victorian writers was so solid that as late as 1913, a Bostonian writing a letter to the editor of the *Nation,* could speak with confidence of "certain canons of good taste which are universally accepted by well-bred people as governing humorous expression of all sorts." [9]

Meredith's ideal of contemplative and restrained laughter had assumed the status of a "natural fact" by the turn of the century. Writers viewed this ideal as the logical end goal of human cultural evolution. Meredith's concept of restrained laughter was completely intertwined with social Darwinism, a discourse that naturalized its aesthetic claims. Burgess Johnson suggested to *Harper's Monthly* readers in 1915 that working-class humor was literally of a lower evolutionary order than that of the more genteel folks. Laughter depends, he suggested, on a stimulation of the nervous system, either through shock and surprise. One of the most primitive mechanisms of the body, laughter appears early in the development of natural organisms:

> Picture this great-grandfather of living things [the mollusk] lying motionless save for those nervous, fluttering, sensitive feelers extended to play the part of sight and hearing. A bit of seaweed bumps against them. A spasm racks the mollusk's whole being, crushing him into his shell until the surprise has abated; then the fact that no further attack follows brings relief. This is the germ of the cause of our laughter spasm—a sudden shock, instantly followed by a feeling of relief. [10]

"The laugh of the mollusk" echoed through the centuries as a crude "racial memory," shaping the pleasures generated by neural stimulation. As humans evolved and developed higher degrees of civilization than their mollusk ancestors, they also developed a more refined sense

of humor. The evolutionarily superior human re
of physical comedy in favor of the subtler, mor
of a perceived incongruity or a contradictory cl
had not developed such a refined taste simply
toward an ideal state of civilization as their
remained on the level of "children and savag

James Sully, a leading child psychologis
in his much-acclaimed treatise on laughter. Sully
evolution in comic sensitivity from the crude laughter ...
savages, and the animal kingdom at the "teasing and taunting" of then
fellow species toward the more "thoughtful laughter" being perfected
in the modern age. He concluded a lengthy discussion of early anthropological research into the nature and function of laughter in tribal
societies with the observation that "in all this mirthful teasing, it is
easy to see much that strikes us as cruel, or at least, as unfeeling. It is
only natural that the hilarity of peoples low down in the scale of culture
should now and again take on this aspect." [11] Such crude humor was the
product of "the simpler feelings of savages, untrammeled by the laws of
decency as civilized people know them." [12] Human progress alters the
nature of laughter: "the primal laugh, devoid of intellectual content,
becomes less general; the laugh of the mind more frequent." [13] Sully
suggested that this cultural evolution would eventually produce "a
certain kind of temperament, a complexion of sentiment, nay more, a
mode of psychical organization," which he linked to Meredith's notion
of "thoughtful laughter." [14] (Dr. Charles Gray Shaw, a New York
University philosopher, took this argument to its logical extreme,
suggesting that "when all men are fully evolved, laughter will die a
natural death. Indeed, it is safe to predict that war and laughter will
depart hand in hand." I suspect few readers held their breaths for either
eventuality.)[15]

"The True Comic Spirit" was at once a mark of individual distinction
and a signpost of a refined society. The term, *refined* was carefully
chosen, since it referred to a purification process, the imposition of a
cultural filter between the individual and the comic stimulants. Refined
humor marked mastery over cruelty, brute emotions and unrestrained
passion. Possession of such humor reflected an ability to think for
oneself apart from the flux of the times, to gain distance from the
immediacy of human experience; humor arose only when we are able to
contemplate actions and attitudes against their fuller context and to find
within them evidence of incongruity. Drawing upon humor's original

30

meaning as a bodily fluid, Sully claims that this humor was a social lubricant facilitating a greater sense of community, a sharing of good cheer between individuals engaged in a common project; such humor was "a thing wholesome, refreshing, and edifying of character."[16]

For Sully and others of his generation, humor was not a property of comic texts nor was it an affective response that could be provoked. Rather, humor was a quality an individual might possess, a form of mental alertness and moral wisdom. W. L. Courtney, a literary critic, defined the quality:

> We laugh at farce, we laugh at all kinds of burlesque entertainment, we laugh at pantomimes, we laugh at the grotesque humor of some of the reviews. But this kind of laughter could not possibly be called thoughtful; it rather rests on the absence of all thought and comes more naturally from a vacuous mind. . . . Thoughtful laughter is a different experience, which does not come to us often. It is an inner experience—a sort of internal chuckle—which does not display external manifestations. It is the enjoyment of the intellect when situations or characters or sometimes, phrases strike one as happy exhibitions of humor.[17]

For this reason, among others, proponents of "thoughtful laughter" frequently expressed disdain for public amusements. Remarked Max Beerbohm, "There is to me something rather dreary in the notion of going anywhere for the specific purpose of being amused. I prefer that laughter shall take me unawares."[18] Personal discovery was an essential element of thoughtful laughter and many felt that such chance encounters with the comic were not compatible with calculated entertainment. Writing in 1898, Gerald Stanley Lee protested "the constant strain of the American people to keep itself amused," suggesting that "three-quarters of the fun of a funny thing is in finding it in the wrong place. The other quarter is the finding it for oneself. What is left after this is the joke."[19] Not surprisingly, advocates of thoughtful laughter saw its greatest potential within the realist theater. The ideal stage comedy duplicated the conditions accompanying the discovery of the comic in everyday life, although those conditions could be altered somewhat to allow for a greater clarity of insight. Courtney declared, "The world as pictured by the true writer of comedy should be the real world, though heightened and adorned by his comic humor. The characters he portrays are real men and women, albeit that for the purposes of his wit their lineaments are exaggerated."[20] Again and again, there were calls for a style of performance that allowed spectators to discover for themselves the humor in a situation "caught unawares" from behind the invisible fourth wall. There were also numerous attacks on the direct address to the audience favored by vaudeville and review performers, since such self-consciousness called attention to the performer's efforts to amuse. All signs of the intentional production of laughter were to be erased; humor was to arise from the interplay of rounded characters within a realistic context and should never be "forced" or "contrived." Jokes were not to exist for their own sake, but rather subordinated to the narrative; jokes were to reveal the character's fundamental comic flaws rather than display the performer's talents.

Sully further insisted that "true comedy" came through a careful melding of emotions, a precise mixture of comedy and pathos: "The art of humorous writing consists in part in selecting characters, incidents, and the rest in such a way as to exhibit the intimate connections between that which amuses and that which touches the serious sentiments, respect and pity; and to develop the reflective consciousness which sustains the mood of humor."[21] Such affective fusion allows not only for the discovery of the comic against a broader contextual background but also for a more subtle and restrained reaction to life's complexities: "The more energetic movements of laughter are without doubt restrained by an admixture of sympathy."[22] Sully, like many of his contemporaries, saw the fulfillment of his aesthetic ideals in the plays of Molière and his contemporaries. The well-made French farce achieved "a perfect fusion of play and gravity, of the aggressiveness of laughter and kindly consideration."[23] This tradition provided a ready set of exemplars by which ethical and moral concerns about the quality and function of laughter could be translated into an aesthetic of comic realism.

THE MECHANICS OF EMOTION

The new mass market publications that emerged in the late nineteenth and early twentieth centuries generated an alternative discourse that challenged the necessity of purposeful laughter and questioned the aesthetic centrality of comic realism. This new discourse represented pleasure as a desirable goal in its own right. Its advocates seemed interested merely in locating the most effective way of stimulating an outward display of laughter. Perhaps the most remarkable thing about this new discourse was how rarely its advocates felt the need to address social, moral, or ethical questions at all. They did not so much challenge the previous discourse as simply ignore it (though traditionalists were less willing to ignore the New Humor). The clash of these two paradigms can be seen in the sharp contrast between two statements: the first by a literary critic for *Blackwood's Magazine,* whose position reflects the norms of the nineteenth century; the second by Brett Page from his guidebook for would-be vaudeville writers, whose position suggests the craft orientation of this new discourse:

> The great men who dared to laugh in an earlier age than ours laughed in moderation. . . . They held folly up to ridicule, not to amuse the groundlings, but to reveal, in a sudden blaze of light, the eternal truths of wisdom and justice. . . . They did not at every turn slap their reader on the back and assure him that there is nothing congruous in the visible world. . . . They kept their humor in its proper place; they used it for a wise purpose; they did not degrade it for an easy round of applause.[24]

> The purpose of the [comic] sketch is not to leave a single impression of a single story. It points no moral, draws no conclusion, and sometimes it might end quite as effectively anywhere before the place in the action at which it does terminate. It is built for entertainment purposes only and furthermore, for entertainment purposes that end the moment the sketch ends.[25]

For the *Blackwood's* critic, comedy must "instruct"; for Page, it need only "entertain." For one, the outward display of emotion is to be distrusted, laughter is to be restrained; for the other, outward affective response is a measure of success in a craft that ruthlessly exploited any and all means of producing a laugh. No longer was the debate over what purpose comedy should serve but rather over whether comedy need have *any* higher purpose; the debate was not over what limits should be placed upon comic material but rather over whether limits were necessary. The moral certainty of Victorian comic sensibility was called into question by these brash new merchants of mirth who found it perfectly acceptable to say that their comic material was "built for entertainment purposes only."

While the traditional aesthetic saw the ability to perceive comic incongruity as a mark of social distinction, the new aesthetic sought to level the classes, appealing to what its advocates saw as basic visceral responses. George M. Cohan and George Jean Nathan wrote in 1913: "The emotional lives of all men follow a fixed norm, precisely as do their physical lives. In the main, the same elemental ideas that got a 'rise' out of our ancestors will do the same for us. . . . If we are normal, we all cry at the same things, laugh at the same things, and are thrilled by the same things."[26] Spectators go to the theater precisely because they wish to have "emotions played upon," to be pulled away from the humdrum reality of their workaday existence and thrust into a situation where they can experience affect without consequences. Through a sophisticated mastery of the "mechanics of emotions," Cohan and Nathan argued, the playwright and performer may control audience response, may shape and mold the emotions of the spectators in a precise fashion. Making explicit references to the developing science of reflexology, Cohan and Nathan suggested that humans possesses "emotional reflexes" that may be manipulated to produce a predictable reaction: "Given the average crowd in a theater, the experienced playwright, in the quiet of his study, can figure out in advance precisely what constituents in his play will produce particular effects. . . . If produced at the right moment and with sufficient skill, they never fail to strike the audience in the midriff."[27] Cohan and Nathan isolated a vocabulary of basic mechanical devices, insertable into any performance regardless of context, and calculated to produce an immediate and outward response. These devices required little intellectual engagement with the material, and not much intellectual honesty or aesthetic integrity:

> [A device] has been utilized arbitrarily by the stage artificer, and it may have absolutely nothing to do with what follows. . . . If subsequently, the audience says to itself, "we were fooled," it does not matter. . . . The secret of stage effectiveness rests in the impression of the moment. . . . Nothing counts in the theater but the impression of the time being. All the mechanics of emotion are based, from the theatrical craftsman's point of view, on this one solid fact.[28]

The pseudoscience of affective "mechanics" dominates the discourse of early twentieth-century show business. Gagwriters and comic performers spoke confidently about "what makes people laugh" listing their "sure-fire laugh-getters" and suggesting their effects upon an audience.[29] Social scientists employed quantitative surveys to measure human receptiveness to different types of jokes and to different bits of comic business. Performers and humorists relied more on their own impressions. Both scholars and performers wrote with certainty about their ability to predict the results of particular tried-and-true materials; both social scientists and comics regarded themselves to be skilled interpreters of human affect. Consider, for instance, how burlesque clowns Joe Weber and Lew Fields characterize the devices that produce a "payoff" from their audience:

An audience will laugh loudest at these episodes:

(a) when a man sticks one finger into another man's eyes;
(b) when a man sticks two fingers into another man's eyes;
(c) when a man chokes another man and shakes his head from side to side;
(d) when a man kicks another man;
(e) when a man bumps up suddenly against another man and knocks him off his feet;
(f) when a man steps on another man's foot.

Human nature—as we have analyzed it, with results that will be told by the cashier at our bank—will laugh louder and oftener at these spectacles, in the respective order we have chronicled them, than at anything else one might name.[30]

Here, as with Cohan and Nathan, no mention is made of the gag's context, of who is poking whom in the eye or why. Such gags functioned as self-contained units; they could be slotted into diverse contexts and could assume many potentially funny meanings. The audience's response does not involve the quick perception of subtle incongruity; it requires a visceral reaction to crude shock, intense stimulation, and immediate sensation. A comic vehicle could be welded together from various affective mechanisms with an eye toward a gradually intensifying response. Brett Page's guide for vaudeville writers observed of ideal comedy sketches: "Merely a thread of plot holds them together and on it is strung the elemental humor of the comedy bits. The purpose being only to amuse for the moment, all kinds of entertainment forms may be introduced."[31] These comic "bits" were not subordinated to the larger narrative, as they might have been within the aesthetic of comic realism; rather, they were to be the entire basis of the entertainment, justified purely through the degrees of laughter they provoke. Jokes were crafted from the "raw materials" of comical sounds; routines or sketches were constructed from the "raw material" of jokes; the whole was aimed at manipulating the spectator's emotions. Laughter was to be precisely orchestrated in order that the most intense wave of response came at the end of a sequence of gags, providing "complete satisfaction in one great

The mechanics of emotion: Weber and Fields. Wisconsin Center for Film and Theater Research.

burst of laughter" so that the audience had a chance to catch its breath, recover its bearings a little before the next onslaught began.

The merits of the program were determined by the performer's ability to manipulate the audience to the point that they suspended conscious thought and simply felt. In 1925, Robert Lytell defined for *New Republic* readers what he saw as characteristic of the best vaudeville performers: "Human horsepower, size, electricity, energy, zingo. . . . These people have a fire in their belly which makes you sit up and listen whether you want to or not, which silences criticism until their act is over and you can begin thinking again. . . . They seize you and do pretty nearly anything they want with you and while it is going on, you sit with your mouth open and laugh and laugh again." [32] Theater managers looked to audience response as a tangible measure of quality, as evidence of the "effectiveness" of a comic performance.

"EVERYTHING IS FUNNY IF YOU ONLY THINK SO!"

Albert McClean, Jr., has characterized this New Humor as a unique product of twentieth-century American life: "The New Humor spoke for the New Folk and was the point of agreement upon which the new mass community might be founded." [33] The shifting population base of the United States, he suggests, required a redefinition of appropriate humor as native traditions came into contact with the folk traditions of the immigrant community. The New Humor expressed frustration and confusion against the inability of American institutions to fulfill their promises. Rapid new styles of living required a more intense, more economic form of comedy than would be desirable or even acceptable in a more leisurely, pastoral era.

McClean's arguments have some merit. The logic of the New Humor was deeply affected by the input of ethnic materials into the national culture and by the rapid pace and harsh life of urban America. Vaudeville's base in oral culture allowed its humor to respond quickly to shifts in popular taste and social practice. It would be a mistake, however, to perceive the New Humor as a total break with the past. Lawrence Senelick, who reviewed the personal gag books of two vaudeville performers, J. C. Murphy from the 1870s, Jerry Cohan from the 1880s, concludes that many of the traits McClean identifies as characteristic of a twentieth-century urban culture were already in place prior to institutionalization of vaudeville: "His [McClean's] hypothesis breaks down under scrutiny. The same cynical quid pro quo pervades Murphy's material, where it appeared on the lips of hicks and hired men. There too the survival instinct predominates, along with an awareness of the harsh exigencies of everyday life." [34] If anything, Senelick finds a muting of these aggressive tendencies, a movement toward less fragmented materials in Cohan's sketches that he attributes to the campaign to attract a more respectable audience for vaudeville. The brutal comedy of *Peck's Bad Boy,* which one contemporary labeled "the vulgarest conception of family life ever penned," [35] and the black humor of the popular "Little Willie" jokes about an impish lad who slaughters his family members can be found in an even rawer form in the nineteenth-century adventures of Davy Crockett, Simon Suggs, or *Mose the Bow'ry B'hoy.* [36] Many of the jokes filling the humor columns of local papers or forming the basis for the strip cartoons could be traced back to *Joe Miller's Jest Book* nearly two hundred years before, and had been recycled endlessly during the intervening years. [37] Indeed, contemporary critics frequently attacked these new comic forms for their heavy dependence upon "old saws." [38] It was the crudity and vulgarity of these earlier native comic traditions that bourgeois critics rejected when they embraced the more "refined" traditions of English and European comedy, when they sought to model American humor magazines like *Life* and *Puck* after *Punch* or tried to reshape American theater on the model of French farce. [39]

What had changed, then, was not so much the nature of comic material as its availability. Materials previously restricted to the masculine culture of the saloons and the oral discourse of the ghetto were now gaining national prominence through the industrialization of amusement. Materials the genteel writers of the late nineteenth century repudiated in their campaign for greater respectability commanded national attention once again. By the early twentieth century, increased leisure time and expanded family budgets had greatly broadened the potential market for commercial entertainment; shifts in technology and corporate organization had created conditions enabling would-be entrepreneurs to exploit this market with much greater success than previously. [40] Mass market magazines provided an alternative voice that embraced rather than rejected the emotional immediacy of popular humor.

The result was a massive proliferation of comic materials, a large-scale commodification of the joke. According to one study, the number of joke books published in the United States grew from 11 in 1890 to 104 in 1907 and continued to expand throughout the first two decades of the twentieth century.[41] More than thirty-five different humor magazines, many of them weeklies, were added to the market in the years, 1883–1920. While some of them folded almost as quickly as they appeared, many others would provide a key base for would-be gag writers for years to come. The period also saw the rise of amateur humor magazines on the campuses of many of the nation's leading universities.[42] For the first time, it was possible to make a good living just writing jokes, and advice for would-be joke writers can be found in the pages of many of the day's leading literary journals.[43] Humorist Thomas L. Masson estimated that he had sold more than fifty thousand jokes in the course of his career, mostly to his own publication, *Life*, but also to various other periodicals.[44] First appearing in American newspapers in the early 1880s, comic strips had become a staple item of popular journalism by the turn of the century. One newspaper editor estimated that the addition of the Sunday comics had increased his circulation by more than a half, adding another fifty thousand to an initial base of one hundred thousand readers.[45] Many newspapers also published daily joke or humor columns. By 1900, there were more than nine hundred theaters in the United States that regularly featured vaudeville performances and another five thousand that sometimes offered variety performances as part of a more varied program. A large chunk of the variety bill was devoted to various forms of comic performance.[46] The number of theaters that predominantly featured variety shows would surpass fifteen hundred by vaudeville's peak years in the mid-1920s.[47] By 1912, the year that Mack Sennett's Keystone studio began active production, some forty comic films a week were being released into the country for exhibition in nickelodeons, making comedy the largest single genre in the early cinema. The number of film comedies produced grew at a much faster rate than the general increase in the number of shorts being produced.[48] Soon the advent of commercial radio would further increase the demand for new gags.

Few could stand outside of this incredible onslaught of jokes and pratfalls. These materials were now being targeted at the middle class as well as at the working class; at women as well as men; at children as well as adults. They were commanding a greater degree of cultural respectability than they had previously been granted. Gag writers, humor columnists, and vaudeville clowns were interviewed alongside prestigious figures of industry, government, literature, society, and education in the pages of popular magazines. A 1916 article asked President Woodrow Wilson, Vice-President Thomas R. Marshall, key cabinet officials, congressional leaders, John D. Rockefeller, and other luminaries to share their favorite jokes and their answers appeared alongside those of humorists Thomas Masson, Thomas Lawson, and Irwin S. Cobb, and comic performer Otis Skinner.[49]

The performers and gag writers themselves displayed a giddiness about their newfound status. Evoking imagery calculated to provoke middle-class ire, Tom P. Morgan, another leading jokesmith, described his craft:

> We do not get our material by inspiration but by theft, assault and battery and otherwise. A solemn, honest, peace-loving commonality is grabbed, thrown down, turned inside out, and reconstructed into an absurdity. A feeble, hoary-headed idea is ruthlessly set upon, crippled, torn to pieces, put together backwards with a new head or tail on it; the King's English is deliberately murdered—all for a joke! Then, too, everything is funny if you only think so.[50]

With an ever-expanding market for the comic, with a highly appreciative audience, with increasing skills in jokesmithing, and with an almost unlimited territory to exploit, these spokespersons for the New Humor had every right to sound cocky.

The New Humor steadfastly refused to remain marginalized, demanding a greater share of America's cultural life; it encroached further upon terrain the middle classes had once regarded as their own and consequently, it provoked a strong, almost panic-stricken response. Theater critics lambasted the strong influence vaudeville and screen slapstick were having upon the traditional stage.[51] Readers hotly debated the advisability of including nonsense verse in spaces traditionally devoted to lyric poetry in the most prestigious literary magazines.[52] Others protested the inclusion of comics in the pages of the daily newspapers, suggesting that those spaces should be reserved for more pressing matters.[53]

Despite such protests, New Humor refused to remain in its "proper place," contaminating all spheres of cultural activity, blurring the taste categories that once built distinctions between different social classes. Writing in 1906, literary critic Jerome K. Jerome predicted that the modern vogue for the comic would demean all aspects of American life. Jerome predicted that the nation would soon confront comic trials, silly sermons, and humorous funeral services.[54] Albert R. Bandini reported in a 1926 *Catholic World* essay that "the per capita consumption of humor is much greater in the United States than in any other country of the world." If spending fifteen minutes a day reading was calculated to improve your word power, as a contemporary campaign for self-education promised, Bandini mused, what would be the moral and intellectual consequences of an American public that spent well over an hour a day laughing at jokes and comics?

> The fetish of humor affects our whole social life; it deprives us of the sense of salutary indignation which we ought to feel against evil and evil-doers. It dulls pity and stunts justice. . . . The public must be amused, it clamors for its daily ration, and therefore any likely or unlikely material, any situation, no matter what its gravity, must be thrown into the cauldron and cooked into some fashion of mirth. Nothing can be spared.[55]

"EVERY JOKE HAS ITS PRICE":
MIDDLE-CLASS ANXIETY AND THE NEW HUMOR

This massive expansion of the potential market for humor and its amoral exploitation by producers and performers intensified the rhetoric against laughter and joking. In such a climate, aesthetic discourse quickly assumed ethical, moral, and social dimensions. Anxieties about industrialization, urbanization, immigration, unionization, women's suffrage, and generational conflicts were rapidly translated into anxiety about the New Humor. Reckless jokes seemed to throw more fuel onto the fires of change. The image of a loss of bodily control in laughter seemed to symbolize for these writers the loss of social control and the decline of their cultural dominance.[56]

Would this onslaught of "purposeless" laughter, of joking that respected no limitations or boundaries destroy the type of civilization late Victorians valued? Would it reshape popular opinion and increase the likelihood of class warfare, lawlessness, and social decay? Educators, clergymen, sociologists, psychologists, literary critics, moral reformers, all had firm (if often hysterical) opinions about the New Humor's consequences. While most acknowledged that a developed sense of humor had become a social necessity, one of the marks of a civilized individual, and a key to business success, many expressed anxiety that the tendency to joke was being pushed to a dangerous extreme. Too much joking would destroy the social cohesiveness of American culture. *Cosmopolitan* contributor Mabel Marion Cox suggested, in 1906, that "nature teaches us that a display of the teeth is always a warning, a threat."[57] A nation composed of "modern heathen who worship the crescent of the smile," a nation unresponsive to nature's warning, Cox predicted, would suffer the consequences of its "ruthless" pursuit of laughter.

James Sully also cautioned about the rampant expansion of the comic into all spheres of social life:

> [If] laughter is an escape from the normal, serious attitude which living well imposes on us, its wise cultivation means that we keep it within limits. Only where there is a real earnestness and good feeling at bottom, will our laughter be in the full sense that of the mind and of the heart. . . . If the laugh grows too frequent and habitual, this respect will be undermined, and, as one result of this moral loss, our laughter itself will shrink into something void of meaning and mechanical.[58]

He insisted that good "humor," laughter within moderation, could be socially unifying, morally uplifting, and physically invigorating, "a useful prophylactic" he describes it at one point. However, he feared the consequences to both the biological and the social body if laughter were taken to an extreme.[59] Laughter, he felt, was refreshing precisely because it broke the normal rhythm of life, accelerated the circulation of the blood, increased the flow of oxygen, and relieved tension on the brain. Because it was such a "violent interruption," however, it should be restricted to an "occasional spurt" of good cheer.[60] If laughter became the normal state rather than a release from normality, the respected doctor warned, one could literally laugh oneself to death or into insanity.

Like many others of his generation, Sully was perhaps even more fearful of the moral and social consequences of prolonged laughter. Restrained laughter helped maintain social customs in the face of outside influence, censored common vices and follies, and facilitated greater social cooperation. However, the corrective power of laughter was blunted when it was used indiscriminately; wit could destroy social unity when used without proper caution: "The laughing impulse, when unchecked, has taken on ugly and deadly forms. . . . Society is right in her intuitive feeling that an unbridled laughter threatens her order and her laws."[61]

Sully was not alone in these beliefs. Educators worried that the acceptance of "anything in the name of a good joke" was destroying classroom discipline as wayward students used joking as an excuse for all conceivable forms of misconduct.[62] Parents expressed concern that the Sunday Colored Supplement might foster delinquency and "destroy all respect for law and authority."[63] Early and prolonged exposure to this unrestrained jocularity would have long-term consequences for the health of the nation: "We are teaching them lawlessness; we are cultivating a lack of reverence in them; we are doing everything we can, by cheapening life, to destroy the American homes of the future."[64] Many feared that the New Humor would eventually destroy all moral judgment, plunging American society into ethical chaos. In 1903, an *Atlantic* writer asserted that

> [joking] carried to excess must mean the sacrifice of serious consideration of life and duty, would do away with reverential thought, and replace fervency with flippancy. There is a national tendency to overdo the funny side, to make a joke at any cost. Every joke has its price and some are too expensive. Their payment means a lessening of respect for sacred institutions, a lowering of the standard of morality, a dulling of the sensibility to coarseness and vulgarity.[65]

If American civilization had been founded upon a seriousness of purpose, rooted in idealism and committed to achievement, then a new "flippancy," with its mixture of cynicism and immediate gratification, would destroy it. Articles with titles like "The Plague of Jocularity," "A Plea for Seriousness," or "Serious Results of the Recent Humor," appeared in publications of every sort.[66] In this age of reform, the quality of American humor, of popular amusement in general, had become a serious social issue. America had become a laughing nation, a country of frivolists and hypergelasts, a culture dangerously out of control. Only a return to self-restraint and discipline, only a resurrection of the nineteenth-century comic aesthetic could divert America from its course toward anarchy and immorality.

The hyperbolic rhetoric and the prolonged struggle against the rise of the New Humor suggests, however, that something more than aesthetics was at issue here. Concepts of good taste, appropriate conduct, or aesthetic merit are not natural or universal. Rather, they are rooted in social experience and reflect particular class interests. As Pierre Bourdieu notes, these tastes often seem "natural" to those who share them because they are shaped by their earliest experiences as members of a particular cultural configuration, reinforced through each and every social exchange and rationalized through encounters with higher education and other basic institutions. Yet access to this "cultural capital" is unequally distributed; differences in taste serve as marks of "distinction" in a realm where some tastes are "naturally" preferable to others.

[Taste] unites and separates. . . . [Taste] unites all those who are the product of similar conditions but only by distinguishing them from all others.
. . . Tastes (i.e., manifested preferences) are the practical affirmation of an
inevitable difference. It is no accident that, when they have to be justified,
they are asserted purely negatively, by the refusal of other tastes. In matters
of taste, more than anywhere else, all determination is negation; and tastes
are perhaps first and foremost distastes, disgust provoked by horror or
visceral intolerance ('sick-making') of the tastes of others.[67]

"Refined laughter" functioned as a central source of social distinction
within the culture of late nineteenth- and early twentieth-century America.
Categories of laughter were one way cultural experience was ordered and
social status was justified. Writers of the period often spoke of one's
sense of humor as evidence of a "natural" propensity toward "good
taste" among those with proper "breeding." Richard Burton suggested
in a *Bellman* article of 1917: "One's sense of the fit time to laugh and
the kind of laughter to indulge in on occasion is one of the sure tests of
culture in the individual and civilization in a people. . . . The coarse
guffaw is a mark of ill-breeding."[68]

Drawing on Herbert Spencer's notion that comic perception required
a momentary sensation of superiority over others, *Nation* critic Louis
Crocker drew a sharp contrast between the intelligence required to
appreciate high comedy and that needed to enjoy more low-brow fare:

He who has brought a critical attitude of mind to bear upon the institutions
and the ways of men will cooperate with the creative activity of a faculty
which he himself possess and has exercised; he to whom all criticism is alien
can evidently find no cause for superiority within himself and must be
flattered by the sight of physical mishaps and confusions, which, for the
moment, are not his own.[69]

High comedy demanded the experience of actual superiority and was
therefore reserved for a higher class audience; low comedy offered only
an illusion of superiority, the only type available to those of low
intelligence and poor social position. Within the rhetoric of social
Darwinism, taste distinctions helped to consolidate differences in class
position and justified inequalities of economic capital; they endowed the
haves with an easy way to rationalize greater access to wealth and power
while outcast labels were used to ensure conformity to social and aesthetic norms.

Such a cultural economy is self-perpetuating, Bourdieu argues, because approved tastes are generally distanced from economic want while rejected tastes make a virtue of economic necessity. The high value the "bourgeois aesthetic" places on aesthetic distance and emotional control "can only be constituted within an experience of the world freed from urgency [and] . . . presupposes the distance from the world which is the basis of the bourgeois experience."[70] It requires slow cultivation of taste and a gradual development of certain cultural competencies. These refinements come only from constant exposure to the aesthetic realm and consistent reinforcement of the preferred taste. Granted a world where time and economic capital can be spent with relative freedom, one can chose to experience the aesthetic in a slow and subtle fashion, one can develop the distance from the world required for thoughtful laughter. "The intention of purifying, refining and sublimating facile impulses and primary needs" becomes a sign of conspicuous consumption, marking possession of sufficient economic capital and leisure to be indifferent to the need for more immediate sensation.[71]

The working class of the country's expanding cities, for whom entertainment dollars were scarce and leisure time limited, placed a greater emphasis upon the "use value" of cultural experience, upon the amount of pleasure received per expenditure. The aesthetic choices of the working class, Bourdieu argues, often reflect a desire for "maximum 'effect' . . . at minimum cost, a formula which for bourgeois taste is the very definition of vulgarity."[72] A hunger for immediate gratification and intense stimulation grows from an insistence on the ultimate return on one's investment and a need for an immediate, though short-lived, release from the rigors of one's environment.

Advocates of the New Humor considered themselves to be responding to the tremendous tensions of urban life and satisfying their patrons' demands for "more laughs for their dollars." Canon Burnett, a sympathetic Boston reformer, saw cheap theater as responsive to the deprivations of working-class life: "They see color instead of dusky dirt; they hear songs instead of the clash of machinery; they are interested as a performer risks his life and the jokes make no demands on their thoughts."[73] Another progressive era defender of the new aesthetic, Paul W. Goldsbury, saw the "stimulation of the senses" and the emotions as a cure for the mental stress, emotional fatigue, and sensory starvation of urban experience:

Foul odors greet the nostrils; harsh cries and quarreling voices strike the ear; too often the roar and rumble of elevated trains add to the din. Food is stale and unpalatable; the body touches hard surfaces and coarse fabrics, and the eye sees dull, grimy colors, straight lines, and sharp angles. It is easy to understand the popularity of the hurdy-gurdy and the moving picture show and the relief sought in the saloon.[74]

Goldsbury argued that the intensity of sensory impression and affective stimulation offered by popular amusements allowed for the recreation of the mental apparatus, refreshing the sensory receptors necessary for intelligent judgment. For Goldsbury, it was more important that the theater stimulate the emotions and jolt the senses than that it provoke serious thought or encourage wise reflection.

It was precisely this intensity that seemed so savage to defenders of the traditional aesthetic and provoked such horror from most other social reformers. Jane Adams warned that the overstimulation of the total urban environment redirected normal adolescent desire in sinful and potentially dangerous directions: "The newly awakened senses are appealed to by all that is gaudy and sensual. . . . This fundamental susceptibility is thus evoked without a corresponding stir of the higher imagination, and the result is as dangerous as possible. . . . Every city contains hundreds of degenerates who have been over-mastered and borne down by it."[75] George Elliot Howard, a respected Nebraska University sociologist, saw tremendous dangers in the commercialization of amusements and particularly in popular entertainment's demand for intense audience response. He feared that mob psychology could dominate the audience under such conditions, resulting in a loss of conscious control and social propriety.[76]

The increased emphasis on spectator's direct emotional response rejected not simply the aesthetic of comic realism and the tradition of the well-made farce but also threatened the strict ethical and moral principles and the implicit social hierarchy reflected in those traditions. Commercial entertainment's rewarding of mass taste challenged the traditional authority of the Protestant establishment to determine what constituted an appropriate jest and what fell outside "good taste." A middle class, already buffeted by dizzying social, economic, technological, cultural, and moral change, saw the development of the New Humor as yet another example of the collapse of their hegemony. Henry Seidel Canby would recall of middle-class experience during this period: "The community in which we had been brought up and the education ground into us was ordered, self-contained, comprehensible, while this new society was incoherent, without fixed aim, and without even a pretense of homogeneity. We were like pond fish who had been flooded into a river." [77] Traces of what a later generation might label *future shock* are reflected in critical attacks on the New Humor. Writing in 1894, Oscar Fay Adams attacked the aggressiveness of the New Humor as an "anathema" to those of the "better sort," suggesting that themes and subject matters abhorrent to "any company of refined men and women" provided the predominant basis of American humor. Adams laments the degree to which the cultivated class had lost the ability to set standards of "good taste" in the face of the new mass humor: "How much weight does your opinion of the matter carry with it? Does not this American humor which you dislike so much become every year more popular?" [78]

Writing in 1910, Katherine Roof protested what she characterized as the "de-Americanization" of native humor, the polluting influence of the immigrant masses:

> We seem to have acquired a class of individuals whose so-called sense of humor takes the form of uncouth flippancy, a type of mind that stares blankly in the face of the real article, and laughs noisily at the things that should command respect. . . . The tremendous influx of Continental foreigners—the raw and often the waste material of the countries they come from—into a democracy, English-speaking and founded upon Anglo-Saxon morality, is a powerful factor in the creation of a new type. . . . Among other changes a perversion of the idea of humor occurs when the American mental habit is grafted upon minds of a different color. [79]

This decline in native American culture, she complained, had been accelerated by the quickening of urban life: "The rapid pace of things, the possibility of swift advancement to the uncultivated, combined with the theoretic ideal of equality, tends to induce superficiality." For Roof, as for others of her generation, New Humor encapsulated the total field of cultural changes, especially those four feared horsemen of the progressive era apocalypse: immigration, urbanization, industrialization and unionization.

By the turn of the century, the comic had become a focal point for a dispute between the displaced and confused middle-class "pond fish," hopelessly lost within the onrush of modern American culture, and the underculture of the "mollusks," looking for their futures in the changes overtaking the nation. Writing in *North American* in 1895, H. H. Boyeson spoke for many of his generation: "How is it possible for a civilized man to live among people who are always joking?"[80] That question arose again and again over the next few decades.

"DO YOUR ROUGHING NICELY": *MOVING PICTURE WORLD,* SIDNEY DREW, AND AMERICAN SCREEN COMEDY

The history of American popular humor in the first few decades of the twentieth century is really the history of attempts to overcome anxieties about the countercultural impact of the New Humor, to construct modes of popular amusement satisfying middle-class decorum while maintaining the emotional intensity of mass art. The early filmmakers and nickelodeon owners responded to the same pressures that beset others who offered mass entertainment; showmen were trying to attract the "classes" without alienating the "masses."

A complete history of the early development of American screen comedy remains to be written.[81] Yet a review of some of the discussion about screen comedy in the pages of *Moving Picture World,* the leading trade publication of the early cinema period, provides insight into the conflicting impulses encountered by film producers and exhibitors. While not necessarily representative of the full range of responses to early film comedy, *Moving Picture World's* editorials reflect many of the same assumptions about the nature and function of jokes and laughter that appear in larger debates of the period. As many historians have suggested, that publication played a central role in promoting classical Hollywood narrative and lobbying on behalf of the interests of a growing middle-class audience. However, its support for the "refinement" of motion picture art was tempered by its role as a trade publication that must also reflect contemporary market conditions. In its pages, the demand for a comedy of thoughtful laughter confronted a more pragmatic recognition of the need to maintain a broad audience appeal and of the necessary centrality of New Humor within commercial entertainment. What its editors promoted was finally not "true comedy," though they were not afraid to embrace that label, nor New Humor, but a hybrid of the two traditions calculated to attract and entertain a diversified film audience.

Its critics negotiated between those competing demands throughout a period of shifting conceptions of screen comedy. The earliest film comedies derive almost entirely from the broad physical comedy of vaudeville and the gag-oriented humor of the comic strip. By the time *Moving Picture World* began publication in 1907, film practice was beginning to shift toward a more "respectable" style of comedy, one aimed at attracting middle-class viewers and therefore more responsive to their tastes. Yet this move toward respectability was inconsistent, met by counterpressures toward greater emotional immediacy; the emergence of Mack Sennett as a key figure in American screen comedy, starting in 1911, revived screen "farce," rejecting refinements in favor of broad slapstick and crudely stereotyped characters. The development of feature-length film comedies, however, led toward more classical narrative structures and characterizations, moving slapstick comedians more fully in line with middle-class taste.[82]

Throughout these shifts, *Moving Picture World* and its leading critic, Epes Winthrop Sargent, consistently pushed filmmakers toward a "higher standard of comedy," characterized by a more realistic tone, more rounded characters, more structured narratives, and more restrained responses from the audience. Sargent wrote in 1915: "For my part I believe that audiences—refined audiences, at least—are tired of rabid slapstick, but there is sadly needed a school of good comedy writers to turn out stuff with stories to them."[83] Sargent consistently spoke of a general evolution in screen comedy from the bodily humor of "water throwing and senseless chases" toward sophisticated comedy directed at "an audience of a higher intelligence and a more discriminating taste." Sargent envisioned a process of cinematic refinement that mirrored the evolution in comic sensitivity claimed by Meredith, Sully, and other writers in the thoughtful laughter tradition.[84] Someday, "rough" comedy would give way to "true forms of light comedy in which the humor is too delicate to bring forth much outward demonstration."[85]

Sargent's optimism about the progressive refinement of screen comedy, however, ran against the increasing popularity of Mack Sennett's Keystone comedy. In November 1913, a little over a year after the studio began regular film production, *Moving Picture World* reported, "If you are in communication with any comedy company and the editor has tried to tell you what is wanted, it's dollars to doughnuts that you've been told, 'like Keystone.' "[86] While Sargent frequently excluded Sennett from such criticisms, claiming that the producer's films displayed a "spark" of comic invention lacking in his imitators, he repeatedly belittled the heavy dependence upon formula gags and the relative disinterest in story and characterization found in "rough" comedy. Sargent objected to the absurdly exaggerated behavior of screen clowns, parodying their highly stylized movements in an 1913 essay: "If your leading character is coming down the street, he no longer should walk;

Girls and grotesques: Mack Sennett comedy. Wisconsin Center for Film and Theater Research.

he should take it on the run and bowl over a policeman or an apple woman as he nears the camera."[87] The intrinsic realism of the cinematic image, he felt, meant that "there is a jarring note struck when they [characters] do things that persons of flesh and blood would not naturally do." Sargent also objected that such rough clowning provoked an immediate and superficial response, rather than allowing for the "sort of comedy that lingers in your mind after you have left the theater."

The critic feared that the fast pace of Sennett comedy prohibited the development of rounded characters or the construction of complex narratives, a view apparently shared by Sennett and his employees. One Sargent column quotes, without comment, Craig Hutchinson, a Keystone story editor: "We are accused of not having much of a story in our pictures, but I think you will find that when the mass of comedy business is scraped away and the bare plot is left exposed, a genuine situation is sticking around in it somewhere. This, however, is usually so skillfully and humorously covered by Mack Sennett's directing, that a careless observer is inclined to overlook it."[88] While Hutchinson claims some commitment to narrative, he concedes it is the gags, not the story, that is the focus of Keystone's creative energies. A classicist like Sargent would surely counter that a narrative unrecognizable as such would fail to provide sufficient guidance to spectators or a coherent structure for the comedy.

This style of comedy evolved, Sargent felt, from the laziness and cowardice of local exhibitors who relied upon laughter and applause as a test of a comic film's merits rather than trust their own judgments: "The greater demand is for comedies that will make the audience laugh so that the exhibitor, hearing the laughs, will know that they are comedies . . . . It is the wrong standard, but since it is so, they must be given material that will bring unthinking roars of laughter rather than keen, silent appreciation."[89] The exhibitors themselves often lacked the sophistication needed to appreciate "true comedy," and fell back upon more raucous forms of entertainment sure to draw easy laughter.

Sargent's dual role—as an advocate for more sophisticated screen techniques and as an adviser for writers interested in producing marketable pictureplays—meant, however, that his response to the Sennett style of comedy remained troubled. Sargent clearly wished to push the cinema toward the adoption of a "higher standard" of film comedy, one consistent with the ideals of the "true comedy" tradition. Yet he recognized and acknowledged that such comedy often did not attract the interests of film producers or the attention of theater owners and patrons. He feared that many of the earliest attempts to introduce "polite comedy" to the screen were largely devoid of comic action and held little in the way of emotional appeal. He protested in a 1915 column: "Once again, let it be said that polite comedy is not too polite. It is not slapstick, but that does not mean it is the exact opposite. It merely means that the idea should not be grotesque and meaningless, but should tell a real story in lively action."[90] Film comedy required comic action; film comedy should provoke audience response but it should do so without violating standards of good taste and social decorum. Some way needed to be found to reconcile the New Humor with the tradition of thoughtful laughter if screen comedy was to be both refined and successful. These conflicting attitudes toward slapstick comedy are explicit in his 1914 advice: "Rough it up but do your roughing nicely."[91]

Sargent's weekly column, The Photoplaywright, instructed his readers how to write marketable slapstick comedy, yet nudged them toward greater refinement of form and content. He pushed for the abandonment of many standard slapstick devices, reporting in 1913 that the comic chase was "so common and . . . so greatly overdone" as to require retirement and declaring in 1917 a "closed season for comedy custard pies."[92] Would-be scenario writers were urged to "see if you cannot find something a trifle newer."[93] Photoplaywrights were encouraged to maintain a consistently high level of comic action: "Until you can get a laugh in every scene you are not writing comedy no matter how funny the central idea may be."[94] Comic action, however, should not be "forced" upon the narrative but should be "germane to the plot and natural to the situation."[95]

Sargent's strategy was to link the New Humor and its demand for affective immediacy with the classical aesthetic's commitment to narrative causality and continuity. Gags, he suggested, often failed to provoke strong emotional responses if they are not fully integrated into the narrative or if they "distract and confuse" the spectator: "[Padding] interrupts the thread of the story at the moment and it persists in this interruption after the scenes pass because you are subconsciously at least trying to find its application to the story being told."[96] An 1916 essay urged his readers to "look at any of the [Sidney] Drew Comedies" for examples of how to successfully integrate gags into a larger narrative structure and how to avoid the meaningless "padding" of lesser comic films: "There are lots of things which Mr. Drew might do that would be as funny as the things he does do, but they would not be as interesting if they did not hold a direct application to the story and one reason why you like Drew comedies is because the stories are direct and without padding."[98]

Sargent's appeal to Sidney Drew and Vitagraph was not an isolated incident.[99] In a 1915 essay, the critic cites Vitagraph, Lubin, and Beauty as exemplars of the new "polite parlor comedy" he sees as the hallmark of screen humor. Sidney Drew was more frequently discussed in the pages of the *Moving Picture World* than any other comic filmmaker except Mack Sennett. Part of a longstanding theatrical family and a relative of the Barrymores, Drew began on the legitimate stage and was one of numerous theatrical stars recruited to appear in vaudeville playlets in the late nineteenth century. Unlike most of the other legitimate players who toured vaudeville once or twice, Drew continued to tour on the circuits from 1896 until his screen debut for Vitagraph in 1915. Drew shifted to Metro in 1917, producing and starring in Metro-Drew

Thoughtful laughter: Polly and Sidney Drew. Wisconsin Center for Film and Theater Research.

comedies at the rate of one per week. He and his wife, Polly, retired from the screen to return to vaudeville and the legitimate stage in 1918 but were recruited back by Amedee J. Van Beuran and began production at Paramount shortly before Drew's death in 1919. His wife, who directed many of the Drew comedies, continued to make films for a

53

"Character, class and prestige": 1917 ad for Metro-Drew comedies. Wisconsin Center for Film and Theater Research.

1917 promotional material for Sidney Drew comedy. Wisconsin Center for Film and Theater Research.

short while following his death. Peter Kramer identifies Drew as an important precursor of romantic comedy, yet Drew also participates in significant ways in the development of the comedian comedy tradition.[100] Drew's insistence on the subordination of gags to plot, the linkage of comic plots to real-world situations, and the need for a higher degree of audience identification made him the ideal champion for Sargent's comic aesthetic.

Sidney Drew was the model of bourgeois respectability and a great advocate of thoughtful laughter. Drew offered an image calculated to ensure stable middle-class support. Advertisements for the Drew comedies adopted the slogan, "They Keep You Smiling," a phrase suggesting a subtler response than the "fun, thrills and girls" promised by Keystone.[101] Drew advocated a "sentimental human comedy" of narrative and situation, a "comedy of inference." He claimed that his films appealed to intellect and sentiment rather than bodily laughter; he insisted that they were characterized throughout by "cleanliness in idea and thought." [102] Drew would have been pleased with his *Moving Picture World* obituary, which praised his comedies because they "never offended the finer sensibilities of the most particular audience." [103]

The following statement from a 1916 interview suggests the long time stage star's commitment to the classical aesthetic of thoughtful laughter: "True comedy . . . is human. It tells of the things that not only can happen, but probably have happened to you and me and all the rest. I aim at stories that find a responsive impulse in the breast of a majority of our clientele. They are not always brilliant episodes, but always I try to make them human—which is more nearly the secret of lasting success." [104] Much like Sargent, Drew felt comic situations should be plausible and should "deal with something that really occurs and not a figment of the imagination." [105] The characters should be identifiable, should be like "real human beings" whom the spectator might encounter. Comic incidents should arise naturally from common problems of domestic life, from "real problems, real good times." [106] Moreover, these comic incidents should be grounded in a coherent plot that maintains a consistent level of audience attention: "No matter how interesting comedy incident may seem to be at the moment or in what proportions it is assembled, there MUST be plot back of the incident if it is to have excuse. . . . It is plot that gains and holds the interest of the spectator and this plot alone can do." [107]

Unlike many other nineteenth- and early twentieth-century writers, Drew required no particular profundity or higher purpose from comic narratives; he did, however, insist that the plot must provide "a distinct and clearly defined objective upon which interest may be centered." [108] Gags must actively contribute to the onward development of a narrative rather than provide a "mechanical appeal" to spectator emotions: "Without a plot there cannot possibly be continuity of interests and where this continuity is lacking, then the laughter rises from what is done at the moment rather than from why a thing is done." [109]

Drew rejected the "gross horseplay" he saw as characteristic of the "knockabout" school of screen comedy; comic incidents did not need to be humorous in and of themselves but could depend upon the plot to "make the action humorous" by revealing contradictory aspects of a character or intensifying a narrative situation. Comic films, Drew argued, required not the rapid escalation of isolated comic antics but the more leisurely unfolding of a comic plot: "Most producers believe the more rapid the action the stronger the humor, but they forget the mental upheaval that is inevitable in the minds of the audiences upon the reception of so much ill-timed and undigested fact."[110] Audiences required time to contemplate the humor; comedy should be restful and relaxing rather than provoking strong and disturbing passions.

Comedy, for Drew, was an art of understatement, one whose primary ideals were "repose, pause, and inference." Ideal comedy allowed an active role for the spectator to find the potential humor in a represented situation: "Every director should credit his future spectators with possessing an average amount of intelligence. He should presuppose that his audiences will have a sufficient sense of humor to be able to infer the point of a situation without having it rammed down their throats."[111] Drew pushed his actors toward a subtlety of gesture and an honesty of emotional expression he hoped would make his films seem natural and convincing: "Sometimes a gesture or a look will convey more than can a series of elaborate actions. . . . Often a wink or a nod is better than a ten-foot scene."[112] Actors were fit to their parts, expected to blend fully into their roles in a performance style already much admired on the legitimate stage. Drew frequently played against his own wife, building a "natural" intimacy and warmth between the characters: "To be natural is to be convincing; to be convincing is to be entertaining, and there we have the essence of all true comedy."[113] The naturalness of his performances and the realism of his narratives allowed spectators a broader range of emotional experiences than could be offered by more gag-centered comedies. His films relied on the humorous perception of his spectators rather than the affective power of individual comic incidents.

Moving Picture World's hopes for a more refined style of screen comedy suffered a setback with the death of Sydney Drew in 1919. Though the publication would promote several other stars and producers as exemplifying an improved standard of film comedy (most notably Taylor Holmes and Al Christie), only Drew fully embraced their particular comic aesthetic.[114] Nevertheless, Sargent's ideals of a more restrained and realistic style of screen comedy reached their fulfillment in the late 1910s and early 1920s, the period Agee labeled "Comedy's Greatest Era." While many accounts represent Mack Sennett as the "father of American screen comedy," the most respected of silent comedies, in fact, were marked by a break with the Sennett tradition and a move toward the notion of comic narrative favored by *Moving Picture World*. Peter Kramer has argued that the "classic comedian comedies" of Chaplin, Keaton, Lloyd, Langdon, and others emerged from attempts at "integrating the persona, the comic and acrobatic performances of the star comedians into seriously presented dramatic story patterns," at repositioning slapstick clowns within the mainstream of the classical Hollywood cinema.[115] Such a development satisfied the studios' interests in standardizing production. It also served the need for screen comedies mixing the liveliness of the New Humor with the respectability accorded traditional theatrical comedy.

Seeking to exploit their shift toward a more classical style of comic construction, filmmakers often characterized their films as breaking with a disreputable past and progressing toward a higher standard of screen entertainment. Filmmakers in the 1920s defended their product in terms clearly borrowed from proponents of thoughtful laughter and comic realism. By the mid-1920s, even Mack Sennett distanced himself from the earlier slapstick tradition: "The slapstick and custard pie have gone forever to their great reward. A comedy in these days has to be built with brains and real drama as a foundation."[116] Now, in contrast to Hutchinson's earlier statement , Sennett stressed the increased importance his studio placed upon the well-constructed narrative and the fully developed character as the "foundation" of screen comedy: "The trick mustache and 'muff' are fast disappearing. . . . A real story needs more or less real characters, believable people."[117]

Such attitudes were echoed by spokespersons for other studios. George E. Marshall, head of comic film production at Fox, insisted that "cleanliness" and realism, rather than "bathing girls and custard pies," were the standard set by his productions: "We have abandoned the old comedy policy of making pictures out of a series of 'gags,' strung together without rhyme or reason. Our plan is to take real stories, funny situations and develop their humorous aspects."[118] Al Christie announced that his comedies sought "the good happy medium of good funny situation stories, with the proper amount of hokum and slapstick to enliven the plots."[119] Harold Lloyd spoke of his efforts to produce a "clean entertaining comedy" grounded in coherent and consistent character development and narrative unity: "When the last reel has been run off, the audience does not remember merely a 'gag' here and there that was especially funny, but while laughing at the humor, still retain a clear idea of and a strong sympathy for the character."

Screen producers and performers did not reject entirely the commercial logic of the New Humor, the demand for affective immediacy and popular pleasure. However, they were willing to embrace aesthetic principles founded upon the ethical assumptions of the thoughtful laughter tradition. The classic silent comedies may be understood as attempts to "do your roughing nicely," to add an air of refinement to popular humor conventions, to merge the affective immediacy of the New Humor with the thematic complexity of "true comedy" and thereby to satisfy the conflicting expectations of a heterogeneous film audience.

3

"A Regular Mine, a Reservoir, a Proving Ground": Reconstructing the Vaudeville Aesthetic

Writing in 1930, George M. Cohan proclaimed that variety had served for more than half a century as "a regular mine, a reservoir, a proving ground" for the legitimate theater and the Hollywood cinema. Cohan cited more than a hundred performers who had gone from the circuits into film stardom or Broadway success. Cohan's list, while extensive, was far from complete.[1] In 1917 alone, *Variety* found that more than one hundred standard vaudeville acts were being featured on Broadway, largely in stage revues such as Ziegfeld's *Follies,* George White's *Scandals,* the Shuberts' *Passing Parade,* or Earl Carroll's *Vanities.*[2] The trade paper announced that "vaudeville is becoming more and more the developing field for the legitimate production managers. All of the new stars of the last few years have been from that branch of the amusement profession."[3]

Not all of these new recruits remained theatrical stars; still fewer went from Broadway to Hollywood. Many performers only hoped to enjoy New York runs long enough and prestigious enough to increase their earning power when they returned to vaudeville. Many ambitious performers, however, found the Broadway revue a more lucrative market and decided to stay. A significant number of the cinema's top musical and comedy stars developed their performance skills in the variety house before moving to the legitimate stage and, from there, to the Hollywood studios. What these stars brought to cinema was a particular style of performance characteristic of the vaudeville tradition.

Aside from the occasional biographical reference, however, film his-

George M. Cohan and family on vaudeville. Wisconsin Center for Film and Theater Research.

torians have extended little effort toward reconstructing the aesthetic norms of vaudeville or tracing how those norms might have shaped the ways Hollywood utilized these stars. Star acting is typically treated as if it were either an outgrowth of dominant traditions within the legitimate theater or an invention of the commercial cinema.[4] In this chapter, however, I propose a model of vaudeville as a specific performance tradition, as a particular aesthetic practice. Historical reconstruction of this now lost tradition is a necessary precondition for a full understanding of early sound comedy.

Such a model will necessarily be schematic. No given act conformed perfectly to these norms. Nevertheless, most of the surviving literature on vaudeville performance confirms the importance and prevalence of these aesthetic assumptions. They appear consistently in primary sources such as guidebooks, theater manuals, and critical essays; they represent the criteria critics, spectators, and theater managers employed in evaluating vaudeville performances. As we will see, the institutional framework of vaudeville, particularly its actor-centered mode of production, encouraged certain aesthetic choices over others and distinguished vaudeville from dominant theatrical practices of the same period.

Any attempt to construct an aesthetic paradigm for vaudeville must first acknowledge the diversity of its materials; the many traditions constituting variety make any generalizations difficult, necessarily requiring the privileging of some classes of acts over others. My focus here is predominantly upon the monologists, crossfire teams, and comic sketches, the acts that most directly influenced screen comedy. However, my emphasis upon modes of performance rather than modes of representation allows me to consider those traits unifying the comic sketch with a range of other acts that were not, strictly speaking, representational. Backflips, pratfalls, magic tricks, and trained chimpanzees might all be viewed as more or less equivalent techniques for provoking audience response within a medium whose primary aesthetic criteria was affective immediacy.

This formal system emerged from nearly half a century of shifts in the institutional structure and formal organization of American vaudeville.[5] From its roots in a masculine saloon culture, vaudeville sought respectability, taming its rawer edges and introducing new elements to attract women, children and more wealthy patrons. From a locally based form, vaudeville developed into a national institution, dominated by a small number of powerful national and regional circuits. The variety stage absorbed declining forms of popular entertainment (the minstrel show, the show boat, and to a lesser degree, burlesque) and attempted to attract top stars from the legitimate stage, opera, ballet, and the circus. Formulas for constructing and arranging acts originated and were refined. Performance conventions and stock characters were developed and perfected. New specialty acts emerged to join the musical and comedy traditions of the saloons until every conceivable form of mass entertainment assumed a precise position upon the variety bill. By the turn of the century, several decades of experimentation by performers and entrepreneurs had come together into a distinctive vaudeville aesthetic, one seeking to intensify the "Impression of the Time Being" and the affective response of the spectator, one setting the model for other commercial amusements. Writing in 1923, theater critic and playwright Vadim Uraneff suggested that the variety stage's aesthetic practices had evolved from the need to produce outwardly recognizable emotional reactions:

> The actor works with the idea of an immediate response from the audience; and with regard to its demands. By cutting out everything—every line, gesture, movement—to which the audience does not react and by improvising new things, he establishes unusual unity between the audience and himself. . . . Stylization in gesture, pose, mise-en-scéne and make-up fol-

lows as a result of long experimentation before the primitive spectator whose power as judge is absolute.[6]

This focus upon immediate rather than long-term response pushed vaudeville toward a very different style of performance than characterized the legitimate theater in turn-of-the-century America.

Variety critic Acton Davis wrote in 1906 that "it is his [the vaudevillian's] business to do and to do quickly everything which an actor on the regular stage is taught and schooled to avoid."[7] Critics of stage realism often promoted vaudeville as an alternative to legitimate theater practices, seeing it as an ideal model for their own aesthetic experiments. Variety, they claimed, rejected the dominant norms of theatrical realism and maintained a broad popular appeal. Flippo Marinetti's "The Variety Theatre," which has been characterized as the first major summation of the principles of Futurist theater, established an explicit contrast between theatrical realism, "a finicking, slow, analytic and diluted theatre worthy, all in all, of the age of the oil lamp" and the variety theater, "the crucible in which the elements of an emergent new sensibility are seething."[8] While the legitimate theater "vacillates stupidly between historical reconstruction . . . and photographic reproduction of our daily life," the variety theater offered speed and "astonishment." Vaudeville rapidly absorbed diverse forms of amusement and provided a constant source of audience fascination. Marinetti wrote:

> The Variety Theatre, born as we are from electricity, is lucky in having no tradition, no masters, no dogma and it is fed by swift actuality. . . . The Variety Theatre is absolutely practical, because it proposes to distract and amuse the public with comic effects, erotic stimulation, or imaginative astonishment. . . . The authors, actors and technicians of the Variety Theatre have only one reason for existing and triumphing: incessantly to invent new elements of astonishment.[9]

Marinetti was not alone in finding vaudeville performance a rich source of artistic inspiration. Sergei Eisenstein founded his concept of "montage of attractions" upon the emotional intensity produced by the fragmented entertainment of popular music hall,[10] while his contemporaries and fellow countrymen, the FEX group, saw variety performance as one of a number of popular antecedents for its own celebration of eccentricity and hyperactivity.[11] The fragmented, frenetic, and emphatic style of variety performance spoke to modernists of all nationalities, to many seeking alternatives to the conventionality of theatrical realism and the banality of the commercial cinema.[12] Its intellectual apologists appropriated it in the name of various aesthetic projects from American folk art to surrealism, futurism, and constructivism. They were united, however, in seeing vaudeville as fundamentally different in character from the dominant conventions of the legitimate stage. This difference was variously characterized in terms of a different performer-spectator relationship, a fragmented structure, a heterogeneous array of materials, and a reliance upon crude shock to produce emotionally intense responses. This chapter will suggest how those various aspects of vaudeville practice might be said to cohere into a particular aesthetic system.

"THE ACTOR IS ALWAYS IN THE FOREGROUND": PERFORMANCE VIRTUOSITY, THE VAUDEVILLE AESTHETIC, AND MODE OF PRODUCTION

The underlying logic of the variety show rested on the assumption that heterogeneous entertainment was essential to attract and satisfy a mass audience. E. F. Albee explained in 1923, "The diversified, contrasted and all-embracing character of the vaudeville program gives it, in whole or in part, an appeal to all classes of people and all kinds of tastes. . . . In the arrangement of the ideal modern vaudeville program, there is one or more sources of complete satisfaction for everybody present, no matter how 'mixed' the audience might be."[13] The vaudeville program was constructed from modular units of diverse material, no more than twenty minutes in length each. These individual acts were juxtaposed together with an eye toward the creation of the highest possible degree of novelty and variety rather than toward the logical relationship between the various components of the program. Each act was conceived as a discrete unit that could be slotted into a customized program and play opposite many different acts in its career. The program as a whole offered no consistent message; individual acts might offer conflicting or competing messages. In the end, what vaudeville communicated was the pleasure of infinite diversity in infinite combinations.

Frederick Snyder has suggested that this notion of compartmentalization, or as he calls it, "theater in a package," led to acts being conceived within generic categories, with standardized lengths and with predetermined stage requirements to assist the stage managers and circuit bookers in the construction of a workable program.[14] Snyder points toward a machine age notion of theatrical production, depending upon the standardization of component parts to ensure ease and speed of assembly. Despite pressures toward novelty, acts packaged themselves within a limited range of performance categories already familiar to the bookers and already structured into the standard program. Snyder argues, "The production format was more than anything else a means whereby the managers could standardize the vaudeville show on a nationwide basis so that acts could play a record-breaking number of daily shows and move from theatre to theatre and from city to city in record-breaking time." [15]

Many factors contributed to the selection and arrangement of the acts for the vaudeville bill. [16] The standard fees of individual acts had to be coordinated to ensure that each week's bill fit within a consistent budget and its production cost would not outstrip its likely box office value. Acts played in front of the curtain needed to be alternated with acts played upon the full stage to allow stage hands sufficient time to adjust the scenery and bring on special equipment without causing a delay in the constant flow of entertainment. So-called "dumb acts," acts without dialogue, were slotted at the beginning and ends of programs as well as immediately following intermission so they would not be disrupted by the movement of patrons to and from their seats. The notion of a diversified program meant the avoidance of booking two essentially similar acts back to back on the bill; songs should alternate with comedy and with acrobatics. Bookers also sought to evaluate the emotional intensity and drawing power of each act so that the program mounted in interest toward a climax as the evening progressed and so that headliner performers appeared later in the program than promising newcomers.

However important to the program's overall impact, the art of booking and managing a vaudeville house was that of the selection, juxtaposition and coordination of preconceived units, not that of direction or creation. House managers might be expected to negotiate between several musical stars who wanted to perform the same song as part of their performance or to ensure conformity to local censorship standards. Otherwise, little effort was made to coordinate the individual acts into an ideologically or aesthetically consistent program.

House managers and syndicate executives made periodic efforts to expand their control over the style and content of the individual vaudeville acts and, on occasion, ventured into the production of acts specially designed to meet the needs of their programs. However, the creative authority as well as much of the financial burden remained largely in the hands of the performers. In a 1907 *Variety* article, William Gould emphasized: "Being left to his own resources, he [the vaudeville performer] becomes creative. He originates. No stage manager gives him personality or individuality. It simply grows. He must be his own manager, buy or write his own specialty production. Then he becomes his own advance and press agent; his own property man." [17]

While performers responded to pressures to produce acts that could fit a standard position on the bill, they also felt the demand for novelty and individualization, for their own unique "specialties." As James J. Morton explained in 1906, "Originality is the first step to recognition. Personality next and an indomitable nerve to withstand criticism last." [18] In a world populated by hundreds of comic acrobats, each sought some competitive edge over all of the others. Such originality was felt to require handcrafting. The vaudevillians were responsible for originating their acts and for negotiating directly with production specialists (songwriters, gagsmiths, costume and set makers, manufactures of theatrical effects, etc.) to ensure proper execution. [19] Performers wrote their own material or assembled it from bits offered them by several different writers and, in some cases, made their own equipment, costumes, and sets. Acts were prepared on speculation with hopes that once perfected, they would attract bookings on one of the major circuits. The constant demand for new talent minimized the performer's risks. Of all the mass arts, vaudeville was the most labor intensive. Will Rogers quipped, "With all the different grades and classes of vaudeville they have nowadays, it's almost impossible to have an act so poor that somebody hasn't got a circuit that will fit you." [20] Bookings on the better circuits, though, meant more money, higher prestige, and better working conditions, the considerable difference between giving two performances a day and giving five. Once booked, the performer was still responsible for the transportation and upkeep of the act's props, sets and equipment as well as for adjusting material to shifting audience tastes and market demands. All refinements of the individual act originated with the performer; structured rehearsals were rare and existed only for the house managers to review the acts for potentially censurable content and to allow stage hands to resolve technical problems in coordinating the diverse demands of these varied acts. Vaudeville gagwriter and performer J. C. Nugent suggested, in 1925, that the absence of rehearsals was, in fact, the saving grace of the variety stage, a major advantage over the more director-centered legitimate theater: "Most actors are ruined in rehearsal and by the adopting of ill-considered suggestions.

Will Rogers. Wisconsin Center for Film and Theater Research.

. . . Try to improve or correct a bee's buzz and you make a bum bee." [21] Nugent felt the independence forced upon the vaudeville artist by this particular mode of production, the fact that "the artist must sink or swim," developed more distinctive performers.

Vaudeville saw the individual performer as the primary creative force even as this concept was being rejected by the legitimate theater. An aesthetic of theatrical realism necessitated the displacement of the audience and the performer from their previous positions of authority over theatrical production and the expansion of the role of the director as the primary source of a homogeneous theatrical effect. [22] The new emphasis upon verisimilitude required an active coordination of all of the elements of the production to ensure the consistency of the illusion; it also demanded the rejection of the virtuosity of the individual performer in favor of an ensemble style of performance. The focus shifted from the individual performer's ability to "stop the show," to "command the stage," toward a theater perceived as "group art," where each element had to assume its particular place within the overall work. Theatrical manuals urged actors to "think less of virtuosity for its own sake and more of artistic unity and sincerity," to reject spontaneous gestures in favor of carefully planned, regularized movements rehearsed and coordinated by the director. Players were to be selected less for their individual talents than for their ability to work together and to accept direction. The most important American advocate of theatrical realism, David Belasco, instructed his actors "not to be selfish but to assist one another because, after all, they are only the component parts of a single picture." [23]

The notion of a unified production striving for a realistic illusion required legitimate actors to meld into their assigned roles, to mask their own peculiarities as performers behind the particularities of their characters. Theatrical performer Richard Mansfield asserted that "an actor has no right to offer his own personality. . . . A man who cannot so envelop himself in the robe of the part, who cannot be this man today and that man tomorrow, no matter how smart a fellow he may be, cannot be considered an actor." [24] While previous generations of actors were noted for the idiosyncracies they brought to more or less stock roles, the broadening of the theatrical repertoire and the emergence of realist playwrights discouraged this personality-centered style of acting. [25] Characters were now conceived not as social types or larger-than-life protagonists but as everyday figures confronting real-world problems, as psychologically complex individuals whose responses to each situation grew from their personal history and their social context. New modes of performance conformed to the demands of these characterizations so that these particularized individuals could "come to life" before the spectator. The old star system came under critical attack as antagonistic to theatrical realism and these new conceptions of character. The insertion of a powerful performer personality placed too great of a "strain" on the realist illusion. Stock companies were criticized because they allowed the audience to develop too much familiarity with individual performers, bringing memories of them in previous roles to each new production. Curtain calls were suspect because they broke the actor from the character, though only momentarily and at the end of the production.[26]

If, as Helen Krich Chinoy suggests, the emergence of the powerful director within the legitimate theater responded to a desire for homogeneity and unity within the production—the illusion of a mirrored reality—vaudeville responded to no such pressure.[27] Vaudeville's player-centered mode of production resulted in a constant foregrounding of the performer's status as an entertainer; variety audiences valued attempts to command the spotlight and produce a strong impression. The vaudevillian, as master of the act from conception to execution, sought material tailored to particular performance skills. Performers were never subservient to the script; rather, narrative, where it existed at all, facilitated their familiar tricks. Vadim Uraneff wrote, "The actor is always in the foreground, the literary form is calculated with a view to the individual possibilities of the actor. The interest of the act never depends upon the plot, for it is the actor that counts."[28] The performer's personal charms were far more important than the quality of the sets or the consistency of the characters. Trade press reporter Hartley Davis explained, "It isn't what he says or what he sings that makes a monologist a success, but the way in which he does it. It is their personality which is their chief stock in trade."[29]

Vaudeville was, as one Chicago newspaper critic suggested in 1917, "the field of the expert."[30] Performers were expected to execute their specialties with a consistently high level of speed and precision. Frequently, acts were designed to focus attention upon the performer's skills, having little or no other justification or interest.[31] Such was certainly the case with the protean or quick-change acts, where the star might perform an entire one-act play, alone on the stage, shifting gestures, vocal patterns, and costumes to convey as many as forty or fifty different characters. Impressionists, quick sketch artists, male and

Vaudeville juggler W. C. Fields. Wisconsin Center for Film and Theater Research.

female impersonators, whistlers, rag folders, cloth drapers, eccentric dancers, impersonators of animals or babies appealed to a fascination with showmanship for its own sake; such acts fed a desire to be impressed by the skill of the performer rather than absorbed within the development of a narrative. Alone, confronting the glare of a single spotlight that isolated them from the rest of the setting, thrust forward in front of the curtain while the full stage was prepared for the next spectacular, these performers depended entirely upon their personal appeal and professional skills.[32] George Burns described the experience: "All you've got is delivery and an attitude and the audience will either defeat you or you will be a sensation."[33]

The fierce competition for the spotlight often pushed performers toward adopting more and more different specialties into a single act. Jugglers like Fred Allen and W. C. Fields, acrobats like Mitchell and Durant, rope artists like Will Rogers incorporated comic material into their performances to give them a creative edge over other acts. The consummate entertainer was one who could do the broadest range of different specialties within the shortest period of time. Tongue planted firmly in cheek, George Jean Nathan described the typical vaudeville act: "the reunion of the old Union and the old Confederate soldiers who celebrate the entente cordial by jointly executing a soft shoe dance interspersed with somersaults and thereafter playing a medley of 'Dixie' and 'Marching Through Georgia' on coronets."[34] Nathan's description is only slightly exaggerated. Many acts similarly combined sentimentality and virtuosity. The Siamese Twins, a 1925 act, showcased a pair of circus "freaks" who engaged in a saxophone and clarinet duets, impersonated other sister acts, sang love songs, cracked jokes, and performed ballroom and tap dancing, all within a fifteen-minute appearance. A jaded *Variety* critic remarked that they were "not bad for an act of this type."[35]

Rejecting the rounded characters preferred by naturalistic drama, the vaudeville performer assumed highly conventional roles, often little more than broadly defined social types. The demand for immediacy pushed the variety artist toward the utmost economy of means. Eddie Cantor told an *American* magazine interviewer in 1924: "A comedian in vaudeville . . . is like a salesman who has only fifteen minutes in which to make a sale. You go on the stage, knowing that every minute counts. You've got to get your audience the instant you appear."[36] The gag-writer and the performer hacked away at their material trying to rid it of every extraneous line or detail. Clutter slows down the rapid flow of laughter. Monologist Frank Fogarty insisted, "The single thing I work to attain in any gag is brevity. I never use an ornamental word, I use the shortest word I can find, and I tell a gag in the fewest words possible."[37]

This brutal economy weighed against the exposition necessary to develop rounded characters or particularized situations. Instead, characters and situations needed to be immediately recognizable. An elaborate system of typage developed: exaggerated costumes, facial characteristics, phrases, and accents were meant to reflect general personality traits viewed as emblematic of a particular class, region, ethnic group, or gender.[38] For example, a stock Irishman could be recognized by a collarless shirt, an oversized vest, a pair of loose workman's pants with a rope belt, a battered hat, all predominantly green; a red wig and a set of red (or sometimes, green) whiskers arranged as a fringe around the face; a propensity for epithets and slang, a sing-song vocal pattern, and a thick brogue. The redundancy with which these accumulated features marked a stage character as a stock Irishman allowed almost instant recognition; spectators could just as immediately draw assumptions about the character's propensity to drink, his fiery temper, his sentimental nature, and his love of tall tales and loud laughter. Any or all of these ethnic traits could be made the punch line of a joke or the point of a sketch. Whatever its racist implications, such stereotyping was a necessary aspect of the highly economic style of vaudeville performance.

Such characters made few claims at complex personalities, psychological motivations, or even much individuality. Indeed, Brett Page warned would-be sketch writers that they did "not [have] much chance of making new characters," but that their contributions came from employing the prefabricated types in a novel fashion.[39] He wrote, "There is a wealth of ready material waiting not only in varying combinations but in placing the characters in new business. . . . Make your combination within the limits of plausibility and use characters that are seen upon the stage often enough to be hailed with at least a pleasant welcome."[40] Eddie Cantor won considerable praise for placing a pair of wire-rimmed glasses on the traditional blackface character and thus making him more intellectual and "sissified" than previous renditions. Cantor also attracted attention by writing a sketch about a Jewish aviator who failed to cross the Atlantic because he couldn't eat the ham sandwiches preferred by Charles Lindbergh, mixing traditional stereotypes with a topical situation for novel results.[41]

Actors made only minimal efforts to blend into such characters and often evoked sharp contrasts between their personality and their chosen roles; the very Jewish Fanny Brice, for example, appeared as an Indian squaw, a French courtesan, or a black housewife, lapsing into occasional Yiddish phrases to underscore the effect.[42] Performers won praise not for their ability to assume the "cloak" of a character but rather from their ability to project a unique personality that transcended stock roles. An anonymous *Variety* critic suggested in 1923 that "most blackface comedians do an Al Jolson with a touch of Cantor, the 'Dutch' copy the mannerisms of Sam Bernard, the nuts copy one another and so on. That is why, when a Joe Cook, Bert Wheeler, or Tom Patricola comes along with something a little new, he is acclaimed to the skies."[43] As this passage suggests, the conventionality of character was accepted as part of the general representational system of vaudeville, yet the conventionality of performance was to be avoided where possible. The goal was to be the Cantor or Jolson whom less creative artists imitated or better yet, to be the Cook or Wheeler who had a personality seen as so vivid and unique that no one else could imitate it with success.

Nut comic Joe Cook. Wisconsin Center for Film and Theater Research.

"LIKE SENSING THE PRESENCE OF A FRIEND IN THE DARK":
READING THE VAUDEVILLE AUDIENCE

Vaudeville's emphasis on the performer led to a cult of personality, a fascination with the artists' power to shape spectators' emotional response. J. C. Nugent rhapsodized in 1926, "With his audience well in hand, the seasoned actor holds them, moves them, stops them and starts them." [44] Cohan and Nathan compared the spectator to a crystal goblet that shatters if the performer strikes the correct notes: "The 'coordinated tone-clashes' that reach an audience's inner recesses and cause it to collapse into tears, laughter or horror are just as much a matter of mechanical preparation as the one that reacted upon this goblet." [45] Vaudevillians were masters of the "mechanics of emotion," always pushing for bigger roars of laughter and applause, living and dying from their ability to move an audience to outward response.

Celebrations of the affective force, the "human horsepower, size, electricity, energy, zingo" of the individual performer, however, give only a partial picture of the aesthetics of vaudeville performance. [46] Variety entertainment also required that entertainers remain constantly aware of the tastes and interests of their audience and adjust their performances to feedback from the gallery. The small size of the typical house allowed a high degree of intimacy between performer and patron. Performers built upon this intimacy through direct interaction with the audience, moving as close to the edge of the stage as possible to allow for maximum communication. Vaudeville performer Walter De Leon explained, "Actor and audience are closer together, know each other better [than in the legitimate theater]. . . . therefore he aims to be as simple, as direct and as genuine as the medium of his art permits." [47] Fanny Brice characterized her relationship to a supportive audience as "much like sensing the presence of a friend in the dark," [48] while Nora Bayes spoke of her act as "like an intimate chat with one or two close friends who sit around a table and enjoy themselves." [49]

These attitudes contrast sharply with those advanced by legitimate theater performers and directors during this same period. Alexander Bakshy, writing in 1929, drew a sharp contrast between "the art of direct and personal appeal to the audience [vaudeville] and the art of indirect and nonpersonal appeal [legitimate theater]." [50] Such a sharp contrast could not have been drawn fifty years earlier. Richard Sennett has traced the process by which "the openness and spontaneity of audience response," previously empowered to stop the show and to demand a repetition of a particularly favored bit, gave way to a more restrained response and an imagined separation between the stage diegesis and the spectator space.[51] By the turn of the century, principles of theatrical realism required performers to proceed as if they were ignorant of the audience's presence and as if events were occurring for the first time. Theater architecture was reconceived to emphasize the gulf that separated the house from the stage. Consistency of illusion displaced the moments of heightened emotion, the playing for "points," the direct communication between actor and audience. British theater critic Leigh Hunt, writing in 1887, urged the actor to "divest himself of the audience, to be occupied not with the persons he is amusing but with the persons he is assisting in the representations."[52] The actor was not to play to the audience nor to allow its response to shape the performance; total concentration was to be focused upon conveying the character and maintaining the demands of the overall production. The audience was to wait till the end of the show to express its appreciation of a performance rather than allow its applause to disrupt the play's progression.

The vaudevillians, on the other hand, were unwilling to wait for the curtain call to determine how the audience was responding. Nugent wrote, "The well-edited approval of an audience means nothing. The unconscious and involuntary response is proof of the recognition of a master."[53] Experienced performers learned to "read" the audience, to assess spectator tastes and preferences, and to recognize the precise instant when they fell out of harmony with the house. Trade press reporter Marian Spitzer perceived the need to interpret and respond to the audience as a major difference between variety and legitimate theater: "Most legitimate audiences are pretty much alike. . . . But vaudeville audiences are different all the time. It's almost impossible to set a performance and to play it that way forever. Each town seems different. Every neighborhood in the same city needs different handling. So the vaudevillian has to be forever on the alert, to feel out his audience and work accordingly."[54]

Vaudeville entertainers developed different techniques for assessing audience taste. Mae West would question house managers about the characteristics of particular audiences: "I would try to figure out what the audiences looked like, what they did, what problems of life they faced." She soon realized that "every city and every town set its own standard for entertainment." No fixed act could possibly satisfy the diversity of the variety audience so instead, the performer had to be flexible, conforming to the different standards of local communities. West wrote, "I learned to adjust the mood, tempo and material of my act. I did whatever seemed necessary to get the best response from each type of audience."[55] Leon Errol suggested in a 1922 interview that vaudeville comics frequently focused upon a single spectator who functioned as a measure of the taste and response of the whole house: "I watch every expression on the person's face and I know that I am really seeing my whole audience. For as that one human being responds, so will the hundreds of others out there in front."[56]

No vaudeville text was ever permanently fixed; all material remained flexible and fluid, open to a process of constant revision and reworking. Texts were scripted for performers who showed little reverence to the written word but sought only material that would "come alive" for the variety house audience. Performers were constantly tinkering with their acts. Jack Haley described this process: "You'd get a funny idea and you tried it out. If it was any good, got audience approval, you kept it in. If not, you throw it out. Consequently, a perfection was attained because you could polish a bit, keep it smooth, and make it part of your act."[57] While a performer might exploit a particular routine or character for years, the material would evolve through the performer's efforts to reflect contemporary taste and adjust to local interests. Fanny Brice recalled:

Three months after the first performance of the 'Spring Song,' I realized with surprise that the business I was using was altogether different from the business with which I had started out. . . . My comedy, to be successful, must be spontaneous. Whenever it isn't, the feel of the audience tells me and I throw out that particular piece of business and work out something else to use in its stead. . . . When a piece of business occurs to me, I do it instinctively. If it is successful, I keep it till it is stale. If it is not, I discarded it for something new.[58]

This description suggests the active role of popular response in shaping vaudeville performances.

Staging techniques built on this intimate exchange with the audience, incorporating spectators even more fully in the act. Singers and musicians played requests from the audience; magicians asked for vol-

Ziegfeld Follies star Fanny Brice. Wisconsin Center for Film and Theater Research.

unteers to come onto the stage; dancers would swing over the audience on trapezes or drift just barely beyond reach in hot air balloons. Confederates planted in the audience broadened the playing space beyond the stage itself. In a 1922 act entitled "The Intruders," the house manager appeared on the stage to announce the cancellation of the scheduled performers. Two plants in the audience, a man and a woman, created a fight, criticizing the theater and its policies, finally charging the stage to perform their own song and comedy routine.[59] The so-called Nut Comics experimented with even wilder intrusions of spectator space.[60] Olson and Johnson hurled raw eggs, rubber snakes, and live chickens at the audience, planted confederates who heckled them from the house and ticket scalpers who romped the aisles selling passes to rival shows, attacked spectators with gusts of air from the stage, and broadcast comments and jokes through an intercom system to patrons waiting in line to buy tickets for the next show.[61]

Such practices were accepted and even encouraged as part of the general push toward intensifying emotional experience. The clowns shoved their gags, literally and figuratively, into their patron's faces, refusing to accept a complacent or indifferent response. No other aspect of the performance was more important than establishing and maintaining a bond between performer and patron. Brett Page warned would-be vaudeville writers against undue emphasis upon scenic effects: "Scenery has no artistic meaning. To the vaudevillian, scenery is a business investment."[62] Most commentators suggested that sets should minimize details that might distract attention from the performer. Constance Rourke, writing in 1919, argued for the "simplification of stage settings" to allow the vaudeville spectator greater concentration: "Settings must not overshadow the performance . . . if the essentials of movement and active diversion are to be kept."[63] Marsden Hartley, in 1920, called for "large plain spaces upon which to perform and enjoy their own remarkably devised patterns of body."[64] While vaudeville periodically produced more elaborate stage settings, the cost of manufacturing and transporting scenery, borne by the individual performers, reinforced this aesthetic preference for simplicity. Monologists and comic teams whose appeal was primarily verbal frequently played in front of the curtain with no sets or props whatsoever. Other acts played against the limited number of stock backdrops they found at the local houses, perhaps performing in a woodlands setting at one stop and in a castle or a victorian parlor at the next. The absence of other stage effects sharpened the focus upon the performer.

"No Time for Plot": The Structure of the Vaudeville Act

Vaudeville's emphasis upon affective experience often meant that concern with narrative or character development fell by the wayside. The comic sketch or monologue depended more upon the comic "bits," the component parts, than upon the sense of the whole. Vaudevillian Wilfred Clarke told *Variety* readers in 1906 that an ideal sketch "must be full of business and situations, not one but many; no time for plot; no time for scenic effects."[65] Each part was expected not to contribute to the overall development of a narrative but to assist in the gradual intensification of audience response. Clarke continued, "Each sentence should create a laugh, so as to never allow the ball to stop rolling. To obtain such continuous laughter, a sketch must border on the ridiculous, but if played seriously by the actors engaged . . . the audience forgets the lack of plot and story and laughs!"[66] What mattered was "the impression of the time being," not the larger context in which a particular comic "bit" might be placed. Trade press reporter Hartley Davis suggested that these principles of compression and fragmentation were the major differences between theatrical realism and vaudeville performance: "The artistic 'legitimate' actor wastes too much time in working up to his points, but the skilled vaudevillian strikes them with a single blow and scores. A successful vaudeville sketch concentrates in one act as many laughs and as much action as are usually distributed over a three-act comedy."[67]

The vaudeville sketch, monologue, or crossfire routine was to be built from component parts much as the whole program was constructed from various acts. These "bits" of comic business or patter could be drawn from many different sources and yoked by the performer into some loose structure. Performers were constantly searching for new gags or bits and often fought fiercely for the right to be the sole employer of a particular twist or gimmick. Some comics added new jokes on a weekly or biweekly basis, excising material that no longer drew laughs, inserting new jokes where they seemed to work best. Others would include topical references to local figures or institutions or to contemporary events to add a degree of timeliness to an otherwise preset routine. Censorship of vaudeville material was not centralized but rather left in the hands of local theater owners who had widely divergent standards about what constituted acceptable stage fare. Consequently, the act had to be constructed in such a way that almost any given gag or bit of business was expendable should a manager insist that it be removed. The performer might also be expected to compress or expand the material to conform to the time constraints of a particular program. Page explained, "The monologist can vary his playing time at will by leaving out points and gags here and there, as necessity demands, so the writer should supply at least a full fifteen minutes of material in his manuscript."[68]

To achieve these results, the vaudeville act required an accordionlike structure. Certain moments in the performance were more or less fixed and inflexible. The introduction needed to quickly establish the characters and their immediate situation or perhaps to define the theme from which other variations would be derived. The act sought to build toward a "Wow Finish" that would top all preceding gags and end on a note of peek emotional intensity.[69] Closure was of little importance to the vaudeville performer but climax was, since the audience's final response to the act would be the major determinant of the house manager's report. Page summarized, "A routine is so arranged that the introduction stamps the monologist as bright, and the character he is impersonating or telling about as a 'real character.' . . . The final point or gag rounds the monologue off in the biggest burst of honest laughter."[70] Other elements could be added, subtracted, or rearranged with far greater flexibility, having little to do with the act's overall structure or logical development. Brett Page's instructions for writing a vaudeville monologue suggested such a conception:

> Have as many cards or slips of paper as you have points or gags. Write only one point or gag on one card or slip of paper. On the first card, write "Introduction" and always keep that card first in your hand. Then take up a card and read the point or gag on it as following the introduction, the second card as the second point or gag, and so on until you have arranged your monologue in an effective manner. . . . By shuffling the cards you may make as many arrangements as you wish and eventually arrive at the ideal routine.[71]

The companion volume to the Page book in the Home Correspondence School series, Carlton Andrews' *The Technique of Play Writing,* offered very different advice for the writing of legitimate theater scripts:

> Some preliminary sketch—usually written down, though perhaps occasionally merely mental—is invariably the forerunner of a successful drama. . . . Before beginning work upon any plan, accordingly, the dramatist should

determine the scheme of division, the locale, and the importance and appeal of his leading characters. Singleness of theme or purpose and perhaps, symmetry of structure should be utilized to insure unity of idea, of impression and of tone.[72]

A vaudeville sketch could be, and often was, prepared by shuffling index cards. Many gagwriters kept an index file of potential jokes, frequently clipped from the humor magazines, comic strips, and joke magazines of the period; stored jokes could be quickly reworked and inserted into a new routine. Jokewriter David Freedman estimated that he had from forty to sixty thousand jokes on index cards awaiting just such needs.[73] A theatrical play, by contrast, required careful blueprinting to satisfy demands for causal integration. Theatrical manuals often employed organic or architectural metaphors to describe the logic of a stage play's construction. W. T. Price's 1897 guidebook describes the well-made play as an "organism with connected, articulated parts . . . all with distinct functions, all co-related, none of which can be taken from the chain without breaking the continuity."[74] Elizabeth Woodridge suggest that each scene within the play "resembles not one brick in a straight wall, but one stone in an elaborate arch; the form of the stone will be determined by the point in the arch at which its placed and the purpose . . . which it serves."[75] Each element contributed something unique and irreplaceable to the overall effectiveness of the play; the parts worked together to build a whole that was characterized by its unity and continuity.

Page and others who advised would-be vaudeville writers did not necessarily share this same commitment to causal and thematic integration. For Page, the "pearls" of comic material remained more important than the plot "strings" to which they happened to be attached. The sequencing of the various comic bits had less to do with their logical relationship or narrative function than with their emotional impact. Laughter was to grow with each point until it reached a crescendo, then a few throw-away lines allowed the audience to catch its breath before the onslaught began again.

The structure of the individual gag, on the other hand, was much tighter. Page suggested a tripartite structure for each joke: the first line introduces the situation and invites a slight grin; the second intensifies the situation and provokes a chuckle; the final segment delivers the punch that pushes the laugh over the top.[76] Only on this microlevel did the sequencing of the component parts depend upon their logical function within the act's larger structure. Beyond the level of the individual joke, only the most minimal linkage material could hold these comic units together. A phrase like "Speaking of . . . ," "Which reminds me that . . . ," "But after all is said and done . . . ," "Just to illustrate . . . , " or "My! How times have changed . . . " might have been all that was needed to link one joke to those that preceded and followed it.[77] These connectives worked most effectively when they directed little attention to themselves but still created some unity for the act. Such cohesiveness was more frequently achieved through the association of gags around a principle of theme and variation or the structuring of episodes around the continuity of a central figure than through the linear development of a causally integrated narrative.

"Extinct Volcanoes": Legit Players in Vaudeville

The differences between the vaudeville aesthetic and theatrical realism may be illustrated by a brief reconsideration of the role of legitimate players on vaudeville. The so-called Headliner policy, the recruitment of leading stars of the legitimate theater for vaudeville appearances, began at the turn of the century. While its origins are disputed, Robert Grau traced the approach to J. Austin Fyne's bookings of such stars as Maurice Barrymore, Robert Hilliard, Sidney Drew, David Warfield, Edwin Royle and Vernona Jarbeau in 1894. Grau characterizes the move as "the great element that uplifted it [vaudeville], dignified it and strengthened it."[78] Through such bookings, Fyne was successful in attracting the attention of the "respectable" press to vaudeville, a key to wining a middle-class audience. Fyne's strategy was quickly imitated by his leading rivals, Keith and Pastor, and eventually became a standard vaudeville practice.

Variety appearances by such legitimate stage stars as Sarah Bernhardt, Mrs. Patrick Campbell, Amelia Bingham, Elbert Hubbard, and Gertrude Hoffman were widely touted as a measure of vaudeville's increased respectability and its audience's growing sophistication. In a 1926 interview, E. F. Albee spoke of a national tendency to desire "to make ourselves familiar with better things" that was fed by vaudeville's recruitment of legitimate stars.[79] Albee conceded that "the public had to be educated by vaudeville," but once educated, they had become more "demanding" than any other audience. What Albee's comments conveniently ignore is the nature of the "demands" theater owners and the vaudeville audience made upon the legitimate stars.

The modularity of vaudeville allowed for the easy insertion of short bits of dramatic performance onto the bill alongside more traditional variety acts, much as the program would at other times include film exhibition, military drills, Salome dancers, or jazz bands in response to the shifting interests of its audience. Percy Williams explained the logic of the Headliner policy in a 1908 *Variety* article: "A 'drawing card' is of value for two reasons. One is 'reputation'; the other 'novelty.' "[80] While the bulk of the vaudeville house income came from the regular patronage of a small number of hardcore fans, Williams argued, the use of a big name "drawing card" could ensure their return week after week and could attract patrons who otherwise would not attend the show. Williams would surround the legitimate star with top variety acts to ensure that the new patrons were exposed to the potential pleasures vaudeville offered; such a strategy was calculated to broaden the pool of regular customers for his theaters.

These additions did not demand any substantial reconceptualization or restructuring of vaudeville's standard practice. This modularity, however, had several other consequences. The need to compress a dramatic performance into the time frame previously allowed for a trained dog act meant a reduction of many elements of narrative, character, and thematic development seen as desirable by advocates of theatrical realism. It also meant that a dramatic performance on vaudeville was judged by the same standards as any other act; emphasis was placed upon the performer's ability to move an audience toward an outward display of emotion, not toward the more thoughtful or contemplative reaction promoted by the legitimate theater.

Critics frequently charged that these dramatic sketches stopped the flow of the entertainment dead, requiring a response incompatible with the vaudeville aesthetic. *Variety* critic Acton Davis protested in 1905 that "the greater part of the headliners are made up of dramatic extinct volcanoes, names which in many instances have outlived their usefulness and cleverness on the legitimate boards and now, distended out of all proportion to their worth, are starred at the head of the performance."[81] Davis charged that theatrical stars who could not excite an audience caused "mental dyspepsia" and drained the whole program of its potentially vitalizing function. Those who wanted to survive on the vaudeville circuits were forced to adapt to its norms. Davis expressed pessimism that the current practices of the legitimate theater could ever be made compatible with the demands of the vaudeville audience: "The whole method of the variety stage is so different to that of the regular boards that I cannot see why the average actor should ever expect that he could score with it. . . . It needs an exceptionally strong and magnetic actor to hold a variety audience for eighteen or twenty minutes."

Compression and intensification of the narrative was needed to make the dramatic playlet compatible with the tone and structure of the overall bill. J. C. Nugent suggested that "a playlet must go from its beginning through its conflict or argument to its conclusion by the most direct route."[82] Brett Page's description of the playlet suggests a balance between the "organic unity" of a legitimate play and the immediate impact of a vaudeville performance: "A playlet is a stage narrative taking usually about twenty minutes to act, having a single chief character, and a single problem which predominates, and is developed by means of a plot so compressed and so organized that every speech and every action of the characters move it forward to a finish which presents the most striking features; while the whole is so organized as to produce a single impression."[83] Page's description of the playlet is almost indistinguishable from that found in the guides for legitimate playwrights, including the mandatory discussion of Freytag's pyramid, the dramatic "unities" and the subordination of character to narrative. Yet he put much heavier stress upon the emotional impact of the performance. The playlet was to consist of a series of emotionally intensified "moments" of drama, building toward a wow climax, yet unified around a single character, a single dramatic conflict, and a causally integrated chain of events. Page recommended, "Pick out from life some incident, character, temperament . . . and flash upon it the glare of the vaudeville spotlight. . . . Dissect away the needless; vivify the series of actions you have chosen for your brief and trenchant crisis; lift it all with laughter or touch it all with tears."[84] Such a compressed performance did not allow for the development of rounded characters. Characters were to be streamlined for immediate impact and the pace of their conflicts was to be quickened to a level approaching hysteria.

Moreover, these playlets encouraged a return to the presentational style being rejected by the legitimate stage. Indeed, vaudeville attracted many stars who were accustomed to commanding their own stock companies and who found it difficult to adjust to the increased authority of the director within the legitimate theater. Like all other vaudeville acts, the performer had central authority over the production and frequently commissioned scripts to showcase his or her particular performance "tricks." Often, the act would consist of little more than a series of short speeches or scenes drawn from a number of the plays upon which the actors had built their reputations. Here, the focus was placed upon the distinctiveness with which the actors tackled their assigned roles and the emotional intensity with which a given speech was delivered. Given little chance to develop a full characterization, the actor was encouraged to play for "points" with the audience, to create a vivid and compelling personality. J. C. Nugent commented, "Vaudeville is good for projection. One learns unction, pause, timing, emphasis, 'clicking' as they say. But so much effort is given to that, necessary on account of big noisy auditoriums and the larger, lower and more mixed grades of intelligence which is the general vaudeville audience, that mood is often sacrificed for superficial effect."[85] Ethel Barrymore fretted over the difficulty of satisfying an audience accustomed to "the perfection of the slack-wire artist." She recalled in her autobiography, "If you follow him, you've got to be as good at your job as he is in his or you might as well be dead."[86] The result was frequently a broadening of performance style, the development of a "histrionic" approach calculated to produce audience response, and a shedding of the subtlety and restraint of a more ensemble-oriented staging. As Acton Davis explained, "In the legitimate play, this same actor would have secured important scenes strung through three or four acts. In vaudeville, if he doesn't hit out straight from the shoulder at once he is lost."[87]

Far from remaking vaudeville into a more respectable form, these actors were remade by vaudeville. Vaudeville absorbed those aspects of the legitimate theater compatible with its existing aesthetic practices, adopting them as a new set of options by which to stimulate and arouse audience response. Over time, the place of the legitimate performer on the circuit diminished. A survey of the reviews of new acts, published weekly in *Variety*, points toward a steady decline in the number of dramatic, seriocomic, and operatic acts available for vaudeville bookings.[88] In 1907, there were 71 new dramatic acts, a figure just a little less than the number of acts spotlighting performances on musical instruments (78), song and dance men (89) and acrobats (95), but far smaller than the number of singers (118), or of comic sketches (130). The number of legitimate dramatic players in vaudeville peaked in 1912 when 96 such acts appeared, yet these performers were swamped by comedians (219), singers (152), song and dance acts (118) and song and crossfire acts (129). After 1912, the number of new dramatic acts declined sharply until 1927 when there were only 15 such acts introduced. Despite its hype by the entrepreneurs, opera never constituted a significant category within vaudeville, declining from 15 new acts in

1.1 - 1.3 *Stand Up and Cheer* (1934): James Dunn and Shirley Temple (*top*), Stepin Fetchit (*middle and bottom*).

1.4 - 1.10   *Stand Up and Cheer* (1934): the backflipping senators sequence.

1.11   *Stand Up and Cheer* (1934).

4.1 - 4.3 *Hollywood Party*
(1934): Charles Judels (*top*)
and Jimmy Durante
(*middle*) romance Polly
Moran while Charles
Butterworth watches
(*bottom*).

4.4 - 4.5 *Hollywood Party* (1934): Jimmy Durante in Schnarzan preview.

4.6 *Hollywood Party* (1934): Jimmy Durante.

4.7 *Hollywood Party* (1934): Schnarzan locked in struggle.

5.1 *Duck Soup* (1933): Groucho Marx as President Rufus T. Firefly.

5.2 *Show of Shows* (1929): Winnie Lightner and Frank Fay.

5.3 - 5.4 *International House* (1933): Peggy Hopkins Joyce and Bela Lugosi (*top*); Lumsden Hare, George Burns, and Gracie Allen (*bottom*).

5.5 - 5.8 *International House* (1933): W. C. Fields.

5.9 - 5.11 *Dixianna* (1930):
Ralfe Harolde, Bebe Daniels,
Everett Marshall (*top*);
Jobyana Howland and
Frances Cawthorne (*middle*);
Jobyana Howland and
Everett Marshall (*bottom*).

5.12 *Dixianna* (1930): Bert Wheeler and Robert Woolsey.

5.13 - 5.16 *Monkey Business* (1931): The Marx Brothers.

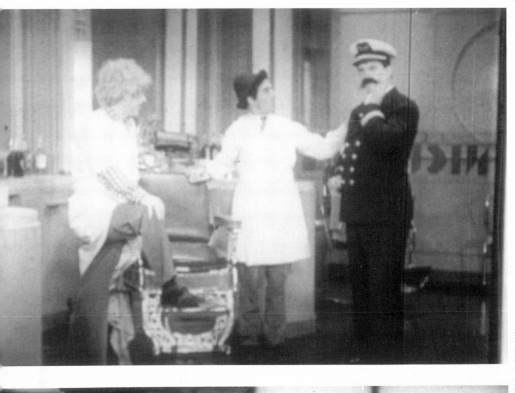

5.17 *Circus Clown* (1934): Joe E. Brown as father and son.

5.18 *Local Boy Makes Good* (1931): Joe E. Brown

5.19 *Monkey Business* (1931): Groucho Marx.

1912 to 5 in 1927. As these statistics suggest, vaudeville appearances by legitimate performers was a short-term response to the perceived composition of the variety audience. This effort to attract middle-class patronage was no longer necessary after 1912. Recruitment of legitimate players might be seen as comparable to the significant, though even more shortlived, increase in the number of jazz band performances in the 1920s. Such acts were believed to attract younger patrons from the nightclubs and dancehalls. The structure of the variety bill made it relatively easy to absorb new types of acts without much reconsideration of its general logic. The demands of the vaudeville audience and the pressures to conform to established act lengths forced legitimate actors to reject many of the norms most closely associated with theatrical realism and to return to or retain earlier acting styles more compatible with the vaudeville aesthetic.

FROM VAUDEVILLE TO BROADWAY, FROM BROADWAY TO HOLLYWOOD

Vaudevillians were a nomadic tribe. By this, I refer not simply to the fact that variety performers spent many long months traveling the circuits, providing entertainment to widely scattered audiences, "living out of a trunk." Stories about late night hash houses, cheap boarding houses, Pullman cars, and lost luggage pepper the autobiographies of vaudeville performers and remain part of the folklore of American show business. Vaudevillians were nomadic in a second and perhaps more important sense: they moved with remarkable fluidity across the many branches of the American entertainment industry. From the very beginning, vaudeville raided other forms of show business, bringing to its patrons the best stars of the English music hall, French cabaret, and Italian circus, the headliners of the legitimate theater, the veterans of burlesque, the minstrel show, the wild west show, sports, and the silent cinema. Vaudeville, in turn, provided a training ground for Broadway, Hollywood, nightclubs, radio, and television; its impact on popular culture could be felt for years after its demise as an institution. Stars did their apprenticeship in vaudeville and then marketed their performance skills elsewhere for higher money. Most of the stars of early sound comedy spent some time on Broadway, most often with the Ziegfeld *Follies* or one of the other New York revues. Hollywood rarely recruited directly from vaudeville, with Burns and Allen or Olsen and Johnson notable exceptions; rather, Hollywood periodically raided the

New York stage and netted a large number of displaced vaudevillians. Of the stars who will concern us in this book, almost all of them were appearing in major Broadway productions at the time they were recruited from the cinema; almost all of them had spent some time with Ziegfeld and his *Follies*.

Contrary to show business mythology, Florenz Ziegfeld did not originate the Broadway revue.[89] Irish entertainer John Brougham enjoyed considerable popularity on the American stage in the 1850s with a succession of lively stage productions featuring a loosely structured mixture of song, dance, and comedy. A more immediate predecessor was George Lederer's *The Passing Show* of 1894, billed as a "topical Extravaganza" and described by the New York *Times* as "a variety show with some touches of burlesque."[90] Lederer's success spawned imitators throughout the late nineteenth century (*In Gay New York, The Whirl of the Town, The Merry World, The Giddy Throng, The King's Carnival, A Little Bit of Everything,* and *About Town*), though few matched his popularity and most received only lukewarm notices. It is suggestive of the status of the stage revue that well into the twentieth century such productions were reviewed as vaudeville shows rather than as a wing of the legitimate theater. Indeed, from the outset, these shows casts were mostly recruited from vaudeville. Lew Field's *About Town* (1906), one of the most successful revues to emerge in the wake of *The Passing Show,* included such former vaudevillians as Louise Dresser, Jack Norworth, and Vernon Castle. Many of these early revues used the loose plot of a tour of New York as a string upon which diverse performance numbers, both musical and comic, could be strung. The excitement and heterogeneity of contemporary urban life provided a background against which to exploit the spectacle and showmanship of the variety stage.

Florenz Ziegfeld's *Follies of 1907* marked a dramatic turning point in the development of the stage revue and would be much imitated by subsequent productions. Ziegfeld's previous experience as a promoter of circus and variety acts, including famed strongman Eugene Sandow and singer Anna Held, meant that he maintained strong connections to vaudeville, even as he aspired toward acceptance within the legitimate theater.[91] Ziegfeld had, as well, known Broadway success with a revival of Charles Hoyt's *A Parlor Match* and with a series of stage vehicles for his wife, Anna Held. The Paris-born Held suggested to her husband the idea of a summer show, modeled after European cabaret yet appealing to American tastes.

From the beginning, Ziegfeld's shows combined continental sophistication with American showmanship, visual spectacle with rapid-fire comedy and toe-tapping tunes. As Ethan Mordden notes, "In devising a unique and extremely popular revue format, Ziegfeld gave vaudeville a venue of esteem next to rather than within the musical. . . . All revues before Ziegfeld were little better than vaudeville with a title. The *Follies* gave revue dignity and latitude. They weren't vaudeville's exile, but vaudeville's apotheosis.[92] The first *Follies* spotlighted such vaudeville veterans as Grace LaRue, Emma Carus, Bickel and Watson, and Nora Bayes. The tremendous success of the first *Follies* set the model for subsequent Ziegfeld extravaganzas. Between 1907 and 1931, Ziegfeld mounted twenty-one editions of the *Follies* and gained an international reputation for his lively blend of sophisticated spectacle, shimmering costumes, lavish sets, beautiful showgirls, delightful scores and remarkable comedy. The first *Follies* cost only $13,000 to produce; that figure had grown to $289,000 by the 1927 edition, a staggering budget for a stage production of the period.

It would be difficult to overestimate the impact of the Ziegfeld *Follies* on the history of American popular entertainment. Altogether Ziegfeld commissioned more than five hundred songs for his revues, drawing on the talents of Jerome Kern, Victor Herbert, Rudolf Friml, and especially Irving Berlin; among songs the *Follies* added to the repertoire of American popular music are "By the Light of the Silvery Moon" (1909), "Row, Row, Row" (1912), "Hello, Frisco" (1915), "Mandy" (1919), "A Pretty Girl is Like a Melody" (1919), "Second Hand Rose" (1921) and "My Man" (1921). The much-glorified Ziegfeld girls included in their ranks Marion Davies, Vera Maxwell, Peggy Hopkins Joyce, Mae Murray, Barbara Stanwyck, Paulette Goddard, and Irene Dunne. Although Ziegfeld professed to be indifferent to comedy and devoted much of his attention to the selection of chorus girls and the development of elaborate stage spectacles, almost all of the major musical comedy performers of the early sound period were in one way or another touched by Ziegfeld, including Eddie Cantor, W. C. Fields, Maurice Chevalier, Lupe Velez, Fred Astaire, Jimmy Durante, Paul Whiteman and his Orchestra, Leon Errol, Jack Pearl, Will Rogers, Fanny Brice, Ed Wynn, Ole Olsen and Chic Johnson, Bert Wheeler and Robert Woolsey.[93] Many of these stars were featured in the *Follies*; others appeared in the more intimate *Midnight Frolic* performances on the New Amsterdam Theatre roof; a few were included in his many book musicals, including *Sally* (1920), *Kid Boots* (1923), *Rio Rita* (1927), *Show Boat* (1927), *Whoopee* (1928), and *Show Girl* (1929). When these stars came to Hollywood, responding to the demand in the early sound period for stage-trained voices, they brought with them the vocabulary of vaudeville, yet they also brought with them the polish and sophistication of Ziegfeld.[94]

Nor was Ziegfeld the only producer who drew heavily upon vaudeville talents in casting his revues. As others began to imitate Ziegfeld's formula and to initiate their own stage revues, they triggered a stampede of vaudeville performers onto the "great white way." Vaudeville managers would periodically complain of shortages of comedians, citing the lure of the New York revues as draining away their best talents, much as Broadway producers would later make these same complaints in response to Hollywood's recruitment of their prized comic stars. The Shubert Brothers mounted a rival show, *The Mimic World,* as early as 1908, just one year after the first *Follies* premiered; they, however, would not sustain an annual stage review until *The Passing Show,* which first appeared in 1918 and ran for eleven more editions. Vaudeville stars who appeared in the Shuberts' productions included Charlotte Greenwood, Jobyna Howland, Trixie Friganza, Robert Woolsey, Ned Sparks, Ed Wynn, Marie Dressler, Ethel Shutta, Fred Allen, and George Jessel. The thirteen editions of *George White's Scandals* spotlighted such vaudeville veterans as W. C. Fields, Winnie Lightner, Tom Patricola, Will Mahoney, and Willie and Eugene Howard. *Earl Carroll's Vanities,* which ran through eleven editions, offered the talents of Patsy Kelly, Joe Cook, Frank Tinney, Ted Healy and his Three Stooges, Charles Butterworth, Moran and Mack, W.C. Fields, and Joe Frisco. Irving Berlin's *Music Box Revue* boasted appearances by Clark and McCullough, Charlotte Greenwood, William Gaxton, Robert Benchley, and Fanny Brice. Altogether, more than 154 stage revues were presented on Broadway between 1920 and 1930, compared to 279 book musicals produced during this same period.[95] There were "black and tan" revues, such as *Africana* (with Ethel Waters) or *Blackbirds of 1928* (with Bill "Bojangles" Robinson), and "intimate revues" aimed at a more literate and sophisticated audience, such as *The Garrick Gaieties* (which featured music by Rodgers and Hart and performances by Sterling Holloway, Lee Strasberg, Imogene Coca, and Rosalind Russell), *The Greenwich Village Follies* (which introduced Joe E. Brown), or *The 49ers* (which drew on the writing talents of the famed Algonquin Round Table). For the most part, however, these Broadway revues followed the formula developed by Ziegfeld and refined through subsequent editions of the *Follies.*

The revue's dependence upon vaudeville talent has led many to describe these productions as little more than elaborately mounted vaudeville shows. Revue shared vaudeville's quick pace and heterogeneous material, its immediate appeal and its emphasis upon spectacle over narrative. Gilbert Seldes could just as easily have been writing of vaudeville when he celebrated the virtues of a Ziegfeld show: "The good revue pleases the eye, the ear and pulse; the very good revue does *this so well that it pleases the mind.* . . . It does not have to send them away laughing or even whistling; all it needs to do is to keep the perceptions of the audience fully engaged all the time, and the evaporation of its pleasures will bring the audience back again and again."[96] Ziegfeld also spoke of the formulas for his shows as an elevation of variety entertainment, emphasizing the novelty and diversity of his materials, while hinting at the larger budgets he had to spend on stagecraft: "We've got to give them something out of the ordinary—something on a little higher plane than formerly, but with enough snap and go to it to prevent the suspicion of being high-brow. We'll let Ben Ali Haggin stage a couple of his gorgeous tableaux, turn Joseph Urban loose with a ton of paint and a battery of colored lights, commission Victor Herbert to write some of his most tuneful music and then get Irving Berlin, Gene Buck, Dave Stamper, W. C. Fields, Van and Schenck, Ray Dooley and the rest of 'em to supply the jazz and the laughs."[97] The fragmentation of the revue, much like vaudeville, permitted the insertion of many different styles of entertainment; the *Follies'* compartmentalization made it possible for elements to be added or subtracted to keep the show fresh for repeat audiences.

Yet it is important to note the differences between these two styles of variety entertainment. Vaudeville, as we have seen, was an actor-centered mode of entertainment; each act was conceived separately as a modular unit, which might play against any number of other acts in the course of its run. The Broadway revue, however, was often dominated by the personality of its producer, be it Ziegfeld, Earl Carroll, George White, or the Shubert Brothers. Ziegfeld and his production assistants recruited the performers, the writers, the composers; they carefully supervised the stage designs and costumes; they proposed ideas for sketches and approved all of the material presented in their shows. Some performers, notably Will Rogers, Eddie Cantor, and W. C. Fields, still wrote at least some of their own material for the *Follies,* yet they did so under the strict supervision of the show's all-powerful producers. Ziegfeld's name appeared before the title and critics who praised the show looked upon him as the guiding intelligence. Seldes wrote, "He [Ziegfeld] makes everything appear perfect by a consummate smoothness of production. . . . It is not the smoothness of a connecting rod running in oil, but of a batter where all the ingredients are so promptly introduced and so thoroughly integrated that in the end a man may stand up and say, 'this is a show!' "[98] The artistry of the Ziegfeld *Follies,* thus, combined the showmanship and spectacle of vaudeville with the unity and coordination of the legitimate theater. George Jean Nathan wrote that all of the basic elements of the Ziegfeld show could be found in variety, yet "it remained for Ziegfeld to orchestrate it, to take its separate ingredients and fashion them into a warm composition."[99] It is suggestive that both Seldes and Nathan spoke of the revue not in terms of component parts that functioned separately (a common metaphor for vaudeville) but rather in terms of appetizing ingredients that would be mixed together. If the vaudevillian often stood alone in front of a stark backdrop, the *Follies* star had to share the public's attention with Ben Ali Haggin's tableaus, Urban's lushly colored backdrops, Erte's stylized costumes, Irving Berlin's scores, and Ziegfeld's trademark parade of showgirls.

The many remarkable performers who passed through the *Follies* developed individual sketches suited to their particular talents, sketches that formed the basis for their later screen personas, yet they also appeared opposite other performers within one of the most remarkable ensemble companies ever assembled. To take the 1919 *Follies,* for example, Eddie Cantor stole the show with his "You'd Be Surprised" number and a sketch that cast him as a nervous patient at an osteopath's office (a scene later reworked for his 1931 film, *Palmy Days*). Yet he also played opposite Bert Williams in a minstrel number. The show's three hour length gave Ziegfeld ample opportunities to showcase his performers both individually and collectively.

The individual scenes strove for a broad range of backgrounds and themes, allowing for the lavish display of sets and costumes. The 1921 *George White's Scandals,* for example, featured twenty scenes with settings that included New York, the South Seas, the Moscow Winter Palace, the Panama Canal, the North Pole, the deck of the Flying Dutchman, and Biblical Jerusalem. The revue also integrated these diverse materials into a unified program, frequently through the introduction of an overriding theme or a loose plot. The 1907 *Follies* played upon public interest in the Jamestown Centenary Exposition, casting John Smith and Pocahontas as masters of ceremonies and taking them on a tour of modern-day New York. There, they encountered such contemporary public figures as Teddy Roosevelt, Anthony Comstock, Andrew Carnegie, John Philip Sousa, Commodore Perry, Enrico Caruso, and Mark Twain. *Fashions of 1924* organized its entertainment around the display of new ensembles by foremost designers with scenes devoted to forecasts of sportswear, beachwear, afternoon wear, furs, and footwear. The Marx Brothers' first stage vehicle, *I'll Say She Is* (1924), fit revue acts into a simple narrative about a woman's misadventures in Chinatown, her trial for murder, and her opium-induced dreams (including a sequence where Groucho plays Napoleon and his brothers Josephine's suitors). Ed Wynn's *Simple Simon* (1930) centered around a Coney Island news dealer who dreams of living in the world of fairy tales, with individual sketches parodying familiar children's stories.

Minimally, a revue show was held together by running gags that cut across the various acts. *The Gaieties of 1919* got a great deal of comic mileage from its lack of plot with host Ed Wynn introducing Mr. Plot in the performance's opening sketch, only to dismiss him as unwanted; Mr. Plot returned several times in the course of the evening with Wynn each time chasing him away. The 1919 *Follies* focused on prohibition: Cantor sang "You Don't Need the Wine to Have a Wonderful Time (While They Still Make Those Beautiful Girls)"; Bert Williams took the opposite position in "You Cannot Make Your Shimmy Shake on Tea"; The Ziegfeld girls strutted in "A Saloon of the Future," dressed to represent Sassparilla, Grape Juice, Lemonade, and other soft drinks. George Jean Nathan protested that this narrow topical focus diminished the pleasures of the Ziegfeld productions: "It would seem that this exceptional professor of the tune stage knows no sounder use for two hundred thousand dollars' worth of magnificent scenes, costumes, rights and girls than to place them in their positions upon the stage, crack the whip and bid them in combination work themselves up in a smashing two-hour crescendo to a joke about Henry Ford."[100]

As the Broadway revue evolved, producers put less and less emphasis upon these unifying themes or plots, allowing the personalities of their comic stars to cement the various segments. Sometimes, stars acted as masters of ceremonies, introducing the performers and offering playful commentary between the acts. John Corbin wrote of the *Gaieties of 1919* that "Everytime it is necessary to shift the scenery he [Ed Wynn] comes out with his conversation and the audience is in no hurry for the next act."[101] W. C. Fields dominated the 1925 edition of the *Ziegfeld Follies,* which drew heavily upon sketches from his failed musical, *The Comic*

Supplement, while Eddie Cantor became the all but exclusive focus of the 1927 show.

These practices led logically to the development of revues and musicals centered around the talents of individual performers. Ed Wynn performed in a succession of such shows, including *Ed Wynn Carnival* (1920), *The Perfect Fool* (1921), *The Grab Bag* (1924), *Manhattan Mary* (1927), and *Simple Simon* (1930). Other performers also followed this route, including Fred Stone, Raymond Hitchcock, Eddie Cantor, Frank Tinney, Al Jolson, Elsie Janis, Nora Bayes, and Joe Cook. Some of these shows, Joe Cook's *Rain or Shine* or the Marx Brother's *The Cocoanuts* and *Animal Crackers,* were book musicals, with the stars' performances fit into a narrative context; Wynn's shows were more often one-man revues making little or no pretense at plot. Here, the pleasure lay entirely in performance.

These shows were the logical culmination of the vaudevillian's push toward the mastery of diverse performance skills. As Gilbert Seldes explained, "The theory of the one-man show is apparently that there are individuals so endowed, so versatile and so beloved, that no other vehicle will suffice to let them do their work." [102] If the vaudeville performer might combine several different specialties within a single twenty-minute act, the revue format asked performers to return again and again to the stage, adopting diverse roles and demonstrating many different specialties. In the 1921 *Follies,* for example, Fanny Brice, one of several comic stars, performed in a spoof of *Camille,* engaged in a comic boxing match, appeared as a young Scottish maid with a mysterious Yiddish accent, and sang two of her most famous numbers, "My Man" and "Second Hand Rose." The one-man shows pushed this tendency to the extreme, devoting a single evening to displaying the talents of a single performer. In the course of *The Perfect Fool,* for example, Ed Wynn sang, played the piano, danced, told jokes, performed as an acrobat, and engaged in a mind-reading act. As Alexander Woollcott noted, *"The Perfect Fool* is for those who like to take their Ed Wynn straight. . . . He has seen to it that nothing should distract you from the main business of the evening—the business of listening to and laughing at Ed Wynn." [103] Such shows brought the star full circle, with Wynn regaining the control over his own performance that he had enjoyed in vaudeville and lost as a performer in the 1914 and 1915 editions of the Ziegfeld *Follies,* the 1916 edition of the Shubert Brothers' *Passing Show,* or *The Gaieties of 1919.* Wynn wrote, scored, pro-

Ed Wynn backstage at *The Grab Bag* (1925). Wisconsin Center for Film and Theater Research.

duced, directed, and stared in his own shows. As Stark Young explained, "He did everything it is possible to do, even to giving a hand with the scenery and props." [104] Not all the revue stars regained this same degree of autonomy when they appeared in theatrical vehicles; Ziegfeld continued to dominate the careers of his contracted performers, even when he choose to feature them in their own shows, as he did for Eddie Cantor in *Kid Boots* (1923) and *Whoopee* (1928).

The introduction of talking pictures lured the former vaudevillians away from Broadway and toward Hollywood. Some revue stars, notably Will Rogers, W. C. Fields, and Eddie Cantor, had enjoyed some popularity in the silent cinema; most were too dependent upon their vocal skills to be attractive to film producers. The coming of sound, however, meant that the studios needed to reassess their talent rosters and to recruit stars who could exploit the commercial potentials of this new technology. Hollywood invested heavily in the assumption that it could market New York-style entertainment to movie audiences. [105] In one week, Metro offered contracts to no less than seven cast members of Joe Cook's musical comedy, *Rain or Shine.* Cook hired Ted Healy and His Stooges to replace some of the departing cast members, only to lose them to Hollywood as well, before Cook accepted a contract to appear in a 1930 Columbia screen adaptation of the play. [106] By 1929, Fox alone had more than two hundred stage-trained people under contract; the full scale of recruitment industry wide would be hard to estimate. [107] Edgar Selwyn, a noted stage producer, succinctly summarized the situation: "Motion picture moguls have combed the stage of its good players, have baited the best with juicy contracts and have left the Broadway mart as dry of excellent actors as a glass eye." [108] Revue stars appeared alongside classical musicians and opera singers on the early Vitaphone programs, and their connections to Broadway remained a major selling point in the promotional campaigns for early talking pictures. Hollywood bought the rights for many of the period's most popular musical comedies, including *Sally* (with Marilyn Miller and Leon Errol), *Poppy* (with W. C. Fields), *The Cocoanuts* (with the Marx Brothers), *Rio Rita* (with Bert Wheeler and Robert Woolsey), *So Long Letty* (with Charlotte Greenwood), *Whoopee* (with Eddie Cantor), *Simple Simon* (with Ed Wynn), and *Rain or Shine* (with Joe Cook). In some cases, the film versions of these stage hits retained their original theatrical casts; in other cases, such as *50 Million Frenchmen* (which was remade as a screen vehicle for Olsen and Johnson) or *Hold Everything* (which put Joe E. Brown in the role Bert Lahr originated and rebuilt the narrative as a vehicle for Winnie Lightner), the films were recast and reworked to exploit previously contracted talent (though here, as well, Hollywood drew extensively on New York and vaudeville veterans). The hope was that these stars and their stage successes would represent presold commodities, already familiar to the urban audiences who were the dominant market for the early talkies. These comic stars brought with them well-developed stage personae, a repertoire of basic tricks and gags, and a vocabulary of performance skills they could exploit in their screen vehicles. Hollywood initially cast these stars in screen versions of their previous stage successes. The problem would come when it had to construct new narratives to exploit their performance specialties, when they had to negotiate between the competing demands of the classical Hollywood narrative and the vaudeville aesthetic. That problem will be the focus for the remainder of this book.

4

"Assorted Lunacy . . . with No Beginning and No End": Gag, Performance, and Narrative in Early Sound Comedy

The importance of vaudeville both as an early exhibition outlet and as a model for early filmmaking practice has been well documented.[1] What Tom Gunning labels the *cinema of attractions* was at least partially a response to the presentation of early films within existing forms of variety entertainment; the formal practices of early cinema reflected the need to appeal to audiences schooled in the vaudeville aesthetic. Gunning suggests that early cinema was characterized by its emphasis upon spectacle rather than narrative, its conglomeration of heterogeneous material, its emotional immediacy, and its self-conscious showmanship:

> The cinema of attractions directly solicits spectator attention, inciting visual curiosity, and supplying pleasure through an exciting spectacle. . . . Theatrical display dominates over narrative absorbtion, emphasizing the direct stimulation of shock or surprise at the expense of unfolding a story or creating a diegetic universe. The cinema of attractions expends little energy creating characters with psychological motivations or individual personality. Making use of both fictional and non-fictional attractions, its energy moves outward towards an acknowledged spectator rather than inward towards the character-based situations essential to classical narrative.[2]

Drawing on Sergei Eisenstein and Marinetti, Gunning ascribes many of these aesthetic principles to early cinema's borrowings from vaudeville, circus, and other forms of variety entertainment. He could just as easily be drawing on Brett Page, Nathan and Cohan, Weber and Fields, and the other advocates of the vaudeville aesthetic. Early cinema apes many aspects of variety performance, offering a heterogeneous appeal to a heterogeneous audience and pushing emotional immediacy over narrative coherence. Historically, Hollywood's construction of a system of classical norms and its push toward middle-class acceptance meant a conscious rejection of the vaudeville aesthetic. As Kristin Thompson writes, "One of the main causes in the shift from primitive to classical cinema involves a change in influences from the other arts, from an initial close imitation of vaudeville, to a greater dependence on short fiction, novels and legitimate drama."[3] While she insists that the shift toward classical cinema cannot be explained entirely in relation to outside influences, Thompson documents how the realist theater and the magazine short story market served as models for the well-constructed screenplay. Vaudeville's subsequent influence upon the American cinema was restricted either to certain marginalized classes of films (B-movies, serials, comic shorts, cartoons) or to short sequences of slapstick or spectacle safely sequestered within larger story structures (as in the silent comic features of Chaplin, Keaton, Lloyd, et al.).[4]

The comic film tended to lag behind the rest of the American cinema in its acceptance of classical Hollywood norms, remaining one of the places where marginal film practices enjoyed the greatest acceptability. The genre nevertheless experienced and ultimately capitulated to the same pressures shaping all of classical cinema. The shift between the loosely structured slapstick shorts of Chaplin and Keaton and their "mature" feature films (i.e., the development of more elaborate narratives, more complex characters, the mix of comedy and pathos) reflected these performers' assimilation into the mainstream of the classical Hollywood cinema.[5] David Bordwell and Kristin Thompson demonstrate, for example, that "virtually every bit" of Keaton's *Our Hospitality* (Metro, 1923) "functions to support and advance the cause-event chain of the narrative."[6] Their analysis suggests that Keaton, like other comic filmmakers of the late 1920s, operated fully within classical norms and showed few signs of his previous allegiance to the vaudeville aesthetic.

The recruitment of vaudeville and revue performers in the early sound period and the effort to construct appropriate vehicles for their talents represented a conscious return to an aesthetic previously rejected, a new effort to appropriate devices from variety entertainment and to integrate them into the classical system. Pressures toward standardization of product and normalization of star image eventually resulted in the formal and thematic conservatism of the late 1930s comedian comedy. In the short run, however, the studios were prepared to tolerate a certain degree of experimentation, provided these experiments found a large and receptive audience.

The vaudeville aesthetic, as I have suggested, contrasts sharply with the formal norms Bordwell, Staiger, and Thompson have identified within the classical Hollywood cinema:

> We find that the Hollywood cinema sees itself as bound by rules that set stringent limits on individual innovation, that telling a story is the basic formal concern . . . that unity is a basic attribute of film form; that the Hollywood film purports to be "realistic" in both an Aristotelian sense (truth to the probable) and a naturalistic one (truth to historical fact); that the Hollywood film strives to conceal its artifice through techniques of continuity and "invisible editing."[7]

A comedy that sought to integrate some central aspects of the vaudeville aesthetic into dominant studio practice would be a strange-looking film, indeed. It would be a text shaped by competing if not directly contradictory aesthetic impulses. Such a film would assert the centrality of narrative only to puncture that narrative with a series of self-contained performance sequences that are often far more memorable than any story the film might tell. Such a film would rupture character consistency to allow for a constant display of performer virtuosity.

Contemporary critics frequently characterized early sound comedies as "sloppy" (*Duck Soup*), "scattered and shapeless" (*High Flyers*, RKO, 1937), "noisy, hectic, absurd, overlong and witless" (*Half Shot at Sunrise*, RKO, 1930), "just thrown together without rhyme or reason" (*Cracked Nuts*, RKO, 1931), and "stretched out endlessly" (*Everything's Rosie*, RKO, 1931). The plot of *So This is Africa* (Columbia, 1933) was dismissed as "so much padding," while *Diplomaniacs* was panned as "strictly a series of gags." More favorably inclined critics suggest that early sound comedies are "loose . . . but hilarious" (*Animal Crackers*), "overflowing with situations" (*Half Shot at Sunrise*), "senseless but clever" (*Phantom President*, Paramount, 1932), and "pleasantly irrational" (*The Cuckoos*, RKO, 1930). One critic described *Monkey Business* as "assorted lunacy . . . [with] no beginning and no end," while another characterized *Day at the Races* as "giddy goofiness and aimless goings-on."

All of these phrases represent different responses to similar aspects of these comedies' formal organization—their fragmentation, heterogeneity, and disunity; their excessive concentration on gags and comic performance at the expense of story and character development; their deviation from the norms of classical Hollywood cinema. One group of critics finds these breaks with standard screen practice an obvious source of pleasure while the other writers find them unpleasant and distracting; one group reads them as a necessary component of the films' overall style while the other group treats them as marks of incompetence. Both sets of critics drew upon classical criteria to understand the unusual character of early sound comedy; both groups clearly saw these films as operating at the margins, at the outer limits of acceptable screen practice. And, it should be noted that many critics expressed uncertainty about the relative importance of these two sets of aesthetic criteria. *Motion Picture Herald* critic Edward Churchill's reaction to *Going Wild* (Warner Brothers, 1930) suggests this indecision: "There is little enough attention paid to reasonableness in the construction of the story, which is merely a thread on which to string the comedy, but it does not matter particularly, since it's entertaining."[8]

Hollywood's assimilation of this alien aesthetic was approached with tentativeness and indecision, resulting in far more artistic and popular failures than successes. Neither filmmakers nor critics were certain how to respond to these films or how to create stable formulas for their production. Yet this creative tension also gave rise to remarkable works that gain their vitality and fascination from their ability to break free from Hollywood narrative conventions—even if only temporarily. This chapter will examine gag and performance as potential sources of comic excess within the classical cinema, examining ways early sound comedy balances a fascination for performance virtuosity with a desire for narrative cohesiveness. A case history of the making of *Hollywood Party* (MGM, 1934) will suggest how these two aesthetics shaped the scripting process and reception of this troubled film.

"His Mind Runs on Gags": Gag Logic and Narrative Structure

All textual systems involve a contest between homogeneity and heterogeneity. As Kristin Thompson explains, "Every film contains a struggle of unifying and disunifying structures. . . . Every stylistic element may serve at once to contribute to the narrative and to distract our perception from it."[9] Thompson adopts the term *excess* to refer to formal elements that are "counter-narrative" and "counter-unity." Excess disrupts the coherence of the textual system and reveals "a gap or lag in motivation."[10] Thompson concedes that moments of excess may have "some unpleasant consequences for the act of viewing," if a film is approached exclusively through the grid of classical narrative conventions, although these same moments may be pleasurable if "one looks beyond the narrative."[11] In her accounts of cinematic excess in *Ivan the Terrible* (1945) and *Playtime* (1967), Thompson concentrates primarily upon stylistic elements that invite a perceptual play with the materiality of the signifier: the textures, colors, and shapes of costumes, certain disruptive or distracting sounds,and the shifts between color and black-and-white footage in *Ivan the Terrible,* the dense and cluttered compositions in *Playtime.*[12] Other writers locate additional places where classical attempts at narrative unity break down and excess becomes a focus for the audience's fascination. Donald Crafton has argued that gags found in early slapstick comedies constitute a potential source of narrative excess; these sudden bursts of comic spectacle impede or disrupt the narrative's syntactical development and command attention beyond their functions within the plot:

> Slapstick seems to me to be defined by this failure of containment and resistance to bourgeois legibility. . . . [The gags' purpose] is to misdirect the viewer's attention, to obfuscate the linearity of cause-effect relations. Gags provide the opposite of epistemological comprehension by the spectator. They are atemporal bursts of violence and/or hedonism that are as ephemeral and as gratifying as the sight of someone's pie-smitten face.[13]

Crafton's analysis of the "dialectical" relationship between systems of gag ("the pie") and narrative ("the chase") in the Charlie Chase short *His Wooden Wedding* applies equally well to the construction of many early sound comedies. In the W. C. Fields vehicle *The Man on the Flying Trapeze* (Paramount, 1935), for example, Fields's narrative goal is relatively modest: he wishes to leave office early one day to attend a wrestling match. Such a plot is not much of a basis for a feature-length film, as critics of this work have been quick to note. Yet the movie's pleasures lie not with the development of this premise but rather with everything that happens (a series of encounters with the police, flat tires, runaway wheels, misplaced tickets) to block his progress toward his desired destination. What commands audience attention are devices that derail the syntagmatic movement of the narrative and allow for a succession of what Crafton (following Eisenstein) calls comic "attractions."

Crafton acknowledges that certain gags may indeed carry bits of narratively relevant information, though these gags may not be reduced to those narrative functions and serve these roles only at a high cost to narrative economy. In *The Man on the Flying Trapeze*, Fields's car develops a flat and he stops to change it. Another car backs into his, and unbeknownst to him, sends his wheel rolling off down the street. An old woman rather timidly interrupts the two men's dispute to inform Fields of the runaway tire, and after much fumbling with his hat, Fields chases after it, racing down a long hill and onto the railroad tracks into the path of an oncoming train. First the tire and then Fields hops onto the other track just as the train is about to bear down upon them. No sooner has Fields escaped the path of one locomotive than another comes upon him from behind, as he races across a long bridge in hot pursuit of his runaway wheel. Again, he only barely escapes certain death by leaping onto the other track where the chase continues a good hundred yards. Then, for no apparent reason, the wheel stops and collapses onto the ground.

In one sense, of course, Fields's pursuit of the runaway wheel is a necessary ingredient of the plot, little more than a blocking device; the protagonist must reclaim the tire and reattach it to his car in order to achieve his goal of reaching the wrestling match. Viewers are reminded of this goal by periodic cutaways to the already started match. At the same time, the absurd lengths to which Fields must go to satisfy this goal and the denial of cause-effect logic in the behavior of an inanimate object makes the runaway tire a source of interest and affective intensity far in excess of its causal functions. We want to see what new obstacle Fields will confront far more than we want to see whether he will make it to the match before it is finished. Moreover, the narrative consequences of this gag are purely cumulative; that is, we could have more or fewer gags involving the runaway tire without really altering the plot development. Individually, they do not change much about the plot; rather, they depend upon a repetition of the same basic man/tire opposition until its comic potential has been exhausted and the forward movement of the narrative may resume.

Crafton errs, perhaps, in his steadfast assertion that gag and narrative are always "antagonistic," that there is "an unbridgeable gap" separating them.[14] Rather, gags and narrative are independent (though often interacting) formal systems. Gags were often written by gagwriters who inserted them into the preexisting structure provided by the narrative scriptwriters. Or, conversely, gags were conceived as autonomous moments of comic spectacle with scripts constructed to provide a framework within which they may be displayed. Comedy producers spoke of plots as "strings" or "frames" that could contain and show off the comic bits. Consider for example how producer Sam Goldwyn characterized his relationship to comedian Eddie Cantor:

> I would see that Eddie Cantor's scripts were pretty much completed before we started production as Cantor as a rule would try to get away from the story and come on the comedy side of it and my belief is that the most important thing in a comedy is to have a story first and follow that story. . . . Cantor never had an idea on stories because his mind runs on gags. . . . Situations are written by authors. [15]

Cantor viewed the story as an excuse for songs, dances, and gags, as a showcase for his performance skills; his lifetime commitment to the vaudeville aesthetic reinforced his tendency to stress gag over story. Goldwyn clearly viewed "story" as a matter of fulfilling narrative conventions necessary to standardize production; his commitments to the norms of the classical Hollywood cinema strengthened his insistence on the importance of plot over gags. Goldwyn also suggestively distinguishes between gags that are irrelevant to the plot development and situations, scenes that play a central role in the unfolding story. Both Cantor and Goldwyn recognized an explicit separation between story and gags, viewing them as two separate elements (or systems) that interact in the film's construction.

Gags may be opposed to narrative in some slapstick comedies, as Crafton shows in *His Wooden Wedding*; they may impede its progression or parody its underlying assumptions and conventions. Gags may introduce alternative patternings—categorical, spacial, associational—that compete with our interest in causality and plot progression. They may also serve narrative purposes, may intersect and motivate future plot developments. Extended comic spectacles (such as the proverbial pie fight that Crafton evokes in his argument), no less than the gunfight in the western, may resolve character conflicts and provide narrative closure. Gags may become devices for characterization, suggesting a problematic relationship between the comedian and the larger social order, or mapping a series of oppositions between comic protagonist and antagonist. They may participate in the process of narration, signaling a particular relationship between the textual world and the realm of lived experience, or marking the authority of the narrational system to withhold or provide relevant information. Or, as Peter Kramer has

"His mind runs on gags": Eddie Cantor. Wisconsin Center for Film and Theater Research.

noted, they may actively contribute thematic significance to a particular film, may be semantic as well as narrative elements within the textual system.[16] Gags may serve a variety of narrative purposes and may be more or less integrated into the causal structure.

GAGS, EVENTS, AND DETAILS

Steve Neale and Frank Krutnik offer a useful distinction between "comic events," which "can exist only within a narrative context—as a consequence of the existence of characters and a plot"[17]—and "gags," which "constitute digressions within a story or story-based action."[18] As chapter 2 suggests, the tradition of thoughtful laughter respected comic events (i.e., narrativized gags that reflect on character relationships) while advocates of the New Humor promoted gags (like "poking one finger in a man's eye") as insuring immediate audience response regardless of their context. Historically, there have been periods of screen comedy that depend heavily upon comic events and situations, such as the so-called Golden Age of silent feature comedian comedy or the late 1930s and early 1940s, and others, such as early slapstick or the anarchistic comedies of the early 1930s, where gags were only loosely integrated into the narrative structure. Similarly, romantic comedy depends far more on situation than comedian comedy, which has tended to be focused around gags. Even within individual texts, jokes and gags are often only intermittently oppositional to narrative and character development. Integrated or not, narrativized or not, however, gags retain an affective force apart from those functions; gags remain a source of audience fascination that competes directly with plot and character development.

One explanation for their antinarrative potential, paradoxically, is that gags are already self-contained narratives following their own logic, independent of the larger plot. (Recall, for example, Brett Page's account of the tripartite organization of the vaudeville joke and his suggestion that individual gags were more tightly organized than the sketch's global structure.) As Steve Neale and Frank Krutnik write:

> One of the reasons why many jokes, wisecracks, and funny lines are rarely integral to a plot is that they all require formal closure, often in the form of a punchline. Because of this degree of closure, they are structurally unsuited to narration. They can, and often do, involve narrative preconditions. But it is difficult to use them as a springboard for narrative development. They are

instead much more suited to constructing or marking a pause or digression in the ongoing flow of a story.[19]

Another reason is that gags often direct attention at points of vulnerability within the narrative logic, making it harder to accept the film's basic premise. Sylvain du Pasquier suggests that gags "disturb" and "subvert" the "normal operation" of the plot by "revealing the fragility" inherent in its assumed order and implied meaning: "The gag, like a parasite, corrupts the plot . . . and the multiple meanings hidden in normal or realistic discourse are exposed, unmasked, laid bare."[20] The gag foregrounds aspects of the plot that would normally be taken for granted. As a result, gags block and often derail narrative development. Gags and jokes, as Mary Douglas notes, are always "potentially subversive" since they call into question the common sense categories by which we make sense of our everyday experience: "The joke merely affords the opportunity for realizing that an accepted pattern has no necessity. Its excitement lies in the suggestion that a particular ordering of experience may be arbitrary and subjective."[21]

We might usefully contrast this conception of the gag with Roland Barthes's account of the narrative detail. In his influential essay, "An Introduction to the Structural Analysis of Narrative," Barthes insists that every element within an narrative "in one way or another, is significant" to our understanding of the narrative's structure and content.[22] Cardinal functions serve as the "actual hinges of the narrative," establishing and resolving moments when an "alternative" arises that has "consequence" within the story; cardinal functions are "risk-laden moments" within the narrative's forward development.[23] Other elements serve to "fill in the narrative space separating the hinge type functions," serving as catalyses that "precipitate, delay, or quicken the pace of the discourse," as indices of character or narrative atmosphere, or as informants of "pure, locally relevant data."[24] These noncardinal elements, such as a reference to James Bond puffing on a cigarette before answering the telephone that Barthes cites as an example, are the spear carriers of the narrative, attracting limited attention to themselves; they make their small contributions while the nuclei stars take all the "risks" and propel the plot. The secondary narrative details, while open to analysis, are generally consumed by the text; readers are typically more concerned with the plot development and thus purely local details are soon forgotten.

While gags may assume the function of a catalyse, indice, or informant, they direct the spotlight onto themselves, attempt to upstage the narrative nuclei, and remain in our memory when the plot is resolved. We may not remember that Bond puffed on a cigarette before answering the phone; we have already translated that action into abstract data about his character and his attitudes toward story situations. We would remember, however, if Bond was struck by a pie before answering the phone and that unexpected image would linger in our mind longer than the phone call or even the entire event chain within which it participates. While not always "hinges" upon which the causal narrative depends, gags nevertheless become "risk-laden" emotionally saturated moments that command spectator interest. Gags are not simply or purely narrative blockage or digression, not "duplications, paddings, convolutions," but focal points of our cognitive and affective experience.[25]

A classical narrative may absorb a certain number of these affective "distractions" without substantial disruption to its coherence and clarity; it may even benefit from the momentary "relief" from narrative consequence such elements provide. Once a certain critical mass is reached, once the gags develop in sufficient number and demand sufficient interest apart from their consequences, these comic details cease to be servants of the narrative; they instead assume a greater affective charge than the storyline within which they are embedded. If, in other words, the runaway tire (a gag) attracts far more interest than the wrestling match (the narrative goal), the logic of this relationship is reversed; narrative causality becomes subordinated to the popular demand for comic spectacle. In such situations, plot exists primarily to create opportunities within which gags and comic performances may occur. One may recall Brett Page's description of the narratives of vaudeville sketches as a "thread" upon which "the elemental comic bits are strung." Such plots hold little interest in their own right but exist merely to facilitate the logical accumulation of gags. The same relationship between narrative and spectacle carries into early sound comedies; this disinterest in causality and this fascination for gag and performance is what is being described in the quotations opening this chapter. Here, causal narratives are almost always either totally streamlined (as in *The Man with the Flying Trapeze*), highly formulaic (as in the Eddie Cantor vehicles described in chapter 6), or extremely convoluted (as in films like *Diplomaniacs* or *Duck Soup*). Novelty is introduced instead at the level of gag and performance; these elements are the primary focus for audience attention. Nobody ever went to see *The Cocoanuts* (Paramount,

1929) to learn whether Polly Potter (Mary Eaton) marries Bob Adams (Oscar Shaw) or whether Mrs. Potter's stolen necklace will be recovered. Rather, they went to see a succession of performances by the Marx Brothers—a series of gags, jokes, wisecracks, and other comic bits— that gain minimal coherence by being attached to a flat and predictable plot. Critics who admired these films praised the inventiveness and the subversiveness of their gags while those who disliked them emphasized the gags' poor integration into the plot or argued that constant disruptions and interruptions made it impossible to follow the narrative.

We must not be too quick to dismiss the necessary role causality plays within the films' construction. The pleasurable "excess" of the Marx Brother's performances only becomes apparent against the flatter background of their films' conventional plots.[26] As I will show in chapter 6, the traditional romance plot also serves significant thematic roles within anarchistic comedy. Moreover, simply as a matter of historical fact, many viewers reacted negatively to the films' "incoherence," just as others responded positively to their apparent dismantling of classical conventions. Perhaps, the habits of watching classical Hollywood texts had become so ingrained that spectators looked for causally integrated narratives even within films not primarily interested in telling stories. Perhaps, too, the displacement of plot interest placed so great a demand upon the variety and virtuosity of performance that it became impossible to satisfy. The film suffered a fatal loss when the gags failed to provide an alternative or compensatory interest. At any rate, the tension between comic spectacle and comic narrative gives these films their vitality and fascination. The challenge was how to integrate the non-narrative aesthetic of vaudeville comedy into the narrative tradition of the classical cinema.

"NOT MUCH OF A STORY BUT . . .": *HOLLYWOOD PARTY* (MGM, 1934)

Hollywood generated no single prototype, no ideal compromise between these competing aesthetic systems. Rather, a period of formal experimentation gave rise to a succession of fumbling attempts to make the techniques of the variety stage functional within the existing set of classical Hollywood norms. The formal organization of any given film was arrived at only tentatively, through a process of experimentation and revision; performance sequences, gags and story situations were coordinated into a whole that, hopefully, satisfied the dual demands of heterogeneity and unity, novelty and coherence. Such an ideal balance could not always be achieved.

In September 1934, A. E. Hancock, the manager of the Columbia Theater (Columbia City, Indiana), wrote an angry letter to the *Motion Picture Herald* attacking MGM's *Hollywood Party:* "Never have I seen a worse mixed-up mess than this picture was!" [27] The film was "jumbled as to story, [and] direction" and left his audiences "foggy as [to] what was happening." Hancock's distaste for this particular release was apparently shared by many other exhibitors. A number of them wrote to the *Herald* s What the Picture Did For Me column to express their outrage over its shapelessness and incoherence: "Not much of a party. Too many stars and no entertainment" (Adair, Iowa);[28] "One of the poorest excuses for a picture we have ever played" (Monticello, Kentucky);[29] "More stars than the Milky Way, less story than Mother Goose" (Lebanon, Kansas).[30] A Mellon, Wisconsin exhibitor, directing his anger toward the film's lead star, grumbled, "I can't figure out why they don't take Jimmy Durante out and shoot him." [31] Of more than a dozen exhibitors' reports on *Hollywood Party,* only one, from a Sumas, Washington showman, expressed a favorable response: "Not much of a story but the customers liked it and the box office sure was above the average so it must be a good picture." [32]

Hollywood Party did little to alter the studio's reputation for lackluster comedian comedies. MGM had achieved some success with romantic and social comedy, including its vehicles for Jean Harlow, Marie Dressler, and Polly Moran, but it had not yet recruited a comic star who could compete with Paramount's Marx Brothers, RKO's Wheeler and Woolsey, Warner Brothers' Olsen and Johnson, or United Artist's Eddie Cantor. Jimmy Durante was the only MGM star who had shown the potential to develop into a top screen comedian and the studio depended upon him to carry most of its efforts. Durante first attracted national attention when he toured vaudeville and appeared in New York nightclubs with Lou Clayton and Eddie Jackson as one third of a musical-comedy team. Ziegfeld hired them to appear in a backstage musical, *Show Girl* (1929), with Ruby Keeler. Durante introduced his trademark song, "Can Broadway Do Without Me?" and attracted a great deal of critical enthusiasm. After appearing in a rather forgettable film, *Roadhouse Nights* (MGM, 1930), Durante and his partners returned to Broadway to appear in *The New Yorkers.* As with their first stage show, Durante wrote the team's numbers, and several scenes were added to the book to incorporate bits of material from the vaudeville and night

Hollywood Party (1934): Surrounding Lupe Velez are Charles Butterworth, Harry Rapf, Ned Marin, and Richard Boleslawsky. Wisconsin Center for Film and Theater Research.

club acts. Durante consistently upstaged his partners, resulting in MGM offering Jimmy a five year film contract if he would appear without Clayton and Jackson.

MGM starred him in *The New Adventures of Get-Rich-Quick Walling-ford* (1931), a film designed to play upon his stage persona as the "Schnozzle," a man of the streets with aspirations toward upward mobility. Stanley Green describes Durante as "the grotesque Punchi-nello, mocking the pretensions of his betters, assaulting those who would assault him, loudly proclaiming his frustrations, yet at all times retaining the inherent winsomeness that made him as much a figure of affection as he was a figure of fun."[33] Durante's oversized nose, sparse yet somehow shaggy hair, battered fedora, and scratchy voice gave the performer a humble quality that contrasted sharply with his self-impor-tant proclamations and pretentious vocabulary; Durante spoke the language of high society and the academy, yet he spoke it in the accents of the streets, mispronouncing words, mangling syntax, and garbling grammar. Durante tried to pass himself for "Jimmy da well-dressed man," but his stooped walk and rambunctious gestures suggested that he did not "naturally" fit the part. Fan magazine profiles exploited this same contradiction: one picture showed Durante in his posh Hollywood home with the caption, "Just the kind of shack for a big corned beef and cabbage brawl with a keg of beer"; another pictorial featured Durante modeling the attire of the "well-dressed man," offering advice on how to improve your squash game and how to dunk a doughnut.[34]

His screen vehicles construct narratives that exploit his previous stage persona, that place him in situations where he must outstep his social position; his comedy almost always centered on the pleasures and problems of class mobility. He assumed the roles of a noted explorer in *Meet the Baron* (MGM, 1933), a campaign director in *Phantom President* (Paramount, 1933), the manager of a brewery in *What! No, Beer?* (MGM, 1933), or a polo-playing film star in *Hollywood Party*. Each time, his character is unable to fully fit into his new social milieu and often betrays himself with signs of inappropriate upbringing or faulty cultural assimilation. The films intensify this conflict by their casting strategies. Most often, the studio sought a foil for the rough-hewn Durante, someone a bit more refined and a good deal more soft-spoken. Durante had been cast against Buster Keaton (*The Passionate Plumber,* MGM, 1932; *Speak Easily,* MGM, 1932; *What! No Beer?*), George M. Cohan (*Phantom President*), and Charles Butterworth (*Student Tour,* MGM, 1934). By dividing screentime with such low-key performers (and next to Durante, even Cohan seemed low-key), the films found welcome relief from his high-intensity performances and exaggerated the vulgarity of Durante's self-presentation. Conversely, other Durante vehicles accented his disruptiveness by casting him against equally flamboyant costars such as Jack Pearl and the Three Stooges (*Meet the Baron*) or Lupe Velez (*Strictly Dynamite,* RKO, 1934). Here, the clowns reinforced inappropriate tastes and encouraged rowdy conduct, resulting in progressively broader transgressions of social standards. Neither strategy was fully successful in building a strong audience following for this difficult performer, though both occasionally produced interesting results. Critical consensus was that Durante worked best in supporting roles (such as his much praised appearance in *Cuban Love Song,* MGM, 1931) and would be tolerated only in small doses. As one exhibitor wrote to the *Motion Picture Herald,* "Our folks do not like so much of

Durante. He is in too many pictures and his stuff is the same in every picture. He has not [got] enough on the ball to carry the star part of any feature film. I hope it is a long time before we see him again." [35]

Hollywood Party was yet another attempt to showcase Durante's already overexposed talents. Durante plays Schnarzan, the "Mighty Monarch of the Mudlands," star of a series of jungle adventure movies. Although once popular box office attractions, the Schnarzan films have lost their following because, as one exhibitor explains in the film's opening scene, "the public's fed up with those mangy toothless moth-eaten lions he's been fighting." Goldfarb, his producer (Richard Carle), sees hope for salvaging the star's reputation if he can only get him some better lions; he convinces Schnarzan to host a lavish party for the globe-trotting Baron Munchausen (Jack Pearl), who is arriving with his menagerie: "I'll get a flock of beautiful dames and give him a real African welcome. We'll throw the biggest affair since the Boston Tea Party." Much of the film centers around that party. Liondora (Charles Judels), a rival screen star, disguises himself as a foreign nobleman, Archduke Nickel-Louse. He crashes the festivities and offers a competing bid for the Baron's lions. The Clemps, an oil-rich Oklahoma family (Charles Butterworth, Polly Moran, June Clyde), are invited guests who knew Schnarzan before he had a "kettle to cook in." They become embroiled in the struggle for the lions. Clemp watches with bemused interest as his wife is romanced first by Liondora who proclaims his love with mangled poetry, "You sweet honeybuns and doughnuts / The moon casts a marshmallow fragrance on your hair," and then by Schnarzan who serenades her with an equally nonsensical crooning song (figs. 4.1, 4.2). Both men hope to use the Clemp fortune to gain control over the lions, yet Mr. Clemp seems indifferent to their efforts. Watching from behind the rose trellis as the aptly named Nickel-Louse seduces his wife, Clemp (fig. 4.3) offers a running commentary on her lovemaking, "Hey—this is going to be good. We're in a very good position. I can see everything. . . . Interesting technique. Henrietta's always improving her mind." The Clemp daughter has a brief love scene with a movie star (Eddie Quinlan), which forms the basis for another comic love song, "My One Big Moment." The legitimate owners of the lions (Laurel and Hardy) arrive to announce that they have been cheated by the Baron and plan to repossess the much coveted beasts; they are side-tracked, however, when they encounter Schnarzan's feisty former girl-friend (Lupe Velez).

Hollywood Party offered Durante many opportunities to display his performance skills, providing him several musical numbers and casting him against many of his previous costars, including Pearl, Butterworth, Velez, not to mention Ted Healy and his Three Stooges (who play autograph hounds pestering the arriving guests) A mock trailer for one of the Schnarzan films allows Durante and Velez to parody MGM's successful *Tarzan* series with the Schnozzle absurdly miscast as a heroic he-man, "nature's forgotten man who never forgot the call of nature."[36] Durante pounds his hairy chest and issues a resounding cry that summons forth from the jungle depths (and the studio vaults) stock footage of African wildlife (figs. 4.4, 4.5). Later in the film, Durante performs a high-intensity musical number, backed by a massive chorus of beautiful blondes and accompanied by a tribe of Zulu warriors, greeting the Baron to his home ("We give my friend a Mazaltov, a Bon Jour and other high hat stuff.") This number was clearly modeled after *Animal Crackers'* "Three Cheers for Captain Spaulding" but displays MGM's characteristic overkill; its overblown production value swamps both its comic potential and its narrative importance. In another sequence, Durante lectures a chorus of learned professors on his theories about reincarnation and appears in dream sequences as Adam in the Garden of Eden and Paul Revere's horse (publicity photographs show him dressed in drag as Marie Antoinette, almost certainly part of the "Reincarnation" number, but this footage does not appear in the final film).[37] Mickey Mouse stretched his nose and jumbled his syntax to impersonate Durante in one delightful scene, an act that the Schnozzle found typically "mortifyin'."

Much of the comedy stems from the same basic joke: the earthy, semi-literate Durante as the host of a high class party, the focus of a literary salon, and the star of action-adventure epics. This contradiction is vividly captured in an early scene where Durante returns from his polo game, bragging to his servants about how he "moidered 'em," while looking admiringly at a classical bust whose noble Roman profile bears the performer's own distinctive proboscis (fig. 4.6). Durante dominates the film and gives one of his most likable performances; Schnarzan and his on-again, off-again efforts to purchase the lions provided the narrative framework for the film's often unrelated comic sketches and musical numbers.

Although this strategy was successfully adopted in many comedies of the period, most notably in Paramount's *Big Broadcast* films, *Hollywood Party* never fully resolved the competing demands of story and spectacle. Early in the film, *Hollywood Party* insists on the importance of character conflicts and plot development. Indeed, it becomes quite repetitive in establishing the jungle star's desperate need to salvage his career and focusing narrative interest on the Baron's long-awaited arrival. The second half of the film, however, becomes so preoccupied with nonintegrated performance sequences that it fails to satisfy our narrative expectations. Lupe Velez spends much of the film trying to confront Durante, her former costar and boyfriend, who is trying to dump her from his pictures and his life; a series of obstacles (each manifested in another comic exchange) blocks her from ever getting together with Schnarzan. Fans are thus denied a much anticipated scene between two comic performers who had proven popular in their previous screen encounter (*Strictly Dynamite*) and stage appearance (*Strike Me Pink,* 1933) together. Similarly, the baron receives very limited screentime, despite the fact that the film's plot hinges on his decisions. Jack Pearl arrives in the arms of his trained gorilla, "Ping Pong, son of King Kong," offers a few lackluster jokes, and dances a tango with Durante.[38] He soon gets lost in the party crowd. The struggle over the lions is also continually deferred and never fully resolved. Clemp, backing Liondora, successfully outbids Goldfarb for the lions. The negotiations, however, are quickly interrupted and upstaged by the Walt Disney sequence with the result that we never get to see the characters' reactions to this turn of events. Later, Durante romances Mrs. Clemp, hoping to use her influence to gain access to the beasts, yet again their conversation is interrupted and leads nowhere. This time, Laurel and Hardy set the lions free and the runaway beasts wreak havoc at the party. Laurel and Hardy's actions are motivated by an unrelated chain of events: trying to crash the party and confront the baron, the two clowns ran afoul of the butler, who pursues them in subsequent scenes. They unleash the lions to evade his chase and in doing so, they bring the entire narrative to a halt.

Upstairs, Schnarzan pretends to wrestle a lion skin rug to display his prowess to Mrs. Clemp, only to find himself locked in a struggle with a real lion (fig. 4.7). He is knocked unconscious during their fight, and a reprise of scenes from the film is superimposed across his reeling head. *Hollywood Party*'s final scene finds Durante asleep on a sofa, a *Tarzan* novel propped on his chest, with the suggestion that all of the previous events have been simply a dream. As he awakens, we discover that Durante is, in fact, married to Polly Moran and the two are preparing to go to a swank Hollywood party at Lupe Velez's house. Filmgoers were invited to invest their interest into a series of convoluted plot developments that finally had no basis other than Durante's feverish imagination. We never see Laurel and Hardy's confrontation with the baron, the reconciliation of the Clemps, the culmination of their daughter's romance with a young film actor, Liondora's humiliation and defeat, or Schnarzan's encounter with an angry Lupe Velez.

The film's production history offers some explanations for its peculiar plot structure. Whatever else one may say about *Hollywood Party,* the script was clearly not rushed to the screen, as some of the local exhibitors suggested. Rather, the script underwent extensive revisions over nearly a two-year period, from the film's initial inception in early 1933 up until its release in May 1934; its scripting involved creative and conceptual contributions by three producers, more than two dozen gagsmiths and screenwriters, and many leading composers and choreographers. At one time or another, virtually every major MGM star was signed to appear, though the final release depended heavily upon second-string performers. Directors Alexander Leftwich and Edmund Goulding both left the production before shooting a single frame. *Hollywood Party* began filming in July 1933 under Russell Mack, but he resigned only three days later in a dispute with producer Harry Rapf. He was replaced in succession by Richard Boleslawski, George Stevens, and Allan Dwan, though none of these directors lasted more than a few weeks. Charles Riesner completed the production, though Roy Rowland also shot some scenes. As Eddie Quinlan explained, "I think we had every director on the lot! And when it was finished, nobody wanted the credit!"[39]

These long delays and extensive reconceptualizations make *Hollywood Party* an extreme yet particularly informative example of the ways in which the clash between classical Hollywood norms and the vaudeville aesthetic was confronted and compromised within the scriptwriting process.[40] While far from complete, the extensive documentation on *Hollywood Party* contained in the MGM Scripts Collection at the University of Southern California allows us to trace some points of tension that contributed to the unsatisfying construction of this muddled text.

"THREADING TOGETHER THE INDIVIDUAL SCENES"

The precise origins of the project remain obscure, but by early February 1933, producer Harry Rapf had begun collecting ideas for a follow-up to his successful *Hollywood Revue of 1929* (MGM, 1929). Like earlier revue films such as *Paramount on Parade* (Paramount, 1930) or *Show of Shows* (Warner Brothers, 1929), *Hollywood Revue of 1933* was intended to showcase the studio's large stable of stars through a series of unrelated comedy acts and musical numbers. The USC files contain a number of one-to-two page sketch ideas, occasionally fleshed out with sample dialogue or suggestions about possible casting submitted by a number of different writers.[41] In addition to utilizing the studio's stars, the initial proposals sought topical interest or novelty. Charlotte Wood, for example, predicted a return to "the graceful Irene Castle type of woman," and recommended a musical number based on this anticipated shift in feminine fashion.[42] Others exploited contemporary fads, such as bridge, jigsaw puzzles, technocracy, the construction of enormous theaters, and monster movies. Among these early submissions came several recommendations from Rapf's fellow MGM producer and personal friend, David O. Selznick. Selznick confided that he was negotiating with Walt Disney to provide animated material (including a scene featuring Mickey Mouse) for his planned Jack Pearl vehicle, *The Adventures of Baron Munchausen* (later retitled *Meet the Baron*); he suggested that "it might be swell in your review to include a complete cartoon sequence in color along the lines of the reel that Disney exhibited at the Academy dinner."[43] Selznick's advice was to have Disney animate a typical film party, burlesquing "a Mayfair Club or a Hollywood opening"; such a segment would provide room for caricatures of "all the stars of the studio, and perhaps all the stars of the industry."

Although the earlier revue films were non-narrative, Rapf's initial call for sketch ideas (which is not included in the USC collection) may have included a request for suggestions about a possible frame story. Several of the early submissions include unrelated proposals for "threading together the individual scenes" into a larger structure.[44] Walter Wise proposed that the revue might center on a New Year's Eve celebration in a major city: "The crowds, excitement, comedy and spectacle of that hectic night can be the basis for fast moving and interesting revue sequences, all tied together by the underlying theme."[45] Robert Hopkins and Gus Kahn submitted a possible opening sequence for the revue set in the throne room of King Leo's palace, in which the court jester (Jimmy Durante) attempts to amuse the sour-faced King of Beasts and is forced to call for assistance from the studio's other star entertainers.[46] The earlier revue cycle, many believed, had been short-lived precisely because it made the format itself into a novelty that was quickly exhausted rather than focusing its appeal around the novelty value of the individual components.[47] A loose narrative structure, motivating a series of related or semirelated performance units, might gain broader acceptance. Such an approach would not be alien to the revue tradition; New York stage revues, as chapter 2 suggested, often depended on thematic or narrative structures to unify their heterogeneous materials. Such an approach would, however, pull the revue film into closer harmony with the narrative traditions of the classical Hollywood cinema.

The notion of a frame story was discussed at an April 11 story conference, involving theater director Alexander Leftwich, film director Edmund Goulding, composers Richard Rodgers and Lorenz Hart, gagwriter Ritchie Craig, and longtime vaudeville sketchwriter Edgar Allen Wolff.[48] The participants concluded that they should abandon the revue format and focus their attention on constructing "a fast, mad musical comedy" like the successful Marx Brothers' vehicles. A decision was made at that meeting to change the film's title to *Hollywood Party* and to focus its narrative around "a weekend in Hollywood." The idea to use a film party as the frame story may have come from several sources, including Selznick's proposed cartoon sequence, Wise's New Year's Eve celebration suggestion, and another submitted sketch parodying the studio's own *Dinner at Eight* (MGM, 1933) (which was to have been called "Dinner at Two" and, like the finished film, to have featured Jimmy Durante as the party's host). Andy Skretuedt suggests that the project evolved from a spoof of *Grand Hotel* (MGM, 1932) proposed by Buster Keaton; there is, however, no mention of this earlier project in the story conference minutes.[49] Another possible source might have been the opening scene from *Strike Me Pink,* a Ray Henderson—Lew Brown revue in which Durante had played a starring role; the stage show introduced its cast members as guests at a Hollywood film premier. The story conference notes specifically called for the film to follow the "form of *Dinner at Eight*," a recent success.

The April 11 session, apparently, proved highly productive; the assembled writers also roughed out a possible narrative, including some proposed casting. Jimmy Durante, "the mastermind of Hollywood," hosts a party for a Texas oil man (Frank Morgan) and his wife (Lula McConnell), who have come to Hollywood to visit their movie star son (Buddy Rogers):

> This very quiet party, from word being passed on, develops into a large party. Half of Hollywood arrives at Durante's house. . . . Every time the party is about to break up, someone else always invites them over to do something else. It is at the [Hollywood] Hotel that we get our comedy. . . .

When it reaches its greatest point again, the hotel catches fire. . . . The fire department is called and Ed Wynn starts out for the fire. He is putting on his broadcast at the time of the fire and can't interrupt it. . . . When they finish broadcasting and are ready to put out the fire, we see that the hotel has burned to the ground.

Several story conferences, held in mid-April, tried to integrate the proposed sketches and numbers into this frame narrative, culling those lacking sufficient entertainment value: "At the hotel, someone starts singing 'Black Diamond' and then is when [Clifton] Webb starts telling the story. . . . Jean Harlow is an operator in the hotel . . . . She falls asleep and we go into the 'Dreams of Hollywood' number." [50]

"ANY ACT COULD BE INCORPORATED INTO THE PARTY"

Rapf and his writers apparently continued to perceive the narrative as a loose structure into which they could insert various more or less self-contained performance units. As Edmund Goulding suggested at an early story conference, "Any act could be incorporated into the party. It is only necessary for someone to say 'oh, look!' The lights black out and the act goes on." [51] Few of the accepted sketches were causally integrated; most were simply miscellaneous activities at the weekend-long Hollywood party, with the celebration moving arbitrarily from place to place to facilitate the introduction of this varied material. Although the studio's writers had already developed a profusion of ideas, Rapf called for new sketch proposals, particularly for new musical numbers. The producer hoped to match the number and range of sequences offered by the original *Hollywood Revue*. Throughout late April and early May, numerous gag writers submitted additional ideas. [52]

A May 13 document (possibly prepared by Howard Dietz) inventoried the proposed scenes, dividing them into four categories: sketches, plot scenes, music, and comedy. The logic behind this classification seems cryptic, since many of the proposed sequences, in fact, could have been grouped in several different categories. However, this breakdown is interesting for two reasons. First, it suggests that the film was still conceived as a series of routines and numbers rather than as a integrated narrative, and, indeed, that plot development was regarded as simply one element among others. Second, far fewer entries in this list fell under the category of plot scenes than any of the other classifications, indicating that the bulk of the scriptwriting to that point had concentrated on spectacle rather than narrative.[53] This list formed the basis for the earliest located story outline, prepared by Dietz and dated May 15; that outline included all of the listed sequences, weaving them together into a loose sequence.[54]

In turn, Goulding reviewed Dietz's outline, producing a rough continuity outline by June 7 that reflected his analysis of the earlier script.[55] In keeping with his contributions to the earlier story sessions, Goulding's commentary consistently treats narrative exposition as a necessary evil, potentially threatening the comedy's quick pace yet important in providing some cohesiveness to the film. He complains, for example, that one expositional scene "reads like a drop," yet concedes that it "may be necessary here" to resolve a subplot involving two young lovers. A Three Stooges sequence is to provide only a "faint flavor of plot" but should "mention Durante, etc., to tie in" the rest of the film. Goulding's discussion of the opening scenes calls for a clear and speedy establishment of the character relationships so that "we could start the party at the proper speed, and not be held up to explain anyone or anything." A later sequence involving Polly Moran and her daughter was designed "to set the thin plot on its wheels so that we can pick it up whenever we want at any spot outside." Frequently, he justifies the inclusion of performance sequences purely on the basis of their spectacular appeal, noting that one scene "throws the feeling of the party into one of glamour." Goulding's aesthetic preferences may perhaps best be suggested by his description of the "Hollywood Party" number: "The foregoing scene is one of absurd excitement and should be cut so fast that we should have a very vague idea of what has actually happened, except that we have a feeling of Durante's pumping a lot of loud music and laughs."

Goulding's revised outline and analysis apparently formed the basis for a June 15 script, which closely follows its scene breakdown and conforms to his goal of a more streamlined narrative.[56] The June 15 script, probably the first complete draft for a *Hollywood Party* screenplay, was closely scrutinized in a series of story conferences held in mid- to late June. Minutes for these conferences suggest a continued concentration on spectacle: "I would like a little comedy scene after 'the Hot Chocolate' number. It's bad construction to go right into a song, one song right on top of another."[57] Rapf, nevertheless, expressed increasing dissatisfaction over the film's narrative structure, concluding the June 29 meeting with the statement that "the construction of the whole script is poor."

"MERELY A SKETCHY OUTLINE HASTILY THROWN TOGETHER"

Just a few weeks before shooting was to begin, in early July, Rapf began to reassess the film's structure and contents, passing the finished script to Charles Riesner and Endre Bohem for comments. Riesner, who had directed the earlier *Hollywood Revue* and had become the leading director of MGM comedies, applied criteria consistent with that employed by earlier contributors. He concluded that *Hollywood Party* will be "good from an entertainment and box office value," since it included in its cast eight comic stars and "laughter is one of the most important [factors] in a revue's success."[58] Bohem, whose previous and subsequent screenwriting credits were mainly for dramatic films, produced a succession of memos focused primarily on story logic. Bohem expressed great dissatisfaction with the script's failure to integrate the performance sequences:

> The numbers are more or less as independent as they were in your first revue, yet, something resembling a story runs through. The story in itself is not a good one, but what is more harmful is that on one hand, it does not serve its purpose. It does not tie the various numbers together and on the other hand, it slows up the revue terribly. . . . It gives one the impression that it is merely a sketchy outline hastily thrown together.[59]

Bohem found implausible the rationale of the party, which by this point had come to focus around Durante's efforts to discredit a rival star (Jack Pearl); the romantic subplots involving various members of the oil-rich Clemp family also seemed "boring and tiresome."[60] He concluded, "The thing as a whole is a series of jerky, incoherent vaudeville skits."[61]

While acknowledging that his suggestions would probably be unacceptable given their proximity to the scheduled beginning of production, Bohem called for a radical reconceptualization. He rejected altogether the party frame and proposed structuring it instead as a Hollywood equivalent of *Berlin: Symphony of a City*. *Berlin*, Bohem suggests, "had no story yet it held your interest as well as the fastest moving gangster picture."[62] *Hollywood Party*, he proposed, could represent "24 hours in the life of a major studio's lot," from the night crew's work on building the sets to the arrival of the stars in the morning and the rehearsal and production of a various films on the sound stages.[63] This frame story, he argues, would "show in an entertaining fashion things that interest every moviegoer and things that they have never seen in any picture before"; it could also utilize many of the better numbers already scripted and would allow Durante to act as "some sort of unofficial master of ceremonies."[64] Bohem evaluated *Hollywood Party* according to classical criteria of coherence, consistency, and plausibility, focusing on narrative causality and continuity rather than simply on the entertainment value of individual component parts. He still acknowledged the difference between this film and standard Hollywood narrative, proposing as his model not a classically integrated film like *Dinner at Eight* but an experimental documentary. [65] Increasingly, attention was being shifted from the merit of the parts to the quality of the whole, as institutional pressures began to push *Hollywood Party* into greater conformity with classical norms. Rapf acted on relatively few of Bohem's suggestions; many of the problems Bohem identified still surface in the finished film. The producer apparently rejected Bohem's proposed restructuring of the film as impractical.

Just two days after the last of Bohem's memos was issued, Rapf met with Goulding and Dietz to discuss the problems he saw in the current script and to review the production costs for the various sequences. Rapf foresaw a potential waste of $250,000—an unacceptably high figure—if they filmed all the scripted material before deciding which sequences would be incorporated into the final film. The conference minutes record that Rapf told his writers, "You can't possibly shoot everything you've got here. It's a terrific amount of stuff. The question is—what do you want to eliminate?—What do you want to tell? By pulling the whole thing down, you are going to help on your construction."[66] Rapf was obviously concerned about the script's lack of focus; *Hollywood Party,* the producer felt, developed so many different plot lines and contained so many performance sequences that Durante "gets lost" in the film's second half. Rapf cited the final hotel fire as a prime example of the ways the scriptwriters "let your imagination run wild without thought of how to get that entertainment nor the cost of it."[67] The producer demanded that the scriptwriters find a simpler way to resolve the various storylines and give his film a "wow finish."

Rapf argued that narrative clutter detracted from the entertainment value; too much spectacle created unnecessary spectator distraction and confusion; such a weak plot failed to spotlight those elements of spectacle carefully developed for the film. Despite increased emphasis on narrative integration and production economy, Rapf expressed continued concern about the need to diversify the material. The producer protested that "all your entertainment is bunched together of the same kind" and that "at no place do you show beautiful girls."[68] Rapf's ideal was apparently a film that offered varied entertainment yet was sufficiently integrated to allow easy spectator comprehension; such a position still subordinated narrative causality to spectacular display yet nevertheless pushed the film toward greater conformity with classical Hollywood norms.

The USC script files include two revised outlines, both clearly reflecting Rapf's reservations about production costs and his desire to streamline the narrative.[69] The first of the two outlines makes only limited changes, primarily concentrating on the film's increasingly troublesome ending. The second outline, prepared by Howard Dietz, makes more substantial changes. The Dietz outline still includes many of the nonnarrative elements from previous drafts. Dietz, however, considerably tightened the script, eliminating sixteen previously proposed units and changing the entire rationale for the party. Many of the basic elements of the finished film appear for the first time in this script. Jack Pearl was recast from the rival Tarzan to the owner of a group of man-killing lions; both Schnarzan and Liondora (now to be played by Charles Judels) seek to purchase the beasts for use in their films. Durante holds the gathering in hopes of winning favor with the baron; his rival, disguised as the archduke, crashes the party and becomes ensnared in a romantic triangle with the Clemps. As for the oil man and his wife, the Clemps no longer have a movie star son, but instead, wish to back a Hollywood film as a business investment and soon become participants in the struggle for the possession of the great cats. Dietz's proposed climax centers around the substitution of fierce circus lions for the tame lions and the baron's attempts to recapture them when they escape from their cages. The crowd returns in time to see the baron standing over the caged beasts and crowns him a hero, although actually the circus trainer has returned them to their confines when the baron faints. In the film's final moment, the baron seals a deal for the sale of the lions to Durante with Clemp to back the upcoming Schnarzan production. (Ironically, while Dietz's proposed ending was the source of much dissatisfaction from the producer, it actually provides a much stronger sense of narrative closure than the ending included in the finished film.)

Rapf apparently favored the Dietz outline over the July 10 document; it served as the basis for a revised script prepared by Dietz and dated July 22, while Goulding's involvement with the production ended.[70] Subsequent revisions would refine but not radically alter Dietz's July 12 outline. However, the film's conclusion remained a problem. A number of studio writers offered their own proposed endings throughout early August. Seasoned comedy writer Arthur Caesar proposed a conclusion borrowing many of the key elements from Dietz's final reel but reassigning the narrative roles: rather than the baron, it is Liondora and Durante who seek to recapture the runaway lions; his rival is knocked cold by a lion's swat, but Durante sings to them and leads the dancing lions away "like the pied piper."[71] Dietz, working with Broadway playwrights Frances Goodrich and Albert Hackett, suggested that the baron might inadvertently connect his cages to a circus wagon, resulting in a climactic chase to reclaim the lions,[72] while gagwriter and sometime comic performer Richy Craig proposed a totally different type of ending: the police raid the party and an unexpected earthquake rips away the front of Durante's house, "revealing . . . the entire cast all in action in different rooms."[73] Each of the proposed endings confronted but failed to resolve the dual demand of providing closure to the frame story (the primary requirement of a conclusion within the classical Hollywood norms) and of offering some large-scale comic spectacle that would wow the audience (the major function of the "finish" within the vaudeville aesthetic).

When production began again on August 10 with Richard Boleslawski directing scenes involving Durante and Pearl, *Hollywood Party* still lacked a finished script. Subsequent revisions of the script would be constrained by the need to incorporate already shot material while creating necessary exposition and connecting scenes. An August 23 outline not only reordered some of the key sequences, but also provided a report of which scenes had been shot, which had been written, and which remained undeveloped (a category that included the film's elusive climax).[74] New writers were called upon to flesh out the as-yet-unwritten sequences throughout late August and early September, while production on the film was stalled, not to resume again until September 21.[75]

"THE GATHERING UP OF STORY THREADS"

The USC records become much sparser after this point, making it harder to trace the process of script revision. Apparently, Rapf remained dissatisfied with the film's screenplay and asked that script writer Henry Myers analyze the story problems and prepare a revised scenario. Myers's task was to bring *Hollywood Party* into greater conformity with the norms of classical Hollywood narrative, to provide stronger character motivation, and to tighten the plot construction. Myers clearly perceived the project less as a revue film than as a conventional comedian comedy; he consistently wanted to ground comic spectacle in character conflicts and to integrate performance sequences into plot development. In a December 7 letter to Rapf, Myers argues that the current script does not make the character's goals and actions "seem important enough to the audience."[76] He expressed concern about the film's erratic tone and the performance sequences' potential disruptions of story development. He was troubled, for example, that the opening sequence, a mock trailer for Durante's ape-man film, "gives the audience the impression that the whole piece is to be a burlesque; belief in a story cannot be established if that is the first impression."[77] Myers proposed that a scene be added that established a narrative context for the trailer in terms of the rivalry between the two jungle movie stars. The remainder of this initial letter detailed the motivations behind the character's actions, attempting to transform comic stereotypes into more rounded figures.[78] Six pages of purely expositional material predates the first musical number, which, in many of the previous drafts had opened the film. One paragraph, for example, explains that "the envy which Durante feels toward Liondora has three-fold roots" and proceeds for a solid page to motivate the rivalry between the two would-be Tarzans.

Walt Disney's animated "Hot Chocolate Soldier" sequence posed a particular problem for Myers:

> The reason why the Chocolate Soldier number is so troublesome is that it is so good, and the better it is and more entertaining, the more it will disrupt and prevent a return to plot, as is invariably the case with a particularly good specialty. But if its merit requires that it be used, then I can only see it as a climax, led up to and carefully planted throughout the entire picture."[79]

Myers was initially "stumped" by this dilemma, tentatively suggesting that Mr. Clemp and/or his wife might be characterized as having a "passion for chocolate" and gorge themselves on a box of chocolates before going to sleep: "The Chocolate Soldier number is the dream that they have and which practically decides them in favor of Durante's proposition" to back his next film. Although Myers initially characterizes this dream sequence motivation as "dragged in by the heals," he continued to pursue and bolster it in subsequent correspondence. By December 14, Myers was proposing that Clemp become a "chocolate king" who was known for making chocolate soldiers and who regards the success of this product to be "emblematic of everything he does."[80] The final dream, which has been suggested by a chocolate soldier motif throughout the earlier segments of the film, would reflect his "symbolic victory" over his competition and predict the success of his new film ventures. *Hollywood Party* would, thus, "finish with the Chocolate Soldier number, the gathering up of story threads such as the unmasking of Liondora, the victory of Durante, etc."[81]

Other musical numbers received far less attention and sympathy from Myers, who at one time or another insisted that each of the remaining performance sequences be removed from the film as "deadwood" in favor of strengthening the character relationships and adding "more love interest." Myers particularly wanted to expand the interaction between Durante and Moran (who, he suggested, should have been previously in love with Durante prior to her marriage to Butterworth). In a December 18 memo, Myers even proposed that the entire film could be framed through testimony at a Clemp divorce trial, during which scenes from Durante's party are offered as evidence for the events leading up to the collapse of their marriage.[82]

Although Rapf did not accept many of Myer's more extreme recommendations, his influence can still be recognized in the final script.[83] Following Myer's advice, Rapf removed several of the musical numbers—those which apparently had not been shot as of the end of 1933—and jettisoned a scene involving Durante and Velez, which, though already shot, had troubled the Production Code Administration and otherwise disappointed the producer. The finished film placed more attention on the romance between a Clemp daughter and a rising young Hollywood leading man (June Clyde and Eddie Quinlan); their relationship is now developed through a "mushy love song" of the sort Myers suggests in one of his letters. The final script also places greater attention on the Durante-Moran relationship with the star romancing Mrs. Clemp and offering her a role in his next film in return for the use of the Baron's lions. Expositional sequences were added to the film's opening scenes to better motivate the rivalry between Schnarzan and Liondora. Despite Myers's extensive efforts to integrate the Disney footage into the narrative, however, Clemp remains an oil tycoon, not a "chocolate king," and the "Hot Chocolate Soldier" number stays a totally unmotivated diversion.[84] In fact, most existing prints of the film circulate without this sequence and one would be hard pressed, without reviewing the original scripts, to tell where it fit into the narrative.

For a year and a half, Rapf, Dietz, and some of MGM's top screen-writers struggled with the script for *Hollywood Party*, only to produce a film that one of its most sympathetic critics described as "a succession of bits and numbers which are none too adroitly dovetailed but which will not bore."[85] Major plot devices were introduced even after production was well underway; numbers were recast and rewritten numerous times, only to be rejected in a last-ditch effort to tighten the plot and clarify character motivation. Rapf and Dietz obsessively fiddled with the ending, even after the final cutting continuity script and pressbook synopsis were prepared. Almost all participants agreed that a musical comedy like *Hollywood Party* did not require much plot, but how much plot was enough? What should be the proper balance between narrative and number, character and performance, climax and closure, unity and heterogeneity? How far could the writers break with the norms of classical Hollywood narrative and still produce an acceptable film?

Their hesitations and missteps reflect the problem of maintaining the vaudeville tradition's affective immediacy, performance virtuosity, and heterogeneity within a causally integrated narrative. It is tempting to see the conflicting advice Rapf and Dietz received from the spectacle-oriented Goulding and the more narrative-centered Bohem and Myers as personifying the two very different aesthetic systems at play behind the construction of *Hollywood Party*. Yet a closer reading suggests that all involved sought some way of reconciling those conflicting demands. Their differing positions may, indeed, have as much to do with the stage at which they entered the production process as any personal predilection toward particular aesthetic options. While Goulding clearly valued the economy and intensity of the performance sequences over the slower, more mundane exposition, he nevertheless acknowledged the necessity of a strong "story thread" to weave together the various fragments. Similarly, while Myers consistently wanted to strengthen the causal logic within the film and to deepen character motivation, he also expressed the position, in more than one letter, that "the mood in a piece of this kind is much more important than the actual plot" and that the narrative links should not come at the expense of a rapid pace or a consistent style of entertainment.[86] In fact, Myers, whose script for *Million Dollar Legs* (Paramount, 1932) was hardly a paradigm example of classical narrative, lobbied heavily for an increased role for the Three Stooges, who he felt possessed a style of humor ideally suited to the production. We find, then, a number of experienced writers, each confronting the need to reach a proper balance between the novelty offered by the vaudeville aesthetic and the narrative coherence promised by greater conformity to classical Hollywood norms. The finished film was unsatisfactory both because its more fragmented style of narrative was already starting to lose favor with film audiences and because the filmmakers failed to adopt a consistent or coherent strategy for integrating narrative and performance; some scenes placed high emphasis upon plot and character development while others dismissed these concerns in favor of long periods of unmotivated comic and musical spectacle. Despite such intensive effort, *Hollywood Party* was, finally, in the words of one displeased exhibitor, "just a lot of nothing, half thrown together."[87]

5

"A High-Class Job of Carpentry": Toward a Typography of Early Sound Comedy

Hollywood Party came at a crucial moment in the development of screen comedy, a phase characterized by shifting strategies for integrating narrative and performance. The production history documented in chapter 4 reflects changing conceptions about the final product's placement within a range of generic options open to filmmakers working in 1934. Rapf's decision to move from a simple revue format toward a frame story posed questions about the possible relationship between performance sequences and plot development. Initially, the producer sought a loose story structure that would allow for the periodic introduction of diversified entertainment; he had little expectations that the performance sequences would be integrated into the larger plot development. However, Rapf progressively pushed the production toward a more conventional narrative centered around Jimmy Durante and showcasing his performance skills; Rapf saw Durante's personality as unifying the heterogeneous material and his character's problems as motivating plot actions. Unintegrated performance sequences would still be acceptable in such a film as long as they did not decenter Durante from the film's interests. Later writers, especially Henry Myers, insisted that all performance sequences be heavily motivated by character psychology and narrative development. By this time, however, the film was too far into production to repair the obvious plot holes. In fact, efforts to bolster narrative causality created more expectations the film could not fulfill. Such a fluid situation argues against any rigid separation between different classes of comic texts, yet it also suggests that directors, writers, critics, and audiences shared expectations about specific styles of film entertainment. *Hollywood Party*'s producers never really decided what kind of comedy they wanted to make and, as a result, failed to develop a systematic strategy for resolving the competing demands of the vaudeville aesthetic and more classical norms.

Hollywood Party's troubled production history suggests the need for a more sophisticated vocabulary for discussing the different generic options available to filmmakers in the early sound period. In this chapter I will propose one set of categories that might usefully be applied to the films of this transitional era. I have focused this proposed typology around issues of comic performance. Performance is certainly not the only potential source of "cinematic excess" within these comedies, as the previous discussion of gags suggests. Yet performance was privileged both in discourse about vaudeville (recall Vadim Uraneff's claim that "the actor is always in the foreground") and in discussions of the film themselves. [1]

While central to the formal operations of many different genres, issues of performance have held a fairly marginal place in most genre studies. [2] We lack adequate terms for discussing different styles of screen acting; the "excessiveness" of performance often makes it difficult to analyze in relation to narrative or thematic issues; film studies' early emphasis upon cinema-specific techniques meant that there was less sympathetic attention applied to techniques such as acting or costuming that linked cinema to earlier theatrical traditions. David Bordwell and Kristin Thompson's *Film Art: An Introduction,* a standard introductory textbook, devotes an entire chapter to sound-image relationships but only a few pages to techniques of film performance; a similar imbalance occurs in most other books providing introductions to film analysis and reflects the lack of attention to performance questions within film studies more generally. [3] While it is beyond the scope of my current project to propose a general framework for discussing film acting across different genres, I would like to isolate a series of five fairly basic criteria that, if not exhaustively, point toward some key issues surrounding performance in the early sound comedy. These five criteria reflect the five central relationships that constitute film performance— the performer's relationship to the narrative, to the character, to the signs of his or her own performance, to the other performers in the production, and to the audience. One might, of course, add the player's relationship to the script and to the director, but those relationships are less open to textual analysis and can be resolved only through historical investigation.

Narrative Integration. Performance within some genres, such as the musical or the comedian comedy, may be foregrounded in certain more or less enclosed sequences of self-conscious spectacle rather than integrated into the overall development of the narrative.[4] Patricia Mellancamp characterizes the song-and-dance numbers within Hollywood musicals as "closed units within the larger narrative, set off by a system of brackets"; the audience's attention shifts at such moments from plot development onto the materiality and atemporality of performance.[5] The interaction of certain codes of visual and aural representation (musical accompaniment, centered framing, elevated staging, internal audiences) mark these sequences as privileged moments of heightened interest. Historians of the musical trace a general movement toward the causal and thematic integration of these performance spectacles. Many comedies, as we have seen, are also characterized by a fairly sharp division between sequences of performance virtuosity and sequences of narrative development and exposition. This heightened attention to performance is partially a product of certain visual codes (frontality, flattening of narrative space, long takes and camera movements, absence of point of view cutting). Much as in the musical, these sequences may be presented as diegetic performances (as in the mangled magic act William Gaxton, Ole Olsen, and Chic Johnson perform in *50 Million Frenchmen,* Warner Brothers, 1931); they may also stand apart from narrative actions because of their qualities of excess, stylization, and exaggeration (as in Mitchell and Durant's acrobatic display in *Stand Up and Cheer* or the Marx Brothers' mirror act in *Duck Soup*). These scenes exceed their narrative motivation through their flamboyance, their refusal of narrative economy, and their prolonged duration. Some such sequences exist in almost all film comedies, though many comedies actively foreground performance as performance while others subordinate performance almost entirely to the demands of narrative and character development.

Character Integration. As Richard Dyer has argued, there is almost always a problematic fit between the film character and the star's image.[6] The star's image is an extratextual construct developed through the audience's familiarity with the performer via other film appearances, promotional materials, publicity discourse, and reviews and commentary. As such, the polysemic and fully articulated star image often overpowers the character played in any given film. Some film movements, such as Soviet montage or Italian Neorealism, cast nonactors who bear no such semiotic traces to maximize the fit between performer and role. Classical cinema minimizes the gap between star image and character, typically by casting stars into roles closely corresponding to their preexisting images. Humphrey Bogart may become Rick Blaine in *Casablanca* (Warner Brothers, 1942), largely because the character is a composite of traits already associated with the Bogart persona; much of the film's dialogue further develops the character as a unique individual. Rick fought in the Spanish Civil War, once lived in Paris, was unlucky in love, owns the Café American, never drinks with his customers, etc. Steve Seidman argues, however, that comedian comedy heightens audience awareness of the central clown's extratextual status at the expense of integration into a specific character.[7] Dialogue functions less to reveal information about characters than to present gags; characters are reduced to stock roles and can be completely overpowered by the performer's own personality. In some cases, as when Groucho Marx is cast as the president of Freedonia in *Duck Soup,* the performer is asked to accept a story role so at odds with our preexisting perceptions of the star that it produces an active gap between performer and role (fig. 5.1). Groucho makes little effort to act presidential, remaining Groucho while being placed into situations where he might reasonably be expected to conform to the demands of his office—if not to the particularities of his character. This focus on the performer's personality was a central component of the vaudeville aesthetic and contrasts sharply with expectations about performance within the realist theater and the classical cinema.

Expressive Coherence. Closely related to the second category, expressive coherence refers to the degree of consistency that exists within an individual performance; expressive coherence occurs when all the performance signs are coordinated into the development of a rounded character. James Naremore argues that realist performance maintains a high degree of "expressive coherence" even in sequences where characters are themselves expected to give diegetic "performances" (e.g., Humphrey Bogart's visit to the bookshop in *The Big Sleep* (Warner Brothers, 1946).[8] Comedy, on the other hand, is marked by "expressive anarchy," as largely unmotivated performance signs (physical gestures, vocal mannerism, etc.) disrupt coherent characterization. Such signs frequently become a source of interest and amusement in their own right (as when Hugh Herbert, playing a Chinese henchman in *Diplomaniacs,* suddenly slips into a Yiddish accent and inflection).

Ensemble Consistency. This term refers to the homogeneity of performance styles among all the actors within a film's cast. Realist theater typically strives for an ensemble effect in which there is a high degree of stylistic consistency across the various performances, while many early sound comedies combine different acting styles (realist, melodramatic, vaudeville) within a single text. Wheeler and Woolsey, for example, adopt a much broader, more exaggerated style of performance, in contrast to the young couples in their romance plots who are more naturalistic; these contrasting acting styles emphasized the clown's eccentricity and the performer's virtuosity. This heterogeneity may occur between different syntagmatic units (as in *Stand Up and Cheer,* where the administrator reviews a succession of different would-be variety acts) or between paradigmatic clusters of characters (as in the example of the Wheeler and Woolsey comedies discussed above).

Audience Consciousness. This category refers to the relationship between performer and the spectator. Theater historians frequently draw a distinction between representational and presentational styles of performance. Representational styles create an invisible "fourth wall" separating actor and audience; the actor displays no awareness of the spectators (or in film acting, of the camera). Presentational styles are directed at the spectators and are shaped by the audience's affective response. As we saw in chapter 2, vaudeville encouraged the maintenance of the presentational style long after it was out of fashion in the legitimate theater; variety entertainment rewarded the performer's direct engagement with spectators. While the extreme transgressions of the separation between spectator and performance space found in vaudeville (Olsen and Johnson's bombardment of the audience, the magician's call for volunteers to come onstage) were clearly impossible within the cinema, traces of that tradition may be found in the frontality of staging, direct address to the camera, muttered asides, and other reflexive gags. Certain gestures mark the comic star's awareness of the potential presence of film spectators. Robert Wolsey punctuates gags with looks into the camera, puffs on his cigar, and raises his eyebrows, sometimes accompanied with a prolonged "Whoa!" Groucho Marx suggests that the spectators might wish to go into lobby for popcorn until a particularly dull scene is completed. Ed Wynn giggles at his own gags and mutters, "Isn't that the silliest thing?" Jimmy Durante mutters, "Ev'rybody wants to get into de act." These performance signs reflect a higher degree of audience consciousness than would be generally characteristic of the classical cinema.

Each of these categories should be interpreted as a continuum of possible choices, not a set of binary oppositions. To take character integration as an example, most film performances maintain some degree of distance between the star's image and the film's character, though certain types of films (comedy, musical) focus audience attention on that gap while others (social problem films, melodramas) efface it as much as possible. The other categories offer a similar range of possibilities. John Mueller has revised traditional distinctions between integrated and nonintegrated musicals by suggesting other different relationships that might exist between a musical number and its larger narrative context.[9]

By focusing on these five categories, one may make fairly precise distinctions between the acting styles preferred by different genres and subgenres. It is possible to identify a set of five different classes of comedian-centered comedies in the early sound period based upon their utilization of distinctive performance strategies. Remember, however, that this particular taxonomy is constructed through critical analysis and does not necessarily reflect the explicit distinctions employed by the filmmakers or contemporary viewers, who typically categorized films from any of the five classes as "comedies" or "musical comedies."[10] Filmmakers, as was shown in the case study of *Hollywood Party,* did make implicit assumptions about the strategies of performance appropriate to different comic texts, and those distinctions are consistent with the classifications proposed here.

"THE MELTING POT OF MUSIC": THE REVUE

Revue films, like *Hollywood Revue of 1929, Paramount on Parade, King of Jazz* (Universal, 1930), and *The Show of Shows,* stand at one extreme in their exclusive concentration on performance at the expense of any attempt at narrative or character development. These films preserved many conventions of the theatrical revue or the vaudeville show. Each presents a succession of totally independent performance units, acts,

Hollywood Revue (1929). Academy of Motion Picture Arts and Sciences.

numbers, or sketches, marked off by such rhetorical practices as the opening and closing of curtains, the use of title cards, the dimming of lights, the crescendo of orchestral music, or the reappearance of a master of ceremony. Only minimal narration creates unity. *King of Jazz,* for example, opens with the image of a giant book announcer Charles Erwin explains is the scrapbook of Paul Whiteman and his orchestra: "Its pages are crowded with melodies and anecdotes, which we are going to bring to life for you by the magic of the camera." The initial segment— an animated cartoon by Walter Lantz—does indeed explain in a humorous fashion how Whiteman became known as the "King of Jazz." Subsequent sequences,however, are linked by the recurring image of the book or by introductions from Whiteman or Erwin. These segments, however, frequently have little or nothing to do with Whiteman and his band. They are selected not to reflect his "melodies and anecdotes" but rather to constitute a varied program. *Paramount on Parade* and *Show of Shows* (fig. 5.2) make far less pretense at thematic coherence, depending upon the periodic appearances of masters of ceremony to introduce the individual "acts" and to create minimal unity between the segments. As Skeets Gallagher, Jack Oakie, and Leon Errol explain at the beginning of *Paramount on Parade,* "Anytime you grow confused or find yourself perplexed, one of us will stagger out and tell you what is next. . . . We're the masters of ceremony—keeping you people in touch with *Paramount on Parade.*"

Performers make few efforts to blend into characters here. Their introductions identify them by name and focus attention on their particular skills and talents. These introductions may range from a simple announcement that "Chevalier's next" (*Paramount on Parade*) to elaborate sequences, such as Frank Fay's prolonged build-up for many of the performers in *Show of Shows*. The most lengthy introductions, in fact, are given to dramatic performers, like John Barrymore in *Show of Shows* or Ruth Chatterton in *Paramount on Parade,* who normally sought to blend more fully into their characters. Here, however, it is the performers' status as performers that is stressed, focusing attention not on the characters they are playing but rather on the skills with which they execute those roles. In *Paramount on Parade,* Skeets Gallagher appears outside Chatterton's dressing room, enters and berates her for being late to the show and keeping the other actors waiting; this scene plays with the disjunction between her slangy talk in the dressing room and the more pretentious language Chatterton employs onstage. She promises to appear in "less than five minutes," so Gallagher steps outside and introduces the sketch, which then builds toward Chatterton's entrance. Barrymore appears before the curtain in *Show of Shows* to explain the context for his soliloquy from Shakespeare's *Richard III,* before disappearing and reappearing again in character as the demented hunchback. This brief introduction also serves to highlight the gap between Barrymore's normal appearance and delivery and his assumption of a Shakespearean role.

Moreover, the revue films actively play with the celebrity status of some of their featured performers, highlighting their extratextual status. Maurice Chevalier's performance of "All I Want Is Just One Girl" in *Paramount on Parade* is immediately followed by an appearance by Mitzi Green who not only impersonates Chevalier's rendition but also shows how the same song might be performed by Moran and Mack. Green's act places attention both on Chevalier's status as a celebrity performer and on Green's impersonation skills—especially given the disjunction between her frilly dress and the male stars she mimics. *King of Jazz* plays extensively with the image of rotund bandleader Paul Whiteman. Not only does Whiteman serve as master of ceremonies but he is also impersonated by a double who does elaborate dances; he is caricatured on the book's cover, on the heads of drums, even on the face of the moon; he is transformed into a cartoon character within the Walter Lantz animated sequence. *Show of Shows* directs attention to the fact that Al Jolson was one of the few Warners stars not to appear and

Paramount on Parade (1929): Mitzi Green imitates Maurice Chevalier.

King of Jazz (1930): Paul Whiteman.

has Sid Silvers impersonate him while Frank Fay jokes about Jolson's characteristic gestures and vocal mannerisms.

Expressive coherence is generally maintained within individual acts, though the same performers may play multiple roles in the same film and adopt different acting styles for different appearances. The revue films, like vaudeville itself, exhibited a diversity of entertainment: everything from Shakespearean drama and poetic recitations to eccentric dancing and acrobatics, from classical music to cartoons and dog acts; these works displayed little interest in stylistic consistency between the various segments. Ensemble effects were, for the most part, reserved for the closing numbers—"Sweeping the Clouds Away" in *Paramount on Parade*, "Lady Luck" in *Show of Shows*, "The Melting Pot of Music" in *King of Jazz*, etc.—which brought the entire cast together in one musical extravaganza. Even here, the numbers were staged so that each performer was allowed one final moment in the spotlight to reprise or introduce a specialty, before blending back into the larger chorus. Such sequences involved a constant play between the ensemble and the individual, between moments of novelty and a general movement toward homogeneity.

The revue films maintain a degree of audience consciousness unprecedented in the classical Hollywood cinema. As a result, they are often dismissed as overly "theatrical." A few sequences—Ruth Chatterton's "My Marine" and Helen Kane's "Boop-Boop-A-Doo School" in *Paramount on Parade,* for example—follow later Hollywood practice of constructing an internal audience to justify the more presentational aspects of performance numbers. More often, the presenters directly address the camera and through it, make concrete references to the "ladies and gentlemen" in the movie audience. Jack Oakie, who appears as a murder victim in a mystery movie parody in *Paramount on Parade,* suddenly breaks character, bursts out laughing, and points directly into the camera; Oakie claims that the sketch was "written especially for me" rather than for its alleged stars—Warner Oland, Clive Brook, William Powell, and Eugene Pallette—each of whom had previously claimed top billing. Skeets Gallagher enters one scene and thanks the audience for an anticipated ovation, holding his ear so that he may hear the applause better; there is the sound of one pair of clapping hands on the soundtrack. An off-screen voice, presumably from the cinema audience, harasses and insults his performance, before he walks off screen, glaring at the camera. Frank Fay adopts a similarly reflexive stance throughout *Show of Shows.* During his introduction of Irene Borodoni, for example, Fay explains that if the audience does not understand the French lyrics of the chanteuse's numbers, they may speak to him after the show and he will be glad to translate. Paradoxically, such devices increase the sense of spontaneity and immediacy, allowing screen performances to substitute more fully for live stage appearances, but they also direct attention upon the temporal and spacial gap between the performance and its reception.

STOP THE MUSIC! THE SHOWCASE FILM

The showcase film embeds the nonintegrated units of the revue film within a frame story. Comedies, like *International House* (Paramount, 1933), *The Big Broadcast* (Paramount, 1932), and *Stand Up and Cheer,* were initially viewed as an improvement upon the earlier revues because their interest was not entirely conditional upon the entertainment value of the individual segments. Yet, as the case study of *Hollywood Party* suggested, the attempt to merge spectacle with narrative, performance with characterization, presents problems not faced by the more openly presentational revue films. First and foremost, there was the problem of how to build narrative motivation for these performance sequences. For the most part, these films solved this difficulty by adopting settings in or around the world of show business; such a context not only provides a narrative rationale for the performances but also presents opportunities for diegetic audiences with whom the performers can interact. In *Stand Up and Cheer,* the central character's job (Secretary of the Department of Amusements) requires him to audition and recruit variety entertainers. *International House* concerns the initial public demonstration of a new form of television, with the revue segments displaying the technological wonders of this novel invention. *The Big Broadcast* films are set in or around radio studios and include "broadcasts" from popular performers. *Thrill of a Lifetime* (Paramount, 1933) concerns the production of a revue at a summer resort and opens in the office of a vaudeville agent— both settings where performances may naturally occur. In *Here Comes Cookie* (Paramount, 1935), a series of miscalculated business transactions leaves Gracie Allen in charge of her father's estate; the ever daffy Gracie mistakes her father's desire that he appear penniless for instructions to spend all his money. As a result, she turns his mansion into a free boarding house for vaudeville troupers. The screen space overflows with performance, embodying the vaudevillians' disruptive presence in the characters' lives. In one shot, the camera pans across Gracie's living room, showing, in quick succession, jugglers, acrobats, trained dogs, magicians, unicycle riders, knife throwers, a jazz band, and a lasso artist, all practicing their acts simultaneously in a cramped domestic space.

In each film, a certain number of performance numbers are intro-duced as part of the general atmosphere of the film's show world setting and are treated as pure spectacle, while others assume a higher degree of narrative significance. In *The Big Broadcast,* the survival of Station WADX depends upon a radio appearance by Bing Crosby, although the star is so embroiled in his romantic difficulties that it seems unlikely he will reach the studio in time to make the broadcast. Station manager Stuart Erwin frantically searches all over town for a phonograph record-ing of Bing Crosby to air instead. Meanwhile, back at the station, a series of performers (Kate Smith, Cab Calloway, the Boswell Sisters, the Mills Brothers, and Vincent Lopez and his Orchestra, among others) delay for time. The film cuts back and forth between the narratively centered actions of Erwin and performance numbers at the studio. Bing's performance is thus doubly marked as the film's entertainment highpoint and the resolution of its plot action.

The showcase film is characterized as well by a high degree of stylistic

The Big Broadcast (1932): Stuart Erwin. Wisconsin Center for Film and Theater Research.

diversification; heterogeneity is introduced not simply between different forms of entertainment within the performance segments but between the presentational style of the explicit performance units and the more representational style of the narrative segments. *International House,* in fact, involves at least four different levels of performance:

(1) Performers who appear only on the radioscope or in the hotel's stage show and who appear under their own names (Rudy Vallee, Cab Calloway, Baby Rose Marie, Sterling Holloway);

(2) Performers who appear under their own names but assume some narrative role (Peggy Hopkins Joyce, George Burns and Gracie Allen);

(3) Performers who appear as totally fictionalized characters but are only minimally integrated into those characters (W. C. Fields as Professor Quail);

(4) Performers who blend into their characters and maintain the

primary narrative responsibilities within the film (Stuart Erwin as Tommy Nash, Bela Lugosi as General Petronovich, Lumsden Hare as Sir Mortimer Fortescue).

The interplay between these four levels of performance is quite complex. Each level involves its own conventions regarding character integration, audience consciousness, and expressive coherence. Sequences of pure performance are explicitly marked through the presence of a diegetic audience, the constant reinscription of the frame of the radioscope during presentations of broadcast material, and the acceptance of a fairly high degree of audience consciousness including direct address. Narratively active characters (i.e., those in categories 2–4) do not appear within the radioscope; rather, their narrative tasks involve an effort to bring the radioscope more fully under their control (fig. 5.3). Dramatic actors, like Lugosi or Hare, are frequently cast as straight men or foils for the more comically exaggerated performers. Comic stars like Burns and Allen or Fields may break the flow of the narrative to engage in more ambiguously marked performance sequences within the story space proper: Gracie Allen interrupts a narratively significant conversation to perform a magic trick that she completely muddles, thus pulling the more serious performers into her comedy (fig. 5.4); George Burns and Franklin Pangborn take turns feeding straight lines to Gracie, their movements choreographed into a near dance. Such sequences fit comfortably neither in the world of explicit performance (i.e., the radioscope broadcasts) nor in the world of the narrative (the struggle for the rights to the invention) but rather work to blur the sharp boundaries between the two.

The greatest ambiguity surrounds W. C. Fields's status. Fields, as an international explorer and inventor, is first shown in a mock documentary presented on the radioscope (fig. 5.5), a scene that strongly evokes his extrafilmic image as a heavy drinker: the ground crew loads barrels of beer and trays of mugs into an airplane (fig. 5.6), a white-gloved hand reaches down to lift a mug of beer from the tray (fig. 5.7), and the camera follows it up to show Fields sitting in the cockpit, downing the drink (fig. 5.8). If the first few images are clearly established as radioscope broadcasts, the frame of its screen soon disappears and their diegetic status becomes more ambiguous. Later, Fields appears in a photograph in a newspaper Gracie reads, again as a representation rather than a narrative participant. Finally, the misdirected explorer appears in person at the International House ("Say, this isn't Kansas

City?"), though he retains a privileged relationship to the broadcast images. When Fields enters the room during one of Dr. Wong's demonstrations, the broadcast image of Rudy Vallee yells at him to stop interrupting his number; Fields shoves his cane into the machinery and blows it out, changing channels to a view of a navy ship, which Fields sinks by firing a pistol into the screen. Fields's actions not only disrupt broadcast performances and narrative developments but also destabilize the space between the two.

This fairly radical (though sometimes unstable) separation of actors according to plot-centered and performance-centered functions distinguishes the showcase film from the backstage musicals of the same vintage.[11] Typically, the plot of a backstage musical, such as *42nd Street* (Warner Brothers, 1933) or *Footlight Parade* (Warner Brothers, 1933), centers upon the process of putting on a show. The performers in the onstage sequences become characters within the frame narrative; their resulting performances are rich in narrative significance. It is not Ruby Keeler the star who steps onto the stage in the climactic moments of *42nd Street* but rather her character, the young dancer who has waited all her life for her chance at stardom. Her musical number primarily marks the young woman's triumph, rather than showcasing Ruby Keeler's virtuosity, though these two cannot be easily separated. For the most part, performances in backstage musicals display a high degree of character integration and a low degree of audience consciousness when compared to the performances in showcase films. A notable exception may be cameo appearances by famous stage stars, such as the appearance of Eddie Cantor in *Glorifying the American Girl* (Paramount, 1929), that often motivate numbers existing primarily to display these performer's talents; the onstage appearance by fictional characters decreases attention to the performer's extratextual status and more fully integrates performance into narrative.

ACTING IN SOCIETY: THE COMIC ROMANCE

The distinction between plot-centered and performance-centered actors breaks down further within the comic romance. While the frame story in the showcase film is merely a device for structuring the performance sequences, plot becomes the primary appeal of the comic romance. Here, comic performance is subordinated to narrative demands and appears only sporadically. *Dixiana* (RKO, 1930), for example, is first and foremost a romance concerning two young lovers (Bebe Daniels,

141

Everett Marshall) who must overcome parental opposition and the threat of a powerful rival (Ralf Harolde) (fig. 5.9). Unlike traditional romantic comedy, such romances are treated melodramatically rather than comically, with particular emphasis placed upon the pain of the lovers' separation. Dialect comic Frances Cawthorne and the bulky Jobyana Howland appear as the boy's squabbling parents, who alternate between comic scenes involving the wife's hopeless efforts to cultivate her immigrant husband (fig. 5.10) and more dramatic sequences involving the couples' reservations about their son's unsuitable choice of a bride (fig. 5.11). Their performance style shifts abruptly between the exaggeration of the comic scenes and the more naturalistic tone of the dramatic scenes. As dramatic performers, Cawthorne and Howland block Dixiana's upward mobility; as comic performers, they pose questions about rigid class barriers. After all, if these two can achieve acceptance in genteel society, the more ladylike Dixiana seems assured of eventual success in her attempts to leave burlesque and join the southern gentry.

Bert Wheeler and Robert Woolsey offer a comic contrast to the romantic couple. Their own buffoonish dispute over Dorothy Lee parallels and parodies the rivalry over Dixiana. This function is particularly apparent during a broadly played duel between the two comic leads that foreshadows the film's climactic and far more serious duel between the two dramatic leads. Like Cawthorne and Howland, however, the two comics also adopt a more restrained and naturalistic acting style during scenes that have greater narrative consequences, as when they must comfort Bebe Daniels following her forceful expulsion from her lover's house. These shifts pose a threat to the expressive coherence of individual performances not present within the revue or showcase films, where individual performers retained a more fixed status. The more performance-oriented sequences must be more restrained, displaying little audience consciousness and a higher degree of character integration if the comic performers are going to be successful in making the transition to more dramatic sequences.

Most of the comic romances share a thematic concern with the problems of social assimilation, with how to "act" in proper society; such a focus helps to naturalize these disjunctions in performance style. In *Dixiana, Her Majesty Love* (First National, 1931), *Rain or Shine* (Columbia, 1930), *Everything's Rosie, Love in Bloom* (Paramount, 1935), and *Poppy* (Paramount, 1936), leading ladies escape from their show world past into high society. Their successful transition is prefigured by their conformity to a more naturalistic style of performance. The comic stars are often cast as the girl's relatives or friends. The comic stars' inability to make a similar transition into naturalistic acting, their tendency to revert back to broader styles of performance, offers not only a source of amusement for the audience but also a tangible threat to the leading lady's own assimilation. Their buffoonery often results in her expulsion from society when their "bad manners" directs attention on her disreputable background. In *Love in Bloom*, Vi (Dixie Lee) has run away from her drunken father and his rundown traveling carnival, finding a place for herself as a song plugger at a big city music shop and winning the love of a young songwriter (Joe Morrison). The father, suffering business difficulties, dispatches her brother (George Burns) and his wife (Gracie Allen) to go to the big city and bring her back with them. The film cuts between Burns and Allen's comic misadventures along the road and the progression of Lee's preparations for her wedding; the two comedians' antics provide comic relief from the more realistic romance plot as well as a vivid manifestation of the world that Lee hopes to escape. By the time they arrive in the city, just in time to make a shambles of the wedding, their disruptiveness can be reread as tragic rather than comic.

The apparent incompatibility of these two very different ways of "acting" is dramatically evoked in many of these films through the device of a disastrous social affair, such as the interrupted wedding in *Love in Bloom*. This sequence often involves an engagement dinner given in honor of the leading lady and attended by characters from both worlds. Initially, the playfulness and spontaneity of the comic stars is accepted by the other guests as a refreshing novelty. Soon, their enthusiastic reception pushes the clowns toward broader and broader performances. Joe Cook in *Rain or Shine* showers the dinner guests with spaghetti, while W. C. Fields in *Her Majesty Love* tosses pastry across the table, alarming other diners. Bert Wheeler in *Dixiana* does a ballancing and juggling act with fancy china and crystal, smashing it against the floor (fig. 5.12), while Robert Woolsey in *Everything's Rosie* engages the guests in the old shell game and takes all their money. The leading lady's embarrassment at the clown's performances, usually followed by the revelation of her disgraceful ties to show business, gives these sequences a melodramatic edge. Their consequences for the romantic couple colors our perception of what otherwise might be read as pure comic spectacle. Performance has intruded too abruptly into the narrative space, and, as a consequence, not only the comic stars but also the upwardly aspiring female lead must be expelled; expressive performance must be suppressed in favor of rigid conformity to plot demands. The irreconcilability of these two spheres allows only two possible resolutions: either the leading lady must reject the stuffiness of high society and return to show business or she must break totally with the realm of exotic performance and enter completely into the space of narrative accountability.

Comic romance serves as an interesting intermediary category between the comedian comedy and the screwball comedy traditions. While the plots of films like *Poppy* and *Her Majesty Love* follow the same story conventions as screwball comedies like *You Can't Take It with You* (Columbia, 1938) or *Bringing Up Baby* (RKO, 1938), their performance style is fundamentally different. The screwball comedy owes relatively little to the vaudeville aesthetic, representing the translation of theatrical farce into classical Hollywood narratives. While the comic romance still contains some nonintegrated performance sequences, specifically those centered around the star clowns, screwball comedy always endows impersonations or performances with narrative consequences. Clark Gable and Claudette Colbert impersonate a bickering married couple in *It Happened One Night* (Columbia, 1934); this scene, however, contributes to the plot development in a way that Wheeler and Woolsey's performances in *Dixiana* generally do not. The characters' ability to act as a married couple prefigures their own union at the film's conclusion. Stage-trained performers like Katharine Hepburn and Cary Grant melded directly into their characters, with casting designed to maximize the match between performer and assigned role. Screwball comedy, moreover, maintains a high degree of stylistic consistency between the film's performers, while comic romance is characterized primarily by the thematization of multiple styles, the radical separation between comic and dramatic performers. For the most part, the screwball comedy tries for a style of performance that is less naturalistic than the dramatic segments of the comic romance and less exaggerated than the comic sequences.

"Like a Playful Child": The Anarchistic Comedy

If the revue and showcase films display the performance skills of various entertainers, the anarchistic comedy is constructed as a vehicle for a particular comic personality; it consistently creates opportunities for a comic star or team to demonstrate the full range of their abilities. Comic director Norman McLeod has characterized the development of

Roman Scandals (1933): Eddie Cantor. Wisconsin Center for Film and Theater Research.

such a film project as "a high-class job of carpentry"; the stars' repertoires of existing stage business provided raw materials that could be assembled into a flimsy narrative structure.[12] This reuse of already familiar material ensured that the comic performer remained imperfectly integrated into any particular character role. Certain sequences (Eddie Cantor's blackface numbers, Harpo's harp solos, Bert Wheeler's female impersonation, W. C. Fields's golf or pool tricks) stand apart from the rest of the film, marked as star turns inserted into the narrative with only the most transparent attempt at motivation. These moments invite comparison with previous films and thus direct attention away from their context within this particular story. In *Ali Baba Goes to Town* (Fox, 1937), Eddie Cantor resorts to blackface, jive, and jazz when his efforts to communicate with a group of Nubian slaves prove unsuccessful, while he poses as an "Ethiopian Beauty Specialist" in *Roman Scandals* (United Artists, 1933). The resulting numbers are totally anachronistic and have next to nothing to do with the plot; they do, however, showcase Cantor's trademark singing style and incorporate jazz performers and tap dancers. Audience members often expressed dissatisfaction if these specialties did not appear in a particular vehicle, expecting their repetition regardless of narrative context. [13]

Individual scenes are conceived as set pieces, opportunities for performance, with their narrative significance often added as an afterthought. Story information is compressed into tight units of intrusive exposition at the beginnings and ends of scenes; the bulk of each sequence is spent on largely unmotivated and unintegrated comic performance. Unlike the previous categories, however, anarchistic comedies do not create a fixed separation between narrative space and performance space. The comic performers act within the diegesis, entering narrative spaces so they may be transformed into an impromptu stage for their clowning. Frank Krutnik writes of these films:

> It is as if the comedian—the disruptive element in the smooth functioning of the genre—has been dropped into the fictional world by accident, and, like a playful child, proceeds to toy with its rules. The comedian refuses to act "straight"—unlike the other characters in the film—or is incapable of doing so. . . . Thus two sets of expectations come into conflict: the comedian "interferes" with the ostensible fiction, the fiction "constrains" the comedian. It is the play between the two which is responsible for much of the comedy. [14]

The Marx Brothers in *Monkey Business* are almost literally "dropped into the fictional world by accident," having stowed away on a luxury liner inside barrels of kippered herrings (fig. 5.13). By this somewhat unorthodox means, the brothers enter a world with which they would ordinarily have little contact. The captain and his men try to capture the stowaways, resulting in a series of chase scenes in which the various clowns burst into new rooms and disrupt the other passengers' ongoing activities. Running across the ship's ballroom, the brothers pause long enough to play a short musical piece and bow to their astonished audience, before darting away again. Harpo stumbles onto a children's puppet show and assumes a puppetlike persona, integrating himself into the entertainment; he draws first the ship's steward and then the captain himself into the Punch and Judy act (fig. 5.14). Harpo and Chico seize control of the barbershop, shaving away a customer's mustache in their attempts to "even it up a little," (fig. 5.15) while Groucho takes command of the captain's quarters and devours his lunch. Trying to sneak past customs, each of the brothers impersonates Maurice Chevalier with varying degrees of success (fig. 5.16). Every nook and cranny on the ship poses new possibilities for comic appropriation; divorced of its usual functions, the ship becomes an ideal space for the Marx Brothers' performances and each plot action provides new opportunities for the display of their virtuosity.[15]

Moreover, the comic stars exist almost entirely outside of the restraints of stable characterization. Characters have names and social positions, serve particular narrative roles, yet they offer little competition for the stars' engaging personalities. In extreme cases, as when Wheeler and Woolsey, cigar, glasses, and all, are inserted into historical settings in *Cockeyed Cavaliers* (RKO, 1934) and *Silly Billies* (RKO, 1936), the films play upon a tension between their extratextual personae and their narrative roles. The comic stars are literally reduced to icons in the films' opening credits, where caricatures of the central performers rely upon certain familiar facial and costume details (Groucho's cigar and painted mustache; Harpo's fright wig and horn; W. C. Fields's red nose, top hat, white gloves, and cane; Robert Woolsey's glasses; Eddie Cantor's owlish eyes; Joe E. Brown's big mouth) to evoke audience's extratextual knowledge of their familiar personae. While additional character information particularizes that persona to the needs of a specific narrative, this information is minimal and may be disregarded later, if the characterization interferes with the filmmakers' desire to introduce a particularly entertaining sequence. Little in the common man characters Eddie Cantor plays in his films justifies his ability to suddenly burst into song and dance or don blackface. At such moments, established characterization simply dissolves to allow Cantor the performer to emerge. One might contrast that fluidity between characterization and performance to the complex narrative motivations surrounding Marlene Dietrich's stage appearances in films like *Morroco* (Paramount, 1930) or *Blonde Venus* (Paramount, 1932).

Anarchistic comedies places a relatively low value on expressive coherence, openly creating disjunctures between character and performer or allowing for fairly abrupt shifts in performance style. In the course of a single scene in *Monkey Business,* Groucho Marx adopts the style and rhetoric of a patriotic stump speaker, a dance instructor, a gangster, a quiz show host, a little boy, and a flirtatious woman, all while remaining one step ahead of a mobster and his seductive moll. This "expressive anarchy" creates space as well for the performer to break character and confront the audience directly, as Groucho does in almost all of his films, though the performers generally display far less consciousness of the audience than do the stars of revue or showcase films.

"TAKING ONE'S PLACE IN THE SOCIAL ORDER": THE AFFIRMATIVE COMEDY

Steve Seidman and Frank Krutnik have advanced a model of the comedian comedy that sees the clown's antics as signs of "identity confusion" and "behavioral disfunction," an inability to integrate into adult society.[16] The comedian comedy, they argue, depicts the comic protagonist's efforts to work through these personality difficulties and gain social acceptance.[17] The normalization of the character's conduct is mirrored by a normalization of performance; the performers are more fully assimilated into their narrative roles as the characters fit more perfectly within their social roles. Such a model of the comedian comedy implies not a contestation between performance and narrative but rather a final subordination of performance to plot demands. The comedian's virtuosity must yield to the demands of a character role; "expressive anarchy" must be transformed into "expressive coherence." Such a model seems inadequate to classes of comic films that either maintain a radical separation of performance-centered stars and plot-centered actors (as in the showcase film or to a lesser degree, the comic romance) or make the demands of character and story subservient to spectacle and showmanship (as in the anarchistic comedy). There is, however, another group of early sound comedies more closely conforming to the Seidman-Krutnik model. Perhaps best represented by the films of Joe E. Brown, the affirmative comedy contrasts sharply with the anarchistic comedy both in its thematic of social integration and in its emphasis upon plot and character over spectacle and performance.

Joe E. Brown's comedies depend less upon extended sequences of comic performance than upon small bits of character business. Even in films like *Circus Clown* (Warner Brothers, 1934) or *Six Day Bike Rider* (Warner Brothers, 1934), where Brown must perform onstage, these performances are heavily determined by their story situations and have direct consequences on future plot actions. In *Circus Clown,* Brown plays Happy Howard, the son of a famous circus performer. Happy, like his father, aspires toward stardom under the big top. Periodically, the film shows Happy rehearsing on a trampoline, allowing Brown to display his acrobatic abilities. These moments of performance are so closely bound with the protagonist's personal goals that they read as reflecting the developing abilities of Happy Howard the character, not the already well-developed talents of Brown the former circus performer. Similarly, Happy's appearances in the circus ring later in the film enact the character's efforts to gain professional recognition and romantic acceptance; such actions are so rich in narrative interest that the audience is inclined to forget the virtuosity of the clown who performs them (even in remarkable scenes where Brown plays both Happy and his father) (fig. 5.17). The opening of *Six Day Bike Rider* establishes the rivalry between Harry St. Clair, a vaudeville performer, and Wilifred (Joe E. Brown), the baggage clerk at the local railroad station. When Harry performs stunts on his bicycle during the variety show, Wilifred insults him from the audience and is challenged to come onto the stage to show whether he can do any better. Blindfolded, Wilifred performs such stunts, much to the embarrassment of his girl friend, and ends up riding his bike into the orchestra pit. Again, this performance is thoroughly integrated into the story action, serving to alienate Wilifred from his fiancée and to intensify his hostility toward the film's antagonist. This performance thus motivates his subsequent decision to enter the six-day bike race and to challenge St. Clair for the hand of the woman they both love.

Unlike other performers who played essentially similar characters in all of their films, Brown adopted various personae: fast-talking young playboys (*Broad-Minded*, First National, 1931), bespectacled buffoons (*Six Day Bike Rider, You Said a Mouthful, Local Boy Makes Good*, First National, 1931) (fig. 5.18), gangling athletes (*Alibi Ike*, Warner Brothers, 1935; *Elmer the Great*, First National, 1935; *Sit Tight*, Warner Brothers, 1931), and ill-fated braggarts (*Son of a Sailor*, Warner Brothers, 1933; *Earthworm Tractors*, Warner Brothers, 1936). Brown adjusts his limited vocabulary of grimaces, gawks, and guffaws to the particular needs of each role. Brown more fully submerged his own personality to the demands of characterization than any other early sound comedian. As a result, Brown, like the classical silent clowns, can move from comedy to pathos, where such a shift would be impossible for a performer like Groucho Marx. Frequently, the films ask us to share Brown's pain at his inability to gain social acceptance and his temporarily frustrated ambitions, as in a sequence in *Circus Clown* when Brown is unjustly fired from the show. The film lingers on a close-up of Brown's tear-streaked face as the circus train pulls away into the night, leaving him alone and dejected on the open road.

Moreover, Brown's comedies develop a high degree of stylistic consistency. Brown's body movements and vocal mannerisms are certainly broader and more stylized than other cast members, making his character appear eccentric, clumsy, and ill-adjusted to his social environment, yet those gestures shed insight onto his characters. We find here none of the more radical breaks with naturalistic performance style that we associate with other film clowns. Brown remains oblivious to the presence of the camera, avoiding not only direct address but also the frontal staging so common in early sound comedy. The internal monologues in *You Said a Mouthful,* modeled after a similar device in *Strange Interlude* (MGM, 1932), are the exception that proves this rule. Here, Brown steps momentarily out of the story action, the background movement is suspended, and he strikes a thoughtful pose. The camera pulls into a tight close-up, while Brown's voice on the soundtrack reveals his character's thoughts. Groucho Marx parodies *Strange Interlude* in *Animal Crackers,* using the device to comment on the constructedness of the plot and to engage in his familiar wordplay; Brown's internal monologues, like those in *Strange Interlude* itself, reflect the character's thoughts and convey plot information; they are not a reflexive gag. As the narratives progress, Brown adjusts his acting style into closer conformity with the other characters, frequently concluding with sequences where he displays the physical prowess and social grace previously denied his characters. The normalization of Brown's performance becomes a measure of his character's social integration; earlier moments of stylization and expressive incoherence are read as signs of the comic protagonist's social immaturity rather than as moments where the performer's personality surfaces. The relative restraint and coherence of Brown's performances may be the product of the limited range of his performance skills. Whatever its origins, this style of comedy, with its high emphasis upon the integration of comic performance into character and narrative development, proved far more compatible with the norms of the classical Hollywood cinema than the other classes of comic texts described above. The comedian comedies of the late 1930s and 1940s (the vehicles of Joe Penner, Abbott and Costello, Bob Hope, Danny Kaye, and Red Skelton) follow Joe E. Brown's example rather than adopting the anarchistic comedy model. Even anarchic performers like the Marx Brothers or Wheeler and Woolsey were forced to restrain the more excessive aspects of their performances and to integrate their comic routines more fully into the plot progression. The gag sequences in *Monkey Business* thwart plot development, interrupting and derailing the gangster subplot, rendering its actions ridiculous (as when Groucho acts as a sports announcer providing running commentary on the final fist fight) (fig. 5.19); similar sequences in *A Day at the Races* further narrative purposes, as when the Marx Brothers create disturbances to

150

allow Allen Jones to sneak the horse away from its stable or to block efforts to investigate Dr. Hugo Hackenbush's credentials. What is read as performance virtuosity in the early Marx Brothers films comes in their later works to signify the characters' eccentricity, with the sudden shifts of performance registers restrained by a greater attention to character motivation.

Each subgenre described above represents a different strategy for reconciling the competing demands of the vaudeville aesthetic and classical Hollywood narrative. The revue film resolves the contradiction by abandoning narrative altogether, offering the film as a substitute for a stage presentation, as a text made of nothing but performances. The showcase film introduces a minimal degree of plot development, yet interrupts the narrative periodically to allow extended sequences of performance that have little or no direct bearing on the storyline. The comic romance transforms the problematic relationship between performance sequences and causal narrative into a dominant thematic concern, depicting the shifting styles of individual performers as a process of class assimilation and posing eruptions into pure performance as a threat to the romantic couple's happiness. The anarchistic comedy provides perhaps the most unstable balance between performance and plot, with each scene transformed into a battleground between these two competing forces. Here, stories exist to be disrupted and overwhelmed by excessive performances, while narrative destabilization is experienced as a liberation of the comic performer's creative potential. By contrast, the affirmative comedy subordinates performance almost totally to the demands of characterization, with the comic star's movement from performance excess to stylistic restraint reflecting the character's increased integration into the social order.

Strictly speaking, these five categories do not represent phases in the historical evolution of the comedian comedy but rather different options available to comic filmmakers within the early sound period. One may find many early examples of the affirmative comedy, such as Ed Wynn's first screen appearance in *The Chief* (MGM, 1931) or the sound films of Buster Keaton; many of its conventions may be traced back to the classic comedian comedies of the 1920s. Similarly, anarchistic comedy survives well into the 1940s, with W. C. Fields's *Never Give a Sucker an Even Break* (Universal, 1941) and Olson and Johnson's *Hellzapoppin* (Universal, 1941) standing as outstanding later examples. For the most part, however, there was a general movement toward increased conformity to classical Hollywood norms, increased narrative integration and stylistic constraint. The revue film exists almost exclusively in the initial period of talking pictures, occurring with frequency only in 1929 and early 1930, while the showcase film represents a later development, seemingly responding to a similar desire for heterogeneity yet reflecting increased pressure toward conformity to classical narrative conventions. The showcase film, as Kevin Heffernan notes, was tied to studio strategies to test and develop a range of potential new performers recruited from vaudeville and radio. Such films allowed the studio to pull back from substantial investment into any one performer by providing a supporting structure that allowed audience interest to shift across a number of potential attractions.[18] The comic romance primarily appeared in the early 1930s, deriving its stories for the most part from preexisting theatrical or literary works. The majority of the anarchistic comedies appeared between 1930 and 1934, after the studios had determined which stars would be strong enough to receive their own vehicles and before studio pressures and audience resistance led toward greater conformity to classical norms. The affirmative comedy increasingly came to dominate comic production in the second half of the decade. The next two chapters will look more closely at the historical and institutional factors that determined these shifting conceptions of screen comedy.

6

"Shall We Make It for New York or for Distribution?" *Eddie Cantor,* Whoopee, *and Regional Resistance to the Talkies*

On March 23, 1930, Broadway patrons opened the *New York Times* entertainment section to discover that Eddie Cantor, a fixture on the local stage since 1917, was abandoning the legitimate theater for the cinema. In an open letter to his loyal followers, Cantor proclaimed, "This is to certify that I am in my right mind, white, free and rearin' to go to Hollywood."[1] The alert reader was probably not very surprised by this proclamation, having watched for more than two years as the Hollywood studios drained the top talent from the eastern stage for talking pictures.

Of all the current Broadway stars, Eddie Cantor seemed the most likely to achieve cinematic success. *Photoplay* wrote in late 1928 that Cantor "appears to be the only possible contender to Al Jolson anywhere on the horizon."[2] Cantor had spent twenty of his thirty-nine years in show business, moving from Brooklyn amateur night contests to vaudeville appearances, with the popular team of Bedini and Arthur, in Gus Edwards's "Kid Kaberet," and as part of a two-man comic act, "Master and Man," with Al Lee. A brief engagement with the *Midnight Frolics* led Florenz Ziegfeld to offer Cantor a featured spot in the 1917 *Follies,* commencing a close (although often rocky) association that would continue until 1930. Cantor continued to make occasional forays into vaudeville but with each subsequent Ziegfeld show, he played an increasingly prominent role. New York critics and audiences consistently found Cantor a standout, the "life of the party," even within a company that included Will Rogers, W. C. Fields, Bert Williams, Bert Wheeler,

George Jessel and Eddie Cantor at the RKO Palace, 1930. Wisconsin Center for Film and Theater Research.

and Fanny Brice.[3] His success as an aggressive caddie in his first book musical, *Kid Boots* (1924), attracted the interest of Paramount, which adapted the play to the screen as a silent comedy casting Cantor against Clara Bow. *Kid Boots* (Famous Players, 1926) drew considerable praise and reasonable box office, causing many to predict that Cantor might enjoy a long screen career.

Unfortunately, his second film, *Special Delivery* (Paramount, 1927), failed to attract the same response. Unhappy with the story for *The Girl Friend*, which Paramount proposed for his next vehicle, Cantor chose instead to return to Broadway as the sole headliner of the 1927 *Ziegfeld Follies*, the first time total responsibility had been granted to a single performer. The Boston *Transcript* wrote of the show's premier performance: "Upon the shoulders of Mr. Cantor alone settle the farcical responsibilities of the entire show. . . . He is here and everywhere, adding a jesting comment, interpolating an impromptu quip, jiggling and prancing and cutting capers."[4] His tremendous success in what was one of the best-received *Follies* in several seasons motivated Ziegfeld to prepare another book play, *Whoopee,* to showcase his talents. *Whoopee* was Broadway's top grossing musical throughout the 1928–29 season, with weekly ticket sales averaging in excess of $40,000, making Cantor again highly attractive to film producers.[5] His March 1930 "open letter" merely confirmed what had already seemed inevitable: Cantor, like many Broadway names before him, was going to see whether his local appeal could translate into national success as a film star.

Historical accounts of the early sound era and Hollywood's raids on Broadway underestimate the tentativeness with which Cantor and other stage stars approached their entry into the film industry. In what has remained the definitive account of the Broadway raids, Benjamin Hampton asserted that "the tottering star system received its death blow from the talkies. . . . For a while it appeared to film folk that they were to be replaced in toto by their brethren of the footlights."[6] The "brethren of the footlights" shared none of Hampton's confidence. Just a few months after the *Times* announcement, on the eve of the New York premiere of the Goldwyn film version of *Whoopee* (United Artists, 1930), Cantor told a *Times* reporter, "It's like standing trial. I've been good, the judge is nice, but how do I know what's going to happen?"[7] The film's success in the major eastern seaboard cities seemed certain, but its appeal in the hinterland, in cities that had little or no familiarity with Broadway stars and little taste for New York's particular style of entertainment, was unpredictable. Regional opposition would eventually force Cantor to reformulate his screen persona, a process that was initiated by *Palmy Days,* his second sound vehicle.

While widely discussed at the time, these regional differences in the ways audiences responded to Broadway-centered talking pictures have vanished from historical accounts of this transitional period. The tendency, since Hampton, has been to focus upon the destructive impact of this recruitment of stage talent upon the careers of established film stars and to exclude any detailed consideration of what happened when Broadway names attempted to achieve screen success or how audiences responded to these changes.[8] Hampton's 1932 vantage point might explain his failure to predict accurately the long-term consequences of these recruitment efforts, yet it does not justify his accounts' uncritical acceptance by subsequent historians.

For one thing, Hampton predicted a more enduring and stable relationship between stage and screen than eventually evolved. In fact, the attrition rate for existing screen stars during these transitional years was only slightly higher than in any other five-year period during the silent cinema and considerably lower than that experienced by the Broadway recruits themselves over the next few years.[9] The "raids" constituted an expansion of the overall talent pool rather than a cleaning of the ranks from the silent cinema or a fundamental change in the star system.

Second, Hampton underestimated the number of stage-experienced players already under contract in Hollywood at the coming of the talkies, arguing that the absence of stage-trained voices was the primary reason for the recruitment of additional Broadway stars to work in sound movies. The talent raids of the late 1920s represented an intensification of an existing policy and not a radical change in traditional studio practice.[10] Of 286 players under contract to the majors in 1928, roughly half (146) had some prior stage experience, a group that included some 60 percent of those who survived the first five years of the sound era.[11] Presumably, these stars could have been used more extensively to ensure a smooth product flow during that transitional period without necessitating the massive new recruitment effort. Moreover, as Alexander Walker has shown, many of the silent stars who lacked stage experience were able to adapt fairly easily and quickly to sound cinema, once they were given a chance, because of their existing familiarity with the techniques of screen performance.[12] A contemporary observer echoed the logic of Walker's argument: "If the screen player must become accustomed to a microphone, the stage actor must also learn the camera." [13] The demand for stage-trained voices, then, cannot be viewed as providing a necessary and sufficient explanation for Hollywood's massive recruitment efforts.

Third, Hampton failed to consider the possibility that film audiences might remain strongly attached to existing screen stars and express a preference for traditional screen genres. [14] Hampton perceived the film audience as a "progressive" force that accepts all new innovations with great enthusiasm and pushes the more conservative segments of the film industry toward their more rapid adoption. Yet, as we will see, the talkies faced considerable audience resistance, especially outside of the key urban areas.

Finally, Hampton's account ignored the adjustments demanded of the Broadway stars in adapting their performance techniques to existing screen conventions and audience expectations. Like other early critics who felt that exposure to legitimate stage stars would develop a more "sophisticated" audience, Hampton offered an elitist conception of the "quick minds" of the urban, well-educated audience "pushing" their "slower" rural and working-class counterparts into an acceptance of a "higher standard" of film entertainment. [15] Instead, theatrical talents had to learn to adapt to the demands of the existing film audience if they wished to maintain long-term screen careers.

This chapter provides an alternative account of the early talkie period, one that considers the social and cultural implications of Hollywood's talent raids and not simply their economic or personal consequences. What motivated the studios to place so much emphasis upon the procurement of New York-based performers during the early sound period? What strategies did Hollywood adopt for the utilization of these Broadway and variety performers? How were their films received by the existing film audience? What long-range impact, if any, did the recruitment of such stars have upon cinematic and generic conventions? My primary focus will be upon Eddie Cantor, who, like many of the Broadway stars recruited during the early sound period, faced a rocky transition to the cinema and was forced to make substantial shifts in his star persona, performance style, and generic placement in order to maintain a stable career in Hollywood. That Cantor remained one of United Artist's top box office draws throughout much of the 1930s suggests the success with which he was able to execute the necessary changes to broaden his appeal from its initial New York base toward a national film audience.[16] A closer look at his film career should shed light upon the immediate and long-term consequences of Hollywood's talent raids.

"THE BIGGEST STARS WHILE THEY ARE STILL PLAYING ON BROADWAY": HOLLYWOOD'S URBAN STRATEGY, 1928–1929

The eventual displacement of the silent cinema by the talkies did not seem nearly as inevitable to industry insiders in the late 1920s as it has appeared to later historians. By early 1928, the "novelty" value of the talking pictures had already declined as a factor at the box office; survival of the new technologies depended upon finding potential functions for sound to justify the high costs of its adoption.[17] While most trade press reports asserted that sound would continue to be a factor in the commercial cinema, there was considerable debate about its possible role(s) within the studios' total production output. Few insiders envisioned a time when talking pictures would become the sole film fare.

One early strategy saw sound as enabling the cinema to encompass several new functions: 1) recordings of performances by opera stars and variety performers could displace small-time vaudeville and vaudefilm exhibition practices, and 2) recordings of stage successes could provide a less expensive alternative to theatrical roadshows.[18] Silent movies, accompanied with optional canned music and sound effects, could continue to appeal to traditional movie fans and to offer the genres that had become a staple of Hollywood production. What was being proposed, in effect, were two American cinemas: the first focusing on traditional screen genres, targeted at regional and small-town exhibitors and relying almost exclusively upon silent film production; the second offering traditional stage entertainment, targeted at Northeastern and major city exhibitors, and exploiting the potentials of a talking cinema as a replacement for live entertainment. As one studio insider explained in a September 1928 interview, "Silent pictures will go one road, talking pictures another. There will be two kinds of theater to suit two different tastes."[19]

This strategy would expand the potential urban market of the movies without endangering its existing following. Broadway was suffering a serious economic crisis and was therefore vulnerable to Hollywood's moves on its markets.[20] The number of roadshow productions on national tour in an average week had declined from a high of 339 in 1900 to 61 in 1926.[21] Vaudeville was also undergoing severe economic problems and would be extinct by the mid-1930s.[22] Ambitious studio executives saw sound as a means of broadening their entertainment empire and bringing Broadway and vaudeville under their corporate control. Moreover, the expansion of the majors' theater holdings, which occurred primarily in major population centers, placed increased importance upon the profitability of urban exhibition.[23] The economics of converting theaters to sound meant that small-town and regional exhibitors were slower than major city exhibitors to abandon their dependence upon silent film; the talkies would remain a predominantly urban phenomenon for some time to come.[24] A concentration on Broadway-style entertainment would allow the studios to provide these urban areas with the amusements that they apparently wanted and that Hollywood had been previously unable to offer.

This strategy's success depended upon Hollywood's ability to offer urban patrons performers and performances otherwise available only on the legitimate stage and at substantially lower admission prices made possible by the cinema's economy of scale. The estimated seasonal proceeds from screen sales of Broadway productions increased from $500,000 in the 1924–25 season to $1,110,000 in the 1928–29 season.[25] The competition for successful Broadway plays became so intense that studios routinely offered established stage talents advance funds to finance Broadway productions in return for a reduced rate on their eventual screen rights.[26] By 1930, Warner Brothers had become the largest individual producer or backer of Broadway plays.[27] Warner Brothers, Paramount, and Metro each opened New York-based studios to allow theatrical performers to work in the movies while continuing to appear nights on Broadway.[28]

Cantor's film recruitment reflected these general production trends. While theatrical commitments prevented Cantor from feature film work throughout the peak years of Hollywood's raids on Broadway, Paramount repeatedly sought talkie vehicles for him.[29] Ziegfeld as consistently invoked his exclusive contract for Cantor's talent.[30] The producer, however, did allow his top star to make a series of Paramount shorts, filmed at their Long Island studios, as long as they did not interfere with his stage work. Ziegfeld, being courted with possible deals from Paramount, Universal, and Fox, probably wanted to maintain exclusive use of his stage stars for his own film productions. As early as 1926, he had explored the prospect of an ambitious Famous Players-Lasky production based on the *Ziegfeld Follies.* Though Ziegfeld offered to provide part of the funds in return for the use of the sets and costumes in later stage productions, Lasky rejected the project when it was estimated that *Glorifying the American Girl* might cost as much as $1,600,000 to produce, a figure that precluded a profitable release.[31] The emergence of talking pictures revived Lasky's interest in the project, but the production seemed ill-fated. *Glorifying the American Girl* went through more than twenty-five different rewrites; directors (including Dorothy Arzner) were hired and fired; its major roles were recast several times.[32]

Finally released in late 1929, *Glorifying the American Girl* was a typical backstage musical of the period, following the efforts of a young woman to move from the five-a-day circuit to success as a "Ziegfeld girl" and the emotional losses she encounters along the way. The popularity of *The Jazz Singer* and *The Singing Fool* (Warner Brothers, 1928) had initiated a cycle of backstage musicals that only escalated with the success of *Broadway Melody* (MGM, 1929). In May 1929, one in four of the films currently under production at the major studios were musical comedies, with the majority offering behind-the-scenes looks at the New York show world.[33] These backstage films' settings allowed them to reproduce or mimic established stage performances and to foreground their "Broadwayness" as a major part of their appeal to urban consumers. Studio publicity highlighted their links to the New York stage. Insisting that "New York is the greatest source in the world for stars," Vitaphone promised to provide filmgoers with "the biggest stars while they are still playing on Broadway."[34] Another Vitaphone ad proclaimed, "Vitaphone links your theater to Broadway. . . . Broadway—mecca of millions now the round the corner resort of all America, thanks to Vitaphone! Vitaphone obliterates the miles that used to separate you from the street of streets."[35] Each week, Vitaphone grew more ambitious. With the release of *Disraeli* (Warner Brothers, 1929), the company announced that the film now "dwarfs the stage," while another ad in the same issue of *Motion Picture Classic* boasted that "the screen has robbed the stage of its most prized possession"–Marilyn Miller![36]

Both Cantor's shorts and *Glorifying the American Girl* reflect this general appeal to "Broadwayness." *Midnight Frolics* featured Cantor in blackface, engaging in "chatter and song" in front of a set representing the Ziegfeld's New Amsterdam roof club and backed by a stage band.[37] In *That Certain Party,* Cantor played himself, negotiating with a Hollywood producer about a possible appearance in a talking picture, wondering aloud, "should we make it for New York or for distribution?" In *Getting a Ticket,* Cantor is stopped by a New York cop who recognizes him as a major stage star and insists that he perform some of his famous numbers. The elaborate closing sequence in *Glorifying the American Girl,* which reproduced the 1929 *Follies,* complete with recorded performances by Cantor, Rudy Vallee, Helen Morgan, and other Ziegfeld stars, is heavily marked with references to its stage origins. It opens with a *Variety* headline, "Ziegfeld gets $25 per Ticket as Revue Opens," followed in quick succession by a close-up of theater tickets (showing an even higher price [fig. 6.1]), a program with a celebrity portrait of the film's star that flips open to show Ziegfeld's name and that of the production's other cast members. A mock newsreel sequence shows a radiocaster announcing the appearance of a number of New York celebrities, including, not coincidentally, Ziegfeld, with his wife, Billie Burke, and Paramount president Adolph Zukor, who are attending the show's lavish premiere. The individual acts are linked both by scenes of the characters backstage, nervously awaiting their entrances (fig. 6.2), and the theater audience, flipping through their programs and offering excited commentary on the performance. The film never lets the audience forget that they are getting glimpses of a show that others have paid considerably more to see on Broadway.

These appeals proved highly successful in establishing a stable base of support for the talking pictures along the Eastern seaboard and indeed, in transforming these northeastern cities into the dominant source of exhibition revenues. Certain films, *The Singing Fool* or *Broadway Melody* for example, proved so successful that they could return a profit on their investment after runs in only a handful of key urban areas.[38] These strategies were not, however, foolproof. All of the production delays meant that *Glorifying the American Girl* was released at the end of a cycle of backstage musicals. By year's end, a steady stream of such films had depleted the novelty value of *Girl*'s melodramatic plot, its technicolor sequences, and its precise recreation of the 1929 *Follies.* Despite extensive pre-release publicity, the film sank without a trace.

"HUNT OUT ALL THE BROADWAYITES!"
REGIONAL RESISTANCE, 1929–1930

In June 1928, *Variety* stressed the need to make films suited to the demands of the more than twelve thousand theaters, mostly in the small towns and hinterlands, not yet wired for sound.[39] That same month,

Universal ran a trade press ad featuring an open letter from Carl Laemmle promising that "I will not be stampeded [by the 'talking picture craze'] into forgetting the needs of the small exhibitors."[40] By early 1930, however, such promises were forgotten in the studios' excitement over the large returns from their urban-based strategy; the studios abandoned their commitment to westerns and the other film genres favored by small town exhibitors in order to increase their investments in special roadshow attractions. Only about a third of the films planned for the 1929–30 season would be available as silent pictures.[41] The studios were no longer producing sufficient silent films to allow the smaller exhibitors to remain open. While independents moved to exploit this situation, their efforts came too late to stem the financial crisis facing local exhibitors.[42] Some two thousand theaters closed their doors in the first few months of 1929; others adopted sound, often with financial support from local businesses. Having forced talking pictures upon small-town exhibitors, the film industry soon discovered that they now needed to factor the interests and tastes of these new audiences into property selection and casting decisions. The box office failure of *Glorifying the American Girl* was simply one of the many indications that Hollywood needed to reconsider its production policies in light of the end of a phase of domination by urban audiences over sound film exhibition.

Industry spokesmen had initially expressed confidence that film fans could be eventually "educated" toward the more "sophisticated taste" required to appreciate Broadway-style entertainment: "It is within vision of reason to believe the talking picture will convert the picture film fan and flap into a lover of good drama or musical."[43] Signs of resistance to talking pictures, however, had been present from the very beginning and would become a major issue as the studio sought to expand the market for talking pictures into the hinterlands. As late as January 1929, a group of Syracuse exhibitors surveyed their audiences and found that only 50 percent of them preferred talking pictures to silent movies and only 7 percent wanted to see silent films eliminated altogether. More than 30 percent wanted to see sound limited to orchestral scores and sound effects.[44] While the significance or representativeness of any one such survey may be questioned, the prevalence of such reports in the trade press suggests, minimally, that the industry closely monitored exhibitor responses and probably drew upon that feedback in making decisions about product selection and star recruitment.

This resistance to the talking pictures became a more significant factor as the studios sought to release dialogue films in the hinterlands. *Variety* recommended that exhibitors examine local audience response closely before committing to sound, noting that the public seemed almost evenly divided in its response to the talking pictures.[45] Film fans frequently cited "confusion" or distaste over "the stage formulas included in new talkers" as a key factor behind their dislike of sound pictures.[46] Throughout 1929, the *Motion Picture Herald* conducted an extensive survey of local exhibitors, publishing dozens of responses each week from throughout the country. Again and again, this concern with genre and star recruitment resurfaced—alongside the high cost of equipment and film rentals—as one of the key sources of their resistance to the new technologies. A Nebraska exhibitor explained that he could continue to show a profit in the face of competition from wired houses nearby if "they will give us good silent pictures and not so much wine, women, song, and moon."[47] An Iowa exhibitor characterized sound movies as "the worst curse that ever fell upon the picture industry,"[48] while a Florida theater owner singled out *The Desert Song* (Warner Brothers, 1929) as an offensive example of "all this 'Broadway' stagey stuff" that "cluttered up" the theaters.[49] An Illinois show owner protested that "the movies are made for the masses and not the classes, but to hear those birds using their blah blah gives everybody a big pain in the neck,"[50] and a Michigan exhibitor declared war on 'sophisticated' talking pictures:

> Seize all the dinner suits and cocktail shakers in Hollywood, load them on a barge and take them out and dump them into the Pacific Ocean. Round up the English and other accents and quietly exterminate them by some humane but effective method. Hunt out all the Broadwayites . . . and send them back to Broadway. Offer a substantial reward for grand opera singers, dead or alive. Chop up 75 percent of the drawing rooms, boudoirs and tea tables into very fine kindling.[51]

More and more exhibitors were calling for a return to traditional screen genres and the abandonment of Broadway entertainment. Tiffany pictures surveyed Pacific coast exhibitors and found that 90 percent felt that their greatest demand was for "stories that will appeal to the kids," noting that the new talkies had pushed "sophistication" far beyond what was desired by this audience.[52] A group of Texas exhibitors lobbied the studios to increase the production of westerns; their audience would prefer silent westerns to backstage musicals.[53] By late 1929, the industry was forced to conclude that the recruitment of Broadway stars had been no shortcut to box office popularity. In fact, the trade press attributed the sharp decline in film attendance to the predominance of stage names and the premature rejection of screen favorites. A year-end review of film stars concluded that 1929 had discovered "no [new] Jolson to startle the folks nor any other magnetic personality thrown to the fore as a result of unique and extraordinary performance to take the laurels away from film B.O. favorites."[54]

Cantor's next screen vehicle, *Whoopee,* a literal adaptation of his successful Broadway musical comedy, seemed particularly ill-suited to these shifts in audience demand. Disappointed in the reception of *Glorifying the American Girl,* Ziegfeld expressed little desire to work with Paramount a second time, and immediately began scouting for alternative offers. In October 1929, he struck a deal with Sam Goldwyn by which the moviemaker would provide financial backing for several as yet unproduced Ziegfeld shows, including Ed Wynn's *Simple Simon* and Cantor's *Whoopee,* in return for their film rights.[55] Such an arrangement provided Ziegfeld with much-needed capital to keep his theatrical operations afloat in the midst of major revenue losses and guaranteed Goldwyn access to several potentially valuable properties. Their first coproduction, *Whoopee,* would begin filming in May the following year with Ziegfeld playing an active (if unspecified) role behind the camera and most of the original cast, including Cantor, repeating their performances. In true Ziegfeld fashion, the film's production cost eventually exceeded its initially generous $1,500,000 budget and drew trade press attention for its lavish sets and costumes. Chorus girls were dressed in $1,200 dresses for the all Technicolor production numbers (including the much celebrated "Invocation of the Gods" finale staged by young choreographer Busby Berkeley.)[56]

Despite the declining box office returns from musicals, United Artists heavily emphasized *Whoopee*'s stage pedigree in its promotional campaign. Exhibitors were advised, "Here's a genuine $6.60 show. Sell it accordingly."[57] Much was made of the collaboration between Ziegfeld, "the genius of the stage and producer of the Theatre's greatest entertainment" and Goldwyn, "genius of the screen and its most consistent producer of worthwhile box office productions." Cantor, "the most famous of New York's comedians in his first full-length audible picture," was also a major theme in the publicity campaign. Promotional material consistently referred to his previous Broadway experience, often painting him as an "outsider" within Hollywood. A fan magazine interview, "His Pace is His Fortune," focuses on Cantor's

Whoopee (1930): pressbook ad.

"phenomenal" energy level as an exotic contrast to the more relaxed California lifestyle.[58] A *Photoplay* article, "Want to Be Funny?" takes a more playful approach, describing *Whoopee* as "That Ziegfeld Thing that he starred in on Broadway, you recall. Or, do you?"[59]

The question was a valid one. Film patrons, especially outside of the northeast, were often unfamiliar with and resentful of the Broadway stars who displaced their established screen favorites. Ernest Rogers, an Atlanta-based editor of *Photoplay,* warned of the trade press's typical short-sightedness in assuming that "a film which was a smash on Broadway will do the same thing on Peachtree. . . . It just don't work that way. Names like Eddie Cantor, George Jessel, Sophie Tucker *et al.* may mean money when put in front of a Broadway house; but in Atlanta, they've got to sell their stuff or miss the trade."[60]

Whoopee's reception confirmed Roger's reservations. Not surprisingly, the film did smash business in New York City, earning $55,000 at the close of its first week of release and sustaining a first-run play of almost two months. *Whoopee* also set house records in major industrial cities, particularly those with sizable ethnic populations and those along the route for Ziegfeld touring shows. Chicago, however, found the film a "mild success," hurt by "musical's bad reputation locally" and an "agency-planned ad campaign [that was] too high brow" for the area's audiences; this report suggests that the promotional emphasis upon its Broadway predecessor may have backfired in the windy city. In many other areas, such as Indianapolis, Louisville, Seattle, and Tacoma, the film did "disappointing" business, "not up to expectation," often playing normal one-week runs with little interest in holdovers. Consistently, *Variety* reports cited local resistance to Broadway musicals and stage stars as a major factor in the film's failure. In the end, *Whoopee* turned a modest profit based on its strong showings in several northern cities and its mild success elsewhere, but it failed to excite interest in the "sticks" or in regional centers.[61]

"A Happy Melding of Sophistication and Hoke": Genre Shifting, Musical Comedy, and the Regional Audience, 1931

By 1931, the studios were reassessing the generic strategies that had been essential for building an urban audience. Trade press reports suggested two alternative ways of approaching the gap between urban and regional genre preferences. *Variety* reporter Robert Brown called for the production of films with "surefire sectional appeal," particularly slapstick comedy, westerns, sports, war, horror, and other genres with strong regional followings: "Take it any way on Earth, there is probably no one combination that will produce a picture okay in New York, okay in Birmingham, okay in Kansas City and other sections as well."[62] Others called for the end of regionally targeted production and the development of stars and genres with national appeal. Comedy was often cited as a genre that might attract both urban and rural audiences. A 1932 *Variety* article proposed genre-mixing as a strategy for producing texts with broad audience appeal, claiming that the ideal film might be a comically focused musical that provided "a happy melding of sophistication and hoke." [63] This call was widely read as placing a particular premium on comic stars, like Cantor, the Marx Brothers, and Wheeler and Woolsey, who could both clown and perform musical numbers. Yet considerable disagreement surrounded the relative value of story and performance within these films, as illustrated in chapter 5. One *Motion Picture Herald* commentator offered this formula for success: "Always a good story, always romance, always comedy, also some acting," yet this critic insisted that "people do not want a comedian to be the entire show and comedy must be incidental to the general plot and as a relief from the romance or heavier dramatic parts." [64] Others seemed prepared, as we have seen, to dismiss plot in favor of a profusion of diverse entertainment. One critic enthusiastically embraced Wheeler and Woolsey's *Peach O'Reno* (RKO, 1932) for its heterogeneous material: "When a picture is so thoroughly ridiculous that it really becomes funny, then it's time to stand up and shout. . . . Here's one that has a little bit of everything except drama. And, of course, it doesn't need any of that. But you get plenty of laughs, some slapstick, musical numbers, scantly clad girls and a courtroom scene that beggars description." [65] Many of the early successes, such as *Animal Crackers* and *The Cuckoos,* placed heterogeneity over narrative cohesiveness and set the model that subsequent filmmakers would follow; only subsequently did exhibitors become more vocal in asserting their demands for greater emphasis upon story and character.

In marketing *Whoopee,* southern exhibitors backed away from the national advertising campaign's heavy focus on Ziegfeld and the show's Broadway success; instead, they sold the film as a fast-paced comedian comedy, promising "laughs, giggles, gurgles and roars" from the "mirthquake of the century." [66] If the comedy elements in Cantor's films could be expanded without altogether abandoning those components of *Whoopee* that drew urban crowds, Goldwyn might be able to create a formula for national success, a formula that could be marketed as a musical in the urban northeast and as a comedy elsewhere. *Palmy Days,* Cantor's next vehicle, initiated this genre-mixing strategy and its example would be followed by his subsequent vehicles. Goldwyn hired Keystone veteran A. Edward Sutherland to direct and Morrie Ryskind,

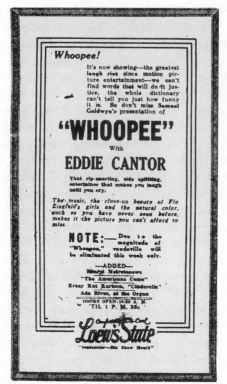

Whoopee (1930): ads from the *New Orleans Picayune* (right) and the *Atlanta Constitution* (left).

who cowrote the Marx Brothers' *Animal Crackers,* to contribute to the script. Studio publicity consistently characterized *Palmy Days* as a "new kind of screen entertainment" that broke with the traditions of the stage musical yet maintained its more desirable qualities; fans were promised "more Eddie Cantor" and "more laughs."[67] Cantor told a *New York Times* interviewer shortly before the film's release, "You may have noticed that . . . the run of the thing is a good deal more like a straight farce than like a stage musical comedy. The music and pretty girls are whipped cream on top instead of the main reason for the show."[68] *Palmy Days* and subsequent Cantor vehicles walked a thin line between the musical and the comic, allowing them to be packaged differently to respond to regional differences in genre preferences.

Like many other musicals of the period, *Whoopee* focused on its romantic comedy plot: A young couple, very much in love, must

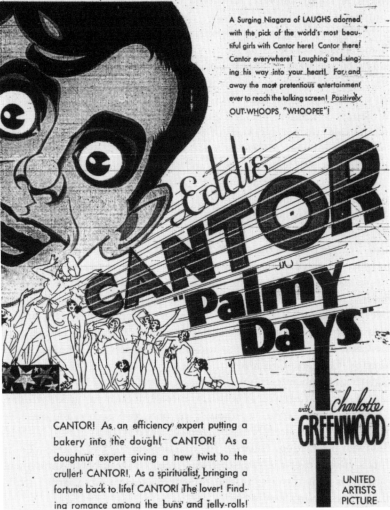

Palmy Days (1931): pressbook ad.

overcome opposition before achieving union. The relationship of the romantic couple is parodied by a second comically constructed couple representing a more plebeian and cynical view of romance. Narrative closure required overturning the obstacles blocking the romantic couple, their happy embrace, and some suggested resolution of the comic couple's relationship. In *Whoopee,* the romantic couple, Wanenis and Sally Morgan, face parental opposition because of their racial difference. Wanenis is a half-breed native American while Sally is a white woman. Sally's engagement to Sheriff Bob Wells threatens to permanently end her romance with Wanenis. Cantor's character, Henry Williams, helps Sally to escape and elude Wells; he eventually reunites the couple. Williams is himself pursued by his nurse, Miss Custer, and their relationship mirrors the twists of the central romance. The finale in the Indian encampment allows for the final defeat of Wells, the revelation of Wanenis's pure white ancestry and the subsequent lifting of the ban on his marriage, the reuniting of the central couple, and Williams's rejection of Miss Custer's advances.

While subsequent Cantor vehicles followed this same basic formula, the emphasis shifted from the romantic couple onto the comic protagonist. In *Palmy Days,* the romance between Steven Clayton (Paul Page) and Joan Clark (Barbara Weeks) is never seriously at risk. The romantic couple has parental approval from the outset, though Eddie Simpson (Eddie Cantor) initially misperceives the situation and believes that Joan loves him instead. The film's action centers around Cantor's encounters with a fake mind reader and his thugs, his efforts to bring efficiency to the Clark bakery, and his romantic entanglements with a health center director (Charlotte Greenwood). Subsequent films paid even less attention to the romantic couple. The lover's quarrel that separates Jerry Lane (George Murphy) and Joan Larrabee (Ann Sothern) in *Kid Millions* (United Artists, 1934) is resolved in only two scenes and has few narrative consequences. *Strike Me Pink* (United Artists, 1936), his final Goldwyn production, collapses the functions of the two couples. Eddie Pink's victory over the gangsters who threaten Dreamland Amusement Park wins him the love of the romantic female lead, Claribel (Sally Ellers) in the film's final scene.

This shift toward greater emphasis upon the comic protagonist was paralleled by a reassignment of musical numbers. *Whoopee* includes several love songs for Wanenis and Sally as well as choral numbers commenting on Sally's impending marriage to Bob Wells. By *Palmy Days,* the majority of songs feature Cantor and are comic in tone.

Subsequent vehicles generally did not devote musical sequences to the romantic couple. An overall reduction of musical production numbers following *Whoopee* was matched by an increased attentiveness to large-scale comic spectacle. *Palmy Days, Kid Millions,* and *Strike Me Pink* end with elaborate chase sequences; *Kid from Spain* (United Artists, 1933) concludes with a bullfight involving Cantor as a comically ill-suited matador; *Roman Scandals* (United Artists, 1933) features a slapstick chariot race; *Ali Baba Goes to Town* (Fox, 1937) involves a flying carpet battle. Such sequences gave exhibitors a high-profile comic sequence to supplant big musical numbers as a focus for their promotional campaigns. The reduction of musical numbers to Cantor's comic patter songs and a few Busby Berkeley productions also signaled a steady movement from the Broadway style of entertainment that made Cantor's reputation. A *Motion Picture Herald* review of *Kid from Spain* emphasized the film's diverse material: "The picture only hazily follows the main plot—with a series of interlude specialties that whirl the story from one sequence to another. . . . You have a girl show, a musical comedy, an enlarged vaudeville show and a bit of thrilling spectacle in the bull-ring."[69] Cantor's vehicles had plots, even classically constructed plots, yet contemporary reviews suggest that these plots hardly mattered; what audiences wanted from a Cantor film was Cantor and more Cantor, Cantor singing, Cantor dancing, Cantor clowning, Cantor romancing.

At the core of this strategy remained the problem of constructing appropriate screen images for stage stars, images that exploited factors appealing to urban theatergoers yet avoided elements alienating to hinterland audiences. Elsewhere, the major studios' decisions to hire Broadway talent on short-term contracts allowed them the flexibility to retreat from their concentration on stage material and to reject theatrical stars who failed to capture film fans' fancies.[70] In one month alone, Fox dropped twenty-two players from its talent lists; almost all of them had been recruited during the initial raids on Broadway. Other studios followed suit. A *Motion Picture Classic* headline colorfully described the situation: "The panic is over; the Broadway hordes are folding their tents and silently stealing away."[71] Goldwyn, however, did not have the option to reject Cantor. Even before *Whoopee's* release, a confident Goldwyn signed a contract with Cantor to produce one film per year for five years, with the star to receive $100,00 per picture and a ten percent share of the profits.[72] If it was to ensure its long-term investment, United Artists needed to oversee Cantor's smooth transition from Broadway celebrity to Hollywood star. Goldwyn was banking on the fact that audiences would be prepared to accept vaudeville-style performances but remained uncomfortable with the sophistication and regional focus of the Ziegfeld tradition. Cantor's image needed to be remade for the movies.

FROM "JEWISH COWBOY" TO "AMERICAN EVERYMAN": *PALMY DAYS* AND THE REMAKING OF EDDIE CANTOR

After more than a decade of performing for Ziegfeld, Eddie Cantor, like many other revue comics, had come to closely identify with his New York audience. Cantor enjoyed the freedom of a more "sophisticated" following; his comedy was sprinkled with cynical remarks about marriage and with eye-rolling double entendres that even hardened local critics sometimes found "too blue" for their tastes. Moreover, Cantor relied heavily upon his Jewishness as an appeal to the city's ethnically diverse theatrical audience. Cantor's 1928 autobiography makes frequent references to his Jewish background, quoting the Talmud on its first page, offering detailed descriptions of Hester Street life and synagogue weddings, recounting crude backstage pranks concerning dietary laws.[73] Such passages suggests how much Cantor's ethnicity was taken for granted as a central component of his public personality.

Glorifying the American Girl treated Cantor's ethnicity as one more exotic aspect of the New York show world. Gloria, the film's protagonist, encounters Cantor backstage as she is preparing to go on for her big number. A sympathetic Cantor acknowledges that he was nervous when he first appeared with Ziegfeld but that "they are a great audience. I've got all my relatives out there and there are a few gentiles, too." Moreover, the producers chose Cantor's Moe the Tailor sketch as one of the highlights of the 1929 *Follies* featured in the film. Cantor, dressed in the bowler and vest of the Jewish stock character, a tape measure draped across his shoulder, tries to help a mousy man find an appropriate suit (fig. 6.3). When the man protests about the price, Cantor tallies his overhead in chalk on the customer's suit. When the man insists on finding a suit with a "belt in the back," the excitable tailor threatens to "belt" him before warning the confused customer, "A suit we're gonna sell you. You wouldn't get out of here without a suit. That you know! That you know!" The poor punter is browbeaten and manhandled until he finally agrees to buy a boy's sailor suit just to escape from the tailor's greedy clutches.

Irving Howe notes how common it was for New York clowns to

"take elements of Jewish self-consciousness and transform—sometimes reduce—them into set-piece jokes and routines" that could attract familiar laughter from fellow Jews and more derisive laughter from gentiles.[74] Following this process, Cantor captures the cadences of Lower East Side shoptalk and peppers his speech with Yiddish phrases, at one point imitating a rabbinical chant as he sings the man's measurements to his partner. His character is excitable to the point of violence, a fast-talking shyster, yet he somehow manages to be a sympathetic character, capable of appealing both to WASP fascination with ghetto exoticism and to upscale Jewish nostalgia for familiar Lower East Side types.

Whoopee also takes Cantor's ethnicity as suitable material for comic exploitation. One pressbook advertisement promised "laughs, giggles, gurgles, roars run riot when Eddie Cantor starts to cut up as a Jewish Indian in the funniest mirthfest ever flashed on the talking screen." Another characterized him as a "Jewish cowboy."[75] Cantor's ethnicity functions more complexly within *Whoopee's* narrative than it does in *Glorifying the American Girl.* Wanenis's racial difference blocks his romance with Sally Morgan. Only at the film's conclusion is it learned that Wanenis, though raised as an Indian, has "pure white blood" and is therefore free to marry Sally. Cantor's character, a New York hypochondriac who has come west for his health, becomes progressively ensnared in the couple's romance, running afoul of Sheriff Bob Wells. To escape, Cantor assumes various disguises, including that of a tough-talking western bandit, a Greek short-order cook, an Indian, and a ɔlackface minstrel.

In a justly famous scene, Cantor, masquerading as an Indian, tries to sell a blanket and doll; he gradually assumes the cadences, accent, language, and gestures of Moe the Tailor: "White man pay'um $40 for two articles. Look, if I sell you for $40, I couldn't make a cent! I should live—it costs me alone thirty-five and a half dollars—so should I sell you for $40? Such chutzpah!" Later in the same scene, Cantor moves gracefully from an Indian war dance into a Jewish folk dance, smiling at the camera and singing "Yiddle-diddle-dee." Such "layering" of performance was characteristic of the vaudeville tradition from which Cantor had emerged, a means of showcasing the virtuosity of the individual comic performer through a complex interweaving of stock characters and dialects. The fluidity with which Cantor assumes and rejects those various ethnic identities undercuts the rigid racial categories and strict boundaries of the romance plot. Cantor's various imper-

Whoopee (1930): Eddie Cantor and Spencer Charters.

sonations make the notion of a fixed racial identity problematic and renders absurd the idea that such an identity might block romantic fulfillment. As Charles Musser writes of the film, "*Whoopee* is an affirmation of diversity and its vicissitudes, a celebration of the dialogic imagination and a burlesque of ethnic and sexual stasis. In short, it embraces the life-generating forces in New York's cosmopolitan culture."[76]

Similarly, his verbal humor contests the heightened emotions and ideological assumptions behind *Whoopee*'s hackneyed story. At one point, he tells an incredulous Wanenis, distraught over the racial difference that blocks the path of true love, that he is also a "half-breed." He adds with appropriate nasal emphasis, "Sure, I breed through one side of my nose. Sinus." When the Indian youth protests that he has some white blood since his grandfather married a white woman, Cantor shrugs and says, "So did mine. What of that?" And, in perhaps the best comic exchange in the film, Wanenis recounts his futile attempts to assimilate into white society: "For this girl that I love, I've studied the ways of your race! Why, I've gone to your schools!" Cantor, with a sudden burst of enthusiasm, claps the Indian on the shoulders and exclaims, "An

Indian in Hebrew school—imagine that!," then adds as an puzzled afterthought, "How did you get along?" In each case, the gags question the meaningfulness of the ethnic and racial categories that structure the film's romantic plot. Cantor's refusal to recognize those boundaries, his play with identity, consistently interfere with the conventional narrative that gives the film its shape and coherence.

Mary Douglas has suggested that jokes work by inserting into popular discourse unstated beliefs and attitudes, repressed desires, unspeakable tensions, social instabilities that otherwise would be denied expression, although these counterdiscourses gain exposure at the expense of no longer being taken seriously. The radical force of jokes is still potentially great since jokes challenge the ability of cultural institutions to naturalize their meanings, questioning the reception community's "common sense" understandings. Nevertheless, these jokes must be somewhat consensual, if they are to be recognized as jokes by their audience. To produce the desired effect of laughter rather than the undesired effect of outrage or shock, the joke must build upon existing though unstated concerns and speak to issues already of vital interest. Jokes, then, are built around potential inversions of the social structure, pushing against the cutting edge of community taste, yet ultimately restrained by the norms of the group they hope to amuse.[77]

While the question of ethnic identity was a central concern of urban immigrant audiences and thus a prime field for the construction of jokes aimed at that group, it did not prove amusing in the hinterlands, which either found the issue irrelevant or threatening.[78] For those viewers, Cantor's Jewishness remained what Douglas calls a "submerged joke," a joke that goes "unperceived" because it lacks congruence with prevailing social thought. Few regional spectators could be expected to understand Yiddish or know enough about Jewish culture to appreciate such gags. Moreover, racial intolerance and anti-Semitism had increased dramatically throughout the 1920s, sparking a revival of the Ku Klux Klan, the imposition of new immigration quotas, and physical assaults against minorities.[79] This chilling climate encouraged a process Irving Howe calls *de-Semitization,* a rejection of the traditional marks of Jewishness, a strenuous effort at cultural assimilation, among performers appearing outside of the safe confines of Broadway.[80] While the success of *The Jazz Singer* may have suggested that movie audiences would accept representations of Jewish culture, the reception of other early talkies soon punctured that illusion. *Variety* cited Fanny Brice's "Hebrew jesting" as a major factor in aborting her much-publicized screen career.[81] United Artists, who had gone to court to break its contract with this problematic star, was reluctant to repeat the experiment with Cantor and pushed him toward de-Semitization.

Publicity for *Palmy Days* shifted attention from Cantor's Jewishness. Although much is made of his rise to stardom from an impoverished childhood on the streets of New York, no mention is made of specific neighborhoods that might bear ethnic connotations, and Cantor is described in several studio biographies as coming from a "Russian background."[82] Though it had appeared in his *Whoopee* publicity, a joke about Cantor having won a ham as a prize in an amateur night contest was scratched from early drafts of his *Palmy Days* pressbook profile.[83] The star, who spent his childhood living over a Hester Street delicatessen, even endorsed Wonderbread in a tie-in campaign emphasizing *Palmy Days'* bakery setting.[84] Cantor's Jewishness was something that could no longer be taken for granted or even directly mentioned in promoting his films.

Palmy Days also avoids any overt references to Cantor's Jewishness while allowing ample opportunities for the comic to display his valued skills as an impersonator of ethnic types. *Palmy Days* featured Cantor in blackface singing a minstrel number, in drag escaping from the gangsters into a woman's dressing room, and as a French psychic outsmarting a rival fortune-teller. Unlike *Whoopee,* Cantor's Jewishness does not intrude into these performances and does not provide the base level of his identity. Here, the character breaks into song whenever he gets nervous, a trait that substitutes for the disruptiveness of Cantor's Yiddish outbursts in the previous film. A similar pattern occurs in subsequent Cantor vehicles. Though these later impersonations may take wildly improbable forms (an appearance as a shuffling, thick-tongued "Ethiopian beauty specialist" at the ancient baths in *Roman Scandals,* for example), they do not directly challenge the film's thematic organization, as they did in *Whoopee,* nor do they require audiences to acknowledge that Jewishness is central to the performer's identity. Ethnicity exists as a form of eccentricity in these later films, a mask to be assumed rather than an identity to be maintained. In fact, Cantor only make one direct reference to his ethnicity in the five Goldwyn-United Artist releases that followed *Whoopee.* There, he identifies himself as "Russian," not Jewish. In *Roman Scandals,* Cantor is captured by the Roman centurions and placed on sale at a slave market. Always the shrewd merchant, Cantor pitches himself to potential buyers, "Look at these skins, imported—all the way from Russia!"

Palmy Days (1931): Eddie Cantor endorses Wonderbread. Wisconsin Center for Film and Theater Research.

Palmy Days (1931): Eddie Cantor in drag (top) and as a French psychic (bottom). Academy of Motion Picture Arts and Sciences.

Whoopee played on the paradox of the "Jewish cowboy," suggesting a clash between two different cultural systems within a single character; much of its humor built on the discomfort of Cantor's positioning within his narrative role. These feelings of dislocation, these anachronisms and comically inappropriate responses to generic situations remained core to Cantor's screen vehicles, though they were stripped of their roots in ethnic difference. Instead, the later films provide various other narrative motivations for Cantor's "otherness." In both *Palmy Days* and *Strike Me Pink*, Cantor is a jack-of-all-trades suddenly placed in charge of a substantial business. In *Kid from Spain*, he is an American who must pass for a famous Spanish bullfighter when gangsters force him across the Mexican border. In *Roman Scandals*, he is a citizen of the contemporary American town of West Rome who finds himself inexplicably transported back to Ancient Rome. Similarly, in *Ala Baba Goes to Town*, he is a movie extra who awakens to find himself in the realm of the Arabian knights. *Kid Millions* removes him from poverty in Brooklyn and into an Egyptian adventure, when it is discovered that he is the only legitimate heir to a much-sought fortune. Unlike the Jewish Indian in *Whoopee*, these later character dislocations actually make Cantor more like the hinterland spectators; they open him to closer identification from predominantly gentile audiences. After *Whoopee*, Cantor's vehicles explore the prospect of a "normal" person being transplanted from an "everyday" world into a more exotic realm. Samuel Shayon, who contributed to the script of *Roman Scandals*, characterized the Cantor persona as "a simple, honest, naive character, an American everyman."[85]

Frequently, the films adopt additional strategies that deny or shift attention from the question of Cantor's ethnicity. In *Kid Millions*, for example, Cantor is shown at home with his very Irish family, including Edgar Kennedy as his bullish stepbrother. *Kid from Spain, Kid Millions,* and *Strike Me Pink* cast Cantor against eccentric ethnic types (Lyda Roberti, Eve Sully, and Parkyakarkus respectively) for dialect comedy sequences that depend upon a sharp contrast between Cantor's bland "normality" and their colorful ethnicity.

This de-Semitization campaign, linked with the shift in generic placement, proved successful in broadening Cantor's base of support beyond the ethnic enclaves of the major east coast cities. While they were slow in labeling the shifts in his character, regional newspapers clearly acknowledged and approved of a difference in Cantor's screen vehicles. A Providence *Journal* review reported, "A new screen star was

Kid Millions (1934): Eddie Cantor in Brooklyn (top) and in Egypt (bottom). Academy of Motion Picture Arts and Sciences.

6.1 - 6.2 *Glorifying the American Girl* (1929): from the *Ziegfeld Follies* sequence.

6.3   *Glorifying the American Girl* (1929): Eddie Cantor as Moe the Tailor.

7.1   *Half Shot at Sunrise* (1930): Dorothy Lee and Bert Wheeler.

7.2 - 7.3 *Diplomaniacs* (1933): the Paris hotel sequence.

7.4   *Diplomaniacs* (1933): The Dead Rat Café.

7.5 *Diplomaniacs* (1933): "Fifi Was My Mother's Name!" (Hugh Herbert).

7.6 *Diplomaniacs* (1933): centering the performance.

8.1 - 8.8 *Hips, Hips, Hooray* (1934):
the anarchistic sequence.

8.9   *Duck Soup* (1933): Margaret Dumont and Groucho Marx.

8.10   *50 Million Frenchmen* (1930): Ole Olsen and Chic Johnson.

8.11 *International House* (1933): W. C. Fields annoys Franklin Pangborn.

8.12 *Hold 'Em Jail* (1932): Bert Wheeler and Robert Woolsey harass
Edgar Kennedy.

9.1 *So Long Letty* (1929): Charlotte Greenwood and Claude Gillingwater.

9.2 *Side Show* (1931): "Lady Beautiful."

9.3 *Side Show* (1931): Charles Butterworth and Winnie Lightner.

9.4 *Side Show* (1931): Winnie Lightner as Princess Mauna Kane.

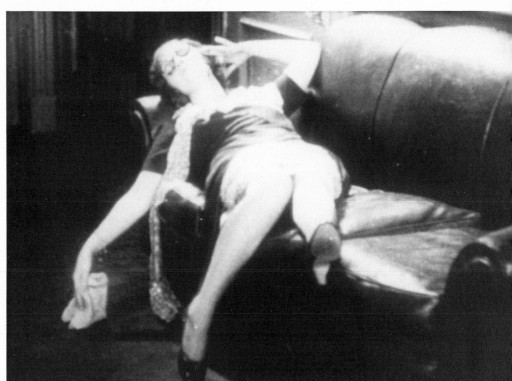

9.5 - 9.6 *Gold Dust Gertie* (1930): womanly masquerade.

9.7 *Life of the Party* (1930): "Poison Ivy."

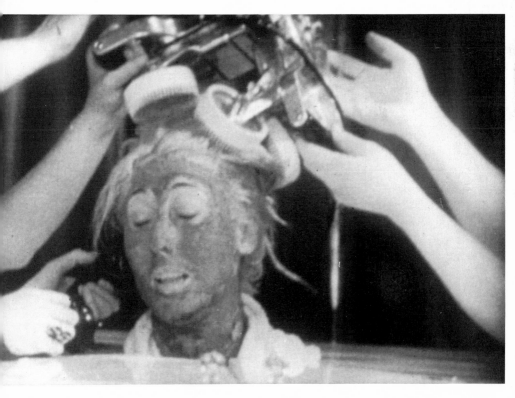

9.8 *So Long Letty* (1929).

9.9 *So Long Letty* (1929):
Charlotte Greenwood.

9.10 *So Long Letty* (1929)
"Clowning."

9.11 *So Long Letty* (1929):
"So Long Letty."

brought in with *Palmy Days.* It is Eddie Cantor. True, he has been with us, photographically, several times in the past. This is the first time, however, that he has been funny. This is the first time he has had a screen personality that jelled."[86] New York critics also noted a marked difference in Cantor's comedy, though they were generally disappointed by it. *Variety* wrote, "It's not a continuous laugh for the steady theater-goer but most of the gags will find the laughs they are after from those who pay to be entertained. That's the kind of picture it is all the way."[87] The New York *Times* suggested that "the wit may not be as nimble as Mr. Cantor's image" but the film would prove especially popular with children and more rural audiences.[88] Cantor himself explained to the audience at the film's New York opening, "I hope you like *Palmy Days,* but it wasn't made for you. It was made for the masses."

This perception of a "new" Eddie Cantor translated into a different pattern of box office returns. *Palmy Days* did strong business in those areas that had lacked enthusiasm for its predecessor.[89] Birmingham went for Cantor "in a big way," Columbus scored a "smash" hit, and returns were "excellent" in places like Kansas City, Providence, Denver, and Minneapolis, justifying holdovers throughout the south and the midwest. *Palmy Days'* box office returns in the industrial north was "lukewarm," and ticket sales in Manhattan, Baltimore, Los Angeles, and Pittsburgh sank below *Whoopee's* records. With each subsequent Cantor vehicle, the pattern was repeated. Hinterland engagements increasingly became the staple market for his comedies while his New York and major Eastern city runs became progressively shorter.[90]

The broadening of Cantor's appeal into the American heartland had been a calculated risk, one that greatly increased his earning power for United Artists. Yet the studio was reluctant to alienate his initial ethnic following and efforts were made, following the successful release of *Palmy Days,* to rebuild his support in the Jewish community. United Artists produced a steady stream of press releases specially targeted to the Yiddish press, publications inaccessible to gentile America, that emphasized his support for Jewish charities, his involvement with a summer camp for economically deprived east side youths, and even his early opposition to Nazism.[91]

The reading of Cantor's ethnicity prompted by these publicity materials was facilitated by subtle textual traces of his Jewishness, all but invisible to regional viewers yet potentially meaningful to minority audiences. These traces can be located in character names (Simpson,

Pink, etc.) that often sound like Americanized versions of traditional Jewish family names; they also surface in individual gags, such as a moment in *Kid Millions* where Cantor, held captive by an Arab sheik, begs, "Let my people go!" Here, however, the reference to Moses is quickly recuperated when Cantor and all of the other characters (including a Southern colonel) burst into a minstrel song about Moses' flight from Egypt. A similar moment occurs in *Ali Baba Goes To Town,* when Cantor speaks Yiddish as part of an ongoing search for an appropriate means of communication with a group of black slaves. For a Jewish audience, this moment would no doubt attract considerable attention and interest, while for a non-Jewish audience, the Yiddish passage might blend into other short bits of Spanish, French, German, and Russian, as he tries a number of different languages to see which provoke a response. In fact, the context—using a foreign language to speak to a group of racial others—might actually distance Cantor from any close identification with Yiddish. This masked address to the Jewish viewer is strikingly different from the ways Cantor had actively played to this same audience in his initial film appearances. Traces of his ethnicity remain but they could be read only by those who knew how to look for them and desired to find them.

Richard Dyer has argued that star images are "structured polysemies" that embody multiple, and often, contradictory meanings producers can manipulate in the construction and promotion of film texts.[92] At a time when the marketing of films was still largely controlled by local exhibitors rather than nationally standardized, this polysemic potential could be used to make specialized appeals to more limited audiences, such as United Artists' Yiddish press campaign, without substantially altering a star's national image. Through such strategies, Cantor's screen persona could be at once Jewish and non-Jewish depending upon the desired audience. The polysemic construction of his screen image allowed him to negotiate between the conflicting demands of urban and rural viewers in building a broad national audience for his screen vehicles.

The de-Semitization of Eddie Cantor was simply one aspect of a complex process by which stage stars were repackaged in order to appeal to a broader national audience. Depression era America was still polarized around regional and ethnic differences and still distrustful of the increasingly important place of the city within its culture. Shifts in studio policies for building and maintaining an audience for talking pictures led to a sudden change in the films' orientation. Star images that had proved popular with northern audiences were potentially alien to filmgoers in the south or the midwest and needed to be "normalized" in order to allow for interpretations more compatible with the interests and desires of those potential audiences. Jokes that were vitally connected with the experiences of urban viewers were either too obscure or too painful to be accepted by regional spectators.

For Cantor, this normalization involved a de-Semitization, the removal of all overt acknowledgement of his ethnic identity, and the development of a new image as an American everyman. Charles Musser similarly argues that the Marx Brothers' abandonment of their ethnic roots and the resulting "weakening of comic aggression" tamed their comedy and undercut its particular appeals to a cosmopolitan audience.[93] For other stars, normalization took other forms. Markers of ethnic, class, regional, or gender difference were effaced to allow for a more "mainstream" construction of the stars image. Joe E. Brown became successful in rural areas only after his initial image as a effeminate urban playboy was replaced by that of a athletic small-town boy, a persona more compatible with the taste and interests of regional audiences. The sexual aggressiveness of female comedy stars like Winnie Lightner and Charlotte Greenwood needed to be muted and counterbalanced by casting them against equally aggressive male stars. The suggestive dialogue of Olsen and Johnson met the censor's blue pencil. Where this repositioning was not possible (as in the case of Fanny Brice) or was unsuccessful (as with Winnie Lightner or Olsen and Johnson), stars were rejected by Hollywood and forced to try to regain a place on the stage.

While Hampton and other early commentators drew a rigid separation between "film folk" and "their brethren of the footlights," stage stars survived in Hollywood only by becoming film folk themselves. Though effective in the short-term in attracting a sizable urban base for the talkies, these star recruitment efforts ran counter to the tastes of the regional patrons needed to broaden that initial base into a national film audience. In the long run, stage recruits did not so much transform the Hollywood star system as become absorbed in its formal and ideological norms. They did not so much create an audience more receptive to New York-style entertainment as adopt star images that held national appeal.

These shifts in star images were accompanied by shifts in generic placement and narrative construction, as techniques and plots derived from theatrical traditions were absorbed into the classical Hollywood cinema. Cantor weathered the transformation with relative ease, since the formula associated with his stage success relied heavily upon theatrical farce traditions that had already become part of the accepted conventions of the classical silent comedian comedies. Cantor's later films bear a distinct resemblance to the comedies of Harold Lloyd and, to a lesser extent, Buster Keaton. Cantor's move from comic *musicals* to musical *comedies* involved a replacement of musical number with comic spectacle without a radical change in the logic of the story construction. Consequently, Cantor's comic vehicles look and feel like classical films in a way that those of many other early sound comedian comedies do not.

The push to broaden the audience for New York entertainers, how-ever, did not always result in a closer assimilation to classical narrative conventions. What the regional audience rejected was not fragmentation but "sophistication," not broad slapstick but ethnic in-jokes, not class antagonisms or sexual suggestiveness but direct appeals to specialized knowledges. In many cases, the demand for a heterogeneous address to a heterogeneous audience led to increasingly fragmented and often incoherent narrative construction; its immediate effect was often to expand rather than reduce the gap between the vaudeville aesthetic and the classical Hollywood norms. The "hicks" and their demand for "hoke," to use *Variety*'s slang, embraced rather than rejected many aspects of the vaudeville aesthetic, particularly its broad physical com-edy and its colorful performances. The strength of variety entertainment was its ability to appeal to a diversely constituted audience, to provide something for everyone, and to move quickly enough so that nobody could remain bored for long. The shifting composition of the early sound audience encouraged Hollywood to experiment with aspects of this tradition, yet its experiments did not necessarily ensure critical or commercial success. The challenge to produce a form of entertainment that mated the diversity and affective intensity of the variety stage with the coherence and clarity of the classical narrative often proved too difficult to be easily resolved.

7

"*Fifi Was My Mother's Name!*" *Anarchistic Comedy, the Vaudeville Aesthetic, and* Diplomaniacs

Written by Joseph Mankiewicz and Henry Myers as a follow-up to *Million Dollar Legs,* directed by William A. Seiter who was one of the top comedy talents of the period, starring Bert Wheeler and Robert Woolsey at the peak of their career, *Diplomaniacs* (RKO, 1933) is a textbook example of anarchistic comedy and embodies both the strengths and weakness of the genre. *Diplomaniacs* was one of a small but significant cycle of early 1930s films that use a political setting as a backdrop for their star comedian's gags and performances; it is closely linked historically with *Million Dollar Legs, Cracked Nuts, Phantom President,* and *Stand Up and Cheer.* Earlier accounts have read the more notable films in this cycle as political satires, as comedies reflecting radical discontent with the political establishment.[1] No doubt, this cycle of films can be read in relationship to the heated campaign between Herbert Hoover and Franklin Roosevelt and to the advent of the New Deal, political developments that dominated newspaper headlines during those years. This topicality, however, was simply one audience appeal among many within a polysemous text designed to attract many different types of spectators—children as well as adults, city dwellers as well as rural and small-town residents, women as well as men, working-class as well as middle-class viewers, etc.—and we probably should not privilege it in our interpretation of such multivalent works.

Of course, these films contain some elements of political satire. *Diplomaniacs* references German munitions manufacturers and their attempts to block any meaningful effort toward world peace; *Duck Soup* points toward the futility of war and the relationship between economic wealth and political influence; *Phantom President* suggested the degree to which showmanship substituted for substance in American politics; *Million Dollar Legs* ridiculed American foreign aid grants. These concerns are not a trivial aspects of the films' interest. Yet content does not give rise to form here. The films' topical content was submitted to the same aesthetic logic that governed the production of all comedian comedies and took its characteristic shape because this particular conception of the political order best served the formal requirements of the genre and best met audience expectations. Politics is read here through the larger thematic of individual license and social restraint, themes that will be discussed more fully in chapter 8. As Groucho Marx would explain in relation to *Duck Soup,* "We were trying to be funny, but we didn't know we were satirizing the current conditions. It came as a great surprise to us."[2] Screenwriter Arthur Sheekman offered a similar explanation: "Comedy is best when you upset stuffy people or notions, but that doesn't mean that you start out with social criticism."[3] The immediate political content of these films can be as readily understood as a response to the popularity of Lubitsch's operetta films as to any real world political crisis; the political context is finally less important as an explanation for the film's general tone and structure than the larger comic logic by which that content was transformed into suitable material for comic performers.

Unlike later writers, contemporary critics paid little attention to the films' ideological content, regarding them primarily as conventional vehicles for their star comedians and judging them according to how well they conformed to the aesthetic demands of that generic tradition. For example, a *Motion Picture Herald* critic noted the "timeliness" of *Phantom President* but treated its satirical aspects as another audience appeal in a film that promised "the farcical comedy of an old-time burlesque show, some of the thrills of a circus, and a lot of that surprise that seemed to pass out of existence with the deaths of the old fashioned carnival and medicine show."[4] This same publication ignored *Diplomaniacs'* political content, describing the film as "a Wheeler and Woolsey musical comedy, put together in the manner of a farcical burlesque show . . . a nutty comedy, a ridiculous farce . . . entertainment for youngsters as well as adults"; its critic characterized the film's leading characters as "a pair of innocent blunderers," seeing them as falling within stock comic roles.[5] *Variety* took a more negative view of the comedy, but still ignored *Diplomaniacs'* topicality: "These boys are practically tossed in a tank and told to give themselves their own swimming lessons. . . . Everything's in but the horn tooting."[6]

These references to earlier show business traditions are yet another reminder of the importance of the vaudeville aesthetic in determining the style and content of these films as well as providing the terms within which were often understood by contemporary observers. This chapter provides a close analysis of the formal structure of *Diplomaniacs,* looking at the Wheeler and Woolsey vehicle as a representative of the broader anarchistic comedy tradition. *Diplomaniacs,* like other anarchistic comedies, systematically subordinates narrative, visual style, and characterization to the desire to showcase performance virtuosity. A close analysis of this film may suggest some of the ways that anarchistic comedy reflects tensions between the classical cinema's emphasis on storytelling and the vaudeville aesthetic's emphasis upon showmanship.

NARRATIVE STRUCTURE

Like many of Wheeler and Woolsey's other films, *Diplomaniacs* positions individual comic sequences within a larger narrative structure, characterized by two distinct lines of development: an intrigue plot and a romance plot. *Diplomaniacs'* dominant plot line concerns the two clowns' efforts to promote the Oopadoop Indians' peace initiative in the face of opposition from munitions merchant Winkelreid and his associates. This plot borrows heavily from their previous vehicles. Some of the team's comedies are structured around a series of confrontations between the anarchic clowns and some controlling agent, such as the army officers in *Half Shot at Sunrise,* the warden in *Hold 'Em Jail* (RKO, 1932), or the landowner in *Cockeyed Cavaliers.* More frequently, the clowns help some failing enterprise, employing their disruptive behavior to foil the film's self-interested antagonists. The boys work to create business for Dorothy Lee's ramshackle hotel in *Hook, Line and Sinker,* save a poor woman's drugstore in *Caught Plastered* (RKO, 1931), back a dude ranch in *Girl Crazy* (RKO, 1932), promote a cosmetics company in *Hips, Hips, Hooray* (RKO, 1934), help a young boy claim his inheritance in *Kentucky Kernels* (RKO, 1934), and bring water to a drought-stricken town in *The Rainmakers* (RKO, 1935). Though perhaps more exotic than these other tasks, their mission in *Diplomaniacs*— to promote the interests of a disenfranchised Indian tribe at the Geneva

Peace Conference—provides a similar focus for the central clowns' antics and justifies a general movement from the pursuit of individual pleasure toward a commitment to public service.

In each case, the threat to the protagonists comes from a corrupt attorney or a double-dealing business manager who places his own interests above his clients' and promotes their hardships to further his own ends. Ma's attorney and advisor in *Caught Plastered* wants to repossess the drug store to facilitate a crooked real estate scheme; Beauchamp, the business manager of Maiden America Beauty Products in *Hips, Hips, Hooray,* receives payment from a rival firm and tries to ruin his own company; John Blackwell, the Marshs trusted family retainer, in *Hook, Line and Sinker,* plans to marry the widowed Mrs. Marsh and gain control over her fortune, he also helps the gangsters steal her jewels. Winkelreid (Louis Calhern), the sinister representative of the High Explosive Bullet Company, in *Diplomaniacs,* follows in this same tradition. Like the other characters, his respectability masks corruption, though Calhern brings to the role a degree of comic exaggeration lacking in similar figures elsewhere.

In *Diplomaniacs,* a series of comic reversals propel two ill-fated barbers, Willie Nillie (Bert Wheeler) and Hercules Glubb (Robert Woolsey), headlong into the realm of foreign intrigue. Their barbershop initially exists outside of temporality, a static space where nothing ever happens. Hercules had instructed his partner to find them a place where there would be "no competitors," but the instruction was misunderstood and they opened a shop that would have "no customers." As the barbershop sequence begins, the two barbers sit in a vacant shop, one combing his own hair, the other manicuring his own fingers, with no prospect of any change in their current situation. The appearance of their first customer, Luke the Hermit, raises the possibility of narrative development. Like the barbers themselves, Luke has existed in stasis, refusing to shave or take any other action until, in an odd gender reversal, his wife returns from the Foreign Legion. Her return motivates Luke to shave and the barbershop springs to life as Willie and Hercules scurry to satisfy their one customer's demands. A group of Indians arrive looking for dandruff relief for their itchy scalps and soon the once empty barbershop overflows with customers. The tribesmen, overhearing the barbers offering their unsolicited opinions on the world situation, decide that they have expertise on foreign affairs and kidnap them, removing them from the world where nothing ever happens into the sphere of story action.

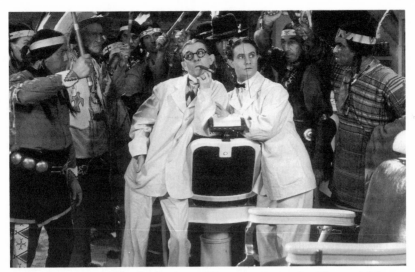

Diplomaniacs (1933): The barbershop. Wisconsin Center for Film and Theater Research.

The film's second scene, set in the Indian encampment, defines the characters' goals. The chief offers them a million dollars, which they accept, only to be told that the funds are expense money they are to use in seeking a peace treaty in Geneva: "If you convince the nations of the world to sign a peace pact, there is another million a piece in it for you. But, if you fail. . . " The boys are shown a gorilla, who the chief claims was once the "most beautiful woman in Paris," and warned that a similar fate awaits them if their mission is unsuccessful.

The following scene, set in a state-room on the USS *Periwinkle,* establishes the conditions that threaten to block the completion of their mission. Winkelreid (Louis Calhern), the sinister representative of the High Explosive Bullet Company, must foil their peace initiative or his munitions company will go bankrupt. He hires first an oriental henchman, Chow Chow (Hugh Herbert), and then a vamp, Dolores (Marjorie White), to assist him in obstructing the barbers' plans: "There are two things that we must get away from them—one is the money for their expenses and the other's a briefcase containing their instructions."

The rest of the narrative evolves from this basic conflict; each scene involves an unsuccessful attempt to stop the barbers' peace mission. Winkelreid sends Dolores to seduce Willie and thus gain the diplomatic papers but instead, one scene later, she falls in love with him. Winkelreid hires a nightclub proprietress, Fifi (Phyllis Barry), to lure the boys to their doom at the Dead Rat Café; she visits them in their hotel room and delivers them into the arms of the waiting thugs, only to have misgivings and to assist them to escape again. Winkelreid and his associates overhear the barbers in the park composing the peace treaty and again, scheme to block its ratification. Winkelreid hires a thug to attack the boys with a battle ax but he is struck from behind by a flying arrow and fails to complete this mission. Fifi tries to kiss Hercules to death, but swoons in a cloud of smoke beneath his passionate embrace instead. Winkelreid tosses a bomb into the assembly hall, and far from killing the delegates, it turns them into a minstrel chorus, united in a song of world peace. Winkelreid forges the signatures on the peace treaty and the barbers, accepting it as a successful completion of their mission, return home, expecting a hero's welcome.

The film's conclusion resolves this plot line through a pair of comic reversals: having failed to destroy the peace conference with a bomb, Winkelreid and associates accidentally drop one of their highly explosive bullets, blowing themselves to smithereens. They reappear in the film's tag as angels, sitting in the clouds and stroking harps. Instead of promoting world peace, the diplomats bring about global conflict, and their tickertape parade turns into a line of soldiers marching off to war.

Like many of the clowns' other vehicles, the central plot is linked to a fairly conventional romance plot in which a young couple unites in the face of parental or social opposition. The duality of the comic team typically requires a doubling of this plot, with the film's resolution involving the formation of two couples. In *Hook, Line and Sinker,* Woolsey helps to overcome parental objections to Bert Wheeler's romancing of Dorothy Lee by marrying the young girl's bullish mother and thus assuming the role of her father; Woolsey then grants permission for his friend's marriage. In *Peach O'Reno,* Wheeler and Woolsey meet the two Bruno sisters, Prudence (Dorothy Lee) and Pansy (Zelma O'Neal), in the course of handling their parents' divorce. The film's final courtroom scene requires the attorneys to reunite their clients and thereby, gain their permission to marry their two daughters. A jazz number in the film's closing moments marks the remarriage of the elder Brunos and the marriage of their two daughters. In *Half Shot at Sunrise,* the boys blackmail a stuffy colonel into giving consent to Wheeler's marriage to his sixteen-year-old daughter (Dorothy Lee), Woolsey's marriage to his longtime mistress (Leni Stengel), and a second daughter's marriage to her beaux who is a war hero. The standard Wheeler and

Diplomaniacs (1933): The Paris hotel. Wisconsin Center for Film and Theater Research.

Woolsey plot pairs Wheeler with a perky, playful, but sexually naive blonde, almost always played by Dorothy Lee (fig. 7.1), and Woolsey either with a sexually aggressive and more mature woman (Leni Stengel in *Half Shot at Sunrise* and *Cracked Nuts*, Raquel Torres in *So This Is Africa*, Thelma Todd in *Hips, Hips, Hooray* and *Cockeyed Cavaliers*) or a threateningly maternal figure (Edna May Oliver in *Hold 'Em Jail*, Jobyana Howland in *Hook, Line and Sinker*). One couple suggests the playful aspects of youthful romance, while the other hints at the repressive qualities of mature marriage. Carlotta (Leni Stengel) tells Woolsey in *Cracked Nuts* that "love is intoxication," to which the cynic responds, "Yeah, and marriage is the hangover." The formula for their vehicles allows Wheeler to experience the "intoxication" and Woolsey to suffer the "hangover."

Diplomaniacs pays little attention to this romantic plot and the relationships are developed in a fairly haphazard fashion. Dolores (Marjorie White) is introduced, meets Willie, and romances him in the moonlight all in the course of three consecutive scenes. Fifi (Phyllis Barry) is introduced, visits Hercules at the hotel and invites him back to the Dead Rat Café; she confesses her love for him in the very next scene, saving him from the trap that she herself has set, only to smash the two clowns' heads together at the end of the sequence and storm away.

Again, all of these shifts in character relationships occupy merely three scenes. In both cases, the women are aligned with Winkelreid's sinister scheme to block the peace proposal and are hired precisely because they are heartless seductresses. Immediately, however, they fall for their intended prey and their allegiances become unstable, shifting back and forth throughout the rest of the film between helping Winkelreid trap the boys and helping them escape again. A few scenes later, the two women help scheme against Willie and Hercules; Fifi tries to kiss Hercules to death on the steps of the assembly hall, only to melt in his arms. The two women watch the peace conference from the gallery and later join in the minstrel number. The women, now dressed as Indian squaws, watch from the sidelines as their men march off to war. While a future romantic commitment is clearly suggested by their costume and behavior during this final scene as well as by conventional representations of troops marching to war, no explicit references are made to this relationship in the dialogue and we never see the women physically united with their would-be lovers.

NARRATIVE DISRUPTION

This account, however, exaggerates the degree of causal integration within the film; *Diplomaniacs* systematically dismantles the causal logic that structures it. The film's "goal-centered protagonists" never complete a meaningful plot action; they are acted upon by outside agents: Winkelreid, the women, the conference delegates. Beginning with their kidnapping in the first scene, they are drawn passively into dangerous situations and then escape without harm, often failing even to recognize the existence of a threat to their lives, as when an unnoticed assailant is struck by a flying arrow from an unidentified source. Indeed, throughout most of the film, they seek a way to abandon their mission and enjoy their newfound wealth, only to be drawn back into the story either by another of Winkelreid's attacks or by a threatening message from the Indians. In the end, the peace treaty is removed from Willie's pocket and handed to them signed not as a result of their performance at the conference (which remains purely a performance), but as a consequence of Winkelreid's final scheme. They do not defeat the antagonists; the villains simply blow themselves up. In those scenes dominated by Wheeler and Woolsey, such as the Paris hotel room sequence or most of the peace conference sequence, plot development is abandoned almost entirely with screen time devoted to the pair's comic performances.

Other elements are similarly emptied of their story significance. Much is made early in the film about the Indians' threat that the barbers will be changed into a gorilla should their mission fail; aside for a few joking references, however, this threat is totally forgotten later in the film, and the only consequence befalling them upon the unsuccessful completion of their peace initiative is that they are drafted. The stateroom sequence establishes the villain's two goals: possession of the diplomatic instructions and the expense money. The boys accidentally discard the papers in a moment of inconsequential slapstick in the very next scene; the papers fall out of the briefcase, which Willie holds upside down, as they enter the ship's dining room. Nevertheless, in subsequent scenes, the characters struggle for possession of the empty briefcase. Similarly, Winkelreid steals the expense money from a drunken Hercules Glubb, only to tear it to bits as so much meaningless paper. The pursuit of the papers and expense money assumes an importance quite apart from the value of the materials sought, which are finally empty markers to be won and lost like the playing pieces of a child's board game.

This same play with causality recurs throughout the film. Willie carefully packs a bag of sandwiches from the ship's dining room, only to casually toss them overboard while romancing Dolores on the moonlit deck in the following scene. Dolores chases Willie around the Paris hotel room but soon loses sight of her objective as first Hercules and then Fifi join into the chase; the four romp around in a circle, taking turns passing each other. A sequence involving a drunken ship's captain who sends the characters spinning aimlessly around the world for ninety days is a blocking mechanism that blocks nothing. The film has set no important deadlines that might be jeopardized by such a delay; the sequence creates no suspense and has no plot consequences, serving only as a transitory gag.

Events introduced in each scene are generally resolved in the course of that or the following scene, prohibiting the braiding of cause and effect typical of the classical Hollywood narrative. The result is a highly episodic structure. The chief's instructions to the two barbers and Winkelreid's state-room scheming establish almost all of the elements of this relatively complex plot. The need for exposition resurfaces when Winkelreid meets with Fifi at the Dead Rat and in the Swiss Park, where the villains overhear Willie and Hercules composing a peace treaty. These moments offer highly compressed chunks of exposition and contrast sharply with the rest of the film, which displays an almost total indifference to the plot developments; the bulk of each sequence is given over to essentially independent units of performance spectacle, leaving one with an overall impression of narrative fragmentation rather than causal integration.

Any given scene's duration is determined less by the amount of plot information it provides than by the amount of funny lines and comic business that can be exploited. The Paris hotel scene, among the film's longest sequences, is particularly bare of plot consequences: the boys awaken in bed together, get dressed, and are met by Dolores and Fifi, who invite them to join them at the Dead Rat Café. The sequence's place within the plot is justified purely by the need to attract Willie and Hercules to the trap that awaits them at the Dead Rat; this function is introduced and satisfied only in its final few seconds. Instead, the film's causal progression stops dead to allow Wheeler and Woolsey to engage in an extended homoerotic parody of the screen operettas of Ernst Lubitsch and Rouben Mamoulian. Their butler minces and lisps, curtsying and announcing that his name is "Marie"; he discusses their hangovers in blank verse and rhapsodizes about "dawn over Paris," his speech punctuated with both music and sound effects. As he prances away, the two men, still in bed together, press their heads cheek to cheek and do a double take, accompanied by Woolsey's characteristic "whoa" and a flick of his cigar. The clowns' responses suggest their uncertainty about the butler's sexual orientation (even as its staging raises questions about their own sexuality). Wheeler teases his hair, which is under a woman's night bonnet, and announces that "we must have our curls up." Woolsey helps Wheeler into his frilly robe and pats him coyly on the bottom (fig. 7.2); Wheeler, not terribly annoyed, shakes his finger, before bursting into a broad rendition of "Isn't It Romantic?" The French maids, who come to help them dress, call the men "Ma'am." The clowns' fussiness about fashion mimics traditional "feminine" modesty, while the the film mocks feminine spectacle with the attention it places upon the display of their new outfits as they strut around the room. The song accompanying this "promenade" also reverses normal gender roles, characterizing the men as "more than an eyeful" and comparing their beauty to the Eiffel Tower, while the men confess that "we have never married," and proclaim that "the girls they come from near and far to wink at us and say Hot-cha-cha" (fig. 7.3).

The scene's excessive quality, its recurrent interest in gender reversals and homoerotic/homophobic parody swamps its narrative significance.

PERFORMANCE HETEROGENEITY

If *Diplomaniacs'* plot is highly conventional, relying heavily upon formulas developed in previous Wheeler and Woolsey vehicles, novelty is introduced primarily at the level of performance. A *Variety* critic charged that "there was a main idea that wasn't so good in the first place, and about all that has been done to help it is the insertion of a couple of crossfire gags and the turning loose of Wheeler and Woolsey." [7] Within the terms of the vaudeville aesthetic, the "turning loose of Wheeler and Woolsey," particularly when their antics display such comic inventiveness, is all that is required to salvage a somewhat ill-considered story line. Of all their vehicles, *Diplomaniacs* allows Wheeler and Woolsey the greatest chance to display the range of their performance skills and devotes the least time to plot development. Each sequence invites its own distinctive type of performance: crossfire comedy, Busby Berkeley-style choreography, tearful Irish ballads, knockabout romantic duets, parodic operetta, comic acrobatics, and minstrel cakewalk. Everywhere they go, Wheeler and Woolsey stumble upon spaces ideally suited for performance. The barber's chair, the Indian blanket, the captain's table, the ship's deck, the hotel's canopied bed and curtained windows, and the conference rostrum each exhibit features of a theatrical stage and function as performance spaces. These impromptu stages come complete with astonished but appreciative audiences (the Indian maidens, the ship's passengers, the conference members) and a steady supply of chorus lines (squaws, French maids, diplomats).

A sequence in the USS *Periwinkle's* dining room gives both members of the team an opportunity to perform their specialties. Woolsey delivers a rambling and nonsensical speech, complete with suggestive remarks to a busty young woman, insults to a matronly older woman, and painful puns for whoever will listen. Woolsey's patter recalls the superior comic speeches Groucho Marx presented under similar situations. Bert Wheeler revises a number he first introduced in the 1924 *Ziegfeld Follies*; he sings a sad Irish song while munching on a sandwich. A bit of bread steadfastly refuses to stay in his mouth, popping out again and again as he sings, though he nimbly catches it and stuffs it back inside. Tears stream down his cheeks and he mops his brow with buttered bread before slamming the slice down onto the table in dis-

Diplomaniacs (1933): Performance spaces. Wisconsin Center for Film and Theater Research.

gust. Breaking down completely, he sobs, "I wish I had a cup of coffee," and receives comfort from Dolores.

The peace conference sequence is another prime example of the process by which narrative space is transformed into performance space and interest in plot development is shifted onto a fascination with bizarre comic spectacle. Woolsey impersonates Ed Wynn, reading a letter addressed to the peace conference from an eighteen-year-old blonde who has "never been kissed" and offering silly advice to the lovelorn. Occupying the rostrum, the men rub their hands together, tossing a

Diplomaniacs (1933): At the peace conference. Wisconsin Center for Film and Theater Research.

cloth back and forth, and prepare to try out their best tricks on this tough house, their political speech completely transformed into a variety act. The two men do flips and acrobatic stunts, Wheeler spinning his partner around on his legs and looking into the camera, proclaiming in a thick German accent, "He's a Beeg success in Europe." The clowns mix their acrobatics with a string of political slogans that are totally disassociated from any meaningful context and assume the quality of one-liners: "Hands across the sea. . . . Can my distinguished opponent deny. . . . The forgotten man—he wants peace. . . . Hey Nonny, Nonny and a hot-cha-cha!" Wheeler bounces into the arms of an an-

197

noyed Edgar Kennedy, who presides over the peace conference with typical ill-temper, and then Wheeler and Woolsey tap dance off the stage while the assembly rises to its feet for a standing ovation. The boys, offstage in the anteroom, hear the explosion of Winkelreid's bomb and mistaking it for loud applause, return for an encore. Finding the delegates with blackened faces from the explosion, and mysteriously wearing white gloves, the comics turn their back to the camera, quickly blacken their faces, and turn around as minstrels. They launch into a jazzy number, "Are You Ready for the Judgment Day?" as the delegates join in the chorus and sway back and forth, waving their gloved hands in the air. Wheeler and Woolsey's performance overflows the stage, engulfing the entire gathering in their showmanship. By uniting the body in a common song, they gain general consensus for universal peace: "No war, no war, no war!"[8]

Such eruptions are not restricted to extended performance sequences; bits of crossfire comedy, flourishes of performance virtuosity, appear in almost every scene, constantly distracting attention from plot development. Even when the clowns confront a direct threat on their lives, as when they are surrounded by armed thugs at the Dead Rat Café, they take time from the plot action to perform for the camera (fig. 7.4). Wheeler begs Woolsey to "sing to me" before "we pass on to the great beyond." The two reprise "Sing to Me," previously offered as a farcical romantic duet between Wheeler and White, rewriting its lyrics from double entendres about sexual coupling into punning references to their impending death. Only when they complete the song's final lyric do the henchmen crash down upon them and the fight begins. Indeed, the scene can be understood as a parody of the way musical conventions posit performance sequences as a break or disruption of the flow of narrative events, stopping the action dead for an absurdly ill-timed song reprise.

CHARACTER FLUX

Diplomaniacs' persistent interest in performance virtuosity results in highly unstable characterization. The whole notion of fixed identity is problematized by this film's constant play with impersonation and masquerade, practices that it shares with a number of other early sound comedies. Steve Seidman argues for a reading of comedian comedy that views the "numerous forms of 'dressing up,' becoming part of a performance" as part of the films' general thematic of "identity confusion" and "behavioral disfunction."[9] This play with the construction of the self, Seidman argues, is "resolved" by the film's conclusions, which "normalize" and "fix" the comedian's identity as he or she is assimilated into the dominant cultural order. Performance signs are reread in this formulation as symptoms of a troubled character. Frank Krutnik encounters difficulty when he applies this model to Bob Hope's *The Paleface* (Paramount, 1948):

> Not all such films end with this smooth imbrication of the comedian into the fiction and such a transparent resolution to the problematic of subjectivity. . . . *The Paleface* ends with a gag which extends the comic pleasure beyond the narrative wrap-up, and celebrates the comedian who is the agent of the comic disruptiveness. . . [*The Paleface*] allows both narrative closure and the dominance of the comedian—the later feeding off the former."[10]

Krutnik's revision of Seidman does not go nearly far enough. The Seidman model presumes a commitment to characterization (and psychologically deep characterization at that) that simply does not exist in many comedian comedies, especially those of the early sound period. Characterization is less a problem the plot works to resolve than a vehicle allowing for a steady stream of even wilder performances. Seidman's account privileges the performer's final state, but these films' constant destabilization of identity prohibits us from attributing any particular fixity even in the closing scenes. Krutnik's reading of *The Paleface* suggest just how volatile and transient this final identity remains if one gag can call it into question.

Much like their counterparts in countless vaudeville and burlesque sketches, Hercules Glubb and Willie Nillie are stereotypical rather than rounded or psychologically deep characters. They are constructed, however, not simply through the invocation of a single stereotype and its associated cluster of traits and values but through a succession of stereotypes held in tension with each other. We accumulate almost no knowledge about these characters in the course of the narrative, and, indeed, what little information we do gather is ignored or contradicted by later developments. The first scene establishes their background as hapless barbers who lack even sufficient intelligence to locate their shop someplace where it might reasonably attract customers. Nothing suggests any particular aptitude or attachment to this line of work; Hercules and Willie are barbers because the narrative wishes to activate one and only one meaning attached to that occupation—the barber's willingness to express a "learned opinion" on any conceivable topic of current interest—and that meaning itself must be forgotten as soon as it outlives its usefulness. The barbershop sequence also allows them to exploit a vocabulary of body gags (jokes about baldness, dandruff, facial massages, shaving cream, etc.) that had been a staple of vaudeville sketch humor and can be found in similar sequences in other films, such as W. C. Fields's *The Barbershop* (Paramount, 1933), Charlie Chaplin's *The Great Dictator* (United Artists, 1940), or the Marx Brothers' *Monkey Business*.

The characters' occupational status carries into the following scene, where they do occasionally make remarks that reflect a poor barber's perspective on the world. Willie suggests that he has been able to cure his "scruples" by using witch hazel, treating "scruples" as a reference to a scalp disease treatable with a traditional home remedy. Confronted with the gorilla who was once the "most beautiful woman in Paris," Hercules suggests that "she needs a shave, doesn't she?" By the time Hercules and Willie reach the USS *Periwinkle,* they (and the film for that matter) seem to have largely forgotten that they were ever barbers, successful or otherwise. Their skilled performance at the peace conference, especially their use of backstage slang, implies that they are former vaudevillians, a background suggested by their earlier film vehicles (which almost always cast them as variety, medicine show, carnival, or showboat performers), but never hinted elsewhere in this film. Their occupation does resurface occasionally. Willie wishes they were "back in the barbershop starving to death," after they are almost murdered by a pack of thugs at the Dead Rat. When Willie offers a plan for wooing the peace conference delegates, Hercules reminds him that "the last idea you had—you opened a barbershop." The film's final scene, which marks their return to the Indian reservation, self-consciously reprises the debate about the shop that starts the film. Looking toward the camera, Hercules protests, "Well, let it go. That's how the whole thing started." Here, though, the character information is redundant, offering no substantial development; it does not deepen our understanding of their characters beyond what we were told in the opening sequence.

Their foreign travels involve not a resolution of the personality conflicts posed in the opening scenes but rather a temporary escape from those conflicts, an escape from characterization into the pure play of performance; their trip returns them precisely in the same state (literally and metaphorically) at which the narrative began. Indeed, the ending, where they march off to war, points toward a generic comedy plot (the enlisted man comedy) and recalls their previous military misadventures in *Half Shot at Sunrise,* suggesting that the play with identity may continue beyond the text itself.

SEXUAL AMBIGUITY

Fundamental aspects of their characterization, most notably indications of their sexuality, fluctuate radically from scene to scene depending upon the comic potentials of each new setting and situation. A certain degree of sexual ambiguity is already posed by the barbershop sequence, where Willie dons a frilly manicurist's cap and apron to serve the customer. When they arrive at the Indian encampment, Hercules sits down and pulls Willie onto his lap, the other man lovingly draping his arm around Hercules' shoulder, again evoking a homoerotic quality in their relationship as well as suggesting the relationship between a ventriloquist and his dummy. This same scene poses an alternative conception of their sexuality, treating them as playboys and ladykillers. Willie flirts with the chief's attractive daughter, whacking her on the bottom with a tomahawk, to which she giggles and exclaims, "I'll bet you do that to all the girls." Later, during a musical number, they warn the braves to "guard your squaws" when they return from their trip to Geneva, suggesting plans for wholesale erotic conquest.

Both versions of their sexuality recur periodically in subsequent scenes. Dolores expresses incredulous surprise upon learning that the scrawny figures in bathing suits in the picture Winkelreid shows her are "men." Willie displays confusion and anxiety over Dolores's sexual advances during a scene in which she assumes the role of the initiator of activity while he struggles like a bashful virgin. The vamp leads the sad-faced barber to the moonlit deck, where she intends to seduce him and gain possession of the diplomatic papers. She begs him to "sing to me"; he resists, asking, "Could you sing if your pants were too tight?" She persists, and he suggests, "How 'bout 'One Hour with You' "; she eagerly agrees but first demands that he sing to her. She breaks into a raucous musical number with exaggerated feminine gestures turning quickly into signs of sexual aggressiveness. She runs her fingers through his curly locks, only to choke him around the throat and yank on his hair; she grabs the cords on his uniform and ties them into knots; she bumps him with her hips and the peevish "boy" bumps her back harder. She swings him around and flings him onto the deck; he pulls her off her feet and she lands sprawling on her bottom. The two begin wrestling on the deck, all the while singing a love duet, and he flips her over his shoulder, before grabbing her in a headlock as the song ends, his virtue seemingly secure despite her persistent advances. The Paris hotel sequence, as has already been suggested, fully exploits the homoerotic aspects of the clowns' relationship, but it ends with them bragging about their charms as dapper gentleman picking up women "along ze Boulevard." They express some romantic interest in Dolores and Fifi outside the Dead Rat but only after they believe the women died protecting them, and even then, they display signs of sexual anxiety. Hercules melts Fifi with a single kiss outside the Peace Palace in an exaggerated display of male potency and the two brag about all the women they "made" following their triumph at the conference. The final scene strongly suggests a romantic resolution to their tenuous relationships with the more sexually aggressive women in the film.

One reading of this film might see a fundamental conflict between the men's fantasies of sexual conquest and the reality of their anxiety and ambiguous orientation, a problem resolved by the suggestion of romantic commitment in the final scene. Such a reading, however, implies systematic development where none exists. The characters never express displeasure with their romantic life; the shifts between sexual aggressiveness and timidity (even homosexuality) are all treated literally, not as a gap between self-perception and reality. Hercules really does reduce the seasoned vamp to mush with one passionate embrace. Hercules really does sleep in the same bed with Willie and treat him as his wife. Moreover, the resolution of the romance plot is so underdeveloped, depending upon audience familiarity with generic formulas rather than onscreen exposition, that it does little to contain the flux of meanings surrounding their sexuality earlier in the film. Rather, play with the characters' sexual identity becomes part of the film's larger interest in baring the devices of its own plot and character construction.

"A FINE WAY TO TALK FOR A CHINAMAN!"

Perhaps the most outrageous example of the ways the film exposes the arbitrariness and conventionality of its character construction comes in the state-room sequence. The scene opens as Winkelreid is being fitted into his tuxedo by his valet: "I must look my best tonight. There's dirty work afoot and I've a little conspiring to do." The valet assures him, "In that suit, you can conspire freely." Deciding that he will require "an especially dirty assistant," Winkelreid rings a buzzer and

Chow Chow pops out of a trap door in the side of the wall, only to be greeted by an impatient villain who demands to know "what kept you." When the valet's services are no longer needed, Winkelreid shouts, "Go," and the man leaps through the portal into the ocean below. Chow Chow calmly reports his fate: "How much water can one man drink?" Learning of the financial instability of his employer, Chow Chow immediately seeks to shift plot roles to realign himself with the heroes, only to be told that he must fulfill story demands regardless of personal inclinations: "See, here, you can't join their side! You're a villain!" Raising his fist and adopting a Yiddish accent and inflection, Chow Chow the sometime Chinaman exclaims, "Then, come the Revolution! See, what, I'll be a hero!" Winkelreid decides that his scheme requires the services of a vamp and orders Chow Chow to procure one, amid much discussion of the specifications required for the present project:

Chow Chow:	What kind of vamp do you want?
Winkelreid:	I want a female vamp!
Chow Chow:	What color?
Winkelreid:	Well, what color have you?
Chow Chow:	Red, yellow, black . . .
Winkelreid:	Any white?
Chow Chow:	How 'bout a nice striped one?
Winkelreid:	I want a white one!
Chow Chow:	The white ones get dirty much quicker.
Winkelreid:	That's fine. She'll have to get pretty dirty. . . .

Chow Chow walks to the wall and orders, "one vamp on rye," a request repeated by an Italian short order cook who promises that one will be "comin' righta down." A slot opens in the wall and Dolores slides out, wrapped completely in cellophane, "untouched by human hands." When the two men "open her up," unwrapping her package, she flings herself on Winkelreid and begins kissing him madly, blindly fulfilling her narrative role as a heartless seducer of men. Winkelreid is still not satisfied, suggesting that the vamp should be "very alluring and foreign." The characters debate what accent she should have before settling on "mixed European": "Yah-yah and Ou-la-la, I will get zem for you, Señor, Yowsah."

The characters are being constructed, fit to the specifications of their narrative roles, before our very eyes. Dolores literally has no life apart from the roles the plot assigns to her; she is pristine, "untouched by human hands," before she is slid into the story. Chow Chow similarly lacks the ability, although not the willingness, to rebel against plot demands, and apparently also has been stored in a kind of limbo outside the story world until he is called to action. Winkelreid freely acknowledges his status as "villain," self-consciously fulfilling the role that has been scripted for him.

Even these transparently stereotypical characters display only the most minimal stability, constantly producing contradictory signs of their identity and status within the text. Dolores's "mixed European" accent exists for only one joke, never to resurface again. This vamp, who has been brought into the story for the sole purpose of heartlessly seducing Willie Nillie into turning over the secret papers, immediately develops a tenderness for the "little fellow" that overrides her initial narrative role. She shifts between an alignment with the villains and an alignment with the protagonists.

Chow Chow's instability is hinted at from the very outset, both by his suggestion that he might join the "other side" and by his sudden reversion into a Yiddish accent when this plan is rejected. Only his name, his costume, and his tendency to speak in proverbs suggest his status as an Oriental henchman, a role he only imperfectly fills. (Hugh Herbert had previously been associated primarily with Jewish roles, and it is likely that this previous association spilled over into the way initial audiences may have read his performance in this very different ethnic role.) Willie stops him mid-proverb during the dining room sequence to demand where "it is written," and the character falls speechless in his confusion, "I-I-I don't know." His dialogue consists mostly of nonsequiters, often linked with sudden shifts in his performance style. Asked for advice, Herbert drops to his knees, impersonating Al Jolson to explain, "East is east and west is west, but I love best my home in Tennessee. Oh, Mammy!" In the next scene, he tries to tell Winkelreid that the ship has docked in Switzerland, only to be told that this is "impossible" since there are no oceans near Switzerland. Without hesitating, Chow Chow adopts a thick German accent, imitating radio's Baron Munchausen (Jack Pearl): "Vas you dare, Charlie?" Winkelreid responds, "That's a fine way to talk for a Chinaman!" and, of course, he is right. In those moments, the Chinese stereotype that forms the initial basis for Chow Chow's character has been displaced by an equally exaggerated German stereotype, one that has nothing to do with the particularity of Chow Chow's character. His Baron Munchausen impersonation is another transient reference in a text composed of many such allusions. German accents are no "way to talk for a Chinaman." Midway through the Dead Rat sequence, when he is told the proprietress's name, Chow Chow kneels, arms stretched out to her, and proclaims with tearful intensity, "Fifi was my mother's name!" (fig. 7.5).

By the time they reach Switzerland, Chow Chow's anarchic energies can no longer be contained within the plot; he has become "sick" of his role, responding with increased curtness to Winkelreid's requests for information or assistance. Finally, he protests that "you are the ugliest villain I ever worked for," jumps from a tree branch, races down to a nearby boat, and proceeds to row to China. He is greeted by his wife, who protests, "Your dinner is cold! You're five-years late!" and produces a string of youngsters, all under five-years-old, explaining that they are a "surprise" for him: "Now that I'm home, you can stop surprising me." From the audience's perspective, it is Chow Chow who will stop surprising us because he has escaped at last from a plot role he has always resisted and has found a "home" for himself, far outside of the story space. Early scripts had Chow Chow inexplicably returning in the parade of soldiers at the films' conclusion, marching alongside the Indian's pet gorilla; the filmmakers chose, in the end, to reject this kind of arbitrary pulling together of story elements and to allow Chow Chow to escape all such containment.

Characterization holds no stability in *Diplomaniacs,* constantly in crisis, unresolved by its conclusion. What remains as our point of identification is not the characters but the performers. Wheeler's wavy hair, earnest eyes, and drooping lips, Woolsey's schoolboy glasses and bony physique remain constant, despite the various masks and costumes they adopt. Familiarity with their performance tricks and personality quirks, developed through previous exposure to their earlier vehicles, allows viewers to override gaping holes in the narrative construction. Wheeler's effeminacy, even the hint of homosexuality, no longer function as symptoms of the character's troubled sexual identity, but stand apart from the narrative as star turns. These moments recall earlier such scenes in other vehicles, such as *Peach O'Reno,* where he performs half the film in drag and parodies ballroom dancing or *So This Is Africa,* where a group of Amazons lock Wheeler, dressed in drag, into a bedroom and order him to "have a honeymoon" with a rather embarrassed Woolsey. The performers' obvious skills even allow us to forget, at least momentarily, the characters' total lack of stage training and to enjoy their virtuoso performance at the peace conference.

So This Is Africa (1933). Academy of Motion Picture Arts and Sciences.

Characters become vehicles for moving the performers from place to place, creating opportunities for the narrative to give way to the pure spectacle of performance virtuosity. Yet those characters are emptied of meaning, just as Wheeler's briefcase is emptied of its secrets, and reduced to their function within the narrative construction. To look toward some extratextual identity for the performers as a source of stable meaning, however, is simply to displace the problem even further; the meanings that accrued around the performers through their previous screen and stage appearances and through extratextual publicity and promotional materials were equally contradictory, appealing not to one stable identity but to yet a broader succession of impersonations and masquerades. All that remained stable, finally, were the performers' physical types and mannerisms—their performance skills, upon which a diverse range of meanings get mapped in the course of their careers.

CENTERING THE PERFORMANCE

Similarly, the film consistently subordinates visual style to the demands of foregrounding these extraordinary comic performances. Gerald Weales has described *Diplomaniacs* as visually "static," a criticism that seems largely misdirected. Weales's complaint reflects a broader history of attacks on early sound comedy as focusing on verbal rather than visual humor.[11] My discussion of the film's performances should already indicate the centrality of physical comedy within Wheeler and Woolsey's repertoire: Wheeler's effeminate gestures, his robust wrestling on the deck with Marjorie White, the acrobatics at the peace conference, the bread that pops from his mouth as he sings, Woolsey's strange postures and flamboyant movements. Such criticisms can be seen as another example of film studies' tendency to privilege visual over aural aspects of film style. Yet even taken on their own terms, as a complaint about visual style, Weales's comments are off the mark.

True, the visual style of *Diplomaniacs* attracts limited interest upon an initial viewing; rarely does the film direct our attention toward its camerawork or editing. Kristin Thompson has argued, however, that the "invisibility" of visual style within classical Hollywood films often reflects not a lack of sophistication in shot composition and articulation but rather the high degree of compositional motivation behind the camerawork.[12] *Diplomaniacs'* visual style is "invisible" on initial viewing, not because it is static nor even because it precisely conforms to classical codes of shot articulation, but because it so fully serves our fascination with the outrageous performances. What we see in *Diplomaniacs* is a set of formal devices that evolved in response to the need to foreground performance.

The camera consistently places the performers quite literally front and center. The staging provides at least minimal motivation for extended sequences of direct address to the camera, preserving the presentational style of vaudeville performance while subordinating it to the classical demand for diegetic consistency and coherence. Woolsey addresses his lines into a mirror, early in the barbershop sequence, allowing simultaneously for a full frontal and an oblique back view of the performer. Other scenes are framed through portals and windows (such as an exchange between Winkelreid and Chow Chow as the ship arrives in Paris or the butler's soliloquy in the Paris hotel scene) or across tables (such as the Irish ballad Willie sings in the ship's dining room); such compositions justify performance frontality and allow for a nondisruptive style of camera address. Similarly, many of the scenes are staged in front of a succession of flat and somewhat abstracted surfaces—the barbershop counter, the railing of the ship, the fence in the park (fig. 7.6), the steps at the conference hall, even a row of Indians or a pack of thugs. These surfaces function like the olio curtain in vaudeville, to thrust the performers forward, restrict their movements, and motivate presentational styles of performance during the delivery of crossfire lines.

This flattening of the playing space has other consequences as well, increasing the legibility of the foreground action by reducing the distraction of a more cluttered or deeper background. (Recall that similar arguments were made on behalf of the simplified scenography of vaudeville; see chapter 2.) The eccentricity of the character movement, the unexpectedness of the choreography, only becomes intelligible against a highly coherent, easily interpretable space. Nothing in the field should require us to shift our attention away from the central performer, lest we miss a comical or spectacular action. Where performances cannot be staged within fairly shallow spaces, the camera is often positioned above the actors so that the background is largely occupied by floor rather than walls or environment, as in a scene where Wheeler and Woolsey sprawl on the ground, working jigsaw puzzles while awaiting word from the delegates about their decisions.

This demand for a high degree of spatial coherence and visual clarity also requires a general dependence upon long takes and camera movements to record action during performance sequences rather than the crosscutting preferred by classical continuity editing. An extreme example of this shot articulation occurs in the Indian camp sequence: Woolsey alternates between addressing lines to the chief and to Wheeler, shifting physically back and forth between two adjacent spaces and the camera continually reframes to keep him constantly centered. Even in sequences requiring a greater depth of field and a more complex performing space, camera movement focuses attention onto pertinent aspects of performance. The dining room sequence requires an acknowledgement of the space's immensity, yet, the camera tracks with Wheeler and Woolsey as they enter the room, never allowing them to slip from the center of attention. Similarly, the Dead Rat scenes create a dense visual environment, a pastiche on Josef Von Sternberg's Marlene Dietrich vehicles, but these scenes also make extensive use of tracking shots to maintain a focus on performer movement. A more complex camera movement is executed in the Geneva Park sequence. After an extended crossfire scene on the bench between Wheeler and Woolsey, the camera starts to follow them as they exit and then moves up to reveal Winkelreid, Chow Chow, the two women, and four corporate executives seated on the branch of a tree, eavesdropping on the two men's conversation. That such elaborate camera movements still do not call much attention to themselves suggests how fully they were motivated by the demand to keep our attention firmly directed on the performer's movements.

This style of shot articulation also helps to preserve the temporal integrity of the performance, allowing the star's virtuosity to unfold without interruption. The "Sing to Me" number, for example, consists of only five shots, with the bulk of the song recorded in two rather extended takes filmed from the same camera position. Only when Wheeler is flung to the deck does the camera move back to encompass more of the performance space, facilitating the presentation of broader physical movements than the previous setup could allow. So thoroughly accustomed to this style of editing do we become that those sequences where the pattern is not followed immediately call into question the credibility of the performance. The tumbling during the peace conference sequence, much shorter in length, requires twelve shots; most of them present the actors from extreme long views or with their backs to the camera, denying us access to their faces. In only a few shots do we see both Wheeler and Woolsey together in the same composition. One immediately suspects that what appears to be the performers' virtuosity was in fact accomplished through the extensive use of stunt doubles, while the recording of the equally physical "Sing to Me" number allows no room for such fakery. An aesthetic centered around audience awareness of performance virtuosity naturally preferred a cutting style that raised no doubts about the authenticity of the performer's actions. There are no such cuts in Mitchell and Durant's performance as backflipping senators in *Stand Up and Cheer,* for example, where it is their skills as acrobats that the scene is designed to display.

One consequence of this heavy reliance upon long takes and camera movements is that point of view editing and reverse field cutting play limited roles here. Point-of-view cutting is used for inserts of written texts and details (the cash register at the barbershop, the signs at the peace conference, a note from the Indians); it also appears in scenes of exaggerated male reactions to female sexual display (Woolsey admires a busty woman during the dining room scene, Winkelreid and Chow Chow react to Dolores's shimmy in the state-room scene and later respond in terror as Fifi blows them a kiss). Reverse-field editing, similarly, is reserved for only a few spots in the film, most prominently during the peace conference sequence. Here, there are cuts between the clowns' performance on the podium and the delegates' reaction from the floor or between the stars and the chorus during the minstrel number. For the most part, the film cuts between adjacent spaces, matching on the performers' movements or it reframes the action through a slight shift in camera positioning, thereby opening the playing space to broader movements or gestures. The "Sing to Me" sequence, for example, involves cuts between a relatively close composition focused on Wheeler's face as he responds to Dolores's assault and a longer view capable of accommodating the couple's entire bodies during scenes where her aggressive choreography takes precedence over his subtler expressions.

Editing is subordinated to performance in other ways as well. During extensive crossfire sequences, cuts punctuate the gap between straight line and punch line or immediately follow a punch line; here, they service the demands of comic timing and create a pause for the audience's laughter. This practice is most noticeable in the gag-heavy barbershop sequence, though it recurs throughout the film and is common within other comedies of the period.

Far from being "static," *Diplomaniacs* makes sophisticated use of camera movement and editing to ensure maximum visual clarity, to preserve spatial and temporal continuity, to direct the audience's attention onto pertinent details, to show relationships within complex spaces, to punctuate the delivery of gags, and above all, to foreground performance. Whereas camera movement is motivated by story information in most classical films, *Diplomaniacs,* like other early sound comedies, subordinates visual style to the demands of performance virtuosity. The influence of the vaudeville aesthetic can be felt in the shot composition and camera movement as readily as in the film's plot construction and character development.

THE DEMISE OF ANARCHISTIC COMEDY

By late 1934, box office revenues for these comedies began to decline sharply, a decline the trade press attributed to the overexposure of their comic stars and their failure to produce a consistently high quality product. *Diplomaniacs* was Wheeler and Woolsey's twelfth film together in four years, the fourth vehicle they made under the direction of William A. Seiter. The stars had exhausted the repertoire of "tried and true" material they developed throughout their independent careers in vaudeville and the New York revues. As the appeal of individual performers declined, the absence of a solid story or particularized characters became harder to tolerate; the number of moments of "astonishment" and virtuosity dwindled beyond the threshold of audience enthusiasm. Local exhibitors, especially those in outlying areas who had initially been the most enthusiastic about this style of broad comedy, now complained of their incomprehensibility and "slap-dash" construction. While, in my judgement, *Diplomaniacs* stands with *Peach O'Reno, Hips, Hips, Hooray,* and *Cockeyed Cavaliers* among the team's most accomplished films, this opinion was apparently not shared by its contemporary audience. Theater owner A. E. Hancock (Columbia City, Indiana) told *Motion Picture Herald* readers that it was "the poorest they have had," complaining that "the same people that made *The Cuckoos* and *Rio Rita* [the team's first successes, both based on Broadway musicals] . . . evidentially have lost what it takes to make a picture with this pair." [13] J. J. Hoffman (Plainview, Nebraska) agreed: "Not as good as their others; seemed to have missed a cog somewhere but couldn't figure out where. We expected a big laugh but only got a few chuckles." [14]

Wheeler and Woolsey faced additional resistance because of their heavy reliance upon scatological humor, a complaint commonly leveled against former vaudeville comics but particularly focused around this team. As one *Atlanta Journal* critic protested, "There are abundant signs that what will be gobbled with salacious greed on Broadway is much below the mental taste and moral psychology of the millions of less cosmopolitan and less sex-obsessed Americans who live outside the atmosphere of the Great White Way in Manhattan." [15] Their previous film, *So This Is Africa* had been the subject of heated controversy because of its allegedly vulgar treatment of sexual themes, especially its homosexual subtexts; this furor eventually provoked an official response from the Production Code Administration. PCA executives sat down with the Ohio and New York censor boards and substantially reedited the film to conform to their far-reaching complaints. The Ohio board alone requested sixty-six cuts, including the omission of twelve entire scenes. [16] Individual exhibitors expressed considerably more ambiguity about the film's violation of audience standards, noting that it shocked many of their patrons ("When college boys think a film vulgar, nothing more can be said about it"), yet acknowledging that the controversy attracted considerable trade: "If you can get it by the 'blue-noses,' grab this one. One of the best nights we've had in a long time." [17] As the *Motion Picture Herald* editors lobbied relentlessly for greater enforcement of Production Code restrictions on film content, local exhibitors seemed to be working through questions of censorship in relation to Wheeler and Woolsey's comedy. One Selma, Louisiana exhibitor suggested that the film's popularity was tempering her own desires for clean entertainment:

> As box office pull, this one beats them all. It got lots of publicity just as I
> was showing it, as the papers had several accounts of an exhibitor being in
> jail in Mississippi for having shown it. There was no doubt about this being
> the best and funniest that Wheeler and Woolsey have ever made, but on the
> other hand, there is no doubt but what it is the wildest and woolliest picture
> that has ever been made. I held my breath on the first showing. I've never
> heard such roars of laughter. They simply ate it up, and never before have I
> known of as much mouth to mouth advertising. . . . I am for clean pictures
> and this one is far from clean, but since I have seen that this type is what a
> majority wants I cannot condemn this picture. [18]

Not all exhibitors agreed and many feared that such comedies posed a
serious threat to their public standing and could speed the movement
for federal censorship of the movies:

> Where are we headed? If pictures like this one [*So This Is Africa*] and *She
> Done Him Wrong* are to be what small-town exhibitors are to offer their
> patrons in 1933 and 34, we might as well close up and quit now, for a
> few more like this one and we will lose our Sunday shows and have
> local censorship. These might be hot shows in the big towns but they mean
> nothing but trouble for us. . . . A few more like this one and we will have
> federal censorship and even the mighty Hays office will not be able "to
> block it." [19]

Diplomaniacs faced an uphill struggle to overcome perceptions both by
the Production Code Administration and by the general public that
Wheeler and Woolsey were "dirty comics." This perception cut deeply
into their box office returns and may account for why they are remem-
bered less favorably today than the Marx Brothers, who somehow escaped similar labeling.

Despite such concerns, *Diplomaniacs* makes extensive use of suggestive humor (the woman in the ship's dining room whose chest bears an
anchor tattoo that speaks to her erotic experiences with the navy;
Dolores's willingness to spend "one hour with you" if Willie will only
"sing" to her; Fifi's passionate kisses that make men's lips smoke and
their legs give way). Sexual appetites surface most dramatically when,
seated on a tree branch with six men, the women suggest, "Let's all
neck," and Winkelreid responds, "There's no time now for sex." It was
the perverse pleasures of such scenes that made Wheeler and Woolsey
such a "hot" property at the Production Code Administration. Reviewing the script, a staff member reported, "This is a typical Wheeler and
Woolsey comedy, full of suggestive dialogue and sequences." [20] James

Wingate urged producer Merian C. Cooper to display unusual caution in his treatment of such materials to avoid the controversy surrounding *So This Is Africa:* "There is no doubt that *Diplomaniacs* will have to overcome some of the unfavorable reactions caused by this previous release."[21] Despite such reservations, the Production Code Administration consistently concluded that "The story is not only highly fantastic but completely impossible and we believe . . . it can emerge as an inoffensive and perhaps amusing musical fantasy, somewhat on the lines of *Phantom President.*" Local exhibitors found the film "a big improvement over *So This Is Africa* inasmuch as they don't go into the gutter (much)," yet suggested that it did not draw as well as the previous Wheeler and Woolsey vehicle, which was "attributed to the bad reaction to the 'dirt' in the *Africa* picture."[22]

Responding to declining box office, exhibitor dissatisfaction and public outrage, the studios either jettisoned declining comic stars or brought their vehicles into greater conformity with classical storytelling conventions and established social standards. The shift in the Marx Brothers' comedies from their Paramount vehicles to those produced for MGM was mirrored by all of the other comic teams who weathered this difficult transitional period. By the fall of 1934, the "bounds of difference," the possibilities for formal experimentation and aesthetic deviation within the classical Hollywood cinema, were narrowing; anarchistic comedy would soon be replaced by a style of comedy that was far more conservative both formally and ideologically, a style of comedy best exemplified by the films of Joe E. Brown or Joe Penner. RKO continued to feature Wheeler and Woolsey in a string of progressively less satisfying vehicles until 1937, when their career ended with Robert Woolsey's death, yet most of those later films lack the anarchic energy, comic inventiveness, and performance virtuosity of *Diplomaniacs.*

8

"If the Whole World Were Created for Our Pleasure": Order and Disorder in Anarchistic Comedy

"The Marx Brothers are not human, not mythological—they are completely fantastic and they seem completely mad. . . . Again and again, the Marx Brothers act as we act in dreams, or as we would act if we dared, if the whole world were created for our pleasure."

Gilbert Seldes[1]

Two medicine showmen, Andy Williams (Bert Wheeler) and Rob Dudley (Robert Woolsey), hope to forge a partnership with Frisbee's beauty products company for the manufacture and marketing of Dr. Dudley's flavored lipsticks (peach for lovers, raspberry for mother-in-laws). In a sequence about midway through *Hips, Hips, Hooray,* Miss Frisbee (Thelma Todd) and her model, Daisy (Dorothy Lee), go to a meeting at "Dr. Dudley's office." Woolsey has temporarily commandeered the space by telling its normal occupant, Mr. Clarke (Spencer Charters) that his home is on fire, thus sending him rushing frantically to rescue "my wife! . . . my goldfish!" (fig. 8.1). Dudley hangs his own shingle outside the office door just seconds before his prospective investors arrive. Their meeting proceeds with more than a few double entendres about "propositions" and "mergers," resulting both in the formation of two romantic couples (Wheeler and Lee, Woolsey and Todd) and the consolidation of their business interests (fig. 8.2).

While the flirtatious Woolsey continues to discuss details of the new arrangements with the playful Todd, Wheeler and Lee withdraw to the balcony where the young man proceeds to serenade his new lover with a sappy romantic song, "Just Keep on Doin' What You're Doin' " (fig. 8.3). At the end of the first verse, Wheeler gives Lee a slight peck; she reciprocates and escalates the lovemaking, kissing him again and again throughout the second verse, as the overwrought Wheeler tries to back away. The second chorus ends with the two, locked in a passionate embrace, hanging by their heels over the side of the highrise balcony.

Inside, the other couple has entered into the music-lovemaking. Todd serenades a very bashful Woolsey, while she proceeds to pull off his tie and rip the buttons from his shirt. He tries to block her advances with his straw hat, but she unravels it into a long string that she casually tosses onto the floor (fig. 8.4). He joins the song, reluctantly at first and then with greater enthusiasm, as the sexually aggressive woman pulls out his shirt tail and yanks his underwear from inside his pants. As the sound of harps appears on the soundtrack, Woolsey twirls and toe dances. He removes the shade from a nearby lamp and wraps it around his waist like a tutu, continuing to prance about the room, leaping onto tables. Soon, Todd joins him, mimicking his frilly gestures, circling around him and striking poses, and leaping through the air with flutterkicks (fig. 8.5).

Racing in and out of the big glass doors that separate the office from the balcony, they trip and fall at the other couple's feet. Wheeler and Lee watch with admiration for a moment before joining into the dance as all four swing and leap about the balcony in sheer exhilaration. Woolsey picks up an urn, dances with it and then smashes it at Wheeler's feet. Taking up the challenge, Wheeler leaps forward, selects a bigger urn, and smashes it, while Todd approaches an enormous vase, kicks it over, and giggles gleefully as it smashes onto the ground. Each of the four approaches the big glass doors and proceed to wash them, only to reveal that, in fact, the doors contain no glass.

Stepping through them, the two couples reenter the office for their next assault. Lee strikes a dramatic pose, arms stretched above her head, while Woolsey dances around her, flinging the piles of papers he has removed from Mr. Clarke's desk. Wheeler removes a coat hanger from the closet, transforms it into Cupid's bow, and fires imaginary arrows at his friends. Todd seizes the tickertape flowing from the stock machine and drags it like a streamer as she swoops in and out of the other dancers (fig. 8.6). There is a drumroll and much elaborate preparation as Lee crouches atop the desk and then leaps spread-eagle into the awaiting arms of Wheeler and Woolsey. Pretending to be vaudeville acrobats, the men swing her body in great loops over their heads, before letting her fly to the chandelier above, where she dangles, smiling and waving to the "boys" below (fig. 8.7).

At that moment, Clarke returns. Opening the door, he finds his office in an absolute shambles, covered with strewn paper and overturned furniture. Lee hangs daintily from the ceiling while her three comrades hold a tiger skin rug as a net for her. Unaware of his presence, the four continue their wild dance, catching Lee as she leaps, swinging around and around in circles with each other, until Wheeler and Woolsey collide head first into the now quite furious Clarke (fig. 8.8). With typical adeptness, they introduce Clarke into their improvised choreography, dance him into a closet, and lock the door behind him before grabbing their briefcases and racing for the elevator. The scene ends with a shot of the locked door and the sounds of an enraged Clarke pounding and screaming for help.

This sequence materializes the process of disordering and reordering that is the logical structure of the anarchistic comedy. The clowns expel the rightful owner from his office, overturn his space, only to escape again when he returns to his proper sphere and attempts to restore order. The number's fascination lies in its transformation of erotic desire into exhilarating destruction; its appeal rests in an anarchic satisfaction in the dismantling of narrative space. The sequence involves a quick succession of comic transformations and reappropriations, some trivial (a coat hanger becomes a Cupid's bow and a tickertape a streamer; enormous glass doors contain no glass), some more fundamental (Clarke's office becomes Dr. Dudley's office; a business proposition becomes a romantic interlude; an innocent peck on the cheek gives way to an orgy of sublimated eroticism as desire finds expression only through destruction). The odd combination of dance and low comedy, love song and slapstick, opens the spectator to the joys of bodily abandon and the pleasures of social disorder. Sequences like this one compress or condense their texts' overall thematic (social constraint against bodily release, hierarchical order against individual spontaneity) into moments of heightened expressivity and emotional intensity, spectacles of unrestrained performance and explosions of visual and verbal comedy.

COMEDY AND UTOPIA

Richard Dyer has emphasized the utopian aspects of popular texts, maintaining that entertainment offers "an image of 'something better' " than everyday experience; popular amusements, Dyer argues, provide an inverted representation of actual conditions that sparks our interest by holding open the prospect of satisfying, if only symbolically, actual lacks and desires.[2] The energy and intensity of mass entertainment stands in sharp contrast to the exhaustion and dreariness of everyday life. An extension of Dyer's analysis would suggest that the ability of the comic protagonists to shatter the tranquility of ordered space expresses impulses that must be suppressed as we go about our daily experience. Anarchistic comedy addresses a desire to break free from restraint, to enjoy an abundance of energy and spontaneity, to challenge authorities who restrain our creative potential, and to negate the logical order. As I will suggest later, these desires reflect the costs of what Norbert Elias calls the "civilizing process," the price of repressing immediate emotions in order to function within a structured society. This tension remains central to the narrative of anarchistic comedy, to the opposition between the clown and various killjoys, dupes, and counterfeits; the desire to break free from restraint is evoked and resolved by anarchistic sequences that represent the triumph of a creative disorder over a repressive order.

Nobody takes seriously the promise of this anarchic freedom; it does not represent a coherently articulated alternative to the status quo, but it amuses us nonetheless. As Dyer suggests, the utopianism of mass entertainment rarely offers alternative models of experience as more classical utopian fiction has done, but rather "presents, head-on as it were, what utopia would feel like." [3] Consequently, for Dyer, utopian elements can be found working both in representational codes (character, narrative situation, plot action) and nonrepresentational codes ("color, texture, movement, rhythm, melody, camerawork"). The utopian aspects of the sequence from *Hips, Hips, Hooray* would include both what is specifically represented (the destruction of an office, the humiliation and deception of its stuffy occupant, the love play of the two couples) and how it is represented (the sweeping camera movements, the lively choreography, the playful music, the sounds of the shattering urns, and even the rather obvious substitution of a dummy for Lee's body during the more acrobatic stunts). Indeed, what gives the scene its "zingo" (as the vaudevillians would say) is the complex interweaving of transgression on the level of representational codes and expressivity on the level of nonrepresentational codes, the linkage of images of chaos with sensations of exhilaration.

The anarchistic moment does not simply depict the clowns' refusal of social and bodily restraint; it allows the audience to experience a similar albeit vicarious escape from emotional restraint through its stylistic excesses and energetic performances. Norbert Elias and Eric Dunning have suggested that "the quest for excitement," for a momentary liberation from rigid affective control, is a central function of play within contemporary western culture. As emotional constraint has become necessary for functioning within a mass society, these sociologists argue, the need has arisen for a socially sanctioned, carefully programmed release from that constraint, for short bursts of intensely felt and out-wardly displayed emotions.[4] The anarchistic sequence acts both as a stimulus and as an aestheticized rationale for this release. This quest for excitement poses certain ideological risks, since it is best achieved by transgressing or throwing into crisis the established order; yet without these more liberatory forms of emotional expression, the tensions be-tween social actors would intensify to such a point that individuals could no longer function within the community. The quest for excite-ment, thus, poses the utopian possibility of existing outside the estab-lished order, even as it reconfirms that order's desirability.

The heightened spectacle of these moments of social reversal and physical mayhem often pulls them away from their narrative back-ground; we are invited to treat these sequences as somehow assuming a significance apart from their context (as many of the theorists of vaude-ville humor spoke of gags as self-contained mechanisms). These complex images of comic destruction encourage us to view them as moments frozen out of time, like Renaissance woodcuts representing "Worlds Turned Upside Down," rather than as parts of a larger textual system. It is important, however, to situate these scenes within the larger patterns of the work's thematic and narrative organization, and, in turn, to understand those textual systems in the context of historically specific meaning structures.

Frederic Jameson, from whom Richard Dyer derived his concept of utopian entertainment, holds that utopianism exists in a "dialectical" relationship to social constraint. Mass texts, Jameson argues, speak to fundamental "social and political anxieties and fantasies," evoke an "frightening and potentially damaging eruption of powerful anarchic desires and wish material," so that they may "subsequently be managed or repressed."[5] Mass culture works to contain these anarchic desires through "the narrative construction of imaginary resolutions and . . . the projection of an optical illusion of social harmony."[6] Problems in the social structure are revealed, exposed to examination, only so that they may be given fictional solutions; their imaginary resolutions regu-late social anxieties and divert attention from needed structural changes. The conception of comic anarchy as utopian entertainment presupposes not only a stepping away from normality but also a return. The return to order is as much a part of the meaning and pleasure of comic inversion as the initial disruption. Order must be demolished for a liberating disorder; disorder must be contained within a more satisfying order.

Umberto Eco adopts a similar model in talking about more classical forms of comedy. Comedy often appears to be antisocial, but, like tragedy, it is a form of "authorized transgression" that ultimately reconfirms our acceptance of normal patterns.[7] Both tragedy and comedy depend upon the violation of a rule "a code, a social frame, a law, a set of social premises."[8] Tragedy requires the explicit statement of the rule as well as a recognition of the consequences of its violation and the need to restore order following the transgression. In comedy, however, the rule must be "presupposed but never spelled out," while our response to the transgression is far more ambiguous: "Our pleasure is a mixed one because we enjoy not only the breaking of the rule but also the disgrace of an animal-like individual [the transgressor]."[9] Eco concludes that the comic effect is finally no more subversive than the tragic effect: "Comedy and carnival are not instances of real transgressions; on the contrary, they represent paramount examples of law reinforcement. They remind us of the existence of the rule."[10] Comedy allows us to court but never fully embrace social disaster, since our feelings toward the clown, the "animal-like individual," remain highly ambivalent. The clown is an object of both fascination and repulsion, "ignoble, inferior and repulsive," a barbarian or an animal; yet we also embrace the clown's transgressions of the established order as "revenge" for our own capitulation to its demands. Eco's insistence on the inhumanity or at least the outsiderness of the clown bears special importance, since it is by projecting our transgressive desires onto this low Other that these fantasies may be simultaneously expressed and contained. Comedy evokes both a desire for transgression and a desire for a restored order.[11]

"Keep on Doing What You're Doing"

The anarchistic sequence is almost always positioned within a double plot: on the one hand, there is a fairly conventional account of a young couple trying to unite in the face of parental or social opposition; on the other, there is the narrative of the clown, who struggles to maintain individuality and spontaneity in the face of institutional restraint. The first narrative proceeds linearly, through the cause-effect logic of classical film narrative; the second proceeds episodically, primarily through gags and performance sequences. The first narrative can be resolved only through the integration of the young lovers into a socially sanctioned couple; the second can best be resolved through an explosion of the existing social order and the liberation of individual impulsiveness. The film as a whole, then, is characterized by a play between narrative elements that push toward integration and narrative elements that push toward disintegration; its trajectory involves a constant shifting back and forth between attention placed upon the romantic couple and attention placed upon the disruptive individual or team.

For all its anarchistic qualities, the office sequence from *Hips, Hips, Hooray*, in fact, acts as a nexus between the two plots. The dance signals the division of the film's four primary characters into two couples; these relationships will develop throughout the film and resolve by its conclusion. Moreover, the sequence establishes the conditions that temporarily block the successful consummation of these relationships. In the midst of their hasty retreat from Clarke's office, Woolsey accidentally picks up Clarke's briefcase instead of his own. The briefcase contains stocks and bonds, which are stolen by Frisbee's corrupt business manager before they can be returned. The threat of arrest for this unintentional crime dogs the comic protagonists while their destruction of Clarke's office means he will probably be unreceptive to a rational explanation for their error. Thus, while itself a moment of exhilarating disruption, the sequence contributes directly to the development of the integrative narrative. In turn, the sequence's narrative consequences motivate a series of subsequent anarchistic moments, as Wheeler and Woolsey seek to escape from being captured by the police or heap indignities upon the real culprit; the narrative builds toward an elaborate sequence of comic spectacle (a cross-country auto race) that both constitutes an explosion of anarchic energies and allows the protagonists to override all the forces that block the formation of the two couples. The film ends with the two couples, driving away, singing a reprise of "Just Keep on Doin' What Your Doin'," while the two proud papas hold babies on their laps. What began as a moment of social transgression ends with the embourgeoisment of the comic protagonists and the narrativization of the comic spectacle. [12]

"This precarious double alliance with pleasure and with social order," Christopher Herbert writes, is a central characteristic of comedy as a generic tradition. [13] Comedy allows for a suspension of normal social constraints upon the "will to pleasure," the desire for a more vital and exuberant life; it does so, Herbert argues, by constructing an abstracted, gamelike world founded upon "the audacious premise that problems are ultimately innocuous."[14] This artificial world provides "a kind of sanctuary," within which individual impulsiveness is "wonderfully free" from social constraint. Our recognition that order will inevitably be restored liberates both reader and character to engage in broader transgressions of social convention than would normally be permitted. Everything can be destroyed with the knowledge that everything will be rebuilt in the end.

Herbert writes of literary and theatrical comic traditions where the competing forces of pleasure and conformity are often played out within the double narrative of the earthy servant and the romantic master. Here, the servant's lustful pleasures finally bow before the need to bring together the master and his mate. The anarchistic comedy of the Marx Brothers reverses the structural emphasis that Shakespearean comedy, say, places upon the master, making the buffoonish servant the center of attention and privileging his narrative of comic disruption over the romantic narrative of comic reordering. Still, the tension between pleasure and social order remains a vital part of these comedies, embedded within the double narrative described above. The next section will examine the anarchistic plot, focusing on the struggle between the central clown and the comic antagonist as an organizing principle both of individual sequences and the larger narrative. The final section will examine the romantic plot and consider the problems that the intersection of these plots create for the construction of anarchistic narratives.

"EVEN THOUGH IT'S LEADING US TO RUIN": CLOWNS AND THE COMEDY OF SOCIAL DISORDER

Reduced to its simplest outline, anarchistic comedy explores the relationship of the "natural," uninhibited individual to the rigidifying social order, of creative impulses to encrusted habit and conventional modes of thought. Disorder is proposed as a utopian solution not because it offers a viable alternative to the status quo but because the existing order is stifling to all that is vital in human life. The abstract forces of law and license, the social and the individual, are embodied within the conflicting figures of the clown and the comic antagonist. The clown personifies change, encapsulating all that is rebellious and spontaneous within the individual, all that strains against the narrow codes of social life. The comic antagonist embodies civilization, all that

221

is stifling or corrupt within the existing social order, all that would block or thwart efforts toward individual self-expression and personal pleasure.

Paul Bouissac finds this basic opposition already present in the crudest form of comedian comedy—the act of the circus clown—where the archetypal dichotomy between the whitefaced clown and the "ugly" clown or "tramp" comes to represent "the cultural norm and the absence of that norm, either as nature or anticulture." [15] The whitefaced clown, Bouissac argues, has completely suppressed all signs of natural humanity beneath a thick coat of white greasepaint and highly stylized, drawn-on lines that "perfect" the shape of his eyes, his lips, his nose. Even his head is completely hairless. His costume is richly made and perfectly fitting, displaying a totally orderly existence. The ugly clown has "a mask that accentuates natural protuberances and colors, enlarges his mouth, and emphasizes the natural symmetry of the human face"; his hair is "abundant and undisciplined" and his costume eccentric and ill-fitting. [16] The confrontation between these two figures, Bouissac argues, constitutes "a metacultural discourse" that allows society to articulate fundamental assumptions about the relationship between the individual and the social order, between nature and culture. [17] One can locate this same basic structure at work within the Marx Brothers' comedies with the figures of the white clown and the ugly clown transformed into those of Margaret Dumont and Groucho Marx (fig. 8.9). [18] Dumont's "dowager matron" encapsulates all that is self-important and stagnant in the existing social hierarchy; her size, her elegant clothing, her perfectly coiffed hair give her a weightiness and immobility that contrast sharply with the constant movement and wild appearance of Groucho and his brothers. She forbids pleasure; he embraces it.

As this description suggests, the social meanings of these two figures are often mapped directly onto their bodies; the excessive, "unfinished and open" body of the "ugly clown" stands opposed to the restrained and cultivated body of the "white clown" or the "dowager." These opposing images of the body will, of course, be familiar to anyone who has read Mikhail Bakhtin's discussion of grotesque realism:

> The grotesque body is not separated from the rest of the world. It is not a closed, completed unit; it is unfinished, outgrows itself, transgresses its own limits. The stress is laid on those parts of the body that are open to the outside world, that is, the parts through which the world enters the body or emerges from it. . . . This means that the emphasis is on the apertures or

the convexities, or on the various ramifications and offshoots: the open mouth, the genital organs, the breasts, the phallus, the potbelly, the nose.[19]

Bakhtin contrasts this grotesque conception of the body with a more classical conception of the body, one which emphasizes limits and boundaries rather than apertures and orifices, closure rather than openness and individuality rather than commonality. Groucho's body is the twentieth-century embodiment of this grotesque realism; Dumont's body, while a bit grotesque in its shape and size, comes closer to the more classical conception of the carefully controlled and tightly closed body.

We must be careful about extending this analogy too far, however. Bakhtin argues that this conception of the grotesque body is historically specific, bound to the carnival and market culture of Europe during the middle ages, representing a specific set of social relations (a communal alternative to medieval hierarchy). These same figures assume different meanings when they appear in Rabelais, native American ritual, nineteenth-century circus, or 1930s screen comedy. For starters, the Marx Brothers films embrace a conception of expressive individualism that would contrast sharply with the communalism Bakhtin identifies in Rabelais. Yet the grotesque body has remained a fruitful site, a "natural symbol" in Mary Douglas's sense, for mapping social relations.[20] Douglas shows how many different cultures use physical aspects of the body (orifices, digestion and excretion, birth, death, illness) as signifying material to express the relationship between the individual and the social community.

The figure of the clown and the grotesque body, thus, has a much longer history and a broader geography; any understanding of the specific meanings of these figures in 1930s screen comedy must remain attentive to both the figure's larger context and its specific inflection within these films. The clown's anarchy cannot be reduced to either a universal aspect of comic performance nor to a specific response to the American Depression; rather, it exists somewhere in between the totally global and the purely local. A fuller understanding of the clown and the comic antagonist will bring us closer to a comprehension of the concept of comic anarchy at work within these films.

The Clown. Our modern word *clown* is actually derived from two Old German terms, *Klonne,* meaning "clumsy lout, lumpish fellow, a countryman, rustic, or peasant" and *Klunj,* meaning "a clod, clot, or lump."[21]

As Louis A. Hieb suggests, these two root words tell us much about the attributes traditionally associated with the clown.[22] First, the clown is a liminal figure, an outsider, a social vagrant or conversely, a representative of the lowest orders of the social hierarchy ("a rustic or a peasant"). In either case, the clown is a "lout," poorly assimilated into the social order that his or her antics constantly disrupt. Secondly, the clown is "lumpish," a "clot" of conflicting meanings and associations, a "clump" of opposing cultural categories, a "clod" of irreconcilable impulses. As in Mary Douglas's classic definition of "dirt," the clown is "matter out of place"; the clown is the master of "mismeaning" whose very existence calls into question the stability and coherence of normal cultural categories. Traditionally, the clown served ritual functions, assumed a spiritual status, speaking to the eternal principles of creativity and procreation, the order that comes from disorder. Later the clown assumed a civic role—that of the court jester—with comic disruption permitted by virtue of official status and access to political power or, later, as the figure adopts a place among the bourgeoisie and the gentry, the clown's authority reflects proximity to economic wealth. The clown in mass culture assumes a more democratic stance, speaking to, for, and about the popular, though this stance masks his or her economic ties to consumer capitalism. Though the figure has been secularized within western culture, has fallen from its high social status, the clown retains many of its traditional attributes and functions, continues to bear traces of its earlier associations.

The clown within anarchistic comedy, like the traditional figure from which it evolved, remains essentially an outsider, a transient, a tramp, or an immigrant. Indeed, these films almost always open with the clown's displacement from one social order to another, a radical shift in status and/or geographic location; the clown is thrown out of his or her familiar environment into another whose rules and conventions have only been imperfectly mastered. The clown has no long-term commitment to the represented lifestyle, and, as a result, may question its values and disrupt its normal activities. Victor Turner suggests that those who occupy a liminal space "betwixt and between" the established strata of the social formation enjoy the greatest freedom to challenge and ridicule the community's sacred values and institutions.[23] Clowns achieve this liminality either because of their transience or marginality within that order or their transitional state between successive social positions (their adolescence or social mobility). Writing about nineteenth-century popular humor, Carroll Smith-Rosenberg has shown, for example, that Davy Crockett displayed multiple forms of liminality: he functioned on the frontier between civilization and the savage beyond; he represented an adolescent rebellion against parental authority; he adopted the traditional trappings of the transient "lower orders." Crockett's behavior invariably contested the categories by which late nineteenth-century America made sense of its social and cultural experience. Smith-Rosenberg concludes that Crockett, by fusing "the antistructural and chaotic power of three liminalities," offers an explicit commentary on the process of change, "the explosive power of formlessness at war with structure at a time when antistructure was still victorious and form in disarray." [24] The clown in anarchistic comedy serves a similar function, speaking to and for the underculture at a time of economic crisis, expressing a discontent with rigidity, hierarchy and emotional repression by opening the prospect of existing "betwixt and between" the normal structures of the social order; the clown in anarchistic comedy embraces the freedom that comes from straddling cultural categories.

This displacement of the comic protagonist may take various forms. The character may be fired from one job and therefore must adopt a new lifestyle. In the opening of *Life of the Party* (Warner Brothers, 1930), Winnie Lightner's singing causes a fistfight at the department store where she works; she decides to pursue the life of the gold digger rather than seek another position. The character may be hired for a new job and must adapt to its demands. Groucho Marx assumes new positions as manager of a new hotel in *The Cocoanuts,* as the president of a college in *Horse Feathers,* as the leader of Freedonia in *Duck Soup,* and as the head of an insane asylum in *A Day at the Races.* In other films, the character escapes from a threatening situation by adopting a new identity. In *Kid from Spain,* American Eddie Cantor must pass as a famous Spanish bullfighter when gangsters force him across the Mexican border. In *High Fliers,* Wheeler and Woolsey accidentally crash their plane onto the grounds of a posh mansion; when they are innocently implicated in a jewel robbery, they assume the role of police investigators. In *Meet the Baron,* Jack Pearl, a "pants presser," poses as a noted African explorer and must fake a lecture to a respected women's college. Sometimes, the characters inherit a sum of money or property that alters their social status. *Kid Millions* removes Cantor from Brooklyn poverty to an Egyptian adventure when it is discovered that he is the only legitimate heir to a much-sought-after fortune. In *What! No Beer?* Jimmy Durante and Buster Keaton, a local barber and a taxidermist, pool their resources to open a brewery on the eve of prohibition's repeal. Perhaps most dramatically, the characters accidentally find themselves in another time and place. In *Roman Scandals,* Cantor plays a citizen of the contemporary American town of West Rome who finds himself inexplicably transported back to Ancient Rome. Similarly, in *Ali Baba Goes to Town* he is a movie extra who awakens to find himself in the realm of the Arabian knights.

The clown's displacement, the movement from outside to inside the social order or the movement between two different social worlds, provides the preconditions for their "lumpish" play with cultural categories and their unrestrained disturbances of the peace. The clown's performance becomes a play with identity, a merging together of often contradictory categories within a single figure. Eddie Cantor is at once Jewish and gentile, immigrant and native-born. Bert Wheeler is at once female and male, straight and gay. The clown is both adult and child, insider and outsider, human and animal, and in some cases, contemporary and historical. In early sound comedy as in ancient ritual, the clown is a shape-shifter, whose creativity is reflected in the ability to alter appearance and mannerisms, to assume, reject, and fuse normally discreet and fixed identities. Steve Seidman treats these fluctuating identities as the signs of an unstable personality, as symptoms of neurosis and madness, and it is clear that they do assume this meaning in the films of Danny Kaye, Bob Hope and Jerry Lewis. Here, however, they are signs of vitality and exuberance, a freedom from fixed categories, a negation or refusal of socially constructed identity rather than an inability to achieve an identity the clown never desired.[25]

Norbert Elias has traced the historical "civilizing process" by which human societies developed rules that constrained impulsivity, affectivity, and expressivity but were necessary preconditions for large-scale social organization; social control, externally imposed rules of conduct, gradually gave way to "self-control" as individuals internalized those codes and learned to "regulate" their emotional and physical lives.[26] The clown, already set apart from the rest of the social order, refuses to participate within this "civilizing process," refuses to exercise the "self-restraint" needed to remain within structured life. The clown is driven by desire—desires of the body for food, drink, sexuality, or more abstractly, for pleasure and creativity—and the clown refuses to accept rules that block gratification.

The clowns are identifiable by their gross and unquenchable appetites. Groucho Marx and Robert Woolsey make no excuses about their desire to marry for money; gold digging female clowns, like Winnie

Lightner, simply reverse the process. Groucho, Woolsey, George Burns, Joe Cook, and W. C. Fields spend much of their time savoring their cigars, sticking them unlit in their mouths or waving them around in their hands. W. C. Fields dives out of an airplane in *You Can't Cheat an Honest Man* (Universal, 1939) when he accidentally knocks his flask overboard. In *The Cocoanuts,* Harpo makes a meal of buttons, sponges, and a desk telephone, washing it down with huge gulps of ink. Jimmy Durante and Buster Keaton literally swim in their frothing alcoholic brew in *What! No Beer?,* an image of excessive consumption prefigured by the Schnozle's antiprohibition bumper sticker, "I'm all wet!" Bert Wheeler often plays with his food, elaborately peeling and devouring bananas throughout *Hips, Hips, Hooray,* chomping apples in *Cockeyed Cavaliers,* tossing peanuts in his mouth in *High Flyers,* singing while munching on sandwiches in *Diplomaniacs* and *On Again, Off Again* (RKO, 1937), even consuming the wax fruit from a woman's hat in *Half Shot at Sunrise.* Groucho's lecherous leer and his hunched forward walk, Ole Olsen's suggestive giggle (fig. 8.10), and Harpo's constant placing of his limbs on other people's bodies suggest barely suppressed libidinous urges of monumental proportions. The smallest provocations will set these desires into motion and send them chasing after the nearest female. Harpo even takes to a bicycle to pursue blondes in *Monkey Business.* Such moments suggest the clown's immediate responsiveness to bodily desire without regard to social custom or self-restraint.

Often, the clowns lose command of their own bodies, responding to impulses even these grotesque characters might ordinarily check. Eddie Cantor starts singing when he gets nervous in *Palmy Days* and strikes out uncontrollably when he hears whistles in *A Kid from Spain.* Bert Wheeler suffers from bouts of kleptomania in *Cockeyed Cavaliers,* turning glassy-eyed and stealing whatever is at hand. Asked if he has "taken anything" for this problem, he responds, "yes—almost everything." A cabinet minister in *Million Dollar Legs* sneezes every time he wishes to speak. Roscoe Ates, in countless comedian comedies, stutters and stammers, spits and grunts, whenever he tries to communicate.

Like the "ugly clown" in traditional circus acts or the grotesque figures in Rabelais, the movie clowns' antisocial desires, their physicality and impulsiveness, are marked directly onto their bodies. The clowns display abnormally large eyes (Eddie Cantor, Hugh Herbert) and mouths (Winnie Lightner, Joe E. Brown), bulbous noses (W. C. Fields, Jimmy Durante), angular and contorted physiques (Groucho

Marx, Bert Wheeler), and unkempt hair (Harpo Marx, Ed Wynn). Their ill-fitting clothes simply exaggerate the odd joints and disproportionate parts of their misshapen figures; Robert Woolsey often seems to be all bottom, Harpo all legs and arms. Makeup (Groucho's painted-on eyebrows and mustache) directs our attention onto the orifices and extensions of the body. The clowns do not walk; they waddle with legs bowed or heads thrust forward, contorted by the degenerate desires that propel them into action.

The verbal humor of these comedies also suggests a preoccupation with bodily desires and physical appetites, a disinterest in social respectability and self-control.[27] The most innocent phrase may be twisted to communicate the most erotic of meanings. Olsen and Johnson overhear two women discussing their plans to groom a dog in *50 Million Frenchmen,* only to misread the conversation as plans for their sexual pleasure. Landing atop the International House, W. C. Fields asks first an attractive woman and then, Franklin Pangborn, to identify his present location. He seems pleased when the woman answers, "Yoo-Hoo," but throws away his corsage in disgust when he elicits the same response from Pangborn. A woman in *The Cuckoos* explains that she smells "sweet" because she always has violet in her bath; Woolsey explains that he would follow this practice as well but "I don't know Violet." Seen through the leering eyes of the clowns, the whole world is ripe with erotic possibilities, though their verbal gags may speak to other appetites as well. A gangster threatens to give them a "pineapple" in *Hook, Line and Sinker* to which they respond with glee, asking only that they be given a "juicy one." A woman in *Caught Plastered* introduces herself as Miss Newton and Woolsey can't resist asking her if she is related to "the fig newtons."

That many of these jokes are bad and predictable, "old saws" as they were called in vaudeville slang, hardly matters. Indeed, in some cases, the clowns themselves acknowledge how "terrible" these jokes are. Robert Woolsey covers his face, laughing hysterically and protesting that he cannot help himself. Jimmy Durante seems more shameless, ignoring protests from nonresponsive listeners and proclaiming, "I've got a million of 'em." What seems significant is that, good or bad, the clowns cannot resist the compulsion to tell these jokes; they respond to an irresistible urge to pull everything down to its most biologically basic level, to read every statement in terms of its relationship to the body. An overheated and ill-tempered border guard in *Kid from Spain* threatens Eddie Cantor and orders him not to tell any more jokes. Again

Kid From Spain (1933): Eddie Cantor. Academy of Motion Picture Arts and Sciences.

and again, Cantor approaches him only to turn their interaction into the basis for some juvenile joke, even though the guard's increasing hostility tangibly threatens his own interests in escaping across the border unnoticed.

The clown opens his mouth and jokes spring forth, jokes that disorganize cultural categories, fracture normal logic, and defy the rules of everyday discourse. The linguistic play, the joking finally signals a refusal to conform to the codes of coherent communication, a refusal to convey stable meanings. In *Half Shot at Sunrise,* Wheeler and Woolsey, two soldiers AWOL in Paris trying to stay one step ahead of the MPs, duck into a fancy restaurant and assume the role of waiters, only to discover themselves seating their colonel and his wife. The colonel rather pretentiously asks about the "specialties du jours" and Woolsey tries to guess whether "du jours" are "animal, mineral or vegetable." The wife crossly calls him an "imbecile" but Wheeler patiently explains that "we are all out of those. . . . Would you like some naturalized Swiss cheese?" The couple are told that the turtle soup is "snappy" but "a bit slow." When the woman orders an "extremely young chicken," Woolsey suggests that she might like "a couple of eggs." Asked about "wild duck," they suggest they could "take a tame one and aggravate it for you." The customers are warned not to even inquire if they have "frog legs," that joke being so old that it need only be referenced to produce a laugh. In the end, the waiters depart without taking their order; the entire transaction has turned inward upon itself, with nothing meaningful communicated and no possibility of progression beyond the exchange of crossfire gags. Speech based exclusively on jokes must necessarily be self-negating, with each new utterance overturning and canceling what has come before.

The clown contests social hierarchy, transforming and reversing status relationships with the same apparent ease and indifference with which logical and linguistic categories are overturned. In *Love in Bloom*, a motorcycle cop pulls over Burns and Allen and writes them a ticket for speeding. Gracie insists on writing a ticket for the confused cop, who necessarily was exceeding the speed limit himself in trying to catch up with their speeding car. Later, in the same film, Gracie enters a shop and proceeds to try to sell it to its owner. When her father has her psychoanalyzed in *Many Happy Returns* (Paramount, 1934), Gracie suggests that the shrink looks "tired" and suggests that she could ask him questions for a while. Her cook quits because the servant doesn't like Gracie's cooking and she holds her kidnappers for ransom. Gracie inhabits a world where social relationships are reciprocal and reversible rather than hierarchical and structured. She strews disorder and confusion in her path because all those around her seek to make sense of her conversation in conventional terms, while her own thought patterns constantly restructure the world. In both *Many Happy Returns* and *Here Comes Cookie*, she reverses the normal rules of commerce; left in charge of her father's fortune, she works to deplete it, rather than to expand it. She tears down his department store and replaces it with a bird sanctuary, importing the birds from local pet shops. She gives away the goods in the store instead of selling them for a profit. Her style of comic anarchy is less aggressive, less self-interested than Groucho's, but she is no less destructive for all her good intentions.

Here Comes Cookie (1935): Gracie Allen and George Burns. Wisconsin Center for Film and Theater Research.

The Comic Antagonist. Gracie's wacky comedy only works when she is cast against a more serious-minded foil—most often against George Burns, but also against a whole string of cops, shopkeepers, hotel managers, fathers, film directors, and psychoanalysts. They struggle to restore or preserve order even as she provokes disorder, to work while she plays. These figures remain committed to the hierarchical and structured world that holds so little meaning for Gracie. The comic antagonists represent the restraints society would exert upon individual spontaneity; they embody the adult order against which her childishness is contrasted. Charles Ruggles and Mary Boland in *Six of a Kind* seek only to enjoy their second honeymoon, though as an economy measure, they are forced to advertise for a second couple to share transportation expenses. George and Gracie arrive to answer the ad and Gracie immediately begins to rearrange their plans. She moves the furniture about their house and unscrews the receiver from the telephone to use as a cookie cutter, even as Boland struggles to maintain a conversation with her husband. Boland and Ruggles represent the orderly existence that cannot coexist with the presence of Burns and Allen. Their twenty years of marriage contrasts sharply with the clowns' rootlessness; Burns and Allen have remained unmarried and seem to flit from one place to another. Boland and Ruggles have allowed themselves only one vacation in twenty years; Burns and Allen seem to never go off vacation. Boland and Ruggles have carefully planned the most efficient route; Burns and Allen have no use for maps or schedules and insist on taking their own "short-cut," which gets everyone hopelessly lost. Boland and Ruggles are more benign than many other comic antagonists; their demands seem so much more reasonable that the comic disruption often seems annoying and unpleasant. Still, Boland and Ruggles assume many of the traditional attributes of the comic antagonist: a deferment of pleasure, a false sense of importance, an insistence upon order and decorum, a slow-witted response to the clown's unpredictability.

Steve Seidman argues that comedian comedy focuses on "oppositions within the individual," while social or romantic comedy centers around oppositions between characters.[28] Yet such a reading of comedian comedy may be self-affirming, since it is the critic, not the films, who has chosen to ignore the secondary characters against which the comedian is opposed. I would argue that comedian comedy, like other forms of popular narrative, depends heavily upon paradigmatic pairings of characters and it is through this implicit contrasting of figures—the clown and the comic antagonists—that the meanings of the comedian comedy emerge. Anarchistic comedy, true to its roots in vaudeville tradition, involves a comedy of social types. As we have seen, there is not an "interior" to which we can appeal in understanding the Marx Brothers' antics. Rather, we discover what these figures mean by looking at them in relationship to their antagonists. These comic antagonists exist to react against the clowns' disorderliness, to be humiliated and disrupted. Their sluggishness and fussiness are as important as the clowns' spontaneity and exuberance. If the clowns represent those qualities that resist conformity, the comic antagonists embody the lifelessness that comes from perfect assimilation of the conventional and the habitual. The clowns retain vitality at the expense of social acceptability; the comic antagonists enjoy social prestige at the expense of personal expressivity. There are three basic types of comic antagonists: dupes, killjoys, and counterfeits. Each type represents a characteristic flaw of the existing social order; each provides a contrast to the central clown's anarchistic tendencies.

Dupes lack the clown's quick mind and original perceptions; they are completely bound by conventional patterns of thought. Dupes are slow to respond to the provocation of the clown's antics and insults and are often an easy victim for comic schemes. Amos (Tom Howard), the slow-witted country bumpkin in *Rain or Shine,* comes to see circus owner Joe Cook about an overdue feed bill; the fast-talking Cook mumbles, waves his cigar around and ensnares Howard in his tangled logical constructions until the man willingly hands over more money as an investment in the bankrupt tent show. Amos's attempts to comprehend the nature of their arrangement in "dollar and cents" terms are constantly thwarted by Cook's ability to derail any and all logical discussion. Dupes are unable to think outside of found cultural categories; the clown refuses to think in those terms at all.

The clowns' greater mental flexibility ensures that they will always be able to outsmart more sluggish counterparts. Wheeler and Woolsey easily stay one step ahead of the dim-witted Military Police in *Half Shot at Sunrise,* stealing their hats and armbands while the MPs stand against a hedge examining the boys' photograph: "Something tells me we almost had those guys." Wheeler and Woolsey stroll aimlessly down the Paris boulevards, ducking into a hotel lobby to attach a new rank onto their uniforms, flirting with "girls" and enjoying a life of freedom; the MPs doggedly pursue them, recognizing them only too late, unable to anticipate their erratic behavior.

A second type of comic antagonist, the killjoy represents social stability as a loss of individual spontaneity and personal expressiveness. Writing of the role played by this figure in classical Greek comedy, Harry Levin writes, "What these killjoys have primarily in common is that they are agelasts. They cannot make a joke; they cannot take a joke; they cannot see the joke; they spoil the game." [29] Humorlessness is a fatal flaw for a character in an anarchistic comedy. Killjoys have become so accustomed to repressing bodily desire that they have lost the ability to feel pleasure. At their most aggressive, killjoys seek to remove all possibility of pleasure from the general environment. Killjoys may seem shrunken and anemic, like Claude Gillingwater in *So Long Letty* and *Gold Dust Gertie* (Warner Brothers, 1931), drained of life, reduced by the constant restraint, or massive and domineering, like Margaret Dumont in *Animal Crackers* and *Duck Soup,* overfilled with her own importance. Killjoys may be nervous and twitchy like Franklin Pangborn in *International House,* who obsessively returns all the room keys to their proper place just in time for W. C. Fields to overturn them again (fig. 8.11), or barking and sarcastic, like Edna May Oliver in *Cracked Nuts,* who constantly belittles Bert Wheeler. Whatever form the killjoy takes, he or she accepts as a lifelong duty the task of restoring order in the face of the clown's chaotic conduct and of crushing all pleasures that stray from the well-trod path.

The clown provokes the killjoy, tests his or her commitment to the orderly life; the clown pushes and prods until finally, belatedly, the killjoy shows evidence of emotionality and irrationality—even if it is only directed against the clown. Edgar Kennedy as the prison warden in *Hold 'Em Jail* struggles to maintain discipline in the face of steady abuse by two novelty salesmen (Wheeler and Woolsey). Here, the confrontation is suggested by the characters' occupations: one is commissioned to maintain order, the others to spread novelty. The salesmen barge into his office as he is trying to light his pipe; they proceed to catch his matches on fire and to extinguish the blaze with a water pistol that soaks his shirt. They rattle noisemakers in his face and blow horns in his ears, put a toy hat on his head and shower him with confetti; they prod him with streamers, cram a whistle in his mouth, and stick his hand into a Chinese finger trap (fig. 8.12). All the while, he glares at them, trying very hard not to succumb to his rapidly rising anger. He fights to fulfill his professional duty to maintain order, until, finally, he springs to his feet and storms from the office, shattering the glass door behind him. Woolsey looks after the retreating warden and mumbles, "what a sunny disposition." Kennedy's famous "slow-burn" personifies the killjoy's struggle to retain tight control over his passions; that Kennedy never perfectly maintains that discipline, that he must finally explode into raw and childish rage suggests the unnaturalness and arbitrariness of those social demands. Kennedy's placid facade must finally collapse as he coughs up everything he has held in check; he reveals in a moment of pure destructiveness everything he has sought to repress.

If dupes represent the mental fixity and killjoys the passionlessness that comes from conforming to the demands of the orderly life, the counterfeit suggests the bankruptcy of the conformist's demands for social status. Counterfeits claim an unearned respectability and hold others accountable to standards they themselves refuse to obey. The colonel in *Half Shot at Sunrise* forces Wheeler and Woolsey to fulfill their duties as soldiers rather than pursue their own pleasures in the carnal carnival of Paris; the colonel, however, is so distracted by his own amorous feelings toward his mistress that he incompetently fulfills his own duties. He sends a perfume-soaked love letter to the frontlines rather than the important orders upon which the lives of his men depend and the clowns brave danger to deliver it. The colonel is saved from disgrace only by the clowns' incompetence at their assigned tasks. The colonel is a benign figure beside Ambassador Trentino (Louis Calhern) in *Duck Soup*; Trentino's treason poses a far greater threat to the order and stability of Freedonia than the monkeyshines of Groucho and his brothers do. The corrupt lawyers and business managers in *Hips, Hips, Hooray, The Nitwits* (RKO, 1935), and *Caught Plastered* use their social positions to further their own interests. These counterfeit figures abound in *Hook, Line and Sinker*. When Wheeler and Woolsey help Dorothy Lee reopen a luxury hotel, all of the guest claim royal blood or high social status; they are actually all gangsters, intent on stealing the jewels from the hotel safe. A massive shoot-out results as the guests struggle for possession of the "loot," which amounts only to the night watchman's lunch. Although such characters endlessly assert their dignity and prestige, the clowns' antics strip away false dignity. The clown, sometimes intentionally, sometimes accidentally, uncovers the counterfeit's deceit and hypocrisy, exposing covert schemes to public scrutiny.

The comic antagonist, no less than the clown, poses a critique of the social order. Conformity to the rules of normal conduct dulls the mind, robs the individual of pleasure, and deprives the social order of innovation. Besides, the social order's values are corrupt and self-serving; the system demands respect for persons who do not merit it. Within such a world, personal expression can come only through comic disruption, only through transgression of social norms and violation of structured relationships. A stifling order must give way for a liberating disorder, a topsy-turveydom where the clown's values reign and the efforts of the comic antagonist to restore order are constantly thwarted. The anarchistic comedy plays out this struggle both globally, in the larger movement of the narrative, and locally, in the structure of individual sequences. The comic antagonist seeks to exercise control over the clown; the clown resists, creating confusion and chaos, eluding control and escaping the demands for conformity.

Steve Seidman offers a very different version of the anarchistic scenario, one that emphasizes the genre's more integrative aspects; Seidman treats the comedian's antics as excessive signifiers of the protagonist's need to establish a stable and acceptable social identity. His account displaces narrative conflict from a social sphere into the psychic sphere, seeing comic misconduct as an outward manifestation of personality conflict, an aberration from social and textual norms. While acknowledging our pleasure in the comedian's disruptiveness, Seidman suggests that narrative resolutions contain these comic transgressions and pull the characters back into the social mainstream; the emotional "risk" posed by comic transgression is too intense to be left unresolved. Satisfactory resolution can be achieved in only two ways: (1) the "cure" and assimilation of the comic figure into society or (2) the comic figure's rejection from society. Seidman concludes:

> Both resolutions stress the value of attaining a cultural identity at the expense of individual creativity. The comic figure must be divested of his creativity—his difference—for the good of the collective. . . . The cultural assimilation of the comic figure permits the attainment of certain valued norms: responsible social position, sexuality, marriage, material goods and so forth.[30]

For Seidman, comedian comedy is finally a conservative genre; comedian comedy raises the prospect of comic disruption only to reassure the viewer that there was no real risk after all. Comedian comedy, in the end, confirms the desirability of operating within social norms and societal rules. The Seidman model presupposes that the comic text aligns itself with the norms of the social order and that the comedian seeks integration and assimilation into those norms.

We might distinguish between the integrative role Seidman assigns to the comedian and the disintegrative role I assign to the clown. The comedian's comedy stems from mistakes and mishaps arising from efforts to conform to social norms, the clown's comedy from disruptions and transgressions arising from a desire or compulsion to break free from constraint. The comedian seeks to redefine the individual's relationship to the existing order; the clown wishes to escape from society and exist outside of its rules and conventions. Such a distinction, however, is more an analytic device than an adequate description of any actual comedy. The disintegrative aspect of anarchistic comedy—a comedy of disorder—almost always coexists with the integrative aspect of romantic comedy—a comedy of reordering—though the emphasis given the two plots shifts from film to film and across historical periods. An overemphasis on either of the two plots blinds us to the more complex relationship between them.

"A STABLE AND HARMONIOUS ORDER":
THE ROMANTIC COUPLE AND THE INTEGRATIVE PLOT

In what remains the definitive treatment of the conventions of romantic comedy, Northrop Frye argues that the genre offers a reformist vision; romantic comedy seeks a more satisfactory rearrangement of existing hierarchies and relationships in order to better accommodate basic human needs and desires. Frye writes, "What normally happens is that a young man wants a young woman, that his desire is resisted by some opposition, usually paternal, and that near the end of the play some twist of plot enables the hero to have his will."[31] Typically, the blocking figures are of an older generation, one presently in power; these figures represent society's resistance to youthful love and vitality, its basic antipathy to healthy desire and personal expression. The movement of the comic text involves not simply the formation of a new couple but the construction of a new and more perfect society. The blocking agents, not the youthful lovers, are "usurpers" of social power; what they offer is a false or illusionary order, actually a perversion or decline from a previous golden age, and what the romantic protagonist restores is a true utopia.

While the anarchistic scenario moves from order into disorder, seeing the greatest potential for personal expression as existing outside of any structured relationship, the romantic comedy involves a movement from disorder—or false order—into a more perfect order, seeing the reorganization of society as the only way to bring about human happiness. The anarchistic scenario ends with a "carnival," a celebration of social inversion; the romantic scenario ends with a "festival," a celebration of renewed social commitment. The hero in the anarchistic comedy is the antithesis of the sheriff of the conventional western: the clown moves into the social order from the outside, uses his or her skills to create disorder, and then moves on in search of another ordered space to disrupt. The hero of the romantic comedy restores order so that he or she may dwell within it.

The clown's relationship to the conventional romantic comedy is troublesome. What is problematic is not simply that the personality of the clown is more compelling than that of the young lovers. Frye finds a similar pattern in traditional romantic comedy; the romantic couple is "often not very interesting," displaying a bland "neutrality" that offers "wish fulfillment" for the spectator. "His real life begins at the end of the play and we have to believe him to be potentially a more interesting character than he appears to be."[32] For Frye, the comic interest lies primarily in the blocking characters, whose larger-than-life flaws and foibles make them a focus of audience laughter. Such figures direct a rebuking laughter against their social deviations. The anarchistic comedy, however, focuses its comic interest on the clown; these comic values, far from being rejected, are upheld and put to the cause of uniting the young couple. What begin as antisocial impulses must be redirected to the task of promoting a new social order.

The romance between Polly Potter (Mary Eaton) and Bob Adams (Oscar Shaw) in *The Cocoanuts* initially simply coexists with the story of Mr. Hammer (Groucho Marx), his Florida land speculations, and his schemes to marry Mrs. Potter (Margaret Dumont); scenes alternate between the two plots without much causal integration. Bob, a young architect, has developed plans for improving Cocoanut City; he dreams of transforming the developing community into a "Heaven for Polly and Me." His aspirations are challenged by a rival, Harvey Yates (Cyril Ring), whose false claims to a higher social standing make him more attractive to Polly's status-centered mother. Groucho's frankly materialistic interest in Mrs. Potter contrasts sharply with Bob's ideal love of her daughter; Groucho confesses that he would love Dumont if she were poor but "I would keep my mouth shut."

When Dumont disrupts the comic auction sequence to announce the theft of her jewels and Bob is falsely accused of the crime, the two plots are pulled together. Her lover publicly discredited, Polly consents to marry Yates and plans to announce her engagement at a party that night. Harpo and Chico, previously presented as forces of comic disorder, come to Bob's rescue, freeing him from jail so that he may prove his innocence; the two clowns create comic disturbances at the party to block the announcement of Polly's engagement. Having implicated the clowns in the romantic plot, their disruptive behavior assumes a more prosocial and integrative function. In the film's climax, Yates's treachery is revealed and the young lovers are reunited as the brothers shake each others' hands and look benevolently into the camera. The romance between Polly and Bob is highly conventional, and played in an uninteresting fashion, reduced to its most formulaic elements by the demand to create space for the clowns' comic disruptions. Still, it serves the function of pulling the clowns back into the social order. Their commitment to the furtherance of young love—and thus, the creation of a new social order—mitigates against their liminality.

The Marx Brothers themselves—with the exception of Zeppo who occasionally assumes the role of the romantic protagonist—stay clear of romantic entanglements. Groucho continually courts Margaret Dumont, but there is no real love lost between them. The exception is in *Horse Feathers,* where all of the brothers marry the same woman (Thelma Todd), in a parody of the typical ending of romantic comedy, with its uniting of multiple couples in a festival of social renewal. The Marx Brothers serve the romantic interests of other lovers—Hal Thompson and Lillian Roth (*Animal Crackers*), Kitty Carlisle and Allan Jones (*A Night at the Opera*), Maureen O'Sullivan and Allan Jones (*A Day at the Races*), Kenny Baker and Florence Rice (*At the Circus,* MGM, 1939)— helping to bring about a social order within which the clowns have no fixed place. The Marx Brothers' bonds to the social order are temporary and end as the film ends; they are free to depart from the story, having overturned the blocking characters and thus facilitated the lovers' union. The brothers stand apart both from the lovers and from the community as they shake hands in the conclusion of *The Cocoanuts.*

Other performers, however, are drawn much more decisively into the integrative plots; these clowns adopt the role of the young lover who will actively participate within the new social order. In *Cracked Nuts,* Wendell Graham (Bert Wheeler) loves Betty Harrington (Dorothy Lee) but her harsh-talking Aunt Minnie (Edna May Oliver) will not approve of her marrying that "insect." The aunt believes that Wendell is "a wealthy idler who produces nothing, achieves nothing and means nothing," who inherited his family fortune and proceeded to squander it; only by accomplishing something meaningful can Wendell hope to win approval for a marriage to Betty. The film's opening follows closely the romantic comedy formula, swerving into anarchistic comedy only with the appearance of Robert Woolsey as a shyster who wins the kingdom of El Dorania from its former king in a crap game. Wheeler has also bought an interest in the kingdom, feeling that as a king, he might command Aunt Minnie's respect. From this basic situation evolves a series of anarchistic sequences, as the two clowns struggle for possession of the government, humiliating or eluding a succession of comic antagonists, only to find resolution through romantic commitment. In the film's conclusion, Minnie stands on the hotel balcony, lecturing her niece and her fiancé about their misguided ways: "Do you remember my telling you to keep away from that runt?" and Betty answers, "I Do," as the camera pulls back to show her responding not to the aunt's ranting but to the minister's wedding vows. Wheeler has accepted his place within the social order; Woolsey remains outside of its dictates. The duality of the comic team allows a double ending: Wheeler's marriage resolves the romantic plot, while Woolsey's clowning keeps alive the possibility of comic anarchy. The scowling Aunt Minnie similarly plays a double role—as a blocking character in the romantic plot and a killjoy in the anarchistic plot.

Other integrative plots may also be added. Eddie Cantor in *Strike Me Pink* wants to keep Dreamland Amusement Park from falling under mob control, helping to protect "Ma," who refuses to allow gambling machines to be installed in the facility. Similarly, Wheeler and Woolsey use their "promotional genius" to help another old woman maintain control over her late husband's drug store in *Caught Plastered* and to assist Dorothy Lee in making her hotel a success in *Hook, Line and Sinker*. In all three cases, this entrepreneurial plot becomes intertwined with the romantic plot, further binding the clown to the demands of creating a new social order. Cantor falls in love with his secretary, who respects him only as long as he remains committed to keeping Dreamland free from gang ties; she agrees to marry him when he finally defeats the mobsters in the film's climactic chase sequence. Dorothy Lee doubles in *Hook, Line and Sinker* as the recipient of their assistance and the object of Wheeler's romantic interests; the success of the hotel and the capture of the crooks paves the way for Wheeler to win her mother's approval for the marriage. In *Caught Plastered*, Dorothy Lee plays the daughter of a small-town police chief who develops a crush on Bert Wheeler. When the clowns are duped into selling a "lemon extract" that is really bootleg whiskey, they fall under the chief's suspicion and he wants to shut down the drugstore. Only by defeating the bootleggers and proving their innocence can the clowns achieve their dual task: keeping the store in business and paving the way for the romantic union between Wheeler and Lee. Each film allows opportunities for some anarchistic sequences, but the clowns' antisocial tendencies must give way to their integrative function as they become fully committed to the need to establish a more perfect social order. Woolsey, who remained outside the romantic plot in *Cracked Nuts*, develops a son's devotion to his adopted "mother" in *Caught Plastered* and himself becomes involved in a secondary romantic plot with Lee's mother in *Hook, Line and Sinker*.

These social commitments not only close down the anarchic possibilities posed by the clown's disruptive conduct but also tighten the film's plot construction. While Wheeler and Woolsey played a relatively passive role within the narrative of *Diplomaniacs*, they become goal-centered protagonists in *Caught Plastered* and *Hook, Line and Sinker* who take actions to resolve narrative problems. Not accidentally, as classical norms reasserted themselves in the face of the challenge posed by the vaudeville aesthetic, the integrative plot played an increasingly central role. Sometimes, the romantic plot almost entirely displaces the anarchistic sequences. Much has been made of the increased narrative integration in the later Marx Brothers' comedies, a shift often attributed to the guiding hand of Irving Thalberg following their move from Paramount to MGM. All of the other clowns included within this study underwent a similar shift in the mid-1930s, with the romantic and service-centered plots becoming the narrative focus and moments of nonintegrated comic performance growing fewer and fewer. The emergence of affirmative comedy and, later, screwball comedy as the dominant comic paradigms of the late 1930s reflects the greater compatibility of these forms to classical norms.

This development largely forecloses the possibility for anarchistic narratives—though clearly not for isolated moments of comic anarchy within larger structures of comic integration. The Marx Brothers may provoke as much mayhem in *A Night at the Opera* as they do in *Duck Soup*; their antics in the MGM film further their narrative task of uniting the young lovers, however, while their clowning in the Paramount film serves only to bring about the collapse of the dominant social order. This integrative narrative was part of the Marx Brother's comedy from the very beginning—though not in *Duck Soup,* the most anarchistic of all screen comedies. *Duck Soup* has no place for romantic comedy; the power of its justly famous conclusion is that it pushes the brothers outside of narrative, essentially outside of causality and continuity, with no hope of assimilating them back again. Only in their later films does the integrative subplot subordinate the clown's anarchic potential to its demands.

The shifting relationship between the anarchistic and romantic plots may best be illustrated by a consideration of these films' conclusions. As we have seen in previous chapters, conclusions posed an aesthetic problem for early sound comedy: the vaudeville aesthetic mandated that the text should build toward a wow finish, a moment of maximum comic spectacle, while classical narrative construction required closure, a shutting down and tying together of the major lines of plot development. A similar tension exists on an ideological level: the anarchistic plot builds comic disruption upon comic disruption toward a final explosion that rips away the remaining structures of the social order, provokes total chaos, and liberates personal expression; the integrative plot, however, unites the social community behind the romantic couple as the corrupt old order gives way to a better new order. Anarchistic comedy privileges the wow climax at the expense of narrative closure, comic anarchy at the expense of community celebration, though both possibilities are usually evoked in the films' closing moments. The ending of *Animal Crackers* may be a classic example. The stolen painting, upon which much of the plot rests, is recovered. The romantic protagonist's talents as an artist are recognized and he receives a big commission. The mother gives her permission to the marriage of the young couple. The police forgive Harpo for his crimes and lecture him on the need to follow the straight path. All of the strains of the integrative plot have fallen into a pleasing order when silverware and pots start to fall from Harpo's body, revealing a whole succession of previously unsuspected thefts. The police try to carry Harpo away, but he squirts everyone with a flit gun full of chloroform and the whole community drops into a deep slumber. Left alone in a room of drugged women, Harpo picks an attractive blonde, sprays himself, and collapses into her arms. The new order promised by the text collapses into a groggy disorder, as, once again, the clown places his bodily desire over social demand. Narrative integration provides the set-up for a final anarchistic gag.

The car race in *Hips, Hips, Hooray* and the horse race in *A Day at the Races*, the chases in *Strike Me Pink*, *50 Million Frenchmen*, or *The Bank Dick* (Universal, 1940), the football games in *Hold 'Em Jail* and *Horse Feathers*, even the battleground sequence in *Half Shot at Sunrise* reverse this process; they are exercises in controlled chaos with comic spectacle linked to the hero's triumph over narrative obstacles. While individual rules may be violated, the goals of these competitions are always of foremost importance. High Hat must win the Grand Steeplechase at Sparkling Springs Track in *A Day at the Races;* Gil Stewart (Alan Jones) has invested in the horse over the objections of his fiancée, Judy Standish (Maureen O'Sullivan). If the horse fails to win, Judy will lose the sanitarium and he will, in all likelihood, lose both the horse and the woman. Morgan (Douglass Dumbrille), the comic antagonist who hopes to repossess the sanitarium, tries to block the horse's entry into the race. The Marx Brothers have aligned themselves with Gil and employ their considerable skills to disrupt and delay the race so that the young lovers may slip High Hat past Morgan's watchful eyes. Harpo puts soap underneath all the saddles so that the jockeys slide off when the race is about to start; he also soaps the starting horn so that it bubbles and froths but cannot sound. He turns on a monstrous fan that blows all the spectators' hats into the track. Groucho and Chico direct cars to park on the race track. The brothers move the fence so that the jockeys go galloping off into open country. The Marx Brothers transgress almost every rule in the book, but the repeated cutaways to the young couple racing to the track remind us that all this disorder is in the name of a higher order. Despite all these momentary disruptions, the institution of the race remains solidly in place; the race must be run and upon its outcome depend all the characters' futures. When Harpo and High Hat win the race, the major characters—united with a community of poor blacks who have won by betting on the horse—join in a celebratory parade. Groucho will marry Margaret Dumont; Gil will marry Judy. Morgan's scheme has been thwarted and the sanitarium will remain under Dr. Hackenbush's control.

Anarchistic comedy is characterized at all levels by a tension between forces for integration and forces for disintegration. The individual gag works to destablize meaning, to disrupt the coherent development of the narrative, yet its transgressiveness is contained by a larger logic that reinforces the validity of normal modes of thinking. The individual sequence plays out a pattern of social disruption, yet is contained within a larger narrative that pulls it back toward social integration. The narrative is marked by the interplay of two plots—one pushing toward the collapse of all social order, celebrating the utopian prospect of existing outside of cultural and bodily restraint; the other pushing away a corrupt old order only to replace it with a better form of social structure.

The temptation, of course, is to read the anarchistic plot as somehow progressive, a radical critique of the dominant social order, while reading the more reformist tendencies of the romantic comedy plot as conservative, a coopting of the resistive force of the clown's antics. Comedian comedy—that is, comedy dominated by the integrative plot— would be anarchistic comedy made safe. We must be cautious, however, about attributing a progressive force to the anarchistic narrative apart from its use of historically specific imagery and its function within a particular cultural context. In a review of the traditional imagery of "worlds upside down," David Kunzle finds that this representation of a collapse or reversal of dominant institutions has "lent itself historically to a variety of interpretations and was capable of fulfilling diverse and even contrary social and psychological needs." While the imagery spoke to "discontented, lower-class elements who sought or fantasized about the subversion of the existing order," it also "served the interests of the newly entrenched bourgeoisie by suggesting the immutability of the social structure," indicating the absurdity of attempts to alter necessarily hierarchical relationships.[33] It is not enough, then, to identify certain thematic structures as disintegrative and others as integrative; we must locate *where* those themes were aligned with particular social forces within historically specific texts. The next chapter considers the ways in which these anarchistic structures were capable of expressing a variety of perspectives on male-female relationships, the ways male and female clowns articulated fundamentally different notions of comic anarchy.

9

"Don't Become Too Intimate with That Terrible Woman!" Unruly Wives, Female Performance, and Gendered Laughter in Early Sound Comedy

The somber Mr. Davis (Claude Gillingwater) checks into the Ardmore Beach Hotel with his two teenaged granddaughters in search of "sunshine, fresh air and plenty of quiet." The young women are staring glumly out the window, frustrated by the restraint their chaperon imposes upon them. Suddenly, the long-legged Letty Robbins (Charlotte Greenwood), a recruiter for the hotel beauty parlor, bursts through the door, slamming its knob into the old man's face. Letty slaps Davis on the back, stalks about the room pumping everybody's hands, cracking a string of jokes at high speed and even higher volume. The teenagers watch admiringly, obviously enjoying the excitement this unruly woman brings to their grandfather's drab grey world. With a little coaxing from the young women, Letty sits down at a convenient piano and sings a raucous song, "Wait Till Letty Gets Through with Them," disregarding the patriarch's stern glare. The grandfather is horrified when "that maniac" turns her attentions on him again, proclaiming his face a "national calamity," manhandling his cheeks, yanking his hair, and finally, swinging her whole leg over his head and scraping her heel along his bald spot (fig. 9.1). Mr. Davis stands, sputtering angrily, and shouts into the telephone, "This isn't a hotel! This is a madhouse!"

This opening sequence from *So Long Letty* offers the kind of anarchistic moment identified in the last chapter—an explosion of comic aggressiveness directed against a carefully ordered space and an emotionally repressive character. Claude Gillingwater's balding head and sunken eyes make his Uncle Claude the very image of a fossilized patriarchal order. His slow, stiff movements and somewhat nasal speech contrast sharply with Greenwood's rapid-fire delivery and rambunctious gestures. With her ear-piercing voice and thrashing movements, her lack of respect for proper authority and her steady stream of slang and wisecracks, Letty is a dreadful negation of everything he regards to be proper and ladylike: "Take my advice and don't become too intimate with that terrible woman," he warns his nephew. What is different about *So Long Letty*, however, is the surprising way in which the film reverses the normal assignment of gender roles within that scenario. We are offered here a sequence in which a spontaneous woman liberates two young women from the control of male authority and invites them to pursue their own pleasure. Letty's engaging performance encourages spectators to judge and ridicule the stiff old man through the eyes of three lively young women in a reversal of the tripartite structure—male jester, female object, male audience—that Freud saw as characteristic of the smut joke.[1] The woman, by becoming the clown and by casting the patriarch in the traditional killjoy role, forces the anarchistic scenario to speak for female resistance, offering women utopian possibilities most other comedian comedies reserve for men only.

We must be careful not to exaggerate, however, the "liberating" potential of this type of female comic performance. If *So Long Letty* opens on a moment of female enunciation that challenges the normality and desirability of patriarchal order and directs women's laughter at a male butt, the film, like many vehicles for female comics, soon refigures the traditional structure of the joke, transforming the female clown back into the object rather than the subject of her own comic discourse. Indeed, the film's second scene represents a fundamental shift in point of view as we are asked to evaluate Letty from her unfortunate husband's perspective. A middle-aged and rather pudgy man (Bert Roach) enters his house to find the living room in total disarray. He shakes his head and mutters to himself, "How could a woman be so neglectful?" Reaching down to the littered floor, he spots an unopened letter informing him that his wealthy Uncle Claude is coming to visit that very day. The husband hopes for a sizable legacy from Uncle Claude, if the older man approves of his nephew's family situation; Letty's antics in the first scene are redefined as a threat to the future well-being of her husband. Letty will have to work throughout the rest of the film to change the "strong impression" Claude forms of her as "that terrible woman." The second scene responds to the first, suggesting the painful consequences of Letty's impulsive conduct—the costs her husband must endure as a result of her pursuit of bodily pleasure. Indeed, the first moment of transgression may be acceptable here only because it is followed by a narrative of repression and containment. The film's overall trajectory works to constrain and redirect the disruptive energies of Letty Robbins into a more properly feminine style of conduct and finally, to reposition her as wife and mother. Greenwood may be allowed to star in several anarchistic sequences here, yet *So Long Letty* cannot be legitimately called an anarchistic comedy; the reassertion of narrative logic and character consistency restrains her play with identity and her ability to suspend the narrative for moments of performance spectacle. Just as we must not exaggerate the transgressiveness of the first sequence, we need not overstate the repressiveness of the second, for the wife's disorderliness may remain an active source of female pleasure even though (or maybe, precisely because) it is represented as a source of male displeasure.

The image of the "disorderly wife," the "woman on top," as Natalie Zemon Davis has documented, was a central motif within western folk and popular comic traditions. While the figure frequently serves misogynist purposes, justifying the exercise of male constraint against claims for female autonomy, Davis suggests that it was a "multivalent image" that also operated to "widen behavioral options for women within and even outside marriage."[2] Following Davis's analysis of the traditional functions of this figure, I want to show how the persistent image of the "woman on top" within early sound comedy became both a target of chastising male laughter and a vehicle for a liberating female laughter, operating both to place women in their "proper sphere" and to allow them to envision alternatives to traditional femininity. I will outline the range of meanings that were assigned to the figure of the "Wild Woman" as she moved from turn-of-the-century debates about suffrage through romantic fiction, popular humor, and film comedy. In the end, I will return to *So Long Letty* to consider more fully the ways the film resolves its contradictory representation of Letty's disorderly conduct and the tension it poses between the spectacle of female comic performance and the logic of narrative resolution.

"THE SCEPTER OF SOVEREIGNTY IS IN
THE HANDS OF THE WEAKER SEX":
WILD WOMEN, THE SENTIMENTAL NOVEL,
AND THE CULT OF TRUE WOMANHOOD

The Nineteenth Century, a journal of social and literary thought widely read both in England and America, published a series of feverish editorials in 1891–1892 by Mrs. Eliza Lynn Linton, a leading British opponent of women's suffrage. Linton attacked and ridiculed the exploits of the "Wild Women" who she felt were pushing Victorian society toward a state of "chaos and topsyturvydom" from which it might never recover.[3] Linton's essays evoke nightmarish images of unrestrained matriarchal power, domestic disorder, and sexual inversion, of "Wild Women of blare and bluster, who are neither man nor woman," and who were determined to overturn the established sexual hierarchy at any cost.[4] Women had begun to act, think, and look like men; upper-class women were voluntarily reducing themselves to "lower forms of ways and works."[5] The home, once sheltering the family from "the darker passions which the contests of life arouse,"[6] was now a center of strife and conflict; men struggled to retain their declining authority in the face of these unruly and tyrannical women, "the masterful domina of real life—that loud and dictatorial person, insurgent and something more, who suffers no one's opinion to influence her mind."[7] Linton depicts man as enslaved, "bound hand and foot . . . the true captive of the woman" in his own home, trembling before the iron fist of his virago wife; the woman, freed from the natural constraints upon feminine passions, exercises a shrill and fickle authority over him: "The scepter of sovereignty is in the hands of the weaker, and the stronger has to beg for bare justice."[8] This "ugly travesty" had occurred because many men had become "too effeminate, too little manly" to exercise their proper authority within the family and to hold in check the unruly passions of their wives:[9] "The unsexed woman pleases the unsexed man. . . . Domineering women choose effeminate men whom they can rule at will. Effeminate men fall back on resolute and energetic women."[10] Man's loss of potency and authority, coupled with woman's desires for "lawlessness and license," would lead to the family's destruction and the nation's downfall.

Linton's extreme rhetoric reflected the rigidity with which the Victorians clung to the ideal of "true womanhood," a contorted effort to explain the failure of actual women to occupy the pedestal proposed for them.[11] Older beliefs about female unruliness persisted as a means of explaining and controlling women who displayed any deviance from socially sanctioned feminine conduct; notions of feminine "disorder" reinforced rather than contradicted the normality and desirability of ideals of feminine domesticity. The virulence of these attacks increased as the century drew to a close and the push for women's suffrage gained ground; these editorials represented a frantic effort to remain true to old assumptions in the face of dramatic social change.

While female participation within home production had been a normal aspect of an agricultural or artisanal economy, industrialization led to a sharp separation between the production sphere and the domestic sphere, between work and home. This redefinition of the economic structure was closely linked to a reformulation of sexual ideology and a redistribution of gender roles, at least among the middle classes. If men were to be endowed with the responsibilities of economic production, women were mandated with the dual responsibility of social and biological reproduction. The ideal wife, Barbara Welter has suggested, was expected to display ample quantities of "piety, purity, submissiveness and a dedication to domesticity," which were the natural attributes of a "true woman."[12] Recent feminist historians, most notably Nancy Cott, have challenged the assumption that the Victorian ideology of "true womanhood" operated exclusively as a means for the social control of women; Cott stresses how this same ideology established a space within the home over which the woman could exercise considerable autonomy, and rationalized limited female authority over men.[13] Presumptions about the virtuousness of women and the home as a purifying agent in American life meant that the man was finally answerable to his wife for his moral transgressions. Women employed that authority to ensure that husbands remained vital sources of revenue for their families, to insist that they abandon drinking and other vices, and to determine that breadwinners did not squander family income or endanger their jobs. The social purity movements of the late nineteenth century adopted this same logic to argue for the increased political activity of women within the public sphere; women demanded political influence in order to protect their husbands and children from temptations that might lure them from approved morality; these movements rallied against the brothel and the saloon as centers of male vice.[14]

So-called domestic feminism, as Mary Kelly notes, remained a dominant theme in late nineteenth-century and early twentieth-century "sentimental" fiction.[15] Expressing female "protest" over the social

position of women as well as providing "prescriptions" for ideal mar-
riages and proper childrearing, these stories represented homes in crisis;
their plots focus upon women's efforts to reform and redeem their
transgressing husbands through the natural exercise of their domestic
influence.[16] Through a glorification of the home as the machine age's
"New Eden" and of the high ideals of true womanhood, these sentimental novels justify the exercise of limited matriarchal power within the
family.

Linton's portrait of Wild Women as domestic tyrants represents the
dark side of the heroic women of the sentimental novels who work so
tirelessly to reform their wayward husbands. Both accounts see the
home as a moral battleground between domestic values and manly
pleasures. But while the sentimental novels approve of women's control
over their husband's morality, Linton rejects female governance as an
undesirable presumption of male privilege.

"No Room in His Own House": W. C. Fields and the Comedy of Marital Combat

If sentimental fiction provided its female writers and readers with a
moral corrective for the failures of society to adhere to feminine ideals,
the dominant comic paradigm of the period offered a male response,
rejecting the restrictiveness of female moral purity and the threat of
matriarchal power. Like the sentimental novel, popular American humor represented the domestic sphere as a moral battleground between
the woman aggressively protecting the purity of the home and the
husband eagerly pursuing bodily pleasure in the face of his wife's
prohibitions. The "will to pleasure" and its inevitable confrontations
with the demand for social constraint was translated into the threat the
Wild Women posed to the stability of sexual identity and domestic
harmony. The comic embodiment of "domestic feminism," these "petticoat tyrants," in works like Robert Barnwell Roosevelt's *Progressive
Petticoats; or Dressed to Death: An Autobiography of a Married Man* (1874)
or Frances M. Whitcher's *The Widow Bedott Papers* (1846–1859), bul-
lied already emasculated men into an acknowledgement of their superior
moral insight and into acquiescence, at least overtly, to their strict
demands. This typography of male-female conflict is exemplified by
Oliver Bell Bunce's "Some Notions About Domestic Bliss" (1870):
"[Her] presence, her individuality, her temper, her ideas, her wishes,
her inches surround and multiply upon him on all sides. Appleby has

no room in his own house, and a very small corner in the outside world, so completely does Mrs. Appleby fill the boundaries of Mr. Appleby's sphere, and crush him into diminutiveness."[17]

Jokes, as we have seen, tend to cluster around points of friction or rupture within the social structure, around places where a dominant social discourse is already starting to give way to an emergent counter-discourse; jokes allow the comic expression of ideas that in other contexts might be regarded as threatening, although they win their public acknowledgment at the expense of their no longer being taken seriously by the listener. Indeed, Mary Douglas suggests not simply that situations of social inversion or transformation provide the preconditions for joking but that the recognition of this kind of instability or potential inversion within the social structure "calls imperatively for an explicit joke to express it."[18] The translation of social conflicts into jokes allows for a smoother negotiation of differences. Viewed from this perspective, the emergence of the comedy of marital combat seems a logical response to the radical shifts in gender roles occurring within American society, to the ways that the "true woman" of the Victorian era was giving ground to the Wild Women of twentieth-century life. These comic texts speak to the crisis in contemporary gender relations; they reassert a masculine desire for feminine submissiveness while recognizing the reality of the increasing power of women. Their influence extends well beyond literary works; comic representations of marital combat played an important role in vaudeville, burlesque, comic strips and early cinema. These works and their blunt treatment of gender relations were among the most controversial aspects of the New Humor, a source of irritation to genteel readers who wanted a more reassuring vision of family harmony.

Frequently, these comic representations of domestic discord made explicit their links to the campaigns for moral purity and female suffrage, connecting, as Linton did, women's increased independence to images of men's victimization; such representations constituted a bold-faced inversion of the harsh reality of Victorian marriage, where women's power was limited by the whims of her often autocratic husband. In *Reforming a Husband* (Lubin, 1909), the comedy stems from the husband's efforts to sneak out of the house to go to a men's club where he can enjoy his favorite vices away from his wife's watchful eye. A husband signs an oath to his wife and mother-in-law in *Bill Jones' New Years Resolution* (Essanay, 1908), vowing that he will "reform his many vices," but he has trouble sticking to the straight and narrow; each time he strays, his wife appears suddenly and unexpectedly to whip him in line. In Minnie Dupree and Theodore Brown's 1898 vaudeville act, "Dr. Deborah's Elixir," a suffragette wife, in this case a chemist, develops a formula designed to turn bad men into good husbands and forces her spouse to consume it with comic consequences, while the husband in "Why Walker Rebelled" (1912), another male-female vaudeville sketch, is ordered by his "New Woman" spouse to do all the housework.[19] The wayward husband running smack into a meeting of angry suffragettes, the drinking man forced to sign a temperance oath, and the henpecked husband required to assume domestic chores abandoned by his "liberated" wife were staple subjects for vaudeville comedy from the 1870s into the twentieth century; these stock situations reflect a predominantly masculine perspective on married life despite the increased presence of women within the variety house audience.

If, as Shirley Staples suggests, these domestic sketches allowed male and female characters to be "pitted against each other to play on the divergent sympathies of their audience," such comedies almost always ended upon moments of masculine triumph and feminine submission.[20] "Dr. Deborah's Elixir," for example, concludes with the wife's abandonment of textbooks for cookbooks and her resumption of normal household responsibilities, a fairly typical pattern in early cinema and vaudeville. Even when women do not retreat into the domestic sphere, the comedies climax with moments of male empowerment; the men regain their lost potency and get their revenge upon tyrannical spouses and monstrous mother-in-laws.[21] The husband learns hypnotism to bring his wife and her mother under control in *Ma-In-Law as a Statue* (Lux, 1910). *Mr. Gay and Mrs.* (Biograph, 1907) ends with the husband trapping his nagging wife in a folding bed. If these comedies toy with the prospect of female dominance, that problem must be resolved by a reassertion of male authority and a restoration of the "natural order" of married life.

The Naggers series, produced by Vitaphone in the early 1930s, suggests the persistence of these same comic conventions nearly two decades later. By this point, comedy of marital combat had been stripped of any explicit links to the suffrage movement but still reflects a male response to female moral authority. *The Naggers* (Vitaphone, 1929) was based on a vaudeville sketch originally developed for W. C. Fields, though later performed on stage and screen by Jack Norworth and Dorothy Adelphi. Its action occurs in and around the marital bed as Mrs. Norworth, the "nagger," keeps her husband awake all night, berating him for alleged infidelity. She charges that he has met with a former girlfriend, Bessie, though he denies the accusation and begs her for silence. Finally, after many threats and entreaties (including many jokes that play on the suggestion of domestic violence), the husband succeeds in coaxing the janitor to lock his wife in the broom closet. This brief moment of masculine victory, however, is followed by her return and the renewal of the assault as the film closes. The husband's disdain for his mother-in-law, the wife's constant verbal abuse, her jealousy over Bessie, and the couple's violent struggles form the basis for comedy in each of the subsequent *Naggers* shorts.

Many of W. C. Fields's best works, especially *You're Telling Me* (Paramount, 1934), *It's a Gift, The Man on the Flying Trapeze,* and *The Bank Dick,* build upon this same tradition.[22] Fields's rotund figure, his raspy voice and bulbous red nose made him the personification of the pleasure-seeking husband, while his sideways mutters and shifty eyes suggest years of keeping half an eye open for the domineering wife. Like Mr. Appleby, Fields "has no room in his own house," which overflows with women—wives, daughters, mother-in-laws, neighbors, customers, moral reformers—all of whom express a complete intolerance for his pet pleasures and a willingness to tell him precisely what he has done wrong with his life. Fields brags in *It's a Gift* that "I am the master of this household," but he looks around cautiously and lowers his voice to a stage whisper when he does so. His daughter intrudes into the bathroom while he tries to shave, shoving him from the mirror with reckless disregard for the razor he has poised at his throat. His wife lectures him throughout breakfast on his bad habits and his inability to manage his own affairs, while he nervously dumps a mountain of salt into his food. Finally, he timidly sneaks a smoke in the other room, muttering to himself, while his wife drones forth a steady stream of complaints and criticisms. He then retreats from the house without a word of explanation.

The films' narratives center on struggles for dominance within the family. *It's a Gift* focuses primarily upon a debate between Fields and his wife over how to spend some inheritance money. Fields wants to purchase a California orange ranch—a lifelong dream—while his wife insists the money should be spent on more "practical" uses, such as buying her and her daughter fancy clothes. In *The Man on the Flying Trapeze,* Fields tries to cut work to catch a wrestling match. Fields pays a stiff penalty for such recklessness: random catastrophes block him from reaching the match; he is fired from his job and kicked out of his house when his ne'er-do-well brother-in-law falsely accuses him of public drunkenness and marital infidelity.

Fields's greatest pleasures—whiskey, poker, pool, tall tales, smoking—all find their outlet within a masculine saloon culture, which is the only space still largely outside the control of women. Joe Guelpe (Shemp Howard), owner and bartender of the Black Pussy Saloon in *The Bank Dick,* gives Fields the loving attention and wide-eyed admiration his wife refuses him. Like the ideal Victorian wife, Guelpe listens to his tall tales of heroic exploits, tolerates his eccentricities (such as a need to wash his fingers in a glass of water after every drink), helps him out of jams (by mixing a Mickey Finn for the bank examiner), and gives him a hero's welcome. Fields transforms the "erring, inferior husband," the drunkard and poor provider of the sentimental novel and the temperance tract into a sympathetic comic protagonist; he endows the saloon with all of the virtues of the Victorian parlor. The refuge provided by the saloon remains only temporary. This New Eden has achieved a state of bliss precisely by locking its doors to the negative influence of the New Eve. Fields, however, can never fully escape from the controlling and belittling eyes of the female members of his family or the constant threat of an emasculating femininity that holds no tolerance for his pet recreations. In *It's a Gift,* Fields enjoys singing around the campfire with a group of other men until his wife silences him with a can of tomatoes.

True to the conventions of the comedy of marital combat, however, the Fields comedies inevitably end with his triumph over the matriarchal order. In *The Man on the Flying Trapeze,* Fields not only regains his lost job but receives a substantial increase in his salary with which he buys himself a new car. In the film's final shot, Fields and his loyal daughter drive happily down the road, while the wife, her mother, and her brother sit in the rumbleseat under a pouring rain that drowns out their nagging. The conclusion of *The Bank Dick* is somewhat more complex, parodying the conventional redemption of the wayward male in the sentimental novels while offering images of greater male autonomy within the family. The off-key rendition of "Home, Sweet Home," first heard in the film's opening, has been replaced by a more melodic version. The family has moved into a mansion and are now waited on by servants who provide Fields with "Café Rum" for breakfast under the approving eyes of his family who call him "Daddy dear." Fields kisses his family, gathers his hat and cane, and walks off toward his new job. His wife and mother-in-law peer through the open door, beaming with pride over his apparent redemption into proper citizenship. The mother nods approvingly, "What a changed man! You deserve a lot of credit, Agatha." Fields seems to have accepted the norms of feminine civilization. No sooner is he out of sight of the house than he pivots and follows Guelpe the bartender to the safe harbor of the Black Pussy, where he no longer needs to maintain the pretense of propriety imposed upon him by his new social status. The final scenes of Fields's comedies of marital combat offer images of a masculine-centered domestic utopia that contrasts sharply with the female-centered dystopia of their openings. If he does not totally convert his domineering wife into "true womanhood," Fields nevertheless gains greater autonomy within the home (signified by his open consumption of alcohol at the breakfast table and by the wife's display of some affection toward him) by dramatically increasing his material standing (the new cars, homes, servants). Fields finally has found "room in his own home," within which he may pursue his own pleasures and restore his self-respect.

Fields's speedy rise from humiliation at the hands of a "petticoat tyrant" to command over a greatly enriched kingdom allowed male spectators to laugh at their own fears, sexual humiliations, and economic defeats. These feelings were apt to be complexly intertwined in the Depression era because of husbands' increasing dependence upon their wives to provide additional or even primary income for the family. This phenomenon was widely read as a sign of the men's inadequacy in fulfilling the traditional breadwinner's role. Mirra Komarovsky, who interviewed unemployed New York families in 1935–1936, concludes that male unemployment led to fundamental shifts of authority within the family and often a rapid deterioration of the father's status: "In addition to sheer economic anxiety, the man suffers from deep humiliation. He experiences a sense of deep frustration because in his own estimation he fails to fulfill what is the central duty of his life, the very touchstone of his manhood—the role of the family provider. The man appears bewildered and humiliated. It is as if the ground has gone out from under his feet." [23] The husband's humiliation often turned inward, reflecting feelings of lost potency and ambition, a fatalistic withdrawal from power; these feelings could also be directed outward against a wife who was seemingly usurping her husband's status, resulting in increased incidents of domestic violence. Class resentments were mapped onto an already festering hostility toward female efforts to regulate and restrain male pleasure. The unemployed husband was forced to ask his wife for money to buy cigarettes or to drink at the saloon; the wife increasing rejected his sexual advances and asserted her own authority.

The masculine utopias of the W. C. Fields film endings provided a symbolic reversal of this painful situation (which, as Douglas's model suggests, already constituted an inversion or instability within the traditional ordering of gender relations); such scenes restored the husband to a central role within the family and resolved his financial hardships. Fields regains his economic dignity by asserting his authority over his wife and breaking with her moral constraint. The comedy stems from "acknowledging" publicly what most other cultural representations of the period repressed—that men were experiencing a diminishing authority within the family; the comedy also provides reassurance that the situation is temporary and reversible. Such a fantasy could not be more calculated in its appeal to unemployed male spectators, giving new affective force to the older appeal of the comedy of marital combat formula.

"A FIRMLY GRASPED TETHER": THE IDEOLOGICAL CONSTRUCTION OF FEMALE COMIC PERFORMANCE

As comic representations of marital combat—of powerful women and "unsexed" men—reached their peak popularity, there were increasing debates about the nature of feminine humor and the possibility of female laughter. Male writers had sought throughout most of the nineteenth century to deny that women even possessed a sense of humor. In 1842, a writer for *Graham's Magazine* stated with certainty that "there is a body and substance to true wit, with a reflectiveness rarely found apart from a masculine intellect. . . . The female character does not admit of it."[24] A 1909 newspaper editorialist stated flatly, "measured by ordinary standards of humor, she [woman] is about as comical as a crutch."[25] This denial of female jocularity was probably tied to the dominant comic tradition's function as a release of male anxieties and fears; a laughing and joking woman posed a potential new threat to male authority and masculine dignity, intensifying the tensions masculine-centered comedy sought to resolve.

By the turn of the century, however, such statements came with much less conviction. As early as 1885, Kate Sanborn published an anthology of women's humor, *The Wit of Women,* compiled with the acknowledged purpose of proving that "women possess both wit and humor."[26] Women were appearing as comics in vaudeville and filling variety house seats, laughing in public at jokes they previously had pretended not to hear. A number of magazine articles, published in the first decade of the twentieth century and written by both men and women, debated the vexing question, "Do Women Have a Sense of Humor?" The writers generally concluded that women were capable of both joking and laughing, concessions that would not have been made a few years earlier. However, they still posited fundamental differences in the joking of men and women: "Women's sense of humor is more sensitive than that of men, but not so broad."[27] For many, the prospect of women's wit seemed antithetical to their nurturing role within the family; these writers insisted that slapstick could never really be appropriate for women audiences. A 1902 article held that the sense of empathy was too strong in women to allow them to find humor in the plight of others: "The tears from the woman's sympathetic heart fill her eyes before the laughter can ripple across her lips."[28] Elizabeth Stanley Trotter adopted a similar position as late as 1922 when she informed *Atlantic* readers that "Feminine witticisms . . . are seldom wholly at the expense of others and cheer oftener than they wound."[29] Many such writers clearly view female comic performance to be a frightening prospect. A 1909 newspaper editorialist insisted, "Woman was made to be loved and fondled. . . . She was not made to be laughed at."[30] Even some female writers like Trotter spoke indignantly of "those women who deliberately imitate the facetiousness of men—often in its coarsest form—for purposes of their own," and characterized female comic performers as stepping outside the norms of femininity.[31]

Already, however, writers were demonstrating how this particular conception of women's sense of humor worked as a powerful tool for social control. Margaretta Newell suggested in a 1931 *Outlook* article that "If she [woman] is so ill-advised as to indulge in mirth at man's expense, she risks the loss of his material support—a consideration of which the woman in the home is very much aware. In the home, the most a humorous woman dare venture is a smile."[32] Writing for *New Republic* readers in 1924, Mary Austin claimed that men feared women's laughter because it could easily be directed against them and that as a result, women were allowed to joke only "at the end of an exceedingly short and firmly grasped tether."[33]

A review of fan magazine profiles of female comic film stars suggests the ways men attempted to "tether" female comic performance and to manage the contradictions between femininity and buffoonery. In a

1914 *Motography* interview, silent comedy star Flora Finch recalled with some incredulousness being asked by a male reporter, "Doesn't your womanly heart revolt at your comic appearance or—or does your art carry you through?"[34] If Finch seemed surprised at the persistence of these attitudes, the same nagging questions resurfaced almost twenty years later in a *Motion Picture Classic* profile of Polly Moran: "Wouldn't any woman rather be known for her beauty than for her wit? When woman's whole aim in life is to be attractive, how must it feel to play the buffoon?"[35] Again and again, these articles treat female comic performance as a problem to be analyzed, as a manifestation to be dreaded and pitied, as a detraction from the possibilities of feminine charm and beauty.

Female performers who appeared with their husbands as part of male-female comedy teams often depicted their comedy as an extension, rather than a contradiction, of their more "worthy" roles as wife and mother. These women imply that film performance was a way they could spend more time with their husbands and thus strengthen their marital bonds. Profiles of Sidney and Polly Drew praised their "splendid partnership" on and off screen; Polly's selection and preparation of screenplays is transformed into a form of choosy shopping and practical home economy, made possible because "she understands her husband so well." Their work together was viewed as an extension of the "harmony" within their marriage.[36]

The comicality of other female stars, notably young and daffy character comediennes, is treated as a natural phenomenon, an unscripted and spontaneous extension of their peculiarly "feminine" perspectives on life. Profiles of Lyda Roberti spoke of her "effortless clowning"; she "giggles on the slightest provocation"; she speaks "her own special brand of English, which has a talent for sounding like a typographical error," the product of a childhood spent in various parts of Europe.[37] The dumb-blond comedy of Dorothy Lee, "pint-sized, wide-eyed, saucy-nosed, nineteen," reflected her immaturity[38,] while Lupe Velez's comic outbursts, on and offscreen, were characterized as the "spontaneous combustion" of a Latin temperament, "an act as natural as the one nature puts on when two clouds collide to produce lightening and thunder."[39] Such organic jocularity does not require female efforts to provoke laughter but is rather open to discovery by superior male viewers who recognize these women's eccentricity.

Perhaps most frequently, however, the movie magazines represented female comic performance as a failure to achieve traditional standards of beauty and grace or in extreme cases, as a form of gender inversion. Marie Dressler told an interviewer that "as a girl, I was handicapped by bulk and no beauty. I had my mother to support—so I traded bulk and laughs for money."[40] Other female clowns retold similar stories of painful self-recognition: "This grand lady [Edna May Oliver] started out in life to be a singer, but she is exceedingly tall and—well—no beauty, as she herself is the first to admit, and people always seemed to think she was funny, so a comedienne she became, thank goodness."[41] Those women who would actively solicit laughter are redefined as the objects of self-initiated male laughter, and, therefore, their comic utterances are stripped of any possible meaning as an expression of their self-perceptions of their own condition.

"HE GOT A POISON IVY INSTEAD OF A CLINGING VINE": GENDERED LAUGHTER, WINNIE LIGHTNER, AND THE POLITICS OF FEMININE SPECTACLE

Winnie Lightner seemed particularly vulnerable to this treatment. Lightner went from a successful career as a vaudeville and New York revue performer to become Warner Brothers' top female star of 1929–31; she ended her career abruptly less than four years later, retiring to become a "housewife."[42] Although a reasonably attractive woman, Lightner, approaching thirty, was older than most female film stars of the period and seemed largely indifferent to her appearance. Her ample figure, large-boned features, loud, raspy voice, and stringy hair were defined as falling outside Hollywood norms of grace and glamour. Even relatively sympathetic profiles tend to ascribe to her the qualities of the proverbial blind date: "Winnie isn't exactly beautiful but her personality is sparkling."[43]

As a vaudeville performer, Lightner had been known as "The Song-a-Minute Girl," and *Variety* had characterized her as "fast, furious and always to the point."[44] Her aggressive and energetic style assumed other connotations within the cinema, where she often overpowered her male costars. Studio publicity tagged her "The Tomboy of the Talkies," claiming that she was "the only feminine star of rough-house comedy." Fan magazine profiles made much of her preference for wearing pants both onscreen and off and her unladylike predilection for enormous dogs.[45] Such profiles repeatedly depict Lightner's decision to become a comic star as the consequence of her dubious gender identity and failure to achieve recognition for her feminine charms as a performer of serious romantic ballads:

> In 1919, she made her stage debut at Shay's Buffalo Theater in what was to be a serious singing act but, being a tomboy by nature, she paid no attention to her personal appearance. She drew gales of laughter from her audience. From that time, she has been a comedienne.[46]

> Winnie Lightner, Tomboy of the Talkies, has been a tomboy all of her life. An accident made her a professional tomboy. Boyish clothes and muddy shoes she wore on her first stage appearance gave her the title.[47]

> I meant to wring their hearts. Instead, I gave Buffalo the best laugh it had had in twenty years. I swallowed my pride and let them laugh at me and I have been doing it ever since.[48]

This story exploits the gap between ideals of "true womanhood" and the reality of Lightner's own persona, a central theme running through her vehicles. A characteristic sequence in *Side Show* (Warner Brothers, 1931) directly reproduces her failure to win audience acceptance. Speaking straight into the camera, a carny barker announces that he is about to unveil a living painting, "the most perfect example of womanly beauty exhibited on canvas today." As the barker continues to describe her feminine charms, a series of close-ups depicts various men in the crowd, eagerly awaiting the erotic display. When the curtain parts, however, we find only Winnie Lightner dressed in an ill-fitting body stocking and striking a painfully contorted pose (fig. 9.2). A dirty-faced man blows a raspberry at her and the crowd begins to laugh. Lightner continues to smile, though her clenched teeth and arched eyebrows betray the difficulty with which she retains this "glamour" pose. A young boy with a pea shooter hits her in the thigh. Scowling and cursing at the audience, she grabs her sore leg as the curtain falls around her.

Lightner offered her body to the camera as a grotesque parody of traditional femininity, as an unfit object for male desire. Low-angle compositions and uncomfortably close shots exaggerate the mass and power of her body and—in her films with Joe E. Brown especially—the size of her mouth and the volume of her voice. She thrusts her face and hands into the camera, often staring unflinchingly into its lens. Assertive and domineering, indifferent to her appearance and lacking in a womanly sense of "fitness," displaying little refinement in speech and manners, Lightner embodies everything that Linton found so dreadful in the Wild Women. In *Sit Tight,* Lightner plays the vigorous and pugnacious manager of a health club, a role that allows her to boss around, assess, and manhandle male bodybuilders. She storms about the club, issuing orders, evaluating the men's fitness, clapping her hands in a commanding way, and slapping the men on the back. When one grossly overweight man complains about the extensiveness of his work-out, she gruffly orders him back onto his exercise bike: "What do you think I'm running here—a nursery?" She tells a scrawny old man, "If your head was turned around, you would have a wonderful chest." Her robust manner, booming voice, and rapid movements exaggerate her physical size and contrast sharply with her male clients, who crumble under the verbal onslaught and shrink before her towering figure. When her assistant, "JoJo the Tiger" (Joe E. Brown) arrives late, she hits him in the stomach with a medicine ball, knocking him over, and chases him about the room. Lightner shoves him around and yanks him to his feet, while he can only giggle and stammer, "What are you trying to do? Make a monkey out of me?" She looks him over slowly and snarls, "No, nature beat me to it." Brown's inadequacy is signaled by a large pansy on his sweat shirt.

In her vehicles, Lightner is surrounded by highly effeminate or physically inadequate men: the fussy Frank Fay in *Show of Shows,* the giggling Ole Olsen and Chic Johnson and the malnourished Claude Gillingwater in *Gold Dust Gertie,* the physically uncoordinated Joe E. Brown in *Hold Everything* (Warner Brothers, 1930) and *Sit Tight,* and most especially, the pasty-faced and dim-witted Charles Butterworth in *Side Show, Life of the Party* (Warner Brothers, 1930), and *Manhattan Parade* (Warner Brothers, 1932). One of the great underrated talents of early sound comedy, Butterworth personifies the atrophied masculinity appropriate for the mate of one of Linton's Wild Women. Simple-minded and slow-talking, consistently out of touch with everything around him, his eyelashes blinking rapidly and his mouth curved in a singularly insipid smile, Butterworth is so totally degendered that he scarcely seems to know the facts of life, let alone display any real sexual urges (fig. 9.3). In *Side Show,* he informs Lightner that his brother has had a baby and then feels compelled to clarify the situation: "Well, my brother didn't have the baby. My brother's wife had the baby." When Lighter asks him whether it is a boy or a girl, he confesses ignorance: "I don't know whether I am an aunt or an uncle." His proposal at the climax of *Life of the Party* expresses a similar degree of sexual ambivalence: "Ever since I met you, I haven't been able to think of anything else. I wondered if you would marry me so that I could forget you." This frail, soft-spoken little man with his effeminate mannerisms and stammering voice was ideally cast as a foil to the energetic and mannish Lightner, completing the process of gender inversion at the core of her comedy.

Indifferent to male pride and traditional femininity, Lightner turns these men's fumbling attempts at lovemaking aside with a shrill comment or a threatening gesture. When, in a flurry of romantic rhetoric in *Sit Tight*, Brown tells Lightner that if she refuses his love, he will sink into the gutter, she stares at him and mutters, "So—go ahead and sink." The shaken JoJo, falling back on false bravado, can only stare back at her and proclaim, "I wish you were a man!" In *Gold Dust Gertie*, she strips Olsen and Johnson down to their pajamas and kicks them out the portal of an ocean liner, leaving them hanging precariously above a stormy sea, with a lobster attached to the seat of their pantaloons, while she romances another man (as vivid an image of castration anxiety as ever graced the silver screen). Twice in *Life of the Party*, she promises to visit Charles Judels in his apartment for a romantic evening, only to stand him up both times. The excitable Frenchman, enraged at his repeated humiliation, smashes the furniture, overturns trays of food, rips the clothes off his male companion's back, and tears the carpet from the floor, dragging it behind him down the hallway of a plush hotel.

Lightner's screen vehicles couple her comic humiliation of men with a broader play with gender identity. In *Side Show*, perhaps her most satisfying vehicle, Lightner plays Pat, the dutiful daughter of the drunken manager of a broken-down traveling carnival, a woman who is prepared to do anything to keep the show on the road. When, in the film's first scene, the bearded lady threatens to shave if she does not receive her back pay, Lightner responds by preparing to attach fake whiskers to herself if it will keep her father's business alive: "Outside of the fat woman and the human skeleton, I've played everyone's part in the show." In the course of the film, Lightner assumes a wide variety of standard circus roles ranging from a blackfaced cannibal king to "The Great Santini," a muscle-bound and mustached high diver. The band plays, the crowd gathers, waiting breathlessly for the dramatic entrance of the "world's champion fire diver," and Lightner enters, dressed in an asbestos jumper. Hoping to avoid difficult questions about her voice, Lightner pretends to be a deaf-mute, making comic and sometimes obscene hand gestures. She "shoots a bird" at the audience and thumbs her nose at the sheriff. She trips trying to climb the ladder to the top of the diving platform; Butterworth fumbles with the matches trying to set her ablaze. When she finally burst into flames and dives into the tank below, Butterworth tumbles after her and emerges from the water with her mustache stuck to his chin. Lightner's transvestism, here and in *Life of the Party,* where she briefly appears as a male jockey, is doubly comic, both because she can so deftly pass as male—yet another sign of her own failed femininity—and because she is finally inadequate to her assumed role, since she lacks what it takes to be a man. "Neither man nor woman," Lightner proves equally ill-suited to either role.

Lightner steps into stock feminine roles, only to destroy them, often with an air of open resistance to the expectations others would foist upon her. In *Side Show,* Lightner appears dressed in a grass skirt and coconut brassiere as Princess Mauna Kane, the carnival's cooch dancer (fig. 9.4). Her grass skirt falls down around her ankles and she rather gracelessly hoists it back up until it covers her entire torso. Once Lightner begins to sing a bawdy song about an uninhibited south sea bombshell, however, what began as a pathetic performance of failed femininity becomes openly defiant. She belts out the song with a raspy voice and exaggerated gestures, challenging the crowd to find erotic pleasure in her display, laughing at the men as much as they are laughing at her: "Look me over here—Look me over there! Say, what do ya' think of me now!" She runs her hands suggestively over her breasts and down the curves of her hips; she grabs her grass skirt in bunches around her crotch or her buttocks and flips it to the audience, all the while singing of the sexual exploits and feminine charms of the Hawaiian princess. At once excessively feminine and awkwardly man-nish, Lightner adopts and exaggerates the traditional demeanor of the burlesque queen, glorying in the exhilaration of self-display and self-mastery while ridiculing the norms by which such erotic performances are judged. Like her discomfort in the "Lady Beautiful" sequence, her zestful disorderliness in the "Princess Mauna" sequence invites questions about the conventions of female sexual display; her unseemly acts point toward the artificiality of the glamour pose, the puffery of show business rhetoric, and the unreasonableness of male expectations.

Writing about female performance in American burlesque, Robert Allen sees "cooch" as reflecting a diminishment of female authority within a form that had once celebrated unruly women. Earlier burlesque performers such as Lydia Thompson adopted "punning speech" to invert gender identity, question traditional standards of feminine conduct, and assert their own sexual desires. The burlesque woman had, by the turn of the century, become a pure "spectacle," attracting the male gaze but unable to express herself:

> The cooch dance linked the sexual display of the female performer and the scopic desire of the male patron in a more direct and intimate fashion than any previous feature of burlesque. Here, all pretense that the performance was about anything other than sexual pleasure was dispensed with. The spectator's desire was not diffused among a company of performers or mediated by drama but focused exclusively on the body of a single woman. She, in turn, played only to him; her movements served no function other than to arouse and please him. Her dance was a pas de deux involving her body and his gaze. She was an exhibition of direct, wordless, female eroticism and exoticism.[49]

The acceptance of such a role tames burlesque's transgressive potential and opens the way for increasingly explicit erotic spectacles. Since Laura Mulvey's memorable formulation of "visual pleasure," feminist film critics have stressed that the classical Hollywood cinema similarly constructs women for the male gaze, as possessing a quality Mulvey awkwardly describes as "to-be-looked-at-ness." Mulvey links this erotic spectacle to much older show business traditions, specifically referencing both striptease and Ziegfeld's glorified girls. Woman as spectacle "tends to work against the development of a story line, to freeze the flow of action in moments of erotic contemplation."[50] Yet such a conception of feminine sexuality denies women any active role within the story, any chance of articulating their own pleasures and desires. As we have seen throughout this book, comic films offer another kind of spectacle—the clown's active authority to disrupt the flow of the narrative, to step out of character and adopt the role of a pure performer. Writers have often spoken of the anarchistic spectacle of the Marx Brothers as a powerful challenge to the formal and ideological coherence of their films' narratives.

The sparsity of writing about female comic performance means that little attempt has been made to link these two kinds of film spectacles. In one of the few essays to address this question, Mary Russo emphasizes the power of unruly or grotesque women to "make spectacles out of themselves" and in doing so, to call into question rigid constraints on appropriate feminine behavior. This power closely parallels the authority Allen claims for female performers in Thompsonian burlesque or that ascribed to the Marx Brothers and other clowns in anarchistic comedy. If Mulvey's notion of spectacle asserts a socially learned desire to be looked at, Russo's notion of spectacle dares men to look while gleefully anticipating male displeasure with what they see. Russo stresses the "liberatory and transgressive effects" of the disorderly woman and her unfit conduct, yet also recognizes the degree to which this unstable figure can be reread in misogynistic terms.[51]

Lightner's often grotesque performances aptly illustrate the resistive potential of feminine spectacle. Lightner certainly makes a "spectacle" of herself, but it is a very different sort of spectacle than that desired or anticipated by male spectators. As Princess Mauna, Lightner violates the set of power relations implicit within the cooch performance, re-claiming her sexuality as a source of personal pleasure while directing attention back onto the dubious desires of her male audience. Lightner has not been rendered mute in assuming the role of the cooch dancer; she speaks and sings in a loud and raucous fashion. "Princess Mauna" asserts her right to determine the meaning of her performance and to direct the male spectators' attention. She proclaims the attractiveness and desirability of flesh that otherwise falls outside traditional standards of beauty. Yet significantly, unlike the ridicule she receives as "Lady Beautiful," Lightner's "Princess Mauna" act is rewarded with her audi-ence's applause; she makes the men respect her performance skills whereas elsewhere her attempts to exploit her sexual appeal provoke only boos and raspberries. Even the internal audience is forced to acknowledge what movie house spectators undoubtedly realized—that far from a humiliation, Lightner's "comic spectacle" expresses her vital-ity and virtuosity as a performer. She becomes a spectacle on her own terms and makes her audience enjoy it. As Kathleen K. Rowe has written of a more recent generation of unruly women:

> The parodic excesses of the unruly woman and the comic conventions sur-rounding her provide a space to act out the dilemmas of femininity, to *make visible* and *laughable* what Mary Ann Doane describes as the "tropes of femininity." . . . Already bound in a web of visual power, women might begin to renegotiate its terms. . . . By returning the male gaze, we might expose (make a spectacle of) the gazer. And by utilizing the power already invested in us as image, we might begin to negate our own "invisibility" in the public sphere.[52]

This ability to disrupt the male gaze and to construct an alternative form of female spectacle is closely bound to the notion of masquerade.

Joan Riviere addressed many of these same ambiguities about gender in her classic essay, "Womanliness as a Masquerade," published in 1929, the same year that Lightner became Warner Brothers' top female star. Riviere's focus was upon women who had ventured into traditionally male professions. Characterizing their unconventional conduct as a kind of "theft of masculinity" that produced strong feelings of guilt and revulsion, Riviere suggested that such women frequently had difficulty maintaining a consistent gender identity; exaggerated feminine gestures and sounds undermined their attempts to perform traditionally masculine activities. Feminine masquerade, excessive flirtation, "compulsive ogling and coquetting," and uncontrollable giggling, Riviere proposed, were defense mechanisms compensating for a false assumption of masculinity.[53] Riviere wrote, "Womanliness therefore could be assumed and worn as a mask, both to hide the possession of masculinity and to avert the reprisals expected if she was found to posses it—much as a thief will turn out his pockets and ask to be searched to prove that he has not stolen goods."[54] One gender identity—a hyperfeminine one—is layered over another gender identity—a hypermasculine one; both have been assumed by a woman who can claim neither as her own and who constantly hesitated, fluctuated, between the two. Riviere described masquerade as an unconscious process, outside the woman's control and betraying her anxieties. Rowe surmises, however, that this same play of identity, when mastered by the comic performer, may allow women to articulate their resistance to those assigned roles and may facilitate an active deconstruction of the basic tropes of femininity: "Comedic forms contain the potential for representing radical inversions of women's relation to power by not only unmasking the myths and heroes of patriarchal culture, but by opening up space for transgression, parody and exposure of the 'masks' of 'femininity.' "[55]

Womanly masquerade provides the central narrative focus of several of Lightner's vehicles; her films are marked by an almost obsessive play with traditional feminine iconography and by the explicit construction and deconstruction of gender identity. In Gold Dust Gertie, the oft-wed Gertie is the very model of the predatory woman, moving from husband to husband in search of good times and easy living. When she discovers that her previous source of revenue—alimony from Olsen and Johnson—has been cut off by the men's recent marriage to a pair of equally demanding twins, Lightner decides to court and wed their conservative boss, Mr. Arnold (Claude Gillingwater). In order to get Arnold to the alter, the wise-cracking, free-living Lightner must mimic his Victorian ideal of womanhood, trying to convince him of her modesty and virtue. The key moment in the film comes when Gertie conceals her own identity behind a masquerade of demure womanliness. Peering into a mirror, she borrows a pair of wire-rimmed glasses from Arnold's desk, pushes her hair back into a bun, and adjusts her face into a more ladylike expression (fig. 9.5). She, then, collapses dramatically on the coach, pretending to have fainted, and awaits the boss's return (fig. 9.6). Here and in *Life of the Party,* the majority of the comic situations stem from the gap between Lightner's womanly masquerade and her masculinized self-identity, from her inability to assimilate herself into traditional modes of femininity. Her urge to insult and to manhandle can scarcely be checked by her need to remain graceful and ladylike. She stumbles when she tries to walk in high heels and she brags about Venice's streetcar system when she tries to impress men with her worldly sophistication. Such sequences foreground femininity as a constructed identity that must be adopted, often at a loss of personal expressivity, comfort, and dignity. One could argue that the instability of this "feminine" identity still points toward a more "authentic" feminine identity beneath the mask, yet anarchistic comedy's foregrounding of the performer as performer further subverts the "authenticity" and legitimacy of that equally constructed identity. Anyone reading between the lines of the studio's press releases finds that the image of Lightner as performer is also constructed, an attempt to force her personality into line with certain expectations about female stardom. Looking for stability, we find only instability. Looking for authenticity, we find only layer upon layer of masquerade.

By making the perspective of the Wild Woman the focus of the narrative rather than that of her inept male victim, Lightner suggests the possibility of transforming tropes of male dread into figures of female empowerment. Her films shift attention from the problem of matriarchal power to the problem of female identity; her comedies offer narratives in which the struggle between men and women comes to focus upon differing conceptions of desirable womanliness. This transformation is perhaps most vividly displayed in the opening sequence of *Life of the Party.* Flo (Winnie Lightner) and Dot (Irene Delroy), two song pluggers in a Brooklyn music shop, are catching a few moments of rest, complaining about the unreasonable expectations of their male customers and boss: "I've got to be Sophie Tucker and Marilyn Miller all in one for thirty dollars a week." When their boss reappears, the tired Flo begins to hawk music once again. He watches her suspiciously as she interacts with the customers, giving a sales pitch, flirting, and joking with the men who crowd around her, and finally agreeing to perform a requested song, "Poison Ivy." The camera continually positions her within the manager's proprietorial gaze, returning again and again to shots of him looking at her, followed by shots of her presentation to the predominantly male customers. This point-glance structure disappears, however, when she begins to sing. Lightner sings and stares directly into the camera and her performance is recorded within a single, rather lengthy take (fig. 9.7). Moreover, as Flo begins her performance, we see on the shelf behind her sheet music advertising songs from previous Winnie Lightner vehicles, some bearing glamour photographs of Lightner herself. The song sequence is thus doubly marked. First, it stands for Flo's submission to male authority; the male customer who repeatedly requested the song later admits that he only wanted to "make you sing it." Second, it serves as Lightner's nod to her female fans, a star turn very much under her own professional control.

"Poison Ivy," a song Lightner had performed previously on the stage, deals explicitly with the contradictory place of femininity within American culture; its lyrics recount the story of a man whose wife grossly fails to satisfy his expectations:

> Once I was just like a clinging vine,
> till some bozo made me sign the dotted line.
> He thought I was young and simple,
> when he said "li'l girl be mine"
> but he got a poison ivy instead of a clinging vine.
> He thought I'd save him money
> but I took him for every dime . . .
> He thought I'd stay at home nights
> singing lullabies
> but all I did was roam nights with fifty other guys
> and when I made him coffee,
> I'd fill it with iodine.
> Say, he got a poison ivy instead of a clinging vine.

The performer shifts abruptly between exaggerated gestures of conventional femininity (pouting lips, fingers in dimples, hands folded demurely in front, fluttering eyelids) and equally exaggerated gestures of female defiance (hands on hips, clinched teeth, shaking fist); Lightner returns to a coy and bashful pose by the song's final image of matricide. Her song contrasts between two alternative conceptions of femininity: a male fantasy of a nurturing and submissive womanliness (the "clinging vine") and a male nightmare of an irritating and independent femininity ("poison ivy"). The bride systematically transgresses all of her husband's expectations and repudiates all of the virtues of "true womanhood." Performed by a male clown with the wife treated as the object rather than as the subject of the song, "Poison Ivy" would represent a fairly conventional expression of male dread. Performed by Lightner, who willingly claims the position of the bad wife, the song suggests something else; Lightner adopts an air of defiance, gleefully documenting the ways the wife escapes the husband's control and the revenge she intends against her "lord and master" (poison in his coffee).

It is no longer possible, of course, to reconstruct how a historically situated audience might have reacted to such a comic spectacle. Lightner's performances are open to several very different responses. On the one hand, she could easily have become the butt of a male joke, assuming unfeminine mannerisms and unsightly appearances to trigger a highly misogynistic reaction, such as that modeled by the internal audience in the "Lady Beautiful" sequence. Her comedy could be read in terms of the semitragic narrative of failed femininity posed by her publicity, a sign of her inability to conform to male expectations about feminine beauty and grace. Yet, from another perspective, her comedy questions the validity of those criteria; her performances are open to a reading privileging a woman's pleasure of resistance, a pleasure personified by her defiant insistence to "look me over here, look me over there." Lightner's comic masquerade could be read as offering a utopian alternative to conformity and repression; it holds open a means of defining one's own identity apart from rigid social categories. What seems even more likely is that the first interpretation—the misogynist reading of Lightner's antics—may have provided an alibi for the second, may have created a context that tolerated transgressive women's pleasure under the guise of rebuking or ridiculing it. What might well have been experienced as a threat in that historical context, as Douglas's model suggests, has been transformed into a joke that both expresses and represses social tensions surrounding the construction of gender.

"SHE STEPS OVER HIGH WALLS": RESISTANT WIVES,
"GIRLISH LAUGHTER," AND CHARLOTTE GREENWOOD'S
LIMBER LEGS

The Charlotte Greenwood vehicle *So Long Letty* also explores the comic possibilities of woman's resistance to masculine demands for propriety and domesticity. Its farcical narrative places the loud and boisterous Letty Robbins at the core of a series of comically futile attempts by men (a husband, an uncle) to remake her into their own ideals of appropriate femininity. The husband fears that if his puritanical uncle "doesn't think I've married a real domestic little homemaker, he'll never give us a cent" and so he tries to pass off his next-door neighbor's wife (the aptly named Grace) for his own. Even as a neighbor, Uncle Claude finds Letty a horrifying figure, warning that "it would be fatal to you or anybody else to be married to *that kind of a woman.*" The pleasure-seeking Letty has little interest in acquiescing passively to their demands—not without having a few laughs at their expense; her rebellious antics lead to wilder and wilder disruptions of domestic tranquility and considerably less "peace and quiet" than either man anticipated.

So Long Letty reverses the conventional terms of the comedy of marital combat tradition, linking social restraint to the patriarchal order and the desire for spontaneity and joy to women's resistance. Letty is a bad wife not because she refuses to allow her husband to have fun but rather because she wants to have fun herself. While her abandoned husband eats Grace's home-cooked meals and sits by her hearth, smoking his pipe and watching Grace knit, Letty spends her time at the Ardmore Hotel, earning free beauty treatments by drumming up new customers for the salon (fig. 9.8). What makes Letty "so hot that my husband can't get fire insurance," as she brags at one point, is her willingness to put her own bodily pleasure (and her economic self-sufficiency) over her wifely duties; she abandons her home to "rack and ruin" while she indulges her desires for physical pampering. Letty is nowhere to be found when the husband expects dinner on the table and sings "Am I Blue?" when she is finally forced to wash the dishes. She flatly refuses to cater to his demands that she exhibit the virtues of "true womanhood," at least temporarily, in order to convince the uncle of the quality of his married life: "I told you when I married you that I couldn't cook and I don't like housework."

Ironically, those traits that make Letty such a frustration for her husband and a threat to his uncle are precisely those qualities that make her such a delight to the audience—Charlotte Greenwood's directness and vitality, her high energy style, her flamboyant gestures and loud voice, her colorful use of language, and especially her unorthodox physicality. Greenwood was a woman who relished her mastery over her own body, frequently challenging local women (and sometimes, men) to footraces as part of the publicity for her vaudeville tours and generally offering women a model for a more fit and limber style of femininity. In one of her most popular songs, one that she performed numerous times on stage, Greenwood openly acknowledged her nonconformity to traditional femininity:

I may not be so pretty,
and I don't dress like a queen.
I may not be so witty;
I am over sweet sixteen.
My face is not my fortune,
(It looks like the morning after),
but I still maintain
that I retain
(Bing! Bing!)
My girlish laughter!

What Greenwood called "girlish laughter" was actually a celebration of a pleasure that transcended traditional conceptions of beauty and glamour; her "girlish laughter" signaled a bodily pleasure for women that did not necessarily translate into voyeuristic pleasure for men. Alexander Woollcott described Greenwood's performance style in a 1919 review of *Linger Longer Letty,* one of a series of Letty plays she performed on Broadway and on tour throughout the 1920s: "The lanky Charlotte sings and romps and bays at the moon. She steps over high walls and walks on all fours and strokes the ceiling."[56] A publicity flyer for one of her stage appearances features a cartoon of Greenwood, her face dominated by enormous eyes and mouth, and her leg stretching from the bottom left to the top right corners, and her long arms, crossed, dangling limply in front of her thin body. Greenwood herself often bragged that she was "the only woman in the world who could kick a giraffe in the eye."[57] Such representations capture both the illusion of gracelessness and the display of virtuosity that made her such a fascinating performer.

As Letty, Greenwood exploits many of these same qualities. In one scene, Letty, juggling a huge pile of packages that block her vision, steps effortlessly over a white picket fence, a movement underscored by exaggerated creaking sounds and by her bungling husband's inability to cross this same fence without tripping. Letty slides down the hallway of the Ardmore hotel, using her outstretched leg to spin her around when she comes to the corner (fig. 9.9). She paces about her house, crossing

271

A limber style of femininity: publicity materials for Charlotte Greenwood. Wisconsin Center for Film and Theater Research.

the room in only a few strides, and when she dances at the party, her arms and legs seem to fly off in all directions. She stands, bowlegged, her knees bent slightly and her arms dangling limp or flung broadly to focus attention on their length. Her gestures and movements are too large-scale to be comfortably contained within the domestic spaces where the men wish her to remain, suggesting a high-spiritedness and spontaneity that will resist all restraint (self-imposed or otherwise). Greenwood's enthusiastic acceptance of her own odd appearance transforms what could be a pathetic or threatening figure into a celebration of spontaneity and self-confidence. Greenwood is most attractive and engaging in those sequences where she strays the furthest from the norms of traditional feminine behavior and causes the broadest disruption of the patriarchal order (her humiliation of Uncle Claude in the opening scene, her "clowning" in the party sequence).

The zestfulness of her performance must have made it hard for even contemporary audiences to accept the legitimacy of the men's oft-repeated demands for decorum and domesticity; the restraint of Letty would rob the film of much of its entertainment, overpowering the logic of the narrative that requires such a capitulation to the husband's demands in order to settle its farcical situations. The problem becomes how to resolve the trouble that this "terrible woman" causes, how to repair the disruption within her family relations without simultaneously robbing the text of its vitality and comedy, how to reconcile the competing demands for performance spectacle and narrative closure.

One titillating possibility the film explores is that Letty may find happiness with her neighbor's husband, Harold; the ukulele-strumming Harold resents Grace's stifling domesticity and favors Letty's Jazz Age playfulness. In a bold plot twist for a 1929 comedy, the two couples experiment at wife-swapping with nightmarish results: Letty's husband gets indigestion from Grace's home-cooked lamb chops while Letty's wildness exhausts her new mate. Over Harold's tired objections, Letty invites all of her friends from the Ardmore (including Uncle Claude's granddaughters and their suitors) to a party at her house. Here, the association between performance spectacle and female resistance emerges most explicitly. As Letty takes full control over the house and becomes "the life of the party," the narrative breaks down into a succession of musical numbers, each celebrating play and pleasure (Letty croons "My Strongest Weakness"; Harold sings "Never Let Me Go"; the nieces do a shimmy). While the lyrics shed indirect light on the characters' relationships, these songs are treated as excuses for pure showmanship, greeted enthusiastically by a receptive diegetic audience and performed frontally to the camera (fig. 9.10).

If Letty's house becomes a stage for flamboyant performances, Grace's house is a place where narrative still commands respect. Bert quarrels with Grace, rejecting the domesticity she offers; he storms across the street to join Harold and Letty for "Clowning," yet another musical number, and then, sings a solo, "So Long Letty," as a kind of plea for his wife's affections. Significantly, Bert's physical movement between the two houses parallels his movement between plot development and performance; his return to Letty's house and his decision to join the party would seem to signal some acceptance of her unruliness, though the narrative will not allow this tolerance to be sustained. Seconds after Bert departs, Uncle Claude comes to visit Grace, bringing a $50,000 check for his nephew, convinced that Bert has at last achieved domestic happiness with a model homemaker. Outraged over the loud party across the street and concerned by the husband's absence, Claude calls the police, before deciding to investigate the disturbance himself. The uncle's appearance at the party disrupts the performance and signals the return of patriarchal plot structures: he lectures all of the assembled characters on their misconduct (specifically their refusal to fulfill their expected social roles); yet even the stern old man seems on the verge of joining the singing when the police arrive and arrest him along with the others.

The police raid ends the last sequence where Greenwood's performance skills are allowed to command interest apart from the demand for narrative resolution, the reestablishment of domestic stability. The film holds open the possibility of Letty's resistance (and the pleasures of her comic spectacle) to the very last second, then forcefully pulls her back into conformity with the demands of male authority and forces her to accept the domestic containment required for narrative closure. Letty must be hauled before a judge, her marriage in total disarray; she must proclaim her love and affection for her husband and tearfully beg to be allowed to return to married life: "He's not much to look at but he does lend atmosphere in the home." The uncle embraces Letty, who leans over and whispers something in his ear that produces a broad smile of satisfaction, suggesting that the untamed woman has finally accepted her maternal and domestic responsibilities. Uncle Claude may yet get his much-desired grandnephew.

So Long Letty ends with a dinner party, one contrasting sharply in its formality and sobriety to the wild party Letty threw just a few scenes before. The entire cast has gathered around the table with Uncle Claude seated at its head, smiling benevolently at his gathered relatives and friends (fig. 9.11). The prune-faced patriarch has at last been shown proper respect by the once-terrible woman. The young granddaughters announce their engagement to two men they met only a few scenes before; the uncle looks upon it all with approval. He even invites his now much-beloved niece to act as a chaperon for his granddaughters' impending trip to Europe, though she refuses in order to remain at her husband's side. All lift glasses and join in a reprise of "So Long Letty," a slow sentimental ballad strikingly different from the more jazzy numbers associated with Greenwood. Letty has accommodated herself to the demands of her husband and her uncle, having learned quite literally to sing a different tune.

A highly unsatisfying resolution, the exaggerated domesticity of this concluding scene and the abruptness with which it was obtained weakens its ability to restrain Letty's subversiveness. Letty seems to be robbed of a victory over her husband and uncle that generic conventions suggest she richly deserves (and that Bert's "clowning" at the party implied was possible); she is denied the utopian release from stifling domesticity W. C. Fields enjoys at the conclusion of his comedies of marital combat. In the film's final scenes, however, Greenwood's performance still pushes against domestic containment. It is Letty, not the uncle, who presides over the table, offering toasts and dominating the dinner discourse. When the uncle urges her to accompany his nieces to Europe, she initially babbles about "mud packs in Paris," before dutifully rejecting the offer. Her hesitation suggests that she retains the desires that had earlier led to her rebelliousness. When Letty joins in the chorus, she does so with the loud voice and broad gestures that have accompanied the other musical numbers, even as she sings about her own capitulation to male demands: "So Long Letty!" Moreover, Uncle Claude seems looser, more lively here, as if he has been revitalized through his encounters with Letty; the capitulation may not have been entirely one-sided. Finally, it is significant, given the alignment of narrative with masculinity and performance with femininity, that the film ends on a note of performance, the singing of "So Long Letty," which simultaneously creates a narrative unity between the opposing forces. The song reconciles, if imperfectly, narrative and performance just as it reconciles, if imperfectly, male restraint and female pleasure. Even Uncle Claude, the motor of the narrative action, now joyfully joins the musical performance.

Greenwood's "girlish laughter" has transformed what could have been another story about the Wild Woman and her pathetic male victims into the tale of a spirited woman's resistance to male restraint. Her physical expressiveness, the joy she obviously takes in her mastery over her body, her refusal to conform to traditional conceptions of femininity, offered spectators an alternative conception of womanliness, one based on the pursuit of rather than the denial of pleasure.

The figure of the disorderly and unruly wife, the Wild Woman, recurs throughout American popular culture, assuming different meanings through its activation in its varied contexts, reflecting different values for the suffragettes and their critics, the sentimentalists and the humorists, the male clowns and the female comediennes. Undeniably, most film versions of the disorderly woman worked to ensure the pleasures of their predominantly male audiences, expressing and exorcising a masculine dread of feminine moral authority. In the course of ridiculing matriarchal power, however, it was necessary to represent it vividly and tangibly upon the screen. Early sound comedy, therefore, abounds with female characters who resist the traditional roles assigned to women, who refuse to allow themselves to be dominated by men: the matriarchs and matrons played by Margaret Dumont, Marie Dressler, Jobyana Howland, and Edna Mae Oliver; the wisecracking and man-hating roommates played by Patsy Kelly, Joan Blondell, and later, Eve Arden; the sexually omnipotent sirens played by Lydia Roberti, Lupe Velez, Ethel Merman, or Thelma Todd. Female comic stars like Charlotte Greenwood or Winnie Lightner pushed this potential even further; their vehicles make the struggles of energetic women to challenge male attempts to define female identity their central focus; their performances direct an "unmasking humor" against patriarchal institutions. Much like the "women on top" Davis finds in earlier popular and folk culture, these "funny ladies" offered alternative models of femininity, suggesting possibilities for a resistance to the domestic containment of women and for an expression of a powerful critique of the social construction of gender. If such figures remained open to a hostile male response, they still held potentials for forms of female pleasure totally absent from the male-centered comedies of the same vintage.

Conclusion:
The Return of the
Backflipping Senators

In *Stand Up And Cheer,* Senators Danforth and Short simply disappear following their sudden display of previously unsuspected acrobatic skills. A narrative problem is finessed in a moment of performance virtuosity that leaves unresolved the challenge the characters previously posed to Lawrence Cromwell and his mission. A scholarly book, however, is not an anarchistic comedy and must answer to its own sets of formal norms and audience expectations. Here, it would be inappropriate and undesirable to allow these perplexing figures to escape from our attention, nor can we so readily ignore the questions they pose for film studies. Their fascination demands closer examination and thus, we must drag them back on stage for a command performance. What began as a joke must be resolved; we must know what did make pistachio nuts.

This book suggests that the episode of the backflipping senators in *Stand Up and Cheer* did not represent an idiosyncratic flourish or an isolated aberration, did not arise spontaneously within this particular film; rather, these tumbling politicians are emblematic of a much larger historical development within the classical Hollywood cinema. Mitchell and Durant drew upon a basic vocabulary of performance techniques that had been assembled throughout decades of vaudeville practice and accommodated to the particularity of the early sound cinema. The trope of politics as performance was a common one in early sound comedy; Senators Danforth and Short would have found kindred spirits presiding over governments in *Duck Soup* and *Million Dollar Legs,* addressing the peace conference in *Diplomaniacs,* or delivering a campaign speech in *The Phantom President*. Their sudden shedding of identity, the explosion of comic energy that rips aside their dignified masks, represents another variant on the layering of performance Eddie Cantor displayed in *Whoopee* or Winnie Lightner demonstrated in *Side Show*; such practices reflect an aesthetic tradition that valued performer virtuosity over character consistency.

As we have seen, the recruitment of vaudeville and revue performers in the late 1920s and the attempt to construct appropriate vehicles to display their particular talents led Hollywood to experiment with ways that aspects of the vaudeville aesthetic might be integrated into existing screen practice. An aesthetic based on heterogeneity, affective immediacy, and performance confronted one that had long placed primary emphasis upon causality and consistency, closure and cohesiveness. Their meeting posed basic issues that had to be negotiated and resolved through the scriptwriting and production process: should comic texts build upon the vaudeville aesthetic's heterogeneous appeal to a heterogeneous audience or should they strive for a greater degree of unity and integration? Should narrative causality determine the arrangement and structuring of individual scenes or should the film provide space for unmotivated performance sequences? Should characters be rounded and fully developed or should they be vehicles through which performers display their skills? Should the film retain the self-conscious qualities of variety performance or should it adopt the self-effacement more characteristic of the classical Hollywood tradition? Should the film build toward closure or climax? Should its narrative celebrate individual spontaneity and personal pleasure or conformity and social integration? Should the films be made for New York or for "distribution"?

With the coming of sound, screen comedy entered a period of formal and thematic experimentation as various strategies for the construction of comedian comedies were tested, reworked, and perfected. Screenwriters, directors, and performers debated ways traditional vaudeville practices might be integrated into screen narratives as scripts were rewritten and revised in response to differing conceptions of proper entertainment. Critics and audiences reacted sharply to these various formal explorations, rejecting some as incoherent while eagerly embracing others as fanciful entertainment. Studios sought to build upon their (often contradictory) response(s), repeating practices that won favor, rejecting practices that confused or offended viewers, until a set of basic formulas for the construction of comedian-centered comedies emerged.

During this transitional period, the Hollywood studio system was prepared to accept formal practices and thematic concerns that might have been rejected as totally unacceptable a few years earlier or later. Hollywood was hoping to develop a style of entertainment that would find a following with both urban and rural spectators, that would preserve the affective immediacy of the New Humor tradition while maintaining some social respectability. Some early sound comedies subordinated narrative and characterization to the need to display the diverse performance skills of their lead clowns, while other films fit the clowns' antics to the demands of a more linear narrative and a more classical conception of characterization.

Within such a climate of exploration, experimentation, and innovation, *Stand Up and Cheer* attracted no special attention, aside from audience interest surrounding the first feature film appearance of Fox's newest child star, Shirley Temple. Like *International House, The Big Broadcast,* and *Hollywood Party, Stand Up and Cheer* was a showcase film; it exploited the talents of many different contracted performers but fit its performance sequences within a larger frame narrative. The resulting film does not fully develop character motivation or resolve central narrative conflicts; it relies heavily upon contrivance and circumstance to bring about narrative closure; it is often disorientating and sometimes disappointing. Despite these shortcomings, the film attracted far less negative press than *Hollywood Party,* a similar film released that same year, if only because individual sequences provided greater amusement than those created for the troubled MGM production.

Even within this context, however, the backflipping senators pose critical problems, not because they violate classical Hollywood norms, which seemed to be broadening to accommodate a variety of different formal experiments, nor because they are outside of generic conventions, which justified a number of similar moments in other early sound comedies. They warrant our interest because they transgress the film's internal norms. Like other showcase films, *Stand Up and Cheer* maintains a sharp distinction between plot-centered and performance-centered actors, between narratively significant moments and moments of heightened spectacle; this approach ensured the expressive coherence of individual performances if not ensemble consistency between the various performance sequences. These distinctions collapse during the Mitchell and Durant sequence. The senators abruptly abandon their narrative roles to engage in a self-conscious display of their acrobatic prowess; expressive coherence is sacrificed for novelty and surprise. Only familiarity with Mitchell and Durant's previous stage career as comic acrobats might prepare spectators for the shift from drama to comedy, from killjoy to anarchist, from representational to presentational styles of performance. Nor does the film find a way to integrate the characters back into the narrative following this sudden disruption. Such reckless disregard for narrative coherence and consistency might go unnoticed in another context, say, in the middle of *Diplomaniacs,* where it would remain as one reflexive element among many. Here, however, it stands out against the background of a more classically conceived narrative, against the dominant performance strategies of this particular text.

Such stylistic inconsistency was far from rare during this transitional period. While I have been able to locate no production records or script files on this particular film, no traces of the circumstances by which it reached the screen, it seems likely that *Stand Up and Cheer,* like *Hollywood Party,* was the focus of a complex process of aesthetic negotiation as competing conceptions of screen entertainment pushed the film in different directions. The backflipping senators might survive from an earlier, less integrated draft of the script, a moment of comic spectacle too rich and provocative to be discarded, much like the "Hot Chocolate Soldiers" number that proved so difficult for Rapf to abandon in *Hollywood Party.* This remarkable sequence might have been simply too fun to abandon despite increased efforts to bring the film in line with a more classical conception of screen narrative. Or, perhaps, the sequence was added later, in a last-ditch effort to intensify the entertainment value of the film. Both possibilities seem consistent with the aesthetic logic of early sound comedy. Performance sequences were often conceived as self-contained units that could be inserted or deleted depending upon audience response. That such a moment could exist at all, regardless of its precise historical circumstances, speaks to the flexibility of classical norms, the willingness of the Hollywood system to suspend its normal expectations. Such a moment would be unlikely to pass unnoticed in a film made even one year later.

Nineteen thirty-four represented the last great gasp of the anarchistic comedy tradition. Box office returns for this style of comedy declined drastically throughout the year, a decline contemporary observers attributed to overexposure of the comic stars, the inconsistent quality of individual vehicles, the exhaustion of familiar stage material, and public distaste for the films' scatological content. Hollywood was prepared to accept and even encourage deviation from standard screen practice as long as those experiments remained commercially successful. Faced with declining box office returns, exhibitor complaints, and public outrage, the studios brought comedian comedy more squarely in line with the dominant norms of the classical Hollywood cinema. The result was the emergence of a more formally and thematically conservative style of comedian comedy, which this book calls *affirmative comedy*.

Stand Up and Cheer already bears traces of these shifts in thematic and formal structure. Cromwell must repeatedly defend the importance of pleasure and amusement in the face of the sterility and conservatism of killjoys like the senate delegation. Yet he is also aligned with the cause of social integration and the restoration of national order. Cromwell is anything but an anarchist; the pleasure he promises can be most fully enjoyed within the civilized community, not outside of social constraint. The film's narrative pits him against those who would place their own ambitions and desires, their personal pleasures, over the national interests. The film's most anarchistic sequence—the now familiar episode of the backflipping senators—focuses not on the disruptive antics of the comic protagonist but rather on the hypocrisy and false dignity of the film's comic antagonists; the senators reject the possibility of public performances and engage in acrobatic stunts only behind closed doors. The film ends not with the collapse of the old order but with the celebration of the restored national order—with a public rejoicing for Cromwell's success in overcoming the Depression through public amusement, with a festival rather than a carnival.

Though the period of its greatest influence ended in 1934, the vaudeville aesthetic left a strong imprint of screen comedy. While more restrained than their pre-1934 films, comic vehicles for performers like the Marx Brothers, Wheeler and Woolsey, Olsen and Johnson, Burns and Allen, Eddie Cantor, and W. C. Fields appeared into the 1940s, retaining traces of the formal and thematic anarchy of the earlier works. On the margins of the studio system, in poverty row productions, short subjects, and animated cartoons, anarchistic comedy remained a viable alternative to the more integrative styles of comedy preferred by the majors. Works like *Hellzapoppin* or *Never Give a Sucker an Even Break* suggest the possibility of anarchistic comedy even in the face of the relative conservatism of late 1930s and early 1940s comedian comedy. The whole vocabulary of anarchistic comedy was inherited by the character cartoons of the 1940s, with Bugs Bunny's humiliation of the stodgy Elmer Fudd a pleasurable reworking of the earlier confrontations between Groucho Marx and Margaret Dumont. Traces of anarchistic comedy may be found as well in the screwball comedies of stars like vaudeville veteran Cary Grant or theatrical star Katharine Hepburn;

here, however, the spectacle of backflips (such as Grant performs in *Holiday*) or trained leopards (such as Hepburn owns in *Bringing Up Baby*) are subordinated to the demands of the romantic plot and fit to the particulars of the fictional characters. The claim has often been made that screwball comedy displaced anarchistic comedy. I remain unconvinced by that argument, if only because it ignores a long-standing tradition of romantic comedy in the American cinema dating back to the early 1910s and perhaps earlier. The writers of screwball comedies, such as Donald Ogden Stewart and Preston Sturges, also came to Hollywood in the midst of the early sound era recruitments, yet they came with a background in stage farce, not in revues or vaudeville. The stories they constructed fit comfortably within the traditions of the legitimate theater and, in fact, many of the most important screwball comedies were screen adaptations of preexisting stage plays. What *is* true is that the stagnancy of post-1934 comedian comedy meant that screwball comedies enjoyed limited competition in the late 1930s, though I prefer to see romantic comedy and comedian comedy as two generally separate traditions with their own lines of development.

By the late 1940s, Hollywood again embraced the more reflexive and performance-centered style of comedy associated with the vaudeville aesthetic. The films of Hope and Crosby, Danny Kaye, Martin and Lewis, and others build upon the formal traditions of early sound comedy. Yet they also maintain affirmative comedy's emphasis upon the social integration of the comedian. The excesses and contradictions that attract scholars to these 1950s comedies might well be symptomatic of a struggle to synthesize the formal practices of anarchistic comedy with the more conservative thematic structure of affirmative comedy. The integrative thematic structure and the more anarchic formal structure of *Stand Up and Cheer* already suggests the possible coexistence of the two styles of comedy within a single text.

My project has not been to construct the early 1930s as this year's candidate for the title of "Comedy's Greatest Era." I have little desire to depict it as another golden age of screen comedy, which, like that offered by the Agee-Mast tradition, was followed by an inevitable slump into mediocrity. Rather, this book has tried to situate the period as a specific moment within the larger development of the comedian comedy genre; I have sought to characterize those films—by a specific style of comic performance and specific thematic concerns—that are distinctive both from the comedian comedies preceding them and following them. Seidman and Krutnik are correct in locating a characteristic comedian comedy tradition that maintains continuity between distinctive periods of comic film production. Affirmative comedy is distinct from anarchistic comedy; anarchistic comedy is distinct from classical silent comedy. Yet there are films existing in the space between these generic subcategories. One could probably trace a strong line of influence from Keaton and Lloyd, say, through the films of Joe E. Brown or Eddie Cantor to the comedian comedies of Bob Hope and Danny Kaye. One would have a harder time tracing such a simple narrative, however, if one began to try to fit films like *Hollywood Party, Diplomaniacs,* or *Duck Soup* into that same pattern.

What made anarchistic comedy anarchistic—what made pistachio nuts—was a complex series of historical determinants that have been identified in the previous pages: the emergence of a new comic aesthetic in the early twentieth century with a focus on immediate affective response; the institutional structure of vaudeville with its particular emphasis upon the individual performer and upon a heterogeneous address to a heterogeneous audience; the film industry's interest in establishing a stable base of support for talking pictures; the recruitment of variety-trained performers to Hollywood and the demand to create vehicles that exploited their performance skills; the presence of a group of film comedy directors who had gained their initial experience working for Mack Sennett and the other producers of silent slapstick comedy; the Production Code Administration's willingness to accept greater transgressions of their moral norms in comic rather than dramatic films; the difficulty screenwriters faced in reconciling the vaudeville aesthetic with the norms of the classical Hollywood narrative; the particular personalities of specific comedians that pushed them to emphasize the most anarchic aspects of the vaudeville tradition; Depression era audiences who demanded the maximization of pleasure for their entertainment dollars. This series of developments did not end in 1934, though the film industry increasingly sought other strategies for responding to these demands, other ways of utilizing these resources.

An awareness of historical specificity must not blind us to continuity within historical development, anymore than we should allow a recognition of some consistency within a generic tradition to prevent us from exploring what was distinctive about each period of its development. I have focused on a particularly interesting period in the development of the American comedian comedy tradition, hoping to understand the factors that led to comedian comedy's development and the aesthetic and ideological norms that shaped its texts and their reception. Along the way, however, I have provided a passing glimpse at how this period might fit into larger patterns of historical development, how it might evolve from classical silent comedy, how it might mutate into a new style of screen comedy. My hope is that other historians may pursue some of these other lines of development, may reconstruct other periods, explore other texts, resurrect other figures. Such revisionist work will contribute to an even fuller understanding of the development of this central film genre.

Mikhail Bakhtin closed his account of the equally anarchistic comedy of Rabelais with the assertion that "every act of world history was accompanied by a laughing chorus."[1] Our task as historians of the comic genre must surely start with an attempt to reconstruct the sounds of forgotten laughter. A key concern must be to understand what made previous generations laugh, to comprehend what laughter may have meant in different contexts, and to gain some understanding of what gave that laughter its particular tone and resonance. The dominant laughter of the early 1930s was undoubtedly the belly laugh, an intense eruption that shook the entire body, an anarchic laughter that challenged the power of institutions to exercise emotional and social constraint upon individual spontaneity, a nonsensical laughter that was meaningful precisely in the way it transcended narrative meaning. Perhaps most important, it was a popular laughter, which entertained without pretenses of moral education or social reform. This laughter arose in a great explosion of affective response, a wow climax to three decades of comic experimentation, only to be forgotten when a new generation of performers pushed the old from the spotlight.

Notes

1. The Strange Case of the Backflipping Senators

1. James Agee, "Comedy's Greatest Era," *Life*, September 3, 1949, reprinted in Gerald Mast and Marshall Cohen, eds., *Film Theory and Criticism* (London: Oxford University Press, 1974), p. 440.

2. Ibid.

3. Ibid.

4. Ibid., p. 455.

5. Donald McCaffrey, *Four Great Comedians* (New York: Barnes, 1968), p. 149. See also Walter Kerr, *The Silent Clowns* (New York: Knopf, 1975).

6. Gerald Mast, *The Comic Mind: Comedy and the Movies* (New York: Random House, 1976), p. 280.

7. Andrew Sarris, *The American Cinema: Directors and Directions, 1929–1968* (New York: Dutton, 1968), pp. 246–248.

8. McCaffrey, *Four Great Comedians*, p. 152.

9. Donald Crafton, "The Pie and the Chase: Gag, Spectacle, and Narrative in Slapstick Comedy," in Eileen Bowser, ed., *The Slapstick Symposium* (Brussels: Federation Internationale des Archives du Film, 1987), p. 50.

10. Ibid.

11. Peter Kramer, "Vitagraph, Slapstick, and Early Cinema," *Screen* 29(2):99–104 (Spring 1988); see also Peter Kramer, "Derailing the Honeymoon Express: Comicality and Narrative Closure in Buster Keaton's *The Blacksmith*," *Velvet Light Trap* (Spring 1989), no. 23, pp. 101–116.

12. Richard Rowland, "American Classic," *Hollywood Quarterly*, April 1947, pp. 267–268.

13. John Grierson, "The Logic of Comedy," in Forsyth Hardy, ed., *Grierson on Documentary* (New York: Harcourt, Brace, 1947), p. 34.

14. Clifton Fadiman, "A New High in Low Comedy," *Stage*, January 1936, pp. 322–328.

15. "The Marx Brothers Abroad," *Living Age*, September 1932, pp. 371–372.

16. Colin L. Westerbeck, "Marxism," *Commonweal*, June 14, 1974, pp. 332–333.

17. Meyer Levin, "*Duck Soup*," *Esquire*, February 1934, p. 131.

18. William Troy, "Films," *Nation*, December 13, 1933, p. 688.

19. Antonin Artaud, *Theatre and Its Double* (New York: Grove, 1958), pp. 142–144.

20. Raymond Durgnat, *The Crazy Mirror: Hollywood Comedy and the American Image* (London: Faber and Faber, 1969), pp. 150–152.

21. Gerald Weales, *Canned Goods as Caviar: American Film Comedies of the 1930s* (Chicago: University of Chicago Press, 1985), p. 78.

22. Robert Warshow, *The Immediate Experience: Movies, Comics, Theatre, and Other Aspects of Popular Culture* (New York: Atheneum, 1975), p. 50.

23. Andrew Bergman, *We're in the Money: Depression America and Its Films* (New York: Harper and Row, 1971), p. 63.

24. Mast, *The Comic Mind*, p. 287.

25. Weales, *Canned Goods*, p. 78.

26. Levin, "*Duck Soup*," p. 131.

27. Phillipe Soupault, "*Horse Feathers*," *L'Europe Nouvelle*, October 8, 1932, p. 1202.

28. Salvador Dali, "Surrealism in Hollywood," *Harper's Bazaar*, June 1937, p. 68; Roland Barthes, *Roland Barthes* (New York: Hill and Wang, 1977), p. 80.

29. For a similar critique of this tradition, see John R. Groch, "What is a Marx Brother? Critical Practice, Industrial Practice, and The Notion of the Comic Auteur," *Velvet Light Trap* (Fall 1990), no. 26, pp. 28–41. Groch's Foucauldian conclusion—that the Marx Brothers are a critical construct—does not go very far toward reconstructing the historical conditions of their films' production and reception or positioning them in relation to a broader performance tradition.

30. Steve Seidman, *Comedian Comedy: A Tradition in Hollywood Film* (Ann Arbor: UMI Research Press, 1981), pp. 8–11. See also Frank Krutnik, "The Clown-Prints of Comedy," *Screen* 25(4–5):50–59 (July-October 1984).

31. Seidman, *Comedian Comedy*, p. 55.

32. Ibid., p. 5.

33. Jean-Luc Comolli and Jean Narboni, "Cinema/Ideology/Criticism," in Bill Nichols, ed., *Movies and Methods: An Anthology* (Berkeley: University of California Press, 1976), pp. 22–30; The Editors, *Cahiers du Cinema*, "John Ford's *Young Mr. Lincoln*," in Bill Nichols, ed., *Movies and Methods: An Anthology* (Berkeley: University of California Press, 1976), pp. 493–529.

34. Comolli and Narboni, "Cinema/Ideology/Criticism," pp. 25–27.

35. For a useful discussion of *Cahiers du Cinema*'s auteurism, see Pam Cook, ed., *The Cinema Book* (New York: Pantheon, 1985), pp. 114–207.

36. Claire Johnson, "Women's Cinema as Counter Cinema," in Patricia Erens, ed.), *Sexual Stratagems* (New York: Horizon, 1979), pp. 133–143; Claire Johnson, ed., *The Work of Dorothy Arzner: Towards a Feminist Cinema* (London: British Film Institute, 1975).

37. See, for example, Jean Pierre Coursodon, "Jerry Lewis," in Jean Pierre Coursodon and Pierre Sauvage, eds., *American Directors*, 2 vols. (New York: Mc-Graw-Hill, 1983), 2:189–190; Dana Polan, "Being and Nuttiness: Jerry Lewis and the French," *Journal of Popular Film and Television* 12(1):42–46 (1984).

38. Paul Willemen, "Tashlin's Method: A Hypothesis," in Claire Johnson and

Paul Willemen, eds., *Frank Tashlin* (Edinburgh: Edinburgh Film Festival, 1973), pp. 117–122.

39. Jacques Aumont, Jean-Luc Comolli, A. S. Labarthe, Jean Narboni, and Sylvie Pierre, "A Concise Lexicon of Lewisian Terms," in Claire Johnson and Paul Willemen, eds., *Frank Tashlin* (Edinburgh: Edinburgh Film Festival, 1973), pp. 89–129.

40. Michael Selig, *"The Nutty Professor:* A 'Problem' in Film Scholarship," *Velvet Light Trap* (Fall 1990), no. 26, pp. 42–56.

41. See Barbara Klinger, "Cinema/Ideology/Criticism Revisited: The Progressive Genre," in Barry Keith Grant, ed., *Film Genre Reader* (Austin: University of Texas Press, 1986), pp. 74–90. Many of the traits Klinger identifies as characteristic of works identified with "progressive genres" are traits that recur within discussions of early sound comedy, though no one has articulated a claim for its status within this tradition: a pessimistic world view; the "demolition" of values held positively by dominant cinema, including notions of romance, marriage, law, and the family; a reduced, fragmented and/or self-conscious narrative; excessive visual styles and performances; stereotypical and inconsistent characterization. Perhaps it is because the "anarchistic" reading of the Marx Brothers is so widely accepted that no one has felt the need to articulate claims for their films within this new paradigm.

42. Ibid., p. 76.

43. Ibid., pp. 86–87.

44. Dana Polan, "A Brechtian Cinema? Towards a Politics of Self-Reflexive Film," in Bill Nichols, ed., *Movies and Methods,* 2 vols. (Berkeley: University of California Press, 1985), 2:664.

45. Ibid., p. 668.

46. Alan Williams, "Is a Radical Genre Criticism Possible?" *Quarterly Review of Film Studies* (Spring 1984), pp. 121–125.

47. Donald Crafton, *Before Mickey: The Animated Film, 1898–1928* (Cambridge: MIT Press, 1982); Lea Jacobs, *Reforming Women: Censorship and the Female Ideal in Hollywood, 1928–1942* (Madison: University of Wisconsin Press, 1991); Paul Kerr, "Out of What Past? Notes on the B Film Noir," in Paul Kerr, ed., *The Hollywood Film Industry* (London: Routledge and Kegan Paul, 1986), pp. 20–44; Tom Doherty, *Teenagers and Teenpics* (Boston: Unwyn and Hyman, 1988).

48. David Bordwell, Janet Staiger, and Kristin Thompson, *The Classical Hollywood Cinema: Film Style and Mode of Production to 1960* (New York: Columbia University Press, 1985), p. 3; see also David Bordwell, "Historical Poetics of the Cinema," in R. Barton Palmer ed., *The Cinematic Text: Methods and Approaches* (New York: AMS, 1989), pp. 369–398.

49. Bordwell, Staiger, and Thompson, *Hollywood Cinema,* p. xiv.

50. Ibid., p. 3.

51. Ibid., pp. 70–71.

52. Ibid., pp. 70–71.

53. Ibid., p. 21.

54. Ibid., pp. 372–337.

55. Ibid., p. 375.

56. Stuart Hall, "Notes on Deconstructing 'the Popular,' " in Raphael Samuel, ed., *People's History and Socialist Theory* (London: Routledge and Kegan Paul, 1981), pp. 227–240.

57. Michael Denning, *Mechanic Accents: Dime Novels and Working-Class Culture in America* (London: Verso, 1987); Lawrence Levine, *Highbrow/Lowbrow: The Emergence of Cultural Hierarchy in America* (Cambridge: Harvard University Press, 1988); Peter Stallybrass and Allon White, *The Politics and Poetics of Transgression* (Ithaca: Cornell University Press, 1986); Robert C. Allen, *Horrible Prettiness: Burlesque and American Culture* (Chapel Hill: University of North Carolina Press, 1991).

58. Norbert Elias and Eric Dunning, *Quest For Excitement: Sport and Leisure in the Civilizing Process* (London: Basil Blackwell, 1986), p. 44.

2. *"How is it Possible for a Civilized Man to Live Among People Who Are Always Joking?" Class, Comedy, and Cultural Change in Turn-of-the Century America*

1. Carolyn Wells, "First Lessons in Humor," *Century*, May 1902, p. 78.

2. Ibid., p. 82.

3. Irwin Edman, "Gaiety for the Solemn," *Bookman*, May 1926, p. 266.

4. F. Treudley, "The Place of Humor," *Educational Review*, June 1910, pp. 92–96.

5. George Meredith, "An Essay on Comedy," in Wylie Sypher, ed., *Comedy: Two Essays* (New York: Doubleday, 1956), p. 4.

6. Ibid., p. 19.

7. Ibid., p. 3.

8. Robert Bernard Martin, *The Triumph of Wit: A Study of Victorian Comic Theory* (Oxford: Clarendon, 1974), p. 1.

9. Willis Boyd Allen, "Etiquette of Humor," *Nation*, June 1913, pp. 570–571.

10. Burgess Johnson, "The Right Not to Laugh," *Harpers Monthly*, April 1915, pp. 762–765.

11. James Sully, *An Essay on Laughter: Its Forms, Its Causes, Its Development, and Its Value* (New York: Longmans, Green, 1902), p. 232.

12. Ibid., p. 232.

13. Ibid., p. 283.

14. Ibid., p. 301.

15. "The Death of Laughter," *World's Work*, January 1925, pp. 244–245.

16. Sully, *Essay on Laughter*, p. 318.

17. W. L. Courtney, "The Idea of Comedy," *Living Age*, August 8, 1914, pp. 348–359.

18. Max Beerbohm, "Laughter," *Golden Book*, March 1927, pp. 355–360.

19. Gerald Stanley Lee, "A Rule For Humor," *The Critic*, October 1898, pp. 291–294.

20. Courtney, "The Idea of Comedy," pp. 355–360.

21. Sully, *Essay on Laughter*, p. 388.

22. Ibid., p. 310.

23. Ibid., p. 314.

24. *Blackwood's Magazine*, "The Limitations of Humor," *Living Age,* August 31, 1907, pp. 485–495.

25. Brett Page, *Writing for Vaudeville* (Springfield: Home Correspondence School, 1913), p. 147.

26. George M. Cohan and George Jean Nathan, "The Mechanics of Emotion," *McClure,* November 1913, pp. 95–96.

27. Ibid.

28. Ibid., p. 99.

29. See, for example, W. C. Fields, "Anything for a Laugh," *American,* September 1934, pp. 126–130; Irvin S. Cobb, "The Trail of the Lonesome Laugh," *Everybody's,* April 1911, pp. 467–473; Hugh Leamy, "A Kick and a Laugh," *Colliers,* August 20, 1927, pp. 13ff.; John E. Hazzard and Robert Gordon Anderson, "The Bag of Tricks," *Saturday Evening Post,* April 27, 1929, pp. 18–19.

30. Joe Weber and Lew Fields, "Adventures in Human Nature," *Associated Sunday Magazine,* June 23, 1912, as cited in Page, *Writing for Vaudeville,* pp. 103–104.

31. Ibid., p. 142.

32. Robert Lytell, "Vaudeville Old and Young," *New Republic,* July 1, 1925, p. 156.

33. Albert McClean, Jr., *American Vaudeville as Ritual* (Louisville: University of Kentucky Press, 1965), p. 107. See also Albert McClean, Jr., "U.S. Vaudeville and the Urban Comics," *Theatre Quarterly* (October-December 1971), pp. 50–57. McClean's terminology has been maintained here to preserve continuity with previous treatments of this phenomenon, although its meaning in the context of early twentieth-century discourse remains ambiguous. Burgess Johnson, who wrote a series of articles on the New Humor, dealt only with the content of contemporary comic magazines and the nonsense poetry of literary magazines. See Burgess Johnson, "The New Humor," *Critic,* April 1902, pp. 331–338; Burgess Johnson, "The New Humor," *Critic,* June 1902, pp. 526–532. Oscar Fay Adams, "Is American Humor Humorous," *Outlook,* June 2, 1894, pp. 961–962, included comic strips and newspaper humor columns under the term. The phenomenon that McClean describes—the humor of the new mass amusements—went by a number of names including "Noodle Humor," "Mad Humor," "Crazy Comedy," etc. See, for example, John Albert Macy, "The Career of the Joke," *Atlantic,* October 1905, pp. 498–510; Gilbert Seldes, "Mad Humor," *Saturday Review,* November 28, 1925, p. 331; John Kendrick Bangs, "In Defense of Old Jokes," *Bookman,* September 1920, pp. 1–6.

34. Lawrence Senelick, "Variety into Vaudeville: The Process Observed in Two Manuscript Gagbooks," *Theatre Survey,* May 1978, pp. 1–15.

35. Adams, "Is American Humor Humorous," pp. 961–962.

36. The single best source on traditions of American humor remains Walter Blair and Hamilan Hill, *America's Humor: From Poor Richard to Doonesbury* (Oxford: Oxford University Press, 1978). Another standard work is Constance Rourke,

American Humor: A Study of the National Character (New York: Harcourt Brace Jovanovich, 1931). For an informative discussion of Davy Crockett, which shares my dependence upon anthropological theories of jokes and comic inversion, see Carroll Smith-Rosenberg, *Disorderly Conduct: Visions of Gender in Victorian America* (New York: Knopf, 1985), pp. 90–108. Excerpts from Simon Suggs, Sut Lovingood, and other twentieth-century forerunners of slapstick comedy can be found in Walter Blair, *Native American Humor* (New York: American, 1930).

37. See Harry B. Weiss, *A Brief History of American Joke Books* (New York: New York Public Library, 1943) for a fuller discussion of the impact of Joe Miller on American jokebooks and humor magazines.

38. For contemporary discussions of the recycling of jokes, see Milton MacKaye, "The Whiskers on the Wisecrack," *Saturday Evening Post*, August 17, 1935, pp. 12–13ff.; W. D. Nesbit, "The Humor of Today," *Independent*, May 29, 1902, pp. 1300–1304; "Humor and the Joke," *Outlook*, July 20, 1912, pp. 615–616; Vincent Engels, "The Mills of Humor," *Commonweal*, January 2, 1929, p. 261; "Card-Index Humor," *Atlantic*, August 1915, pp. 284–286. Anyone who doubts the impact of nineteenth-century traditions on the New Humor should read MacKaye, who provides a list of suggested books for would-be gagwriters that is heavy with volumes of folk humor and native American literary humor (including Montague Glass, Joe Miller, Chauncey Depew, George Ade and Eugene Field, J. G. Baldwin, Horace H. Riley, Stephen Leacock, Robert Benchley, John Neil, and George W. Harris).

39. Robert C. Allen's history of American burlesque finds earlier critics raising many of these same objections in response to nineteenth-century popular theater. See Robert C. Allen, *Horrible Prettiness: Burlesque and American Culture* (Chapel Hill: University of North Carolina Press, 1991).

40. For discussions of the rise of the amusement park, see Kathy Peiss, *Cheap Amusements: Working Women and Leisure in Turn-of-the-Century New York* (Philadelphia: Temple University Press, 1986); John Kasson, *Amusing the Millions: Coney Island at the Turn of the Century* (New York: Hill and Wang, 1981); Lauren Rabinovitz,"Temptations of Pleasure: Nickelodeons, Amusement Parks, and the Sights of Female Sexuality," *Camera Obscura* 23:71–90 (May 1990). On newspaper comics, see Maurice Horn, ed., *The World Encyclopedia of Comics* (New York: Avon, 1976) and Stephen Becker, *Comic Art in America* (New York: Simon and Schuster, 1959). On humor magazines, see Stanley Trachtenberg, ed., *American Humorists, 1800–1950* (Detroit: Gale Research, 1982). On jokebooks, see Weiss, *Brief History*. On vaudeville, see McClean, *American Vaudeville* and "U.S. Vaudeville"; Shirley Staples, *Male-Female Comedy Teams in American Vaudeville, 1865–1932* (Ann Arbor: UMI Press, 1934); Paul A. Distler, "The Rise and Fall of the Racial Comics in American Vaudeville" (Ph.D. diss., Tulane University, 1963); Frederick Edward Snyder, "American Vaudeville—Theater in a Package: The Origins of Mass Entertainment" (Ph.D diss., Yale University, 1970). The most useful sources on the comic in early cinema include Kalton C. Lahue, *World of Laughter: The Motion Picture Comedy Short, 1910–1930* (Norman: University of Oklahoma Press, 1966); Kalton C. Lahue and Terry Brewer, *Kops and Custards: The Legend of the Keystone*

Films (Norman: University of Oklahoma Press, 1968). On the rise of the nightclub, see Lewis A. Erenberg, *Steppin' Out: New York Nightlife and the Transformation of American Culture, 1890–1930* (Westport: Scarecrow, 1981). On legitimate stage comedy, see Stanley Green, *The Great Clowns of Broadway* (New York: Oxford University Press, 1976). On burlesque, see Robert Allen, *Horrible Prettiness: Burlesque and American Culture* (Chapel Hill: University of North Carolina Press, 1991). For an overview of popular amusements, see Robert Toll, *On With the Show: The First Century of Show Business in America* (New York: Oxford University Press, 1976) and Robert Toll, *The Entertainment Machine: American Show Business in the Twentieth Century* (New York: Oxford University Press, 1982). For a discussion of the impact of changing work conditions on American popular culture, see Roy Rosenzweig, *Eight Hours for What We Will: Workers and Leisure in an Industrial City, 1870–1920* (Cambridge: Cambridge University Press, 1983); Cary Goodman, *Choosing Sides: Playground and Street Life on the Lower East Side* (New York: Schocken, 1979).

41. Thomas L. Masson, "Has America a Sense of Humor?" *North American*, August 1929, pp. 178–184.

42. Stanley Trachtenberg, ed., *American Humorists, 1800–1950* (Detroit: Gale Research, 1982).

43. See, for example, Arthur Sullivan Hoffman, "Who Writes the Jokes?" *Bookman*, October 1907, pp. 171–181.

44. Thomas L. Masson, "How I Wrote 50,000 Jokes in 20 Years," *American*, June 1920, pp. 26–27.

45. "Sounding the Doom of the Comics," *Current Literature*, December 1908, pp. 630–633.

46. Robert Allen, *Vaudeville and Film, 1895–1915: A Study of Media Interaction* (New York: Arno, 1980), pp. 36–37.

47. "Only 300 Houses Vaude," *Variety*, October 2, 1929, p. 51.

48. Based on plot synopses published in *Moving Picture World*, 1907–1912, sampled on four weeks out of every year. Figures for 1907 are unreliable because the publication was unsystematic about printing plot descriptions. In 1908, the weekly releases of comedies averaged fifteen. The following year, a slight decline in production puts the figure closer to eleven. Rapid expansion rose the number to fifteen again in 1910, twenty-four in 1911, and forty-three in 1912. Comedy was either the largest genre or tied with drama in four out of five years included in the study; drama surpassed comedy only in 1910 when comic film production underwent a slump. Henry Jenkins, "Film Comedy Before Mack Sennett: Some Observations," Unpublished Seminar Paper, University of Wisconsin, 1985.

49. "The Other Fellow Thought This Funny," *Everybody's*, July 1916, pp. 52–56.

50. La Touche Hancock, "Some Humor of Some Humorists," *Bookman*, September 1902, pp. 498–510.

51. "Disguising Vaudeville," *Bellman*, March 29, 1919, p. 358; Morris Ross, "A Deterioration of the Stage," *Poetlore*, June 1891, pp. 353–356.

52. "I contend that the people who take literary magazines do not want silly words often made to rhyme absurdly. They can look for this to the funny corner of

the penny daily. Such outpourings are out of place when interlarded with sane and serious work. It is the fly in the ointment; the toad in the flowerbed; the one jarring note in the harmony; the one blot on the picture." Edwin Carlile Litsey, "Nonsense Rhymes and Literary Magazines," *Critic*, October 1906, p. 48. For the opposing view, see KAG, "A Plea for Nonsense," *Critic*, April 1906, pp. 45–47.

53. "Material which in no other country in the world would be offered to anybody but infants or semi-idiots is here gravely thrust by newspapers upon their presumably intelligent readers and hailed as a great advance in journalism." "Sounding the Doom of the Comics," *Current Literature*, December 1908, pp. 630–633.

54. Jerome K. Jerome, "You Can't Be Funny All the Time," *Cosmopolitan*, May 1906, pp. 110–112.

55. Albert R. Bandini, "The Fatal Gift of Humor," *Catholic World*, August 1926, pp. 587–591.

56. Anthropologist Mary Douglas has suggested that laughter functions as an important point of intersection between the corporal and the social, the natural and the cultural. Laughter is technically a bodily eruption, like farting or sneezing, yet it almost always signifies something within a specific sociocultural context. It refers outward to some cultural phenomenon or inward to a state of mind; it also directs attention onto the materiality of the body. See Mary Douglas, *Implicit Meanings: Essays in Anthropology* (London: Routledge and Kegan Paul, 1975). Douglas's work consistently explores ways cultural images of the body reflect the perceived order of the social system. See Mary Douglas, *Natural Symbols: Explorations in Cosmology* (New York: Pantheon, 1982). She suggests that within a hierarchically structured, socially rigid cultural system, such as Gilded Age America, there is a felt need to maintain a high degree of bodily control and to protect orifices from outside intrusion, a need intensified when the social system is under actual threat of disruption. To the members of such a culture, the body, racked with uncontrollable laughter, becomes an apt—if terrifying—image of the state trying to recover its equilibrium in the face of changing social paradigms. For a textbook example of this middle-class anxiety about the image of a laughing body, see Robert Lynd, "Objections to Laughter," *Atlantic*, March 1930, pp. 332–341.

57. Mabel Marion Cox, "Propagation of Laughter," *Cosmopolitan*, June 1906, pp. 110–112.

58. Sully, *Essay on Laughter*, p. 422.

59. Ibid., p. 412.

60. Ibid., p. 26. For similar views, see Lynd, *"Objections to Laughter"* and "The Benefits of Laughter," *Literary Digest*, November 5, 1927, p. 25.

61. Sully, *Essay on Laughter*, p. 418.

62. See, for example, Walter B. Hill, "The Psychology and Ethics of Fun," *Proceedings of the National Educational Association* (1902), pp. 286–297; Treudley, "The Place of Humor"; A. Replier, "Our Loss of Nerve," *Atlantic*, September 1913, pp. 298–304. For a later and more sympathetic treatment of the role of humor in education, see Margaret M. McLaughlin, "A Plea and a Project," *Educational Review*, September 1923, pp. 79–85.

63. "The Comic Nuisance," *Outlook*, March 6, 1909, pp. 527–528.

64. "Cultivating Dreamfulness," *Independent,* June 27, 1907, pp. 1538–1539.

65. "The Dominant Joke," *Atlantic,* March 1903, pp. 431–432.

66. See, for example, H. H. Boyson, "Plague of Jocularity," *North American,* November 1895, pp. 528–535; S. B. Wister, "A Plea for Seriousness," *Atlantic,* May 1892, pp. 625–630; F. Pier, "Serious Results of the Late Humor," *Harper's Weekly,* January 23, 1909, p. 31; Elizabeth Woodbridge, "The Humor-Fetish," *Outlook,* November 7, 1908, pp. 540–542.

67. Pierre Bourdieu, "Aristocracy of Culture," *Media, Culture, and Society* 2:253–254 (1980).

68. Richard Burton, "The Mistimed Laugh," *Bellman,* May 19, 1917, p. 544.

69. Louis Crocker, "A Note on Comedy," *Nation,* September 25, 1920, p. 347. Along with Meredith, Herbert Spencer was probably the most oft-quoted theorist of comedy among defenders of the traditional comic aesthetic. If Meredith pointed toward the refinement of laughter, Spencer was cited as evidence of its brute undercurrents, its appeals to savagery and egotism.

70. Bourdieu, "Aristocracy of Culture," p. 251.

71. Pierre Bourdieu, *Distinction: A Social Critique of the Judgement of Taste* (Cambridge: Harvard University Press, 1979), pp. 379–380.

72. Ibid.

73. Canon Burnett, "The Recreation of the People," *Living Age,* 1886, pp. 272–290.

74. Paul W. Goldsbury, "Recreation Through the Senses," *Atlantic Monthly,* March 1911, p. 415.

75. Jane Adams, *A New Conscience and an Ancient Evil* (New York: MacMillan, 1923). See also Richard Henry Edwards, *Popular Amusements* (New York: Associated Press, 1915) and Richard Henry Edwards, *Christianity and Amusements* (New York: Associated Press, 1915).

76. George Elliot Howard, "Social Psychology of the Spectator," *American Journal of Sociology* (July 1912), pp. 42–46.

77. Henry Seidel Canby, *An Age of Confidence: Life in the Nineties* (New York: Farrar and Rinehart, 1934), p. 124.

78. Oscar Fay Adams, "American Sense of Humor," October 8, 1910, pp. 311–316.

79. Katherine Roof, "The American Sense of Humor," *Outlook,* October 8, 1910, pp. 311–316.

80. H. H. Boyson, "Plague of Jocularity," *North American,* November 1895, p. 528.

81. The history of early screen comedy was scarcely considered before the recent attention focused on early cinema more generally. Most accounts treat Sennett, unproblematically, as the "father of screen comedy," often explicitly denying the existence of comic films prior to the 1912 opening of Keystone. Edward Edelson, *Funnymen of the Movies* (Garden City: Doubleday, 1976) opens with the statement: "Movie comedy really started with Mack Sennett and the Keystone films. This is an exaggeration but not too much of one." Kent Eastin writes, in an introduction to Kalton C. Lahue and Terry Brewer, *Kops and Custards: The Legend of the Keystone*

Films, that "there was no true motion picture comedy form, precedent or technique. It was a clear field and what Sennett did with it in that span of five years is what gave the Keystones their impact on the movies of the day and on motion picture comedy for all time to come." The Pordonone retrospective on Italian and Vitagraph comedy, the MOMA symposium on slapstick comedy, and other recent retrospectives help to redefine this terrain, though they have yet to result in a systematic revision of the history of film comedy during this crucial period. See David Robinson, "The Italian Comedy," *Sight and Sound* (Fall 1986), pp. 105–112; Peter Kramer, "Vitagraph, Slapstick, and Early Cinema," *Screen* 29(2):99–104 (Spring 1988); Eileen Bowser, ed., *The Slapstick Symposium* (Brussels: Federation Internationale des Archives du Film, 1987) for some preliminary work on these issues.

82. I am indebted to Tom Gunning for helpful suggestions about formulating this history of early film comedy.

83. Epes Winthrop Sargent, The Photoplaywright, *Moving Picture World,* May 22, 1915, p. 1253. *Moving Picture World* maintained a firm commitment to this notion of refined comedy throughout its publication history. For early examples of such advocacy, see "The Seriousness of Comedy," *Moving Picture World,* April 9, 1910, p. 548; "A Plea for More Comedies," *Moving Picture World,* October 29, 1910, p. 979; "The Dearth of Comedy," *Moving Picture World,* June 10, 1911, p. 1293; F. George Eggleston, "The Comic Film," *Moving Picture World,* April 22, 1911, pp.875–878; Louis Reeves Harrison, "The Comedy of the Future," *Moving Picture World,* February 4, 1911, p. 230; "The Tragedy of Comedy," *Moving Picture World,* January 14, 1911, pp. 72–73; Louis Reeves Harrison, "It Is to Laugh," *Moving Picture World,* December 21, 1912, p. 1166. W. Stephen Bush, "The Mystery of Laughter," *Moving Picture World,* March 11, 1916, p. 1621, takes a different perspective, claiming that "there can be no doubt that the rough kind of screen humor has a strong and unfailing appeal. I have seen men (and women, too) who were outspoken in their opposition to so-called 'Roughhouse' comedy laugh most immodestly at the kicks and cuffs of which this sort of comedy is largely composed."

84. Epes Winthrop Sargent, The Photoplaywright, *Moving Picture World,* April 12, 1913, p. 157.

85. Epes Winthrop Sargent, The Photoplaywright, *Moving Picture World,* August 26, 1916, p. 1398.

86. Epes Winthrop Sargent, The Photoplaywright, *Moving Picture World,* November 11, 1913, p. 490.

87. Epes Winthrop Sargent, The Photoplaywright, *Moving Picture World,* November 11, 1913, p. 490.

88. Epes Winthrop Sargent, The Photoplaywright, *Moving Picture World,* May 16, 1914, p. 962.

89. Epes Winthrop Sargent, The Photoplaywright, *Moving Picture World,* August 26, 1916, p. 1398.

90. Epes Winthrop Sargent, The Photoplaywright, *Moving Picture World,* November 20, 1915, p. 1493.

91. Epes Winthrop Sargent, The Photoplaywright, *Moving Picture World*, January 3, 1914, p. 41.

92. Epes Winthrop Sargent, The Photoplaywright, *Moving Picture World*, December 13, 1913, p. 157; Epes Winthrop Sargent, The Photoplaywright, *Moving Picture World*, February 24, 1917, p. 1170.

93. Epes Winthrop Sargent, The Photoplaywright, *Moving Picture World*, February 24, 1917, p. 1170.

94. Epes Winthrop Sargent, The Photoplaywright, *Moving Picture World*, December 7, 1912, p. 974.

95. *Ibid.*

96. Epes Winthrop Sargent, The Photoplaywright, *Moving Picture World*, February 24, 1917, p. 1170.

97. Epes Winthrop Sargent, The Photoplaywright, *Moving Picture World*, February 24, 1917, p. 1170.

98. Not all critics shared Sargent's enthusiasm for the Drew films. Gilbert Seldes wrote: "In them there was nothing offensive, except an enervating dullness. . . . These things were little stories, not even smoking-room stories; they were acted entirely in the technique of the amateur stage; they were incredibly genteel. . . . Neither in matter nor in manner did they employ what the camera and the projector had to give and apart from the agreeable manners of Mr. and Mrs. Sidney Drew, nothing made them successful except the corrupt desire, on the part of the spectators, to be refined." Gilbert Seldes, *The Seven Lively Arts* (New York: Barnes, 1924), p. 29.

99. Epes Winthrop Sargent, The Photoplaywright, *Moving Picture World*, July 24, 1915, p. 624.

100. Kramer, "Vitagraph."

101. "Sidney Drew, Loved Comedian, Dead," *Moving Picture World*, April 19, 1919, p. 339. See also Ads, Mack Sennett Files, Herbert Blum Collection, Wisconsin Center for Film and Theater Research.

102. Sidney Drew, "How They Put It Over," *Photoplay*, undated clipping, Sidney Drew File, Herbert Blum Collection, Wisconsin Center for Film and Theater Research; Frederick James Smith, "Seeking the Germ: An Interview with the Sidney Drews," *Photoplay*, September 1917, pp. 27–30.

103. "Sidney Drew, Loved Comedian, Dead," p. 339.

104. Epes Winthrop Sargent, "Sidney Drew on True Comedy," *Moving Picture World*, August 19, 1916, p. 1226.

105. Frederick James Smith, "Seeking the Germ: An Interview with the Sidney Drews," *Photoplay*, September 1917, p. 27.

106. Ibid.

107. Sargent, "Sidney Drew on True Comedy," p. 1226.

108. Sidney Drew, "Comedy Picture Production," *Moving Picture World*, July 21, 1917, p. 412.

109. Ibid.

110. Drew, "How They Put It Over."

111. Ibid.

112. Sargent, "Sidney Drew on True Comedy," p. 1226.

113. Drew, "How They Put It Over."

114. "Al Christie, the Comedy King," *Moving Picture World,* July 12, 1924, p. 15; "The Need of Clean, Clever Comedies," *Moving Picture World,* September 20, 1924, p. 209; William J. Reilly, "I'll Take My Comedy Straight," *Moving Picture World,* June 28, 1919, p. 1964.

115. Kramer, "Vitagraph," p. x.

116. "Mack Sennett Says, 'Laugh Is Only Universal Idea,' " *Moving Picture World,* August 22, 1925, p. 845.

117. "Mack Sennett Perfects 1925–26 Plans," *Moving Picture World,* April 18, 1925, p. 682.

118. "Two New Production Units Are Added to Fox Comedy Staff Under Marshall," *Moving Picture World,* November 28, 1925, p. 351.

119. Al Christie, "This Is Going to Be the Biggest Comedy Year in History of the Screen," *Moving Picture World,* November 3, 1923, p. 164.

120. Sumner Smith, "Harold Lloyd, a Real Showman, Discusses Comical Comedy," *Moving Picture World,* November 11, 1912, p. 36.

3. "A Regular Mine, a Reservoir, a Proving Ground": Reconstructing the Vaudeville Aesthetic

1. George M. Cohan, "Vaudeville as an American Institution," *Variety,* January 8, 1930, p. 10.

2. "Vaudeville's Standard Acts Taken for Legitimate Stage," *Variety,* November 6, 1917, p. 1.

3. Ibid.

4. For the best examples of attempts to draw connections between theatrical performance style and screen acting, see Janet Staiger, "The Eyes Are Really the Focus: Photoplay Acting and Film Form and Style," *Wide Angle* 6(4):14–23 (Spring 1985); Roberta Pearson, "Cultivated Folks and the Better Classes: Class Conflict and Representation in Early American Film," *Journal of Popular Film and Television* 15(3):120–128 (Fall 1987).

5. A solid historical treatment of the evolution of American vaudeville as an economic *and* aesthetic institution does not yet exist. Useful sources, however, would include Robert Allen, *Vaudeville and Film, 1895–1915: A Study of Media Interaction* (New York: Arno, 1980); John E. DiMeglio, *Vaudeville USA* (Bowling Green, Ohio: Bowling Green University Popular Press, 1973); Douglas Gilbert, *American Vaudeville: Its Life and Times* (New York: Whittlesey, 1940); Joe Laurie, *Vaudeville: From the Honkey-Tonks to the Palace* (New York: Henry Holt, 1953); Albert McClean, *American Vaudeville as Ritual* (Louisville: University of Kentucky Press, 1965); Anthony Slide, *The Vaudevillians* (Westport, Conn.: Arlington House, 1981); Shirley Staples, *Male and Female Comedy Teams in American Vaudeville* (Ann Arbor: UMI Press, 1984); Charles W. Stein, ed., *American Vaudeville as Seen by Its Contemporaries* (New York: Knopf, 1984).

6. Vadim Uraneff, "Commedia Dell'Arte and American Vaudeville," *Theatre Arts,* October 1923, p. 326.

7. Acton Davis, "What I Don't Know About Vaudeville," *Variety,* December 16, 1905, p. 2.

8. Flippo Tommaso Marinetti, "The Variety Theatre," in Michael Kirby, *Futurist Performance* (New York: Dutton, 1971), pp. 179–186. Kirby, pp. 19–27, notes that Marinetti was concerned with the spirit and content of the variety and not actual details of its style or form. He summarizes the Futurist's major interests within the form: "an emphasis on concrete or alogical presentation, on the use and combination of all modes and technical means of performance, and on the physical involvement of the spectators and the destruction of the 'fourth wall' convention" (p. 20). For a contemporary response to Marinetti's manifesto from a vaudevillian's perspective, see George Jean Nathan, "Marinetti: Theatricalized Theater" in Thomas Quinn Curtis, ed., *The Magic Mirror: Selected Writings on the Theater* (New York: Knopf, 1960), pp. 204–209.

9. Marinetti, "The Variety Theatre," p. 180.

10. Sergei Eisenstein, "Montage of Attractions," *Drama Review* (March 1974), pp. 77–85.

11. For examples of the FEX Group's writings on variety and other forms of American popular culture, see Ian Christie and John Gilbert, *Futurism, Formalism, FEKS* (London: British Film Institute, 1978).

12. For efforts to appropriate variety within surrealism, see Paul Hammond, ed., *The Shadow and Its Shadow: Surrealist Writings on Cinema* (London: British Film Institute, 1978). For American celebrations of the energy and vitality of vaudeville, see Gilbert Seldes, *The Seven Lively Arts* (New York: Barnes, 1924).

13. E. F. Albee, "E. F. Albee on Vaudeville," *Variety,* September 6, 1923, p. 1.

14. Frederick Edward Snyder, "American Vaudeville—Theater in a Package: The Origins of Mass Entertainment," (Ph.D. diss., Yale University, 1970).

15. Ibid., p. 42.

16. Discussions of programing strategies for vaudeville can be found in Hartley Davis, "The Business Side of Vaudeville," *Everybody's Magazine,* October 1907, pp. 527–537; George A. Gottlieb, "Psychology of the American Vaudeville Show from the Manager's Point of View," *Current Literature* (April 1916), pp. 257–258; Marian Spitzer, "The Business of Vaudeville," *Saturday Evening Post,* May 24, 1924, pp. 125ff.; Edward Renton, *The Vaudeville Theatre: Building, Operation, Management* (New York: Gotham Press, 1918), pp. 118–129.

17. William Gould, "Vaude vs. Musical Comedy," *Variety,* December 14, 1907, p. 19.

18. James J. Morton, "The Monologist and the Actor," *Variety,* December 15, 1906, p. 13.

19. For a detailed consideration of the professional lifestyle of the vaudeville performer, see John E. DiMeglio, *Vaudeville USA.* See also Norman Hapgood, "The Life of a Vaudeville Artiste," *Cosmopolitan,* February 1901, pp. 393–399;

Bennett Musson, "A Week of 'One Night Stands,' " *American Magazine*, June 1910, pp. 203–213; Hartley Davis, "In Vaudeville," *Everybody's Magazine*, August 1905, pp. 231–240; Marian Spitzer, "The People of Vaudeville," *Saturday Evening Post*, July 12, 1924, pp. 15ff.

20. Will Rogers, "How to Be Funny," *American Magazine*, September 1929, pp. 61ff.

21. J. C. Nugent, "Vode Versus Legit," *Variety*, June 24, 1925, p. 8.

22. Helen Krich Chinoy, "The Emergence of the Director," in Toby Cole and Helen Krich Chinoy, eds., *Directors on Directors: A Sourcebook of the Modern Theater* (Indianapolis: Bobbs-Merrill, 1963), pp. 14–15.

23. David Belasco, *The Theatre Through Its Stage Door* (New York: Harper, 1919), p. 65.

24. Richard Mansfield, "Concerning Acting" in Toby Cole and Helen Krich Chinoy, eds., *Actors on Acting* (New York: Crown, 1949), p. 490.

25. On shifts in performance style, see Alan S. Downer, "Players and the Painted Stage: Nineteenth-Century Acting," *PMLA* 61(2):522–576 (June 1946); Garff B. Wilson, *A History of American Acting* (Bloomington: Indiana University Press, 1966); James Cleaver, *Theatre Through the Ages* (New York: Hart, 1967); Alan S. Downer, "Nature to Advantage Dressed: Eighteenth-Century Acting," *PMLA* 58(4):1002–1037 (December 1943).

26. John Dolman, *The Art of Play Production* (New York: Harper and Brothers, 1919), pp. 55–59. Dolman characterized curtain calls as "stepping out of the picture" to acknowledge the audience and felt that instead they should be taken in character to ensure consistency of performance.

27. Chinoy, "The Emergence of the Director," pp. 14–15.

28. Uraneff, "Commedia Del'Arte and American Vaudeville," p. 326.

29. Davis, "In Vaudeville," pp. 231–240.

30. "New Material Necessary Says Chicago Reviewer," *Variety*, October 5, 1917, p. 5. Edward Reed, "Vaudeville Again," *Theatre Arts*, October 1933, p. 803, has a similar view of the vaudeville performer: "He was an artist whose material always had a certain universal quality and who was trained to have this material so entirely under his control technically that he was able to mold it to suit the sophistication or simplicity of the audience he faced."

31. Caroline Caffin, *Vaudeville* (New York: Mitchell Kimberley, 1914) offers a similar argument about musical performances in vaudeville. Caffin's essay, like some of the other primary materials cited in this chapter, is reprinted in Stein, ed., *American Vaudeville as Seen by Its Contemporaries.*

32. "Just one single person in the center of the stage, just forming one single subject in a picture surrounded by a frame of steel and brick and gilded and lighted. Be comical, be entertaining, please your audience, be original, and make them laugh—or in a short while you will find another picture in the frame" (Morton, "The Monologist and the Actor," p. 13). For a similar treatment of the role of the vaudeville performer, see Cliff Gordon, "The Monologue Man," *Variety*, December 14, 1907, p. 17. Martin Beck protested the use of the single spot

focused on the performer as detrimental to the sense of community and the call for a responsive audience. See Martin Beck's Opinions, *Variety*, July 22, 1921, p. 11.

33. Larry Wilde, *The Great Comedians Talk About Comedy* (New York: Citadel Press, 1968), p.141.

34. George Jean Nathan, *The Popular Theatre* (New York: Knopf, 1923), p. 197.

35. "New Acts: The Siamese Twins," *Variety*, February 25, 1925, p. 8.

36. Mary B. Mullett, "We All Like the Medicine 'Doctor' Eddie Cantor Gives," *American Magazine*, July 1924, pp. 34ff.

37. Brett Page, *Writing for Vaudeville* (Springfield: Home Correspondence School, 1913), p. 74.

38. My discussion of ethnic characterizations in vaudeville draws heavily upon Paul A. Distler, "The Rise and Fall of the Racial Comics in American Vaudeville," (Ph.D. diss., Tulane University, 1963). His discussion of the Irish stereotype can be found on pp. 68–73.

39. Page, *Writing for Vaudeville*, p. 118.

40. Ibid.

41. For a discussion of Eddie Cantor's stage persona, see Eddie Cantor and David Freedman, *My Life Is in Your Hands* (New York: Blue Ribbon, 1932). Cantor's stage and screen career will be discussed more fully in chapter 6.

42. For a discussion of Fanny Brice's stage persona, see Stanley Green, *The Great Clowns of Broadway* (New York: Oxford University Press, 1984), pp. 3–19, and Linda Martin and Kerry Segrave, *Women in Comedy* (Secaucus, N.J.: Citadel, 1986), pp. 108–115.

43. "Scarcity of Good Comics Now Blighting Small Time," *Variety*, December 6, 1923, p. 6.

44. J. C. Nugent, "The Trouper," *Variety*, February 10, 1926, p. 8.

45. George Jean Nathan and George M. Cohan, "The Mechanics of Emotion," *McClure*, November 1913, p. 70.

46. Robert Lytell, "Vaudeville Old and Young," *New Republic*, July 1, 1925, p. 156.

47. Walter De Leon, "The Wow Finish," *Saturday Evening Post*, February 14, 1925, pp. 16ff.

48. Fanny Brice, "The Feel of the Audience," *Saturday Evening Post*, November 21, 1925, pp. 10ff.

49. Nora Bayes, "Holding My Audience," *Theatre Magazine*, September 1917, p. 128.

50. Alexander Bakshy, "Vaudeville's Prestige," *Nation*, September 4, 1929, p. 258.

51. Richard Sennett, *The Fall of Public Man: On the Social Psychology of Capitalism* (New York: Vintage, 1974), pp. 74–75.

52. Leigh Hunt, *Critical Essays on Performers of the London Theatres* (1887) as quoted in Downer, "Players and the Painted Stage," p. 570.

53. J. C. Nugent, "What Causes Laughter," *Variety*, May 29, 1909, p. 14.

54. Spitzer, "The People of Vaudeville."

55. Mae West, *Goodness Had Nothing to Do with It* (Englewood Cliffs, N.J.: Prentice-Hall, 1959), pp. 49–51.

56. Mary B. Mullett, "Leon Errol Tells What It Is to Be a Comic Actor," *American Magazine*, January 1922, pp. 18–19. For other discussions of "reading" an audience, see Bennet Musson, "A Week of One Night Stands," *American Magazine*, June 1910, pp. 203–213; Mary B. Mullett, "Frank Tinney's Job Is to Make People Laugh," *American Magazine*, February 1921, pp. 34–35; Joe Cook, "What Makes 'Em Laugh," *American Magazine*, February 1931, pp. 38–39ff; Hugh Leamy, "A Kick and a Laugh," *Collier's*, August 20, 1927, pp. 13ff.

57. Staples, *Male and Female Comedy Teams*, p. 160.

58. Brice, "The Feel of the Audience."

59. "New Acts: The Intruders," *Variety*, July 21, 1922, p. 19. By 1923, the use of confederates or plants had become so common that local theater owners protested its overuse. "Audience-Acts with Plants Undesirable for Small Time," *Variety*, September 6, 1923, p. 4.

60. Snyder, "Theater in a Package," pp. 47–90; Gilbert, *American Vaudeville*, pp. 251–268; Laurie, pp. 170–200; Albert McClean, Jr., "U.S. Vaudeville and the Urban Comics," *Theatre Quarterly* (October-December 1971), pp. 50–57.

61. Joe Franklin, *Encyclopedia of Comedians* (Secaucus, N.J.: Citadel, 1979), p. 258; Otis Ferguson, "Vaudeville Marches On," *New Republic*, January 18, 1939, p. 315; "Wisecrack from Backstage to Theatre's Front Lobby," *Variety*, February 25, 1925, p. 7.

62. Page, *Writing for Vaudeville*, pp. 37–38.

63. Constance Mayfield Rourke, "Vaudeville," *New Republic*, August 27, 1919, pp. 115–116. See Brooks McNamara, "The Scenography of Popular Entertainment," *Drama Review*, (March 1974), pp. 16–24.

64. Marsden Hartley, "Vaudeville," *Dial*, March 1920, pp. 335–342.

65. Wilfred Clarke, "The Vaudeville Novelty," *Variety*, December 12, 1908, p. 43.

66. Ibid.

67. Hartley Davis, "In Vaudeville," pp. 231–240.

68. Page, *Writing for Vaudeville*, p. 142.

69. See De Leon for a detailed discussion of the wow finish.

70. Page, *Writing for Vaudeville*, pp. 83–90.

71. Page, *Writing for Vaudeville*, p. 86.

72. Carlton Andrews, *The Technique of Play Writing* (Springfield: Home Correspondence School, 1915), pp. 60–61.

73. Milton MacKaye, "The Whiskers on the Wisecrack," *Saturday Evening Post*, August 17, 1935, pp. 12–13ff.

74. W. T. Price, *The Technique of the Drama* (New York: Brentano's, 1897), pp. 56–64.

75. Elizabeth Woodridge, *The Drama: Its Laws and Its Techniques* (Boston: Allyn and Bacon, 1898), p. 115.

76. Page, *Writing for Vaudeville*, p. 88.

77. All of these examples can be found in Jimmy Lyons, "Nothing in Particular," a sample monologue in Jimmy Lyons, *Encyclopedia of Stage Material* (New York: Self-published, 1925), pp. 81–83.

78. Robert Grau, *Forty Years Observation of Music and the Drama* (New York: Broadway Publishing, 1909), p. 1.

79. Hugh Leamy, "An Interview with Edward F. Albee," *Collier's*, May 1, 1926, pp. 10ff.

80. Percy G. Williams, "The Headliner and the Box Office," *Variety*, December 12, 1908, p. 20.

81. Acton Davis, "What I Don't Know About Vaudeville," p. 2.

82. J. C. Nugent, Legit vs. Vaude, *Variety*, July 8, 1925, p. 4; see also J. C. Nugent, "The Sketch," *Variety*, July 10, 1909, p. 11; J. C. Nugent, "Sketches," *Variety*, October 14, 1925, p. 4; W. C. Lengel, "Advice to Vaudeville Playwrights," *Green Book*, April 1913, pp. 726–731; E. F. Reilly, "Writing Drama for Vaudeville," *Editor* (May 1913), pp. 279–283. For an alternative view of the place of playlets on the vaudeville bill, See McClean, *American Vaudeville*, pp. 165–192.

83. Page, *Writing for Vaudeville*, p. 155.

84. Ibid., p. 164.

85. J. C. Nugent, Legit vs. Vaude, p. 4.

86. Ethel Barrymore, *Memories: An Autobiography* (New York: Harper, 1955), as excerpted in Stein, *American Vaudeville as Seen by Its Contemporaries*, pp. 98–99.

87. Davis, *"What I Don't Know About Vaudeville,"* p. 2. See also J. C. Nugent, "Artists and Performers," *Variety*, July 29, 1925, p. 4.

88. Figures based on reviews of new acts published in *Variety* in the years 1907, 1912, 1917, 1922, and 1927. Classifications are based on the way the acts were listed in the reviews.

89. For background on the prehistory of the Broadway revue, see Gerald Bordman, *American Musical Revue: From the Passing Show to Sugar Babies* (New York: Oxford University Press, 1985); Robert Baral, *Revue: A Nostalgic Reprise of the Great Broadway Period* (New York: Fleet Publishing, 1962); Raymond Mander and Joe Mitcherson, *Revue: A Story in Pictures* (New York: Taplinger, 1971); Cecil Smith, *Musical Comedy in America* (New York: Theatre Arts Books, 1950); Julian Mates, *America's Musical Stage: Two Hundred Years of Musical Theatre* (Westport, Conn.: Greenwood Press, 1985); Gerald Bordman, *American Musical Theatre: A Chronicle* (New York: Oxford University Press, 1978).

90. Bordman, *American Musical Revue*, p. 20.

91. On Ziegfeld, see, in addition to general histories of the revue cited above, Ethan Mordden, *Broadway Babies: The People Who Made the American Musical* (New York: Oxford University Press, 1983), pp. 34–48; Charles Higham, *Ziegfeld* (Chicago: Henry Regnery, 1972); Marjorie Farnsworth, *The Ziegfeld Follies* (New York: Bonanza Books, 1956); Lewis A. Erenberg, *Steppin' Out: New York Nightlife and the Transformation of American Culture, 1890–1930* (Chicago: University of

Chicago Press, 1981), pp. 214–227; Bernard Sobel, *Broadway Heartbeat: Memoirs of a Press Agent* (New York: Hermitage House, 1953); Allen Churchill, *The Great White Way* (New York: Dutton, 1962).

92. Ethan Mordden, *Broadway Babies,* p. 35.

93. For a useful overview of the place of the stage revue within the evolution of American comedy, see Green, *The Great Clowns of Broadway.*

94. These Broadway revues played a pivotal role not only in fostering the talents of countless performers but also in training and refining the talents of writers and directors, such as Bert Kalmar and Harry Ruby, Alexander Leftwich, Morrie Ryskind, Busby Berkeley, William K. Wells, Howard Dietz, George S. Oppenheimer, and Jo Swerling, who would play a key role in the development of early sound comedy.

95. This section draws heavily on information contained in Samuel L. Leiter, ed., *The Encyclopedia of the New York Stage, 1920–1930* (Westport, Conn.: Greenwood Press, 1985).

96. Seldes, *The Seven Lively Arts,* p. 134.

97. Florenz Ziegfeld as quoted in Richard Kislan, *The Musical: A Look at the American Musical Theater* (Englewood Cliffs, N.J.: Prentice-Hall, 1980), p. 82.

98. Seldes, *The Seven Lively Arts,* p. 135.

99. Nathan, *"Marinetti: Theatricalized Theater,"* p. 88.

100. Ibid., p. 87.

101. John Corbin, "Gaieties of 1919 Big and Gorgeous," *New York Times,* July 8, 1919, p. 9, sec. 1.

102. Seldes, *The Seven Lively Arts,* p. 166.

103. Alexander Woollcott, "The Play," *New York Times,* November 27, 1921, p. 1, sec. 6. Stark Young would write of his subsequent vehicle that "there are not more than half a dozen lines in *The Grab Bag* that are not spoken by Mr. Wynn and certainly there are not two scenes in which he does not enter and entering, dominate." Stark Young, "Ed Wynn Almost All the Grab Bag," *New York Times,* October 7, 1924, p. 26.

104. Stark Young, The Play, *New York Times,* September 7, 1924, p. 1, sec. 7.

105. For a fuller discussion of Hollywood's recruitment of New York entertainers, see chapter 6.

106. "Talking Shorts Take Cook Show's People," *Variety,* July 25, 1928, p. 40.

107. "Over 206 Talent People Under Optional Contracts to Fox: Majority from Broadway," *Variety,* June 5, 1929, p. 7; see also "Film Acting Ranks Turned Over," *Variety,* January 2, 1929, p. 26; "Fox Importing All-Eastern Stage Talent For Movietone Coast-Made Productions," *Variety,* May 30, 1928, p. 11; "Legit Stock for Screen," *Variety,* July 4, 1928, p. 5; "Inside on Film Acting," *Variety,* August 28, 1929, p. 1; "Most New Talent on the Screen Came From Legit Stage Within Past Two Seasons—Names of Many," *Variety,* October 1, 1930, p. 2; "N.Y. New Talent Source," *Variety,* October 15, 1930, p. 3.

108. Edgar Selwyn, "Speaking of Talking Pictures," *Theatre Magazine,* January 1930, p. 30.

4. "Assorted Lunacy . . . with No Beginning and No End": Gag, Performance, and Narrative in Early Sound Comedy

1. See, for example, Robert C. Allen, *Vaudeville and Film, 1895–1915: A Study of Media Interaction* (New York: Arno, 1980), and David Bordwell, Janet Staiger, and Kristin Thompson, *The Classical Hollywood Cinema: Film Style and Mode of Production to 1960* (New York: Columbia University Press, 1985), pp. 159–161.

2. Tom Gunning, "The Cinema of Attractions: Early Film, Its Spectator and the Avant-Garde," in Thomas Elsaesser with Adam Barker, eds., *Early Cinema: Space, Frame, Narrative* (London: BFI, 1990), p. 59.

3. Bordwell, Staiger, and Thompson, *Hollywood Cinema*, p. 161.

4. For a similar argument, see Peter Kramer, "Vitagraph, Slapstick, and Early Cinema," *Screen* 29(2):99–104 (Spring 1988).

5. For a useful discussion of this shift, see Steve Neale and Frank Krutnik, *Popular Film and Television Comedy* (London: Routledge, 1990), pp. 96–131.

6. David Bordwell and Kristin Thompson, *Film Art: An Introduction* (New York: Knopf, 1986), pp. 142–146.

7. Bordwell, Staiger, and Thompson, *Hollywood Cinema*, pp. 19–20.

8. Edward Churchill, *"Going Wild,"* *Motion Picture Herald*, January 31, 1931, p. 54.

9. Kristin Thompson, "The Concept of Cinematic Excess," *Cine-Tracts* 1(2):55–56 (Summer 1977).

10. Ibid., p. 57.

11. Ibid., pp. 62–63.

12. See Kristin Thompson, *Eisenstein's Ivan the Terrible: A Neoformalist Analysis* (Princeton: Princeton University Press, 1981) and Kristin Thompson, *Breaking the Glass Armor: Neoformalist Film Analysis* (Princeton: Princeton University Press, 1987), especially pp. 259–262.

13. Donald Crafton, "The Pie and the Chase: Gag, Spectacle, and Narrative in Slapstick Comedy," in Eileen Bowser, ed., *The Slapstick Symposium* (Brussels: Federation Internationale des Archives du Film, 1988), p. 58.

14. Ibid., p. 54.

15. Samuel Goldwyn Testimony, Clara Dellar v. Samuel Goldwyn Inc. et al., Transcript, George O'Brian papers, United Artists Collection, Wisconsin State Historical Society, Box 202.

16. Peter Kramer, "Derailing the Honeymoon Express: Comicality and Narrative Closure in Buster Keaton's *The Blacksmith*," *Velvet Light Trap* (Spring 1989), pp. 101–116, emphasizes the degree to which gags are "meaningful in terms of narrative issues, with a great deal of their humor deriving precisely from this meaning."

17. Neale and Krutnik, *Popular Film and Television Comedy*, p. 44.

18. Ibid., p. 57.

19. Ibid., p. 47.

20. Sylvain du Pasquier, "Buster Keaton's Gags," *Journal of Modern Literature* (April 1974), p. 276.

21. Mary Douglas, "The Social Control of Cognition: Some Factors in Joke Perception," *Man* [new series] 3(3):365 (1968).

22. Roland Barthes, "An Introduction to the Structural Analysis of Narrative," *New Literary History* (Winter 1975), p. 244.

23. Ibid., p. 248.

24. Ibid., pp. 248–250.

25. Ibid., p. 250.

26. For a useful discussion of the role of conventional narrative in the Marx Brothers films, see William Donnelly, "A Theory of the Comedy of the Marx Brothers," *Velvet Light Trap* (Winter 1971–1972), pp. 8–15.

27. What the Picture Did for Me, *Motion Picture Herald*, September 15, 1934, p. 52.

28. What the Picture Did for Me, *Motion Picture Herald*, August 18, 1934, p. 54.

29. What the Picture Did for Me, *Motion Picture Herald*, September 15, 1934, p. 52.

30. What the Picture Did for Me, *Motion Picture Herald*, October 27, 1934, p. 70.

31. What the Picture Did for Me, *Motion Picture Herald*, October 6, 1934, p. 51.

32. What the Picture Did for Me, *Motion Picture Herald*, August 11, 1934, p. 51.

33. Stanley Green, *The Great Clowns of Broadway* (New York: Oxford University Press, 1984), p. 50.

34. Unidentified fan magazine clippings, Jimmy Durante File, Herbert Blum Collection, Wisconsin Center for Film and Theater Research.

35. A. E. Hancock, Columbia Theater, Columbia City, Indiana, What the Picture Did for Me, *Motion Picture Herald*, September 15, 1934, p. 52.

36. *Hollywood Party* plays here with gossip surrounding Lupe Velez's passionate but short-lived romance with *Tarzan* star Johnny Weismuller, a staple of the movie fan magazines. Subsequently, Velez took great delight in poking fun at her former lover. A remarkable publicity photograph of the period showed Velez sitting on a lawn chair, a copy of the funny pages open to *Jungle Jim* propped between her legs. The photograph ran with the cutline, "Carramba! Larrupin' Lupe's lost her Tarzan, now that her Johnee's wed to another. Miss Velez's [sic] views a comic strip with alarm. Where can she find another Tarzan? It is sad, si, si?" (Unidentified movie magazine clipping, Lupe Velez File, Herbert Blum Collection, Wisconsin Center for Film and Theater Research.) Another article of this same vintage promoted a possible romance between Durante and Velez: "You know why I love heem so moch, eh? Because he play more rough than Tarzan. An' Lupe like plenty excitement. No dull moment w'en thees Jee-mee is around, I tell you!" Barbara Barry, "Rougher Than Tarzan," *New Movie Magazine*, April 1934, p. 58.

37. Durante performed in a similar number, "Data," in his stage success, *The New Yorkers*, offering opinions on world scientific research and bragging that he had "breakfast with Einstein, chatted good naturedly about da fourth dimension."

38. The Baron's appearance in this role was yet another "inside joke": Jack Pearl had played a pants presser accidentally mistaken for an African explorer in *Meet the Baron*, a film that cast Durante as his friend and promoter. The baron would also have been familiar to 1930s moviegoers as a popular character on radio.

39. Randy Skretuedt, *Laurel and Hardy: The Magic Behind the Movies* (Beverly Hills: Moonstone, 1987), pp. 273–275.

40. A review of script files for more than twenty other films suggests that neither the types of problems encountered nor the strategies proposed for resolving them were unique to *Hollywood Party*. Rather, the circumstances surrounding the making of this film reflect general difficulties in trying to absorb the vaudeville aesthetic into the existing formal practices of the Hollywood studio system. Other films examined include *Caught Short* (MGM, 1930), *The Chief* (MGM, 1933), *Cockeyed Cavaliers* (RKO, 1934), *The Cuckoos* (RKO, 1930), *Diplomaniacs* (RKO, 1933), *Dixiana* (RKO, 1930), *Fifty Million Frenchmen* (Warner Brothers, 1930), *Gold Dust Gertie* (Warner Brothers, 1931), *Half Shot at Sunrise* (RKO, 1930), *Hips Hips Hooray* (RKO, 1934), *Hold Everything* (Warner Brothers, 1930), *Hook, Line and Sinker* (RKO, 1930), *Just Imagine* (Fox, 1930), *Local Boy Makes Good* (Warner Brothers, 1932), *Manhattan Parade* (Warner Brothers, 1931), *Mummy's Boys* (RKO, 1936), *Oh Sailor Behave* (Warner Brothers, 1930), *Passionate Plumber* (MGM, 1932), *Peach O'Reno* (RKO, 1931), *Politics* (MGM, 1931), *Prosperity* (MGM, 1932), *Rio Rita* (RKO, 1929), *She Couldn't Say No* (Warner Brothers, 1930), *Sit Tight* (Warner Brothers, 1930), *So Long Letty* (Warner Brothers, 1929), *Speak Easily* (MGM, 1932), and *What! No Beer* (MGM, 1933). RKO titles are held in the scripts collection of the Theater Arts Library, University of California-Los Angeles. All other studios are from the scripts collection of the Edward L. Doheny Memorial Library, University of Southern California. These holdings range from one final cutting continuity script to more extensive material on the writing and rewriting of the scenario and screenplay. The *Hollywood Party* files were the most complete I found and therefore I have chosen to focus on them in this chapter.

41. Wm. A. Grew, "The Perfectly Awful Terror," February 21, 1933, in *Hollywood Party* Box, MGM Scripts Collection, Edward L. Doheny Memorial Library, University of Southern California. All future references to this box will be cited as USC. Dwight Taylor, "Idea for *Hollywood Revue*," February 27, 1933, USC; Charlotte Wood, Memo to Harry Rapf, February 28, 1933, USC; Walter Wise, "Idea for *Hollywood Revue*," February 28, 1933, USC; C. M. Nelson, "The Test," February 28, 1933, USC; Robert Hopkins and Gus Kahn, Unidentified Scenario, March 4, 1933, USC.

42. Wood, Memo to Harry Rapf, USC.

43. David O. Selznick, Memo to Harry Rapf, February 27, 1933, USC.

44. Wise, "Idea for *Hollywood Revue*," USC.

45. Ibid.

46. Hopkins and Kahn, Unidentified Scenario, USC.

47. "It's a novelty, good, and a great idea as a once yearly production for one of the big lots. The public can walk in on this one at any time and not have to pick up the script." "*Hollywood Revue*," *Variety*, June 26, 1929, p. 12.

48. Conference Notes, April 11, 1933, USC. Leftwich, unlike the other participants, lacked any previous screen credits although his stagework included directing Joe Cook's *Rain or Shine* and George and Ira Gershwin's *Girl Crazy*.

49. Skretuedt, *Laurel and Hardy*, p. 274.

50. Conference Notes, April 12, 1933, USC.

51. Conference Notes, April 11, 1933, USC. The list of sketches approved by Rapf included parodies of *Bring 'Em Back Alive* (RKO, 1932) and *Dinner at Eight*, a trained bird act, Disney's animated "Hot Chocolate Soldiers" sequence, several song and dance numbers (including "Hollywood Party"), a swimming display by Johnny Weismuller, a murder mystery, a drama performed only by pairs of gloved hands, and an "acrobatic" turn by Healy and his Three Stooges.

52. Harry Rapf, "Misc. Sections of Notes, Skits, Outlines, and Suggestions," April 14, 1933–October 10, 1933, USC; Al Boasberg, "Misc. Sections of Notes, Skits, Outlines, and Suggestions," April 4, 1933–May 2, 1933, USC; Ritchie Craig, "Misc. Sections of Notes, Skits, Outlines, and Suggestions," April 15, 1933—August 14, 1933, USC; Ted Healy and Moe Howard, "Bits and Scenes," April 19, 1933, USC; Howard Dietz, "Misc. Sections of Notes, Skits, Outlines, and Suggestions," April 14, 1933–July 24, 1933, USC; Mitzi Cummings, "Sketch for Adrian," May 13, 1933, USC; Herbert Fields, Unidentified Scene, May 23, 1933, USC.

53. Unidentified Outline, May 13, 1933, USC.

54. Howard Dietz, Story Outline, May 15, 1933, USC.

55. Edmund Goulding, First Rough Continuity Outline, June 7, 1935 [*sic*], USC.

56. Author Unidentified, Script, June 15, 1933, USC. The timing of this script and its similarities to the earlier outline would suggest that it was probably written by Goulding. A June 29 session discussing the script was attended only by Rapf and Goulding, another reason for believing that Goulding was its author.

57. Conference Notes, June 29, 1933, USC.

58. Charles Reisner, Memo to Harry Rapf, July 15, 1933, USC.

59. Endre Bohem, Letter to Harry Rapf, July 3, 1933, USC.

60. Ibid.

61. Endre Bohem, Letter to Harry Rapf, July 5, 1933, USC.

62. Ibid.

63. Ibid.

64. Ibid.

65. A third assessment, undated and unsigned but apparently written around this same point in the production process, echoes many of Bohem's concerns. The writer expressed reservations about the potential confusion caused by casting some stars as fictional characters while others play themselves; he was also concerned by the inconsistent tone and development of the party: "I think it should be one thing or another" (i.e., either a narrative film or a succession of comic and musical performances). The party was insufficiently motivated; its narrative consequences were never fully developed; plot development was getting swamped by the musical

numbers. The writer concluded, "Nothing is accomplished from a story standpoint by having the party."

66. Conference Notes, July 6, 1933, USC.

67. Ibid.

68. Ibid.

69. Unidentified Writer, Revised Outline, July 10, 1933, USC; Howard Dietz, Revised Outline, July 12, 1933, USC. There are significant differences between the two outlines, so it is unclear whether the July 12 document revises the earlier one or whether one was written by Goulding while the second represented Dietz's simultaneous response to the same narrative problems. Both outlines clearly reflect the reservations that Rapf expressed at the July 6 conference, including a substantial streamlining of the number of included production numbers and the excision of the proposed hotel fire.

70. Howard Dietz, Revised Script, July 22, 1933, USC.

71. Arthur Caesar, Proposed Ending, August 11, 1933, USC.

72. Howard Dietz, Frances Goodrich, and Albert Hackett, Ending, August 14, 1933, USC.

73. Richy Craig, Jr., "Suggested Finish for *Hollywood Party*," August 14, 1935 [*sic*], USC.

74. Unidentified Author, Outline, August 23, 1933, USC.

75. Richard Boleslavsky, "Misc. Sections of Notes, Skits, Outlines, and Suggestions," August 29 1933–September 20, 1933, USC; Norman Krasna, Script Fragment, November 15, 1933, USC; Ned Marin, "Misc. Sections of Notes, Skits, Outlines, and Suggestions," September 19, 1933–September 28, 1933, USC; Stan Laurel and George Stevens, Script Fragment, September 10, 1933, USC; Ted Healy, Script Fragment, November 18, 1933, USC; C. Dorian, Script Fragment, November 20, 1933, USC; Seymour Felix, Letter to Harry Rapf, November 14, 1933, USC.

76. Henry Myers, Letter to Mr. Rapf, December 7, 1933, USC.

77. Ibid.

78. Henry Myers, Revised Scenario, December 12, 1933, USC.

79. Henry Myers, Letter to Mr. Rapf, December 7, 1933, USC.

80. Henry Myers, Letter to Mr. Rapf, December 14, 1933, USC.

81. Ibid.; see also Henry Myers, Letter to Mr. Rapf, December 12, 1933, USC.

82. Henry Myers, Letter to Mr. Rapf, December 18, 1933, USC. Myers's position was supported by Harvey Gates, "Notes and Suggestions," December 27, 1933, USC.

83. Howard Dietz and Arthur Kober, Final Dialogue Cutting Continuity Script, April 13, 1934, USC.

84. The Disney sequence was the only part of the film to be made in technicolor and so for technical reasons was stored separately. Nobody has ever restored it to the circulating prints of the film, but I was able to view this material at the Disney Archives. As Clemp is closing the deal for the lions, the female guests start screaming about a mouse. Durante reaches into a hole in the wall to extract Mickey

Mouse, dragging him out by his tail. Following a brief exchange during which Mickey impersonates Durante, the insulted host flings the rodent against the wall. An anthropomorphic piano magically appears. With some urging from the crowd, Mickey pulls up a bench and performs "Hot Chocolate Soldier," which is illustrated by an original Silly Symphony sequence. When the color cartoon is completed, the film reverts back to black and white and the plot resumes, more or less, where it had been abandoned.

85. Abel, *"Hollywood Party,"* Variety, May 29, 1934, p. 12.

86. "The piece should be a musical comedy of a particularly fantastic and grotesque type, with this keynote best exemplified in the maniac antics of Healy and His Stooges. The mood in a piece of this kind is much more important than the actual plot and we should not lose sight of the fact that the story points are being related here merely to make sure that each step is fairly well related to what follows." Henry Myers, Letter to Mr. Rapf, December 7, 1933, USC. "The style which seems most appropriate is the wildest possible kind of comedy (based on some fairly credible beginning) and for this purpose I should like, if I may, to use Ted Healy and His Stooges more frequently than they now appear, as the things they do are precisely in the mood which I have in mind." Henry Myers, Letter to Mr. Rapf, December 12, 1933, USC.

87. What the Picture Did for Me, *Motion Picture Herald,* September 8, 1934, p. 50.

5. *"A High-Class Job of Carpentry":*
Toward a Typography of Early Sound Comedy

1. Vadim Uraneff, "Commedia Dell'Arte and American Vaudeville," *Theatre Arts,* October 1923, p. 326.

2. See Richard deCordova, "Genre and Performance: An Overview," in Barry Keith Grant, ed., *Film Genre Reader* (Austin: University of Texas Press, 1986), pp. 129–142, for an important review of work on screen performance. Recent works to shift focus onto issues of film performance include Richard Dyer, *Stars* (London: BFI, 1979); Richard Dyer, *Heavenly Bodies: Film Stars and Society* (New York: St. Martin's, 1986); James Naremore, *Acting in the Cinema* (Berkeley: University of California Press, 1988); Steve Seidman, *Comedian Comedy: A Tradition in the Hollywood Film* (Ann Arbor: UMI Research, 1981); Frank Krutnik, "The Clown-Prints of Comedy," *Screen* (July-October 1984), pp. 50–59; Peter Donaldson, *Shakespearean Films/Shakespearan Directors* (Boston: Unwin Hyman, 1990). For a range of other useful accounts of screen performance, see Miriam Hanson, "Pleasure, Ambivalence, Identification: Valentino and Female Spectatorship," *Cinema Journal* (Summer 1986), pp. 6–32; Andrew Britton, *Katherine Hepburn: The Thirties and After* (Newcastle upon Tyne: Tyneside Cinema, 1985); Barry King, "Screen Acting: Reflections on the Day," *Screen* (May-August 1986), pp. 134–139; Barry King, "Stardom as Occupation," in Paul Kerr, ed., *The Hollywood Film Industry* (London: Routledge and Kegan Paul, 1986), pp. 154–184; Andrew Higgins, "Film Acting

and Independent Cinema," *Screen* (May-August 1986), pp. 110–132; Grahame F. Thompson, "Approaches to Performance," *Screen* (September-October 1983), pp. 78–90; Charles Afron, *Star Acting: Gish, Garbo, and Davis* (New York: Dutton, 1977); Christine Gledhill, *Stardom: Industry of Desire* (New York: Routledge, 1991).

3. David Bordwell and Kristin Thompson, *Film Art: An Introduction,* 3d ed. (New York: McGraw-Hill, 1990).

4. deCordova, "Genre and Performance," p. 130.

5. Patricia Mellencamp, "Spectacle and Spectator: Looking Through the American Musical Comedy," *Cine-Tracts* (Summer 1977), pp. 28–35. See also Jim Collins, "Towards Defining a Matrix of the Musical Comedy: The Place of the Spectator Within the Textual Mechanisms," in Rick Altman, ed., *Genre: The Musical* (London: Routledge and Kegan Paul, 1981), pp. 134–145; Jane Feuer, *The Hollywood Musical* (Bloomington: Indiana University Press, 1982); John Mueller, "Fred Astaire and the Integrated Musical," *Cinema Journal* 24(1):28–40 (Fall 1984); Rick Altman, *The American Film Musical* (Bloomington: Indiana University Press, 1987), see especially pp. 59–89.

6. Dyer, *Stars,* pp. 38–98.

7. Seidman, *Comedian Comedy,* pp. 15–57.

8. James Naremore, "Expressive Coherence and the Acted Image," *Studies in Literary Imagination* (Spring 1986), pp. 39–54.

9. Mueller, "Fred Astaire and the Integrated Musical."

10. See Altman, *The American Film Musical,* for a useful discussion of the process by which genre definitions are established. My methodology for developing these definitions closely resembled the practices he describes.

11. Altman, *The American Film Musical,* p. 372, lists *The Big Broadcast* as an exemplar of the show musical based on its syntactic and semantic components, though I would argue that its performance style fits more closely with the showcase film.

12. Gerald Weales, *Canned Goods as Caviar: American Film Comedy of the 1930s* (Chicago: University of Chicago Press, 1985), p. 92.

13. Charles Lee Hyde, Grand Theater, Pierre, South Dakota, wrote of *Duck Soup:* "Good entertainment but lots of disappointed people. . . . The usual music furnished by the harp and the piano was missed. Another example of how dumb smart people can be. Would any exhibitor have made a picture with the Marx Brothers in it and kept the harp and piano out?" What the Picture Did For Me, *Motion Picture Herald,* February 17, 1934, p. 65. Similar complaints were heard from other exhibitors.

14. Krutnik, "The Clown-Prints of Comedy," pp. 52–53.

15. A *Motion Picture Herald* ad for the film (May 9, 1931) foregrounds the brothers' performance sequences as a key selling point for the film: "Groucho has a brand new crop of rapid-fire nonsense. Mute Harpo wangs the harp and chases the blondes. Chico, the tough guy, prowls his omnivorous way. Zeppo provides the one sane spot in the lunatic Marxian universe. The buffooning brothers are invading an unsuspecting Hollywood for this opus."

16. Krutnik, "The Clown-Prints of Comedy," pp. 52–53; Seidman, *Comedian Comedy*, pp. 79–141.

17. Seidman, *Comedian Comedy*, p. 146.

18. Kevin Heffernan, "Product Differentiation: Paramount's Use of Radio Talent, 1932–1934," unpublished paper, presented at the Society of Cinema Studies Conference, Los Angeles, Summer 1991.

6. *"Shall We Make It for New York or for Distribution?" Eddie Cantor,* Whoopie, *and Regional Resistance to the Talkies*

1. Eddie Cantor, "Off to Hollywood," *New York Times*, March 23, 1930, p. 6, sec. 10.

2. Ad, *Variety*, November 14, 1928, p. 23.

3. Alexander Woollcott, "Cantor," *New York Times*, April 14, 1922, p. 20. sec. 3.

4. J. Brooks Atkinson, "Mr. Ziegfeld's Newest *Follies*," *New York Times*, August 7, 1927, p. 1, sec. 7.

5. "25 Outstanders of '28–'29," *Variety*, January 8, 1930, p. 110.

6. Benjamin Hampton, *History of the American Film Industry* (New York: Dover, 1970), pp. 401–402.

7. "*Whoopee* on Screen," *New York Times*, September 28, 1930, p. 6, sec. 10.

8. See, for example, Lewis Jacobs, *The Rise of the American Film* (New York: Teacher's College Press, 1939), p. 300; Arthur Knight, *The Liveliest Art* (New York: New American Library, 1957), p. 147; Garth Jowett, *Film: The Democratic Art* (Boston: Little, Brown, 1976), p. 196; David A. Cook, *A History of Narrative Film* (New York: Norton, 1981), p. 243. Even the revisionist J. Douglas Gomery, "The Coming of Sound to the American Cinema: A History of the Transformation of an Industry" (Ph.D. diss., University of Wisconsin-Madison, 1975), takes Hampton's claims about the motives behind the recruitment of Broadway stars at face value.

9. See "Silent Stars Who Lasted," *Variety*, January 30, 1934, p. 3, which finds that of the eighty-four stars on the studio rosters in 1928, twenty-one were still listed as stars and another five remained featured players. More dramatically, thirteen of the featured players in 1928 had been catapulted to stardom by the talkies and another nineteen survived as featured players. "Star Changes Up to Now," *Variety*, February 18, 1931, p. 3, notes that the Broadway recruits had some of the shortest careers in the history of the star system. See also "Talker Stars for a Day," *Variety*, July 21, 1931, p. 5.

10. Robert G. McLaughlin, "Broadway and Hollywood: A History of Economic Interaction" (Ph.D. diss., University of Wisconsin-Madison, 1970), provides a useful overview of the history of Hollywood's efforts to recruit stage stars, although he still tends to view the early sound period through Hampton's account.

11. "Hollywood's Contracted Talent," *Variety*, January 2, 1929, p. 24.

12. Alexander Walker, *The Shattered Silents* (London: Elm Tree, 1978).

13. Inside on Film Acting, *Variety*, August 28, 1929, p. 1.

14. "Audiences poured into movie theaters presenting girl-and-music talkies, neglecting or giving second consideration to the dramas and melodramas that recently had been their choicest film fare" (Hampton, *History of the American Film Industry*, p. 400). "The screen had now definitely moved toward a still higher level of entertainment, and, as had invariably happened in the past, audiences enthusiastically welcomed the improvement and expected the better films to become the rule, rather than the exception" (Ibid., p. 237).

15. Ibid., p. 94. For a similar view, see also "Talkers Changing Fans and Flaps?" *Variety*, June 18, 1930, p. 79; Sid Silverman, "29 and Talkers—1930 and Wide Film," *Variety*, January 8, 1930, p. 78.

16. Tino Balio, *United Artists: The Company Built by the Stars* (Madison: University of Wisconsin Press, 1975), p. 94.

17. As early as September 1928, *Variety* reported that "the novelty era seems on the wane as far as sound and dialogue films are concerned" ("They're 'Shopping,'" *Variety*, September 5, 1928, p. 5). Three months later, it found a return to pretalkies box office returns that it attributed to the decline of the novelty value of film sound. "Sound Grosses Normal," *Variety*, December 5, 1928, p. 9.

18. See, for example, "33 1/2 or 50%," *Variety*, December 19, 1928, p. 41; "As to the Talkers," *Variety*, June 6, 1928, p. 48. Lee Deforest recorded vaudeville acts, including Eddie Cantor, to demonstrate his Phonofilm process as early as 1925. "Canned 'Names' of Stage in Phonofilm's Road Shows," *Variety*, November 4, 1925, p. 1. Reaction to the initial Vitaphone program stresses this potential function of film sound. See, for example, "Vitaphone Bow Hailed as Marvel," *Variety*, August 11, 1926, p. 10; "Better Than Vaudeville Is Verdict on Vita's $40,000 Bill," *Variety*, October 13, 1926, p. 1; "Vitaphone Framing Canned Programs Along Lines of Vaudeville Bills," *Variety*, February 9, 1927, p. 21. The idea of talking features replacing theatrical road shows also was conceived early in the sound era. "Indications are that talking pictures may eventually usurp the place of the legit road show, which has become practically extinct." See "Vita's Play Talking Films as Road Show Substitutes?" *Variety*, March 28, 1928, p. 5; "23 Road Show $2 Talkers," *Variety*, July 3, 1929, p. 5; "Talkers Butcher Road," *Variety*, October 23, 1929, p. 65.

19. Dorothy Calhoun, "The Great Talkie Panic," *Motion Picture Classic*, September 1928, pp. 16–17.

20. McLaughlin, "Broadway and Hollywood"; Alfred L. Bernheim, *The Business of the Theatre* (New York: B. Blom, 1932); Jack Poggi, *Theatre In America: The Impact of Economic Forces, 1870–1967* (Ithaca: Cornell University Press, 1968). For contemporary reports, see, for example, "B'Way Legits Drop 50%," *Variety*, March 6, 1929, p. 1; "New Lows for B'Way Shows," *Variety*, July 17, 1929, p. 75; "Broadway Takes the Slap," *Variety*, November 6, 1929, p. 1.

21. McLaughlin, "Broadway and Hollywood," pp. 278–280.

22. See, for example, "The Rape of Vaudeville," *Variety*, February 17, 1926, p.

6; "How Vaudeville Lost Out," *Variety,* March 24, 1926, p. 18; "Vode Through, Mayer Claims," *Variety,* May 19, 1926, p. 3; "Pictures and Vaudeville," *Variety,* January 5, 1927, p. 22.

23. See, for example, Tom Walker, "The Year in Pictures," *Variety,* January 8, 1930, p. 87.

24. See, for example, "Talkers Too Costly for Small Houses, Southwest Convention Informed," *Variety,* September 19, 1928, p. 23; "Exhibitors Much Interested in Permanency of Talkers," *Variety,* June 8, 1927, p. 11; "More Wire for Sound? Exhibs Not Uniform," *Variety,* July 18, 1928, p. 11; "Small Town's Talker Reaction Found Through Local Showgoers," *Variety,* October 24, 1928, p. 4.

25. McLaughlin, "Broadway and Hollywood," pp. 282–284.

26. See, for example, "Film Biz Plans Backing of Musical Producers for Secure of Rights," *Variety,* March 27, 1929, p. 1; "Seeking Stage Control," *Variety,* September 24, 1930, p. 3; "Talkers vs. Legit on B'Way," *Variety,* July 18, 1928, p. 1.

27. "Warners May Produce 12 Stage Plays For B'Way Next Season with Lewis Warner, Producer," *Variety,* June 18, 1930, p. 73.

28. "1929 Now Looks Pretty Active in Talking Pictures Way in Eastern Film Studios," *Variety,* December 26, 1928, p. 4; "4 Sound Studios in Greater New York Operating Before November 1: Warners, Par., MGM, FBO," *Variety,* October 3, 1928, p. 11; "Studios East and West," *Variety,* August 28, 1929, p. 2; "Pro and Con for the East," *Variety,* September 10, 1930, p. 4.

29. "Par. Shelves *Kid Boots* on Zieggy's Kick," *Variety,* April 24, 1929, p. 6; "Using New Follies in Par's *Glorifying,*" *Variety,* June 20, 1928, p. 5; "Cantor in Sound Short If Ziegfeld Okays Plan," *Variety,* August 15, 1928, p. 45.

30. "Ziegfeld's Actor's Contract Prohibits Talking Pictures," *Variety,* May 30, 1928, p. 4; "Want Zieggy for Talkers," *Variety,* June 13, 1928, p. 5.

31. "No *American Girl* Film by E.P.: Cost Too High, Zieggy's $150,000," *Variety,* July 7, 1926, p. 1.

32. "*Am. Girl* With Dialog At Par's L. I. Studio," *Variety,* June 6, 1928, p. 7; "*Glorifying* Next Year," *Variety,* June 6, 1928, p. 7; "*Am. Girl* Starting, Has $750,000 Cast," *Variety,* January 25, 1928, p. 5; Inside Stuff—Pictures, *Variety,* April 11, 1928, p. 45; "Zieggy's New Premise, Meanwhile—$1,000 Wkly," *Variety,* March 13, 1929, p. 51; "*Glorified Girl* Picture Will Be Decided by Cost," *Variety,* December 21, 1927, p. 1.

33. "One in Four Musicals," *Variety,* May 1, 1929, p. 20.

34. Ads, *Variety,* September 25, 1929, pp. 18–19; *Variety,* November 6, 1929, pp. 14–15.

35. Ad, *Motion Picture Classic,* December 1929, p. 10.

36. Ads, *Motion Picture Classic,* January 1930, pp. 7, 10.

37. Cantor's shorts were not available for viewing. Discussion based upon *Variety* film reviews, "*Midnight Frolics,*" *Variety,* March 13, 1929, p. 14; "*That Certain Party,*" *Variety,* November 14, 1928, p. 17; "*Getting a Ticket,*" *Variety,* February 5, 1930, p. 19.

38. See, for example, "Three Cities Paid Production of *Fool*," *Variety*, February 20, 1929, p. 5; Inside Stuff—Pictures, *Variety*, March 27, 1929, p. 50; "Altered Picture Tastes," *Variety*, January 30, 1929, p. 5.

39. "Talker's Talk Overlapping," *Variety*, June 27, 1928, p. 51.

40. Ad, *Variety*, June 13, 1928, p. 29.

41. "About 1/3 Silent For 29–30," *Variety*, March 20, 1929, p. 7. See also "Fox Only Counting on Ten Silents Next Year," *Variety*, March 20, 1929, p. 7; "Doubt Silent Film Future," *Variety*, June 5, 1929, p. 7.

42. Paul Seale, "A Host of Others: Poverty Row and the Coming of Sound," Unpublished Seminar Paper, University of Wisconsin-Madison, Spring 1988.

43. "Talkers Changing Fans and Flaps?" p.79.

44. "How Talkers Stand With Paying Patrons; Mail Ballot in Syracuse," *Variety*, January 30, 1929, p. 5. See also "Sound or Silent Future?" *Variety*, June 19, 1929, p. 1; "Small Town Off Talkers," *Variety*, July 10, 1929, p. 5; "Sound Pro and Con—50–50?" *Variety*, January 9, 1929, p. 56.

45. "Sound Pro and Con—50–50?" p. 56.

46. See, for example, "The Class All-Talker," *Variety*, November 21, 1928, p. 3; "Main Street Tastes," *Variety*, February 4, 1931, p. 5; "Films Can't Figure Public," *Variety*, April 1, 1931, p. 3; "Musicals and Operettas," *Variety*, June 25, 1930, p. 102.

47. "Sound as Exhibitors Hear It at the Box Office," *Motion Picture Herald*, June 22, 1929, pp. 84–86.

48. "Public Accepts Increased Prices," *Motion Picture Herald*, August 24, 1929, pp. 27ff.

49. Ibid.

50. Jack Greene, Genesco Theater, Genesco, Illinois, "Fawncy Lingo," *Motion Picture Herald*, November 30, 1929, p. 60.

51. K. M. Wickware, Capital Theater, Utica, Michigan, "Whew!," *Motion Picture Herald*, September 6, 1930, p. 66.

52. "Kids Must Have Actions in Films; Don't Want Mush Stuff Now; Must Bring 'Em Back, the Order," *Variety*, June 18, 1930, p. 49.

53. "Westerns, Not Talkers, Wanted by Small Town Exhibs of Texas," *Variety*, September 11, 1929, p. 5; "Big Demand for Westerns in All Sections," *Variety*, October 16, 1929, p. 7.

54. "Leading Film Stars, 1929," *Variety*, January 8, 1930, p. 1.

55. "Ziegfeld and Film; Goldwyn and *Simon*," *Variety*, February 26, 1930, p. 61; "Goldwyn Declared in by Ziegzy on Shows," *Variety*, October 20, 1929, p. 71. The other proposed Ziegfeld-Goldwyn collaborations never materialized. Ziegfeld was soon searching for the backing to start his own independent production company and attempting to market the screen rights to *Simple Simon* to other studios, suggesting some breakdown on the Goldwyn deal. See "Broker Behind Ziegzy: Not Far Behind—Yet," *Variety*, April 2, 1930, p. 1; "Ziegfeld May Film Wynn Show with Cast Intact," *Variety*, June 4, 1930, p. 70; "*Simple Simon*, Where?" *Variety*, June 11, 1930, p. 3.

56. "Costly *Whoopee*," *Variety*, June 11, 1930, p. 31. See also *Whoopee* Press-book, Greenthal Papers, United Artist Collection, Wisconsin Center for Film and Theater Research, series 5.4, reel 14.

57. Ibid.

58. Robert Fonder, "His Pace is His Fortune," undated and unidentified fan magazine story, Greenthal Papers, reel 4, vol. 7.

59. Robert Crawford, "Want to Be Funny?" *Photoplay* (October 1930), Green-thal Papers, reel 4, vol. 7.

60. Ernest Rogers, "The Importance of the Sticks," *Variety*, November 6, 1929, p. 6. For similar views, see "Golden Days of High Salaries for Legits in Talkers are Due to Pass, Says Experts," *Variety*, April 17, 1929, p. 65; Sid Silverman, "U.S. Film Field for 1930," *Variety*, December 31, 1930, p. 7; "Let Your Hair Down," *Variety*, July 14, 1929, p. 62; "Screen Personalities Triumphing Over Stage Stars in Dialog Films," *Variety*, March 20, 1929, p. 6.

61. Based on reports from key cities published in *Variety* between October 8, 1930 and December 31, 1930. As always, *Variety* figures and assessments of box office returns are to be taken with a large grain of salt since reports from regional keys are erratic, and often the trade press does not distinguish between projected and actual ticket sales. Still, I am assuming that they somewhat reflect the general reception of the film in the reporting area. For local responses to the film, see Mordant Hall, "A Frolic with Mr. Cantor," *New York Times*, September 24, 1930, p. 21; "Eddie Cantor in *Whoopee* at Paramount," *Atlanta Constitution*, September 28, 1920, p. 7; "Cantor *Whoopee* Headlines Loew's Film Attractions," *New Orleans Time-Picayune*, September 28, 1930, p. 10–II.

62. Robert H. Brown, "Sticks vs. City on Pix," *Variety*, December 6, 1932, p. 5.

63. "Sectional Sure-Fire Yarns are Out; Favor Stories National in Scope," *Variety*, October 20, 1931, p. 2. See also "If Hoke is Tossed Out, Peasants Won't Go—and That's That," *Variety*, December 24, 1930, p. 2.

64. Philip Rand, "What the Public Wants," *Motion Picture Herald*, August 23, 1930, p. 64.

65. Charles E. Lewis, "Passing in Review," *Motion Picture Herald*, January 2, 1932, p. 27.

66. Comments on the marketing of *Whoopee* in specific regions are based on my review of advertising and reporting in eight local newspapers: the Cleveland *Plain Dealer*, the Providence *Journal*, the Birmingham *Age-Herald*, the Atlanta *Constitution*, the New Orleans *Time-Picayune*, the Indianapolis *News*, the Louisville *Courier-Journal*, and the Chicago *Herald Examiner*.

67. *Palmy Days* Pressbook, Greenthal Papers, series 5.4, reel 16.

68. "Eddie Cantor Discourses on Music Films," *New York Times*, October 25, 1931, p. 7, sec. 10. See also "Original Book for Musical Preferred," *Variety*, August 25, 1931, p. 5.

69. "*The Kid from Spain*," *Motion Picture Herald*, November 5, 1932, p. 42.

70. "Fox Drops 30 from Talent Lists," *Variety*, March 15, 1931, p. 2; "Musical People Are Dropped by Fox," *Variety*, May 27, 1931, p. 2; "Studios' Cuts and

Outs," *Variety*, May 27, 1931, p. 3; "32 Stars Dropped Since 1929 in Producer's Move to Clear Congestion—But 12 Replacements," *Variety*, March 26, 1930, p. 2. The impact of the Depression made some cutbacks in studio payrolls inevitable. The box office failure of the musical comedy stars determined where cuts would fall.

71. Herbert Cruikshank, "The Panic is Over," *Motion Picture Classic*, September 1930, p. 63.

72. "Cantor Signs for Five Years," *New York Times*, July 21, 1930, p. 20; "$100,000 and 10%," *Variety*, February 12, 1930, p. 57.

73. Eddie Cantor and David Freedman, *My Life Is in Your Hands* (New York: Blue Ribbon Books, 1932).

74. Irving Howe, *World of Our Fathers* (New York: Simon and Schuster, 1976), p. 565.

75. *Whoopee* Pressbook.

76. Charles Musser, "Ethnicity, Roleplaying, and the American Film Comedy: From *Chinese Laundry Scene* to *Whoopee* (1894–1930)," in Lester Friedman, ed., *Unspeakable Images: Ethnicity and the American Cinema* (Chicago: University of Illinois Press, 1991), pp. 60–72. Musser finds a similar play with ethnic identity in the Marx Brothers' comedy *Animal Crackers*, although these clowns, like Cantor, later abandoned Yiddish humor in search of a broader national audience. The Marx Brother's ethnic comedy, most explicit in a scene when Chico identifies the sophisticated Roscoe W. Chandler as "Abie the fish peddler," was more "angry" and confrontational than Cantor's Jewish humor, yet, as in Cantor's later films, it remained largely invisible to gentile viewers. Musser writes, "For non-Jews, *Animal Crackers* can be a zany, anarchistic comedy. . . . The Jewish-centered humor could remain invisible to the uninitiated and be attributed to eccentricity."

77. Mary Douglas, "The Social Control of Cognition: Some Factors in Joke Perception," *Man* [new series] 3(3):361–367 (1968).

78. For a useful discussion of vaudeville's movement from ethnic comics, see Paul A. Distler, "The Rise and Fall of the Racial Comics in American Vaudeville" (Ph.D. diss., Tulane University, 1963).

79. For background, see John Higham, *Strangers in the Land: Patterns of American Nativism, 1860–1925* (New York: Antheneum, 1971).

80. Howe, *World of Our Fathers*, p. 567.

81. "My Man," *Variety*, December 26, 1928, p. 11; "U.A. Gets Fanny Brice," *Variety*, February 20, 1929, p. 4; "Fanny Brice's Suit Started for $155,000," *Variety*, March 26, 1930, p. 8.

82. See, for example, Howard T. Brundidgo, "What Eddie Cantor Owes His Grandmother," *Movie Mirror*, undated clipping, Greenthal Papers, reel 4, vol. 7. Also profiles in the Cantor Pressbooks, Greenthal papers, series 5.4, reels 14, 16, and 18.

83. Based on initial and subsequent drafts, "A Short on Eddie Cantor," Greenthal Papers, reel 4, vol. 7, later employed in Cantor pressbooks.

84. *Palmy Days* Pressbook, Greenthal Papers, series 5.4, reel 18.

85. Samuel Shayon, Testimony, Clara Dellar v. Samuel Goldwyn Inc. et al.,

transcript, George O'Brian Papers, United Artist Collection, Wisconsin State Historical Society, Box 202. Raymond Durgnat, *The Crazy Mirror: Hollywood Comedy and the American Image* (New York: Delta, 1969), p. 166, sees Cantor as the heir to Harold Lloyd, characterizing his screen persona as the "Little American."

86. Jack S. Cohen, Jr., *"Palmy Days,"* Providence *Journal,* October 3, 1931, p. 5.

87. Sime, *"Palmy Days," Variety,* September 29, 1931, p. 14.

88. Hall, "A Frolic With Mr. Cantor," p. 21.

89. Based on reports from key cities published in *Variety,* September 29, 1931–January 5, 1932.

90. Based on *Variety* reports on box office returns from key cities for *Kid from Spain, Roman Scandals, Kid Millions, Strike Me Pink,* and *Ali Baba Goes to Town.*

91. See sample press releases, Greenthal Papers, reel 4, vol. 7.

92. Richard Dyer, *Stars* (London: BFI, 1970); see also Richard Dyer, *Heavenly Bodies: Film Stars and Society* (New York: St. Martin's, 1986); Robert Allen and Douglas Gomery, *Film History: Theory and Practice* (New York: Knopf, 1985), pp. 172–189.

93. Musser, "Ethnicity, Roleplaying," p. 70.

7. *"Fifi Was My Mother's Name!" Anarchistic Comedy, the Vaudeville Aesthetic, and* Diplomaniacs

1. Andrew Berman, *We're in the Money: Depression America and Its Films* (New York: Harper and Row), p. 63.

2. Robert Altman, Jon Carroll, and Michael Goodwin, "Groucho Marx, Portrait of an Artist as an Old Man," *Take One* (September-October 1970), p. 14.

3. Joe Adamson, *Groucho, Harpo, Chico, and Sometimes Zeppo: A Celebration of the Marx Brothers* (New York: Simon and Schuster, 1976), p. 210.

4. Showmen's Reviews, *Motion Picture Herald,* September 24, 1932, p. 30.

5. Showmen's Reviews, *Motion Picture Herald,* April 15, 1933, p. 28.

6. BIGE, *"Diplomaniacs," Variety,* May 4, 1933, p. 12.

7. Ibid.

8. This production number recalls similar moments in other comedies, most especially "All God's Chillin Got Guns" in *Duck Soup,* and the rollicking political rally in *Phantom President.* Gerald Weales, *Canned Goods as Caviar: American Film Comedy of the 1930s* (Chicago: University of Chicago Press, 1985), goes so far as to suggest that the peace conference scene may have inspired the better known sequence in *Duck Soup.* Weales, however, insists that *Duck Soup* "transforms any possible borrowings into something completely new" and superior to the "static" treatment of the material in *Diplomaniacs* (p. 66). It seems more likely that both films build upon the prevalent trope of politics as performance, an image that fits well within the films' settings. The scenes serve rather different functions in the three films. In *Diplomaniacs,* the number climaxes a more extended sequence of comic performance and does not stand on its own merits. In *Duck Soup,* the

sequence builds from the more extensive and self-contained musical number into the film's comic climax. The political rally in *Phantom President* stands as a completely independent number and may be the liveliest and most entertaining of the three sequences. Their different placement within the three films means that the scenes receive different degrees of emphasis and are required to produce different levels of audience response.

9. Steve Seidman, *Comedian Comedy: A Tradition in Hollywood Film* (Ann Arbor: UMI Research Press, 1981), p. 80.

10. Frank Krutnik, "The Clown-Prints of Comedy," *Screen* (July-October 1984), pp. 56–57.

11. Weales, *Canned Goods*, p. 66.

12. Kristin Thompson, *Breaking the Glass Armor: Neoformalist Film Analysis* (Princeton: Princeton University Press, 1988), p. 73.

13. What the Picture Did for Me, *Motion Picture Herald*, July 15, 1933, p. 84.

14. What the Picture Did for Me, *Motion Picture Herald*, July 22, 1933, p. 71. An increased concern with narrative coherence resurfaces in exhibitor responses to many of the 1933 comedies. A Virginia theater owner expressed his concerns about *International House:* "Good show, but you will find plenty of kicks for half of them [the audience] cannot follow the picture. It changes too fast for the average patron, and when it is through they do not know what it was all about." Russell C. Dey, Reedville Movies, Reedville, Virginia, What the Picture Did for Me, *Motion Picture Herald*, December 2, 1933, p. 79. A North Carolina exhibitor reported a similar response to *Duck Soup:* "The entire picture was entirely too sloppy and our patrons were displeased. The independents can do better than this." J. J. Medford, Orpheum Theater, Oxford, North Carolina, What the Picture Did for Me, *Motion Picture Herald*, February 24, 1934, p. 52.

15. What the Press Says, *Motion Picture Herald*, October 3, 1931, p. 8.

16. *Diplomaniacs* File, MPPDA collection, Margaret Herrick Library, Academy of Motion Picture Arts and Sciences, Los Angeles.

17. H. A. Griswold, Sewanee Union Theater, Sewanee, Tennessee, What the Picture Did for Me, *Motion Picture Herald*, April 29, 1933, p. 37; Joe Hewitt, Lincoln Theater, Robinson, Illinois, What the Picture Did for Me, *Motion Picture Herald*, June 17, 1933, p. 45.

18. Edith M. Foroyce, Princess Theater, Selma, Louisiana, What the Picture Did for Me, *Motion Picture Herald*, May 20, 1933, p. 45.

19. Steve Farrar, Orpheum, Harrisburg, Illinois, What the Picture Did for Me, *Motion Picture Herald*, April 15, 1933, p. 45.

20. V. G. Hart, Report on *Diplomaniacs*, seen April 24, 1933, at Radio City, *Diplomaniacs* File, MPPDA, Margaret Herrick Library, Academy of Motion Picture Arts and Sciences, Los Angeles.

21. James Wingate, Letter to Meriam C. Cooper, April 20, 1933, *Diplomaniacs* File, MPPDA, Margaret Herrick Library, Academy of Motion Picture Arts and Sciences, Los Angeles. The Production Code Administration initially took a similar position on *So This is Africa:* "Needless to add, the more amusing the scenes, the less danger there will be of offense at certain situations. . . . It will all be a matter

of treatment, as is nearly always the case with comedies." Jason Joy, Letter to Harry Cohn, October 12, 1932, *So This is Africa* Files, MPPDA, Margaret Herrick Library, Academy of Motion Picture Arts and Sciences, Los Angeles.

22. Joe Hewitt, Lincoln Theater, Robinson, Illinois, What the Picture Did for Me, *Motion Picture Herald,* June 17, 1933, p. 45.

8. *"If the Whole World Were Created for Our Pleasure":*
Order and Disorder in Anarchistic Comedy

1. Gilbert Seldes, *The Movies Come from America* (New York: Scribner's, 1937), pp. 44–45.

2. Richard Dyer, "Utopia and Entertainment," in Bill Nichols, ed., *Movies and Methods,* 2 vols. (Berkeley: University of California Press, 1987), 2:220–232.

3. Ibid., p. 222.

4. Norbert Elias and Eric Dunning, *Quest for Excitement: Sport and Leisure in the Civilizing Process* (London: Basil Blackwell, 1986).

5. Frederic Jameson, "Reification and Utopia in Mass Culture," *Social Text* (Winter 1979), p. 141.

6. Ibid., p. 144.

7. Umberto Eco, "The Frames of Comic 'Freedom,' " in Thomas A. Sebeok, ed., *Carnival!* (Berlin: Mouton, 1985), p. 6.

8. Ibid., p. 1.

9. Ibid., p. 2.

10. Ibid., p. 6.

11. For similar arguments, see Richard Terdiman, *Discourse/Counterdiscourse: The Theory and Practice of Symbolic Resistance in Nineteenth-Century France* (Ithaca: Cornell University Press, 1985); Louis A. Hieb, "Meaning and Mismeaning: Toward an Understanding of the Ritual Clown," in Alfonso Oritz, ed., *New Perspectives on the Pueblo* (Albuquerque: University of New Mexico Press, 1972), pp. 163–195; Peter Stallybrass and Allon White, *The Politics and Poetics of Transgression* (Ithaca: Cornell University Press, 1986).

12. Peter Kramer, "Derailing the Honeymoon Express: The Comicality of Buster Keaton's *The Blacksmith,*" *Velvet Light Trap* (June 1989), pp. 101–116, offers a useful analysis of the process by which a similar transformation of the character of Buster Keaton occurs within his short subject, *The Blacksmith.* Although the end result is the same, I would argue that the process is somewhat different in the Wheeler and Woolsey film precisely because of *Hips, Hips, Hooray*'s emphasis upon intentional rather than accidental disruptiveness.

13. Christopher Herbert, "Comedy: The World of Pleasure," *Genre* (Winter 1984), p. 410.

14. Ibid., p. 404.

15. Paul Bouissac, *Circus and Culture: A Semiotic Approach* (Bloomington: Indiana University Press, 1976), p. 151.

16. Ibid.

17. Ibid., p. 7.

18. Ivan Karp, "Good Marx for the Anthropologist: Structure and Anti-Structure in *Duck Soup,*" in Susan P. Montague and William Arens, eds., *The American Dimension* (Sherman Oaks: Alfred, 1981), p. 45, writes of the clowns' interplay in *Duck Soup* in terms that echo Bouissac's description of the archetypal clown act: "Where Teasdale is always impeccably tailored, Firefly is always dressed in an ill-fitting outfit. Both Mrs. Teasdale and Firefly are aware of the rules of etiquette but while she is concerned with upholding the rules of conventional morality, Firefly pokes fun at the people who live by the rules and respond emotionally to their violations. Thus, the net effect of the Groucho-Dumont opposition . . . is to provide the audience with a spectacular and ongoing relationship of continual status reversal" (p. 42).

19. Mikhail Bakhtin, *Rabelais and His World* (Bloomington: Indiana University Press, 1984), p. 26.

20. Mary Douglas, *Natural Symbols: Explorations in Cosmology* (New York: Pantheon, 1982). On a discussion of the role of clowns in Native American ritual, see Hieb, "Meaning and Mismeaning."

21. Hieb, "Meaning and Mismeaning," p. 190.

22. Ibid.

23. See, for example, Victor Turner, *The Ritual Process: Structure and Anti-Structure* (Ithaca: Cornell University Press, 1977), for the definitive statement of his thesis on symbolic inversion and liminality.

24. Carroll Smith-Rosenberg, *Disorderly Conduct: Visions of Gender in Victorian America* (New York: Oxford University Press, 1985), pp. 100–102.

25. Steve Seidman, *Comedian Comedy: A Tradition in Hollywood Film* (Ann Arbor: UMI Research, 1981), pp. 80–100.

26. See Norbert Elias, *Power and Civility: The Civilizing Process,* 2 vols. (New York: Pantheon, 1982), 2:229–336.

27. Patricia Mellencamp, "Jokes and Their Relation to the Marx Brothers," in Stephen Heath and Patricia Mellencamp, eds., *Cinema and Language* (Frederick, Md.: University Publications of America, 1983), pp. 63–78, provides a detailed discussion of the linguistic play found in the Marx Brothers' comedies: "Permutations of language . . . continually and complexly reposition or disperse the spectator/auditor within the film. . . . Harpo literalizes every metaphor, wreaking havoc . . . on the clichés of language and the mise-en-scène; Chico puns with the sounds of speech and is incapable of keeping secrets (his impossibility with societally coded silence or censorship); while Groucho fractures all the rules of reasoning, relishing his own, Chico's and Harpo's derailment of logic and of grammar's proprietary laws" (p. 65).

28. Seidman, *Comedian Comedy,* p. 64.

29. Harry Levin, *Playboys and Killjoys: An Essay on the Theory and Practice of Comedy* (New York: Oxford University Press, 1986), p. 38.

30. Seidman, *Comedian Comedy,* p. 138.

31. Northrop Frye, *Anatomy of Criticism: Four Essays* (Princeton: Princeton University Press, 1957), p. 163.

32. Ibid., p. 171.

33. David Kunzle, "World Turned Upside Down: Iconography of a European Broadsheet Type," in Barbara A. Babcock, ed., *The Reversible World: Symbolic Inversion in Art and Society* (Ithaca: Cornell University Press, 1978), pp. 88–90.

9. *"Don't Become Too Intimate with That Terrible Woman!" Unruly Wives, Female Performance, and Gendered Laughter in Early Sound Comedy*

1. Sigmund Freud, *Jokes and Their Relation to the Unconscious*, trans. James Strachey (New York: Norton, 1960). For useful commentary on the implications of Freud's concept of smut for feminist analysis, see Patricia Mellencamp, "Jokes and Their Relation to the Marx Brothers," in Stephen Heath and Patricia Mellencamp, eds., *Cinema and Language* (Frederick, Md.: University Publications of America, 1983); Patricia Mellencamp, "Situation Comedy, Feminism, and Freud: Discourses of Gracie and Lucy," in Tania Modleski, ed., *Studies in Entertainment: Critical Approaches to Mass Culture* (Bloomington: Indiana University Press, 1986), pp. 80–95; Mary Ann Doane, "Film and Masquerade: Theorizing the Female Spectator," *Screen* (September-October 1982), pp. 74–87; Tania Modleski, "Rape versus Mans/laughter: Hitchcock's *Blackmail* and Feminist Interpretation," *PMLA* (May 1987), pp. 304–315. For a more general application, see Steve Neale, "Psychoanalysis and Comedy," *Screen*, (December 1981), pp. 29–44.

2. Natalie Zemon Davis, *Society and Culture in Early Modern France* (Stanford: Stanford University Press, 1965), p. 131. For a discussion of the feminist implications of Davis's argument, see Mary Russo, "Female Grotesques: Carnival and Theory" in Teresa de Lauretis, ed., *Feminist Studies, Critical Studies* (Bloomington: Indiana University Press, 1986).

3. Mrs. Eliza Lynn Linton, "The Judicial Shock to Marriage," *Nineteenth Century*, May 1891, p. 691. My use of Linton's essays is not meant to exaggerate her historical importance but rather to offer a summary of one representative voice that encapsulated many themes or images found in much broader circulation. My purpose here is not to trace the history of discourse about the shifting role of women in the early twentieth century, a project undertaken more thoroughly and skillfully by many of the other writers cited here, but simply to suggest some links between this imagery and the comic traditions analyzed in this paper.

4. Mrs. Eliza Lynn Linton, "The Wild Women as Social Insurgents," *Nineteenth Century*, October 1891, p. 597.

5. Ibid., p. 598.

6. Mrs. Eliza Lynn Linton, "The Judicial Shock to Marriage," p. 693.

7. Ibid.

8. Mrs. Eliza Lynn Linton, "The Partisans of the Wild Women," *Nineteenth Century*, March 1892, p. 461.

9. Mrs. Eliza Lynn Linton, "The Wild Women as Politicians," *Nineteenth Century*, July 1891, p. 85.

10. Mrs. Eliza Lynn Linton, "The Partisans of the Wild Women," p. 461.

11. Bram Dijkstra, *Idols of Perversity: Fantasies of Feminine Evil in Fin-de-Siècle Culture* (New York: Oxford University Press, 1986).

12. Barbara Welter, "The Cult of True Womanhood, 1820–1860," *American Quarterly* (Summer 1966), pp. 151–174.

13. Nancy Cott, "Passionlessness: An Interpretation of Victorian Sexual Ideology, 1790–1850," *Signs* (Winter 1978), pp. 219–236.

14. See, for example, Carl Dengler, *At Odds: Women and the Family in America from the Revolution to the Present* (New York: Oxford University Press, 1980), pp. 279–327; Carroll Smith-Rosenberg, *Disorderly Conduct: Visions of Gender in Victorian America* (Oxford: Oxford University Press, 1985).

15. Mary Kelly, "The Sentimentalists: Promise and Betrayal in the Home," *Signs* (Spring 1979), pp. 434–446.

16. Ibid.

17. Oliver Bell Bunce, "Some Notions about Domestic Bliss," *Appleton's Journal*, March 12, 1870, p. 295. This discussion of "comedy of marital combat" is based in part on Alfred Habegger, *Gender, Fantasy, and Realism in American Literature* (New York: Columbia University Press, 1982), pp. 126–139. For examples of this type of humor, see Robert Barnwell Roosevelt, *Progressive Petticoats; or Dressed to Death. An Autobiography of a Married Man* (New York: Carleton, 1874); Oliver Bell Bunce, *Bachelor Bluff: His Opinions, Sentiments, and Dispostations* (New York: Appleton, 1881); Frances M. Whitcher, *The Widow Bedott Papers* (New York: Derby, 1856). For an account of a countertradition in American popular humor—one which did allow women a voice—see Nancy A. Walker, *A Very Serious Thing: Women's Humor and American Culture* (Minneapolis: University of Minnesota Press, 1988) and its companion anthology, Nancy Walker and Zita Dressner, eds., *Redressing the Balance: American Women's Literary Humor from Colonial Times to the 1980s* (Jackson: University of Mississippi Press, 1988).

18. Mary Douglas, "The Social Control of Cognition: Some Factors in Joke Perception," *Man* [new series] 3(3):361–379 (1968). Carroll Smith-Rosenberg makes similar use of Douglas's model in her discussion of the construction of gender within the Davy Crockett stories, in Smith-Rosenberg, *Disorderly Conduct*, pp. 90–108.

19. Shirley Staples, *Male and Female Comedy Teams in American Vaudeville, 1865–1932* (Ann Arbor: UMI Research Press, 1984), pp. 110–111, 146.

20. Ibid., p. 241.

21. It is suggestive that in comedy, mothers-in-law are usually the wife's mother, rarely the husband's mother. The mother-in-law thus doubles the matriarchal power across two generations.

22. Wes Gehrig, who has uncovered several previously unpublished scripts from Fields's stage performances, finds that the figure of "the victimized central male—his leisure time usurped by females, machines (especially cars) and the city" was a key element throughout his early theatrical career. Wes D. Gehrig, "W. C. Fields: The Copyrighted Sketches," *Journal of Popular Film and Television* (Summer 1986), pp. 66–75. Gehrig's research might provide an explanation for the persistence of these stereotypes in Fields's later film comedy: in creating screen vehicles that build upon his already recognizable persona, the writers and directors of the W. C. Fields films often inserted bits of his previous stage material and modeled their narratives

after those same conventions, resulting in a style of comedy that looks backward toward the thematic concerns of an earlier era in American humor.

23. Mirra Komarovsky, *The Unemployed Man and His Family: The Effect of Unemployment Upon the Status of the Man in Fifty-Nine Families* (New York: Octagon, 1971; reprinted from 1940). For additional reports, see Elaine Tyler May, *Great Expectations: Marriage and Divorce in Post-Victorian America* (Chicago: University of Chicago Press, 1980); Elaine Tyler May, *Homeward Bound: American Families in the Cold War Era* (New York: Basic, 1988); Glen H. Elder, Jr., *Children of the Great Depression: Social Change in Life Experience* (Chicago: University of Chicago Press, 1974); and Lynn Y. Weiner, *From Working Girl to Working Mother: The Female Labor Force in the United States, 1820–1980* (Chapel Hill: University of North Carolina, 1985).

24. Habegger, *Gender, Fantasy, and Realism*, p. 116.

25. Linda Martin and Kerry Segrave, *Women in Comedy* (Secaucus, N.J.: Citadel, 1984), p. 13.

26. Kate Sanborn, *The Wit of Women* (New York: Funk, 1885).

27. Constant Coquelin, "Have Women a Sense of Humor?" *Harper's Bazaar*, January 12, 1901, pp. 67–69.

28. Robert J. Burdette, "Have Women a Sense of Humor?" *Harper's Bazaar*, July 1902, pp. 597–598.

29. Elizabeth Stanley Trotter, "Humor with a Gender," *Atlantic*, December 1922, pp. 784–787.

30. Martin and Segrave, *Women in Comedy*, p. 13.

31. Trotter, "Humor with a Gender," pp. 784–787. Madahev L. Apte, *Humor and Laughter: An Anthropological Perspective* (Ithaca: Cornell University Press, 1985), pp. 67–81, finds similar attitudes toward female joking across a number of different cultures and sees them as "an important avenue for social control" over gender relations. Apte concludes, "By restricting the freedom of women to engage in and respond to humor in the public domain, men emphasize their needs for superiority. Men justify such restrictions by creating ideal role models for women that emphasize modesty, virtue and passivity" and often even deny the existence of feminine humor and laughter.

32. Margaretta Newell, "Are Women Humorous?" *Outlook*, October 14, 1931, pp. 206–207, 224. See also Helen Rowland, "The Emancipation of the Rib," *The Delineator*, March 1911, pp. 176–177.

33. Mary Austin, "The Sense of Humor in Women," *New Republic*, November 26, 1924, pp. 10–12.

34. Mabel Condon, "Sans Grease Paint and Wig," *Motography*, June 13, 1914, p. 421.

35. Gladys Hall, "Is It Tragic to Be Comic?" *Moving Picture Classic*, May 1931, p. 48.

36. Rose Standish, "Two Is a Company," unidentified magazine clipping, Sidney Drew File, Herbert Blum Collection, Wisconsin Center for Film and Theater Research.

37. Unidentified press clippings, Lyda Roberti File, Herbert Blum Collection, Wisconsin Center for Film and Theater Research.

38. *Screen Play Secrets* cover, December, Dorothy Lee File, Herbert Blum Collection, Wisconsin Center for Film and Theater Research.

39. Ruth Biery, "The Best Showman in Town," *Photoplay*, November 1931, Lupe Velez File, Herbert Blum Collection, Wisconsin Center for Film and Theater Research.

40. Unidentified press clipping, Marie Dressler File, Herbert Blum Collection, Wisconsin Center for Film and Theater Research.

41. Gladys Hall, "It's Fun to Be Fifty! Says Edna May Oliver," *Movie Mirror*, undated clipping, pp. 62–63, 94, Edna May Oliver File, Herbert Blum Collection, Wisconsin Center for Film and Theater Research.

42. Anthony Slide, *The Vaudevillians: A Dictionary of Vaudeville Performers* (Westport, Conn.: Arlington House, 1981), pp. 92–93.

43. "The New Movie Album: Winnie Lightner," unidentified fan magazine profile, Winnie Lightner File, Herbert Blum Collection, Wisconsin Center for Film and Theater Research.

44. Slide, *The Vaudevillians*, pp. 92–93.

45. Winnie Lightner File, Herbert Blum Collection, Wisconsin Center for Film and Theater Research.

46. "Winnie Lightner," unidentified fan magazine profile, Winnie Lightner File, Herbert Blum Collection, Wisconsin Center for Film and Theater Research.

47. "The New Movie Album: Winnie Lightner."

48. Eugene Earle, "Winnie Wows 'Em!," *Photoplay*, Winnie Lightner File, Herbert Blum Collection, Wisconsin Center for Film and Theater Research.

49. Robert C. Allen, *Horrible Prettiness: Burlesque and American Culture* (Chapel Hill: University of North Carolina Press, 1991), p. 231.

50. Laura Mulvey, "Visual Pleasure and Narrative Cinema," in Bill Nichols, ed., *Movies and Methods II* (Berkeley: University of California Press, 1985), p. 309.

51. "Does this comic female style work to free women from a more confining aesthetic? Or are women again so identified with style itself that they are as estranged from its liberatory and transgressive effects as they are from their own bodies as signs in culture generally? In what sense can women really produce or make spectacles out of themselves? . . . The figure of the female transgressor as public spectacle is still powerfully resonant and the possibilities of redeploying this representation as a demystifying or utopian model have not been exhausted" (Russo, "Female Grotesques," p. 217.

52. Kathleen K. Rowe, "Roseanne: Unruly Woman as Domestic Goddess," *Screen* (Winter 1990), pp. 411–412. Allen, *Horrible Prettiness*, pp. 272–274, makes a similar argument in relation to female comic performance within the burlesque tradition. "The isolation of feminine sexuality from feminine insubordination" meant a separation between the sexually expressive yet mute beauty of the Ziegfeld Girl and the verbally expressive yet grotesque "Red hot mama." Performers like Sophie Tucker or Bessie Smith "kept alive something of the insubordinate, inver-

sive spirit of Thompsonian burlesque," but did so in "the shadows of mainstream culture." Lightner, while closer to conventional notions of beauty than Tucker or Smith, took this alternative tradition of the feminine grotesque into the mainstream of classical Hollywood cinema, enjoying a brief reign as Warner's top female performer, but was unable to sustain a career. She was first displaced from comic stardom into secondary roles in melodramas and then later left Hollywood altogether. More important, any trace of her contribution to the early sound period has disappeared from both popular memory and academic history.

53. Joan Riviere, "Womanliness as Masquerade," in Victor Burgin, James Donald, and Cora Kaplan, eds., *Formations of Fantasy* (London: Methuen, 1986), p. 37.

54. Riviere, "Womanliness as Masquerade," p. 38.

55. Kathleen K. Rowe, "Women, Comedy, and the Carnivalesque: Notes Toward a Feminist Investigation of the Genres of Laughter," paper presented at the Society for Cinema Studies conference, Los Angeles, 1991.

56. Alexander Woollcott, "Charlotte Greenwood, Etc." *New York Times*, November 21, 1919, p. 14, sec. 7.

57. Joe Franklin, *Encyclopedia of Comedians* (Secaucus, N.J.: Citadel, 1979).

Conclusion: The Return of the Backflipping Senators

1. Mikhail Bakhtin, *Rabelais and His World* (Bloomington: Indiana University Press, 1984), p. 474.

Index